Constitutional Review in Central and Eastern Europe

Recent confrontations between constitutional courts and parliamentary majorities in several European countries have attracted international interest in the relationship between the judiciary and the legislature.

Some political actors have argued that courts have assumed too much power and politics has been extremely judicialized. This volume accurately and systematically examines the extent to which this aggregation of power may have constrained the dominant political actors' room for manoeuvre. To explore the diversity and measure the strength of judicial decisions, the contributors to this work have elaborated a methodology to give a more nuanced picture of the practice of constitutional adjudication in Central and Eastern Europe between 1990 and 2020. The work opens with an assessment of the existing literature on empirical analysis of judicial decisions with a special focus on the Central and Eastern European region, and a short summary of the methodology of the project. This is followed by ten country studies and a concluding chapter providing a comprehensive comparative analysis of the results. A further nine countries are explored in the counterpart volume to this book: *Constitutional Review in Western Europe: Judicial-Legislative Relations in Comparative Perspective.*

The collection will be an invaluable resource for those working in the areas of empirical legal research and comparative constitutional law, as well as political scientists interested in judicial politics.

Kálmán Pócza is Senior Research Fellow at the Ludovika University of Public Service in Budapest, Research Institute for Politics and Government, and Head of the Center for Constitutional Politics at the Mathias Corvinus Collegium, Hungary. He is the Principal Investigator of the JUDICON-EU project.

Constitutional Review in Central and Eastern Europe

Judicial-Legislative Relations in Comparative Perspective

Edited by Kálmán Pócza

Routledge
Taylor & Francis Group
LONDON AND NEW YORK

First published 2024
by Routledge
4 Park Square, Milton Park, Abingdon, Oxon OX14 4RN

and by Routledge
605 Third Avenue, New York, NY 10158

Routledge is an imprint of the Taylor & Francis Group, an informa business

British Library Cataloguing-in-Publication Data
A catalogue record for this book is available from the British Library

ISBN: 978-1-032-50660-9 (hbk)
ISBN: 978-1-032-50661-6 (pbk)
ISBN: 978-1-003-39948-3 (ebk)

DOI: 10.4324/9781003399483

Typeset in Galliard
by Deanta Global Publishing Services, Chennai, India

The Open Access version of chapters 1, 5, and 12 was funded by Mathias Corvinus Collegium Foundation.

Contents

Figures

Tables

Abbreviations

CrCC: Croatian Constitutional Court
CzCC: Czech Constitutional Court
ESC: Estonian Supreme Court
HCC: Hungarian Constitutional Court
LaCC: Latvian Constitutional Court
LiCC: Lithuanian Constitutional Court
PCT: Polish Constitutional Tribunal
RCC: Romanian Constitutional Court
SCC: Slovak Constitutional Court
SloCC: Slovenian Constitutional Court

Contributors

Polona Batagelj is an assistant at the European Faculty of Law New University, where she earned her Ph.D. She was a member of the research group on a project titled *Ideology at Courts: The Influence of Judges' World-views on Their Decisions*, focusing on how the ideological profiles of judges influence their performance. As part of this research, she co-authored various chapters in the recently published scientific monograph, *Ideologija na sodiščih* (Avbelj, Matej, et al. 2021. Nova Gorica: Nova univerza). Her research interests focus on European Union Law and sports law with a recent publication: "Reforms of the anti-doping system in the light of (better) protection of the athletes' human rights" (*Dignitas* 2021 (89/90): 145–184).

Márton Csapodi is a Ph.D. student at the Faculty of Law and Political Sciences of the Pázmány Péter Catholic University and a research fellow at the Center for Constitutional Politics of the Mathias Corvinus Collegium. He obtained his master's degree in law from the Pázmány Péter Catholic University. He is currently doing research on constitutional adjudication, constitutional pluralism, and constitutional judiciaries in the EU.

Gábor Dobos is a research fellow at the Centre for Social Sciences (Budapest) and at the Ludovika University of Public Service (Budapest). He is primarily interested in local politics and constitutional adjudication. His latest publications include: "Do Constitutional Courts Restrict Government Policy?" in *East European Politics* 39 (3), 2022 (with Kálmán Pócza, Attila Gyulai, and Zsófia Papp); "Hungary: The expansion and the limits of national politics at the local level" in Gendźwiłł A. et al. (eds.) *The Routledge Handbook of Local Elections and Voting in Europe*. Routledge, 2022; and "Municipal splits and hidden amalgamations in Hungary" in *Miscellanea Geographica – Regional Studies on Development*, 25 (2), 2021.

Monika Glavina is an assistant professor of European Union Law at Erasmus School of Law, Erasmus University Rotterdam, and a visiting professor at Paris School of International Affairs, Sciences Po. In addition, she is a member of the Editorial Board of *Erasmus Law Review* and a member of the Steering Committee of the *ECPR Law and Courts Standing Group*.

She obtained her Ph.D. at KU Leuven University and worked as a postdoc on two large-scale projects: the ERC-granted EUTHORITY Project (KU Leuven) and the Horizon-2020 TiGRE Project (University of Antwerp). Her areas of research include empirical legal research, judicial politics, judicial behaviour, judicial protection in the EU, and trust in courts. Her most recent publications include: "Why passive? Exploring national judges' motives for not requesting preliminary rulings" (with Karin Leijon, in *Maastricht Journal of European and Comparative Law*); "The Reality of National Judges as EU Law Judges: Knowledge, Experiences and Attitudes of Lower Court Judges in Slovenia and Croatia" (in *Croatian Yearbook of European Law & Policy*); and "The Voices of European Law: Legislators, Judges and Law Professors" (with Arthur Dyevre and Michal Ovádek, in *German Law Journal*).

Attila Gyulai is a senior research fellow at the Centre for Social Sciences – Institute for Political Science (TK PTI) in Budapest and an associate professor at the Corvinus University of Budapest. He is the principal investigator of the "Political Normativity" project at TK PTI. His most recent publications include: "Do Constitutional Courts Restrict Government Policy?" in *East European Politics* 39 (3), 2022 (with Kálmán Pócza, Gábor Dobos and Zsófia Papp); *The Orbán regime: Plebiscitary leader democracy in the making* (Routledge, 2020, with András Körösényi and Gábor Illés); "It's a fact: the buribunks are the enemies of the political" in *Griffith Law Review* 28 (2), 2019; and "How to Measure the Strength of Judicial Decisions: A Methodological Framework" in *German Law Journal* 18 (2017):6 (together with Gábor Dobos and Kálmán Pócza).

Iga Jeziorska is an assistant professor the Corvinus University of Budapest. Her research interests focus on illicit drug policies and the role of non-governmental organizations in public service delivery in this area. Her most recent publications include: "A Sin or a Health Issue? Morality Policy Framing and the State of Harm Reduction in East-Central Europe" in *Intersections* 7(1):97; "Collaborative Governance Regimes in Illiberal Democracies: A Comparative Case of Drug Harm Reduction Policy in Central-Eastern Europe" in *Transylvanian Review of Administrative Sciences* 62 E/2021 (62 E):60; and "Understanding drivers of illiberal entrenchment at critical junctures: institutional responses to COVID-19 in Hungary and Poland" in *International Review of Administrative Sciences* 87(3).

Alžbeta Králová is an assistant professor at the Department of Constitutional Law and Political Sciences of the Faculty of Law of Masaryk University in Brno. Her research interests focus on human rights, asylum and migration law, effective remedies, judicial review, and constitutional adjudication. She participated in projects related to the application of EU law by national courts and the influence of EU law on the system of remedies in asylum and migration law. She headed the Department of Analytics and

Comparative Law of the Supreme Court of the Czech Republic and works for the Ombudsman´s Office. Her publications include "Legal Remedies in Asylum and Immigration Law: The Balance Between Effectiveness and Procedural Autonomy?" in *Central European Public Administration Review* (2018).

Csongor Kuti is an associate professor at the University of Arts Târgu-Mureş, Romania. SJD in comparative constituțional law and LL.M. in human rights, both obtained at the Central European University, Budapest. His latest publications include: *Five Essays on the Freedom of Speech* (2020); "Between a Rock and a Hard Place: Constituțional Conflict Cases before the Romanian Constituțional Court" in *Hungarian Journal of Legal Studies* 60(3), 2019; and "The Romanian Constitutional Court: Muddling Through Democratic Transition" in *Constitutional Politics and the Judiciary: Decision-making in Central and Eastern Europe* (London/New York: Routledge, 2019, ed.: Kálmán Pócza).

Erik Láštic is an associate professor at the Department of Political Science, Faculty of Arts at the Comenius University in Bratislava, Slovakia. His research focuses on various aspects of politics and policymaking in Central and Eastern Europe, including legislative politics and referendums. He has published dozens of articles and chapters domestically and internationally. Selected publications include: "Into the Labyrinth: The Rewards for High Public Office in Slovakia" (with Katarína Staroňová) in B. Guy Peters, Marleen Brans (eds.): *Rewards for High Public Office in Europe and North America* (London: Routledge, 2012) and "If It Works, Fine, If Not, So What? Initiatives in Slovakia" in Maija Setälä and Theo Schiller (eds.): *Citizens' Initiatives in Europe: Procedures and Consequences of Agenda-Setting by Citizens* (2012).

Dita Plepa studied law at the University of Latvia. In 2011 she was awarded a master's degree in law. Her research focuses on constitutional law and state law, as well as issues of legal theory. Currently, she is a doctoral student at the University of Latvia, Faculty of Law. In 2008 she started working as the senior desk officer with the Department of the Court of Justice of the European Union, Ministry of Justice of the Republic of Latvia. Since 2009 she has been working at the Constitutional Court of the Republic of Latvia. In addition to this, since 2012 she has started teaching "Legal Methods" at the Faculty of Law, Riga Stradins University.

Kálmán Pócza is a senior research fellow at the Ludovika University of Public Service in Budapest (Research Institute for Government and Politics) and Head of the Center for Constitutional Politics at the Mathias Corvinus Collegium. He is the Principal Investigator of the JUDICON-EU project. Previously, he was a senior research fellow at the Institute for Political Science of the Hungarian Academy of Sciences, Associate Professor at the Pázmány Péter Catholic University, and visiting research fellow at the

University of Notre Dame, University of Tübingen, and the University of Fribourg. His most recent publications include: "Do Constitutional Courts Restrict Government Policy?" in *East European Politics* 39 (3), 2022 (together with Gábor Dobos, Attila Gyulai, and Zsófia Papp); *Constitutional Politics and the Judiciary: Decision-making in Central and Eastern Europe* (London/New York: Routledge, 2019, editor); and "How to Measure the Strength of Judicial Decisions: A Methodological Framework" in *German Law Journal* 18(2017):6 (together with Gábor Dobos and Attila Gyulai).

Dovilė Pūraitė-Andrikienė is a senior researcher at the Law Institute of the Lithuanian Centre for Social Sciences and the Head of the Legal System Research Department of this Institute. She is an expert on Lithuanian and comparative constitutional law, constitutional justice procedure, and human rights. Her most recent publications include: *Legal Protection of Vulnerable Groups in Lithuania, Latvia, Estonia, and Poland* (2022, editor and co-authored with Agnė Limantė); "Individual constitutional complaints in Lithuania: an effective remedy to be exhausted before applying to the European Court of Human Rights?" in *Baltic Journal of Law & Politics* No. 15, Issue 1 (2022); *Constitutional Complaints in Lithuania as a Tool for the Protection of Human Rights: monograph* (2022); "The Development and Prospects of the Lithuanian Constitutional Justice Model" in Švedas. G.; Murauskas, D. (eds.), *Legal Developments During 30 Years of Lithuanian Independence* (2021); and "The Legal Force of Conclusions by Lithuanian Constitutional Court and the issue of their (Non-)finality: Has the Time Come to Amend the Constitution?" in *Review of Central and East European Law* No. 44, Issue 2(2019). She is also an associate professor at the Faculty of Law of Vilnius University, where she teaches constitutional law and European Union law. She is also a member of the Young Academy of Lithuanian Academy of Sciences.

Anita Rodiņa is currently judge at the Latvian Constitutional Court and an associate professor at the University of Latvia. Before being elected to the bench of the Constitutional Court of Latvia she was Dean of the Law Faculty and a member of the senate at the University of Latvia. She has been a member of the Committee for Improvement of the Legal Environment established at the State President's office. She is active in several international platforms like the European Public Law Organization; she is a founder of the public analytical centre "Constitutional Culture" and a member of scientific committees of legal journals abroad. At the Faculty of Law, she teaches constitutional law and constitutional court procedure law. Her most recent publications include: "Protection of Fundamental Human Rights during COVID-19 Pandemic: Case of Latvia" in *International Organizations and State's Response to COVID-19* (2021); "Appointment of the Constitutional Court Justice: Some Issues" in *Law*, No. 14, 2021; Le e-Saeima, l'un des premiers parlements au monde a travailler a distance.

L'impact de la crise sanitaire sur le fonctionnement des parlements ne Europe (Fondation Robert Schuman, 2021; together with I. Lībiņa-Eggnere); "Foreign Materials in the Judgments of the Constitutional Court of the Republic of Latvia" in *Judicial Cosmopolitanism. The Use of Foreign Law in Contemporary Constitutional Systems* (2019); and "The Constitutional Court of the Republic of Latvia as a Law Maker: Current Practice" in *Judicial Law-Making in European Constitutional Courts* (London, New York: Routledge 2020, together with A. Spale).

Katarína Šipulová is the Director of the Judicial Studies Institute at Masaryk University's Faculty of Law. She earned her Ph.D. at the Faculty of Social Studies, Department of European Studies, Masaryk University, Brno, and the MSt in Socio-Legal Research at the University of Oxford. Her main areas of interest are judicial governance, transitional justice, and democratization of the Central and Eastern European countries. She has been an active member of several research projects dealing with human rights as well as international law and its impact on domestic jurisprudence (e.g. international human rights treaties in national legal systems, implementation of ECtHR case law against the Czech Republic), including both ERC research grants led by David Kosař. She serves as a member of the ECPR Law and Courts Standing Group Steering Committee (2018–now), the ICON-S CEE Chapter (2018–now), and the Oxford Global Society (2021–now). Her latest publications include: "Comparative Court-Packing" (*International Journal of Constitutional Law*, with D. Kosař); "Judicial Self-Governance Index: Towards Better Understanding of the Role of Judges in Governing the Judiciary" (*Regulation and Governance*, with S. Spáč, D. Kosař, T. Papoušková and V. Derka); and "Between Human Rights and Transitional Justice: The Dilemma of Constitutional Courts in Post-Communist Central Europe" (*Europe-Asia Studies*, with H. Smekal).

Max Steuer is an assistant professor at the Department of Political Science, Faculty of Arts at the Comenius University in Bratislava, Slovakia, and an associate professor at the Jindal Global Law School, O.P. Jindal Global University, India. His research interests focus on questions of democracy protection, constitutional adjudication in Central Europe, constitutionalism in the European Union, and freedom of expression. His interdisciplinary work has appeared in edited collections and encyclopaedias and in journals in political science, law, sociology, and European studies including: *European Constitutional Law Review*, *The International Journal of Human Rights*, and *Review of Central and East European Law*. A member of several academic associations in political science and public law, such as the International Society of Public Law and its Central and Eastern European Chapter (Founding Advisory Board), he received several academic awards, including a Fulbright Graduate Scholarship.

Paloma Krõõt Tupay teaches constitutional law at the University of Tartu in Estonia. In addition to questions of democratic state architecture, she focuses her research activities on issues of data protection, e-government, and digital constitutionalism. Early in 2023, *Artificial Intelligence and Machine Learning Powered Public Service Delivery in Estonia. Opportunities and Legal Challenges*, a book she co-authored with Martin Ebers, was published. Currently, she is working on the completion of a constitutional law textbook. Previously, she has worked as a legal advisor to the Estonian President and also to the Minister of Interior. Recent publications include: "Has the GDPR killed e-government? The 'once-only' principle vs. the principle of purpose limitation" in *International Data Privacy Law* 2023 (together with Monika Mikiver) and "Estonia, the Digital Nation: Reflections on a Digital Citizen's Rights in the European Union" in *European Data Protection Law Review*, 6 (2) 2020, 294–300.

Artur Wołek is a public policy and administration professor and former vice-rector at the Jesuit University of Krakow Ignatianum. Previously he taught at the Warsaw School of Economics and WSB-National-Louis University. In the 1990s, he also worked as an advisor with the Prime Minister's Office for Constitutional Reform and as the director at the Windsor Group, a think tank. Books authored include: *Słabe państwo* [A Weak State] (2012) and *Demokracja nieformalna. Konstytucjonalizm i rzeczywiste reguły polityki w Europie Środkowej po 1989* r. [Informal Politics. Constitutionalism and Effective Rules of Politics in Central Europe] (2002). He also edited a major handbook *Public Policies* (2021); *Nieodrobiona lekcja. Polityki publiczne w Czechach i Polsce* [The Lesson Not Done. Public Policies in Poland and the Czech Republic] with Ondřej Krutílek (2013) and *Udana transformacja na peryferiach*? [Successful Transformation on the Peripheries?] with Justinas Dementavičius (2013).

1 Constitutional review and judicial-legislative relations in new democracies

Kálmán Pócza, Márton Csapodi, Gábor Dobos and Attila Gyulai

1.1 Introduction: taking courts seriously

The least dangerous branch. No purse, no sword. According to the classical and well-known narratives of the two Alexanders, Hamilton in *The Federalist* No. 78 and, following in his footsteps, Bickel (1962), the judiciary is definitely a harmless institution, which might have authority (*auctoritas*) but whose power (*potestas*) depends on the other two branches of government, which possess the purse and the sword. Consequently, Hamilton argued, no one should fear the judicial power; it should be rather considered "as the bulwark of a limited Constitution against legislative encroachments".

Judicial supremacy, *rule of judges*, and *juristocracy*. Over the past four decades, these terms, referring to recently emerging phenomena, have been used either simply analytically or critically by several authors arguing against the global expansion of judicial power. The central points of criticism are the *legitimacy deficit*, the problem of the *counter-majoritarian difficulty*, and the recurring charge of *judicial activism* (to refer once again to terms widely used in legal scholarship).

While arguments against judicial review were formulated in the United States quite early, the flip side of the story was less well known in Europe for several decades. Criticism in the US and Europe had its origins in political conflicts that arose in the wake of highly contested decisions of constitutional courts, but scholarly reflections that normatively (and plausibly) argued against the expansion of judicial power were absent not only in Central and Eastern Europe (CEE) but, with the obvious exception of the United Kingdom, also in Western Europe, where constitutional courts became crucial political actors after two waves of democratization.

Constitutional courts in Western Europe, originally established either as bulwarks against the violation of fundamental rights or (more often) to settle disputes between different levels of government in federal states, have slowly but steadily moved to the centre stage of domestic politics. They faced only occasional backlashes because judges displayed passive virtues (again, explained in detail by Alexander Bickel), because no politicians dared to challenge the institutions created as bulwarks against totalitarianism or simply because they

DOI: 10.4324/9781003399483-1

were sometimes regarded as useful institutions to which politicians could turn to have judges decide thorny questions with potentially disastrous political consequences for elected politicians (a special kind of blame shifting).

At first glance, the story in Central and Eastern Europe began similarly, or more precisely, even more promisingly. In contrast to Western Europe – where constitutional courts played a decisive role only in countries with an authoritarian past and the "judicialization of mega-political issues" (Hirschl 2008) was almost completely absent in the UK, the Benelux countries, and the Scandinavian countries – judicial review of legislative and executive acts was established in all countries of the CEE region without exception. Copying a template (Parau 2018) and giving judges more power seemed like a good idea, because no one really expected a rebellion against governing by the judiciary (Scheppele 2003). In fact, the first constitutional courts established their authority surprisingly quickly, and since politicians in Central and Eastern Europe were hardly aware of the potential power of judicial review, constitutional adjudication based on judicial review became a success story that is proudly referred to in legal scholarship.

However, from today's perspective and with the hindsight of new generations, one could say that the picture in the CEE region is rather mixed. While some courts in Central and Eastern Europe managed to avoid massive political interference in their work and preserved their relative independence (e.g. the Czech Constitutional Court), others faced either milder forms of pushback or serious backlashes (Madsen, Cebulak, and Wiebusch 2018) from political actors who claimed that judges (and not elected politicians) govern their country. Several political actors have argued that constitutional courts have assumed too much power and that politics has been extremely judicialized. Political actions against courts in the CEE region have ranged from verbal criticism of judicial decisions and constitutional courts in general to (un)successful attempts of court-packing and a total reshuffle of the court, showing that politicians took the courts seriously as centres of power that can significantly hinder them achieving their goals.

1.2 The research puzzle

Nevertheless, the question as to what extent this aggregation of power and authority has constrained the dominant political actors, in fact, has never been examined accurately and systematically in the literature. The twin volumes, *Constitutional Review in Central and Eastern Europe* and *Constitutional Review in Western Europe*, are trying to fill this gap in the literature and deal with the practice of constitutional adjudication in Europe, mainly focusing on the puzzling relationship between constitutional courts and legislatures.

It should be stressed, however, that these volumes do not concentrate either on the theory of judicial or legislative supremacy or on institutional design, which of course can affect both constitutional adjudication and the relationship between these institutions. Moreover, they deliberately avoid philosophical questions about the legitimacy of judicial review, and their main approach is certainly not in line with classical works of (European) legal scholarship. They do not aim to find an answer to the question of supremacy, nor do they approach the question of the relationship between the judiciary and the legislature from a purely legalistic point of view. Instead of philosophical, theoretical, and purely legal questions, we have chosen to explore empirically and systematically the practice of constitutional adjudication in Europe, with particular attention to the diversity of judicial decisions and the strength of the constraint they exert on legislatures. Thus, this work is more in the realm of empirical legal research, which has a rich tradition in American legal research but is relatively unknown in the European context.[1]

1.3 The research questions

Both volumes, *Constitutional Review in Central and Eastern Europe* and *Constitutional Review in Western Europe*, are products of the JUDICON-EU research project.[2] The project formulated two aims: first, we developed a new methodology to capture diversity and measure the strength of judicial decisions. Second, based on this coherent methodology and the database created by the project, we studied the diversity and strength of judicial decisions of the European constitutional courts. Based on these objectives, we formulated two research questions concerning the *diversity* and *strength* of judicial decisions: (1) how differentiated are the decisions of European constitutional courts?; and (2) to what extent have these differentiated decisions of European constitutional courts constrained the legislature's room for manoeuvre?

Based on the analysis of the practice of the Hungarian Constitutional Court, we assumed that other European constitutional courts also elaborated (or adopted from the practice of their counterparts) a variety of ruling types and declared legislative omissions or procedural unconstitutionality, complete or partial, *ex tunc* or *pro futuro* annulments, determined constitutional requirements or prescriptions how to remedy the unconstitutionality. Mapping this diversity of judicial decisions is one of the main aims of both volumes.

Although in legal terminology the strength of a judicial decision seems to be a concept rather difficult to interpret, *strength* as used in this research

1 It should be stressed, however, that most recently several initiatives have been launched which indicate that the field of empirical legal studies is getting more and more popular even in Europe. The first and the second Conference on Empirical Legal Studies in Europe held in Amsterdam (2016) and in Leuven (2018), as well as the activity of Law and Court Standing Group of the European Consortium of Political Research (ECPR), along with several research projects at various European Universities like JUSTIN (Masaryk University Brno), ICOURTS (University of Copenhagen), or PLURICOURTS (University of Oslo) are excellent examples which demonstrate that various methods of empirical legal studies are nowadays more widespread in the European research community than a few years ago.

2 The JUDICON-EU research project (2020–2022) has been funded by the Ludovika University of Public Service. For more details: https://judiconeu.uni-nke.hu/. We are indebted to all interns of the project and especially to Adrienn Vajda, who helped us in editing all figures and tables of the volume.

project shows the extent to which constitutional courts constrain the room for manoeuvre of another constitutional organ (in this research project, the legislatures). While all decisions of a constitutional court have the same legal binding force, they may reduce the scope of legislative activities to varying degrees. For example, in cases described as *procedural unconstitutionality*, legislatures made "only" a procedural mistake in the adaptation of the bill. After having corrected this procedural flaw of the legislative process, they might adopt the same law, often even with the same content. On the other hand, in cases of substantive unconstitutionality, the regulation should be changed substantively, i.e. its content should be transformed to meet the constitutionality criteria. In the second case, constitutional courts significantly narrow down the scope of legislative activities, since the court has found the content, rather than the way the bill was adopted, unconstitutional. Consequently, a decision based on substantive unconstitutionality is stronger than one based on procedural unconstitutionality because it might limit the legislature's room for manoeuvre more heavily.

It is important to note that by measuring the strength of judicial decisions, on no account do we want to measure the *impact* of judicial decisions. The term *strength* as used in our research might be best described with a boxing metaphor: measuring strength is measuring the power of a punch, and by no means the kind of impact this punch had on the other boxer. It is not considered whether this opponent could have side-stepped or is only slightly shaken, although it was a very strong punch. To put it briefly, strength is not measured by the intensity of the impact of a decision.

In what follows, we first briefly give an overview on the existing literature on constitutional review in Central and Eastern Europe, focusing on judicial-legislative relations (Section 1.4). Second, we summarize the methodology of the JUDICON-EU research project, which is essential for understanding the country studies included in both volumes (Section 1.5). Third, we clarify the structure of the country studies since we asked the authors to follow the same coherent structure in writing the chapters (Section 1.6). In addition to the coherent methodology of the research project, the semi-structured chapters based on predefined questions facilitate the comparison of the performance of European constitutional courts with regard the question of their constraint on the legislature. Nonetheless, we have also included a special comparative chapter at the end of both volumes that attempts to provide a first (and rather preliminary) answer to the question of whether institutional design, political context, or event-related variables influence the strength of court decisions or dissenting opinions.

1.4 Literature overview

1.4.1 Institutional design

There is an extensive literature on the development and origins of the *institutional design* of European constitutional review, with a significant body of research on Central and Eastern European countries' constitutional design, including comparative analysis of institutional patterns, origins, and evolution of constitutional courts in post-communist countries established during the democratic transition (Brunner 1992; Utter and Lundsgaard 1993; Magalhães 1999; Smithey and Ishiyama 2000; Procházka 2002; De Visser 2014; Ernits et al. 2022). In this context, Sadurski's work is particularly significant (Sadurski 2002, 2014). While Schwartz has also conducted extensive historical and comparative research in this field (Schwartz 1992, 1998, 2000), Parau provides a comparative analysis of the institutional pattern and the circumstances surrounding the emergence of constitutional judiciaries in CEE from a specific political science perspective, seeing the empowerment of judges as the self-empowerment of transnational elites (Parau 2018).

One prominent approach to studying the activity and functioning of constitutional courts is from the perspective of *federalism*, political centralization, or decentralization. In addition to single-country studies (Benz 2017; Dalla Pellegrina et al. 2017; Popelier and Bielen 2019), Vaubel's cross-country research, including European countries, examines how specific features of constitutional adjudication, such as the degree of independence, difficulty of amending the constitution, and length of time a constitutional court has been in existence, relate to the degree of political centralization (Vaubel 2009). Popelier et al. (2013) also analysed the effects of judicial decisions in time.

1.4.2 *External factors: the political context*

Some examine the functioning of constitutional justice in the light of contextual, *external factors*. For example, Hönnige argued that judges make decisions according to their political preferences and that this can be measured by party affiliation (although the investigation covered two constitutional courts from Western Europe, not from CEE) (Hönnige 2009). This somewhat nuances the picture that European constitutional jurisprudence is not (or is much less) politicized than in the US (Forejohn and Pasquino 2004). Hein and Ewert used quantitative methods to investigate the extent to which European constitutional courts may be politicized in three countries (Germany, Bulgaria, Portugal) and concluded that the type of procedure has a strong influence on the degree of politicization (the extent to which extra-legal considerations play a role in the decision). For example, abstract review is more likely to be politicized than individual constitutional complaints (Hein and Ewert 2016). Garoupa and Ginsburg have examined how judges respond to different "audiences" (e.g. the public, politicians, lawyers) in terms of reputation (Garoupa and Ginsburg 2015) and how the presence of a supreme court coexisting with a Kelsenian-style constitutional judiciary might affect the internal fragmentation of the constitutional court (Garoupa and Ginsburg 2011). Garlicki has also analysed the power dynamics and tensions between centralized constitutional courts and co-existing supreme courts from a comparative perspective (Garlicki 2007).

Vanberg classified the contextual factors of the political system that lead to the preservation of the authority of constitutional courts into two groups according to whether the court's authority benefits policy-makers (endogenous explanation) or would only come at a too high price if it were undermined or eroded (exogenous explanation) (Vanberg 2015). Based on the German Federal Constitutional Court, Vanberg used a combination of quantitative and qualitative methods to investigate the impact of political factors such as transparency and public support on the decisions of constitutional courts. He found, for example, that low levels of transparency (e.g. lack of public attention, complexity of the case) reduce the likelihood of a law being annulled (Vanberg 2004). Bricker and Wondreys (2018) examined the relationship between public opinion and constitutional review through a quantified analysis of opposition-initiated constitutional court decisions in four countries (Germany, Poland, Slovenia, Czech Republic) and concluded that it may not be possible to see constitutional courts as exclusively countermajoritarian institutions. Indeed, their results show that constitutional courts are responsive to changes in public preferences. Public preferences can change over the course of a term, or they can support the opposition in specific policy areas, and a constitutional court can be receptive to public opinion and shape public policy accordingly (Bricker and Wondreys 2018). Garoupa argues that, overall, empirical research on constitutional review clearly points in the direction of constitutional courts being politicized in the sense that the behaviour of judges can be predicted along ideological lines, while other contextual factors can also be identified (Garoupa 2019). Herron and Randazzo (2003) conclude, in the context of post-communist constitutional courts, that the formal strength of judicial review is less, and external circumstances (e.g. economic situation) are more influential on judges' decision to overturn legislation (Herron and Randazzo 2003).

However, based on his quantitative analysis of post-communist constitutional courts, Bumin (2017) concluded that for the activism of judicial review, the institutional development of the court seems more determining than external factors, although his results also showed correlation between the activism of the constitutional court and the political system or even the economic situation. Bumin quantified the extent of judicial activism by compiling data on the constitutional court's jurisprudence in 19 post-communist countries, looking only at the "on the merits" decisions and the constitutionality-unconstitutionality dichotomy in the outcome of the decision (Bumin 2017). Taking the Bulgarian Constitutional Court as a case study, Bagashka and Tiede examined the influence that the attorney general, alongside other political actors, can have on the constitutional court's decision-making (Bagashka and Tiede 2021). External factors influencing constitutional jurisprudence can also include decisions of other countries' constitutional courts, and there is empirical research (combining qualitative and quantitative methods) in the literature on the extent to which European countries use decisions of foreign courts in their own practice (Groppi and Ponthoreau 2013).

A special aspect of research on constitutional adjudication in Central and Eastern Europe is often the role of constitutional review in the democratic transition and in strengthening and maintaining democracy (Epstein, Knight, and Shvetsova 2001; Jovanović 2015). Although by no means exclusively in the context of the post-communist region, but from a global perspective, Daly has done extensive work exploring the role courts play in democratization, encouraging to rethink what tasks we entrust to the courts in the process of democracy building (Daly 2017). However, constitutional review is now being examined not only in the context of building, but also in the context of dismantling democracy: most recently, one can find studies on Hungary and Poland that aim to examine the role of constitutional courts in so-called illiberal political regimes, often claiming that the political branches of power are abusive towards the constitutional judiciary (Castillo-Ortiz 2019; Drinóczi and Bień-Kacała 2019; Dixon and Landau 2021; Kovalčík 2022).

1.4.3 Internal dynamics: dissents

Some studies focus on the *internal dynamics* of constitutional courts, which, due to institutional design, means examination of judicial dissents where possible. Kelemen has done extensive comparative work on the use of dissents in European constitutional review (Kelemen 2013, 2018). Hein and Ewert have used quantitative analysis based on the dissenting ratio of constitutional court decisions in order to investigate the extent to which decisions are politicized (Hein and Ewert 2016). Bricker has carried out a large-scale study combining qualitative and quantitative methods for the German and some Eastern European (Poland, Latvia, Slovenia, Czech Republic) constitutional courts. His research was twofold: on the one hand, he investigated the influence of various contextual factors on the tendency of a constitutional judge to issue a dissenting opinion, and on the other hand, he examined the impact of dissenting opinions on the quality of the resulting decision (Bricker 2017).

Related to internal dynamics, a separate empirical research area is the study of constitutional court reasoning from a comparative perspective. Jakab, Dyevre, and Itzcovich (2017) have made a serious attempt at a comprehensive comparative mapping of constitutional court reasoning, using both qualitative and quantitative methods based on "leading judgments" drawn from selected countries (Jakab, Dyevre, and Itzcovich 2017).

1.4.4 Judicial-legislative relations

By focusing more closely on the research question of the present volume, we find that a long-established type of *qualitative approach* is examining the impact of constitutional courts on the policy-making process and policy-outcome. It thus already relates to the relationship and *dynamics* of constitutional review and the legislature, although there is also research that seeks to measure specifically the impact of constitutional review on the quality of policy outcome (Feld and Voigt 2003).

In terms of the relationship between constitutional review and the legislature, earlier literature naturally focuses on Western Europe (most prominently the work of Stone Sweet from the perspective of comparative judicial politics) (Stone Sweet 1990). Regarding the dynamics of constitutional review and legislature, he identified the constitutional judiciary as the *third legislative chamber*, with regard to both institutional design and empirical experience in specific policy areas (Shapiro and Stone 1994). Stone Sweet has concluded that the entry of constitutional review into the legislative process has caused the death of the legislative sovereignty, with governance taking place alongside or in competition with judges (Stone Sweet 2002, 2012).

Brewer-Carías also finds in his comprehensive comparative work based on national reports of European (and non-European) countries that constitutional courts have acquired a role that is most closely associated with the legislature or the constituent power (Brewer-Carías 2011). Taking the "constitutional courts as legislators" approach as a starting point, Florczak-Wątor has edited a volume of studies on the law-making activities of constitutional courts in Western European and Central and Eastern European countries (Florczak-Wątor 2020). Sadurski addressed the impact of the constitutional courts in CEE countries on the legislative process, approaching the strength of constitutional court decisions by examining the structure of the legislative process, suggesting that some features of this process (e.g. political fragmentation) are decisive for the degree of conflict between the constitutional courts and the legislature (Sadurski 2014).

The concept of a "veto player" has also emerged in the context of a game-theory-based conceptualization of the role of constitutional review in legislation. Although the term was first introduced in the context of studies on Western European courts, as a general theorization of constitutional review, it is also worth mentioning in the context of CEE countries. Volcansek proposed this approach based on the Italian Constitutional Court's jurisprudence (Volcansek 2001), later Hönnige and Brouard nuanced the picture, if not on the Italian, but on the role of the French and German constitutional courts. Using quantitative methods, they concluded that they play the role of a veto player only under certain conditions, and their role may be influenced by, for example, the legislative procedure or the ideological composition of the court (Brouard and Hönnige 2017). However, Tsebelis, for example, did not count (constitutional) judges as veto players (because they are absorbed by other political veto players) but added that they could be included in this role under certain conditions (Tsebelis 2002).

Lijphart conceptualized judicial review as part of a "consensus model of democracy" and also attempted to group 36 countries of the world (including a significant proportion of Western European countries) according to the strength of judicial review. He sets up four groups, the first group comprising those lacking judicial review. Those with judicial review are classified by Lijphart into "strong", "medium-strength", or "weak" categories based on the "degrees of activism in the assertion of this power" (Lijphart 2012). Vanberg used game-theory analysis to conceptualize the relationship between abstract judicial review and legislation, how different judicial behaviours influence the behaviour of the legislative majority, while the latter aims to ensure that legislation passes abstract review or that the opposition does not initiate the review process. Vanberg's results show that abstract review fits Lijphart's model of consensus democracy only when the court is not overly deferential. If it is somewhat restrictive, then legislative self-limitation is directed towards avoiding nullification by the constitutional review process, but if it is very restrictive, self-limitation means taking into account the opposition's viewpoint in order to avoid them initiating the review (Vanberg 1998).

In terms of the literature of empirical research on European constitutional courts, the parallel work of legal and political science is clearly visible, which, according to Garoupa, has moved closer together than the rigid separation that existed before. Garoupa has also systematized the English-language literature using quantitative methods in research on constitutional courts, most of them of course being single-country studies (Garoupa 2020). Garoupa and Bagashka draw attention to three prominent difficulties with empirical research on constitutional courts: the first is the availability (and processing, coding) of data; the second is the openness of the constitutional law scholarly community in this direction; and the third is the fact that such empirical research is not always popular with constitutional courts (Garoupa and Bagashka 2021).

Given that existing literature has not elaborated a consistent methodology for comparing the performance of constitutional courts, the JUDICON-EU research project developed a methodological framework for measuring the strength of constitutional court decisions and for mapping the relationship between constitutional courts and the legislature. In the next section, we describe this new methodology, which served as the analytical framework for all country studies in this volume.

1.5 Research methodology

A constitutional court decision is a complex piece of judicial text which cannot be quantified unless disaggregated into smaller yet distinct and meaningful units. Neglecting the fact that one judicial decision frequently consists of several rulings might seriously distort any kind of empirical legal research since this leads to an unjustified and unacceptable aggregation of units of observations. A decision issued under a single identification number consists of one or more rulings, references to various legal documents (laws, earlier decisions issued by lower courts, etc.), and a more or less detailed justification. Within the same decision one ruling might reject a motion dealing with certain legal regulations while another ruling in the same decision might declare unconstitutional some other parts of the same (or another) legal regulation. The decision of the court might also contain a ruling that declares an *ex nunc* procedural unconstitutionality annulling a whole law, while another ruling of the same decision declares *ex tunc* substantial unconstitutionality of a paragraph of a different legislative act. Added to these, decisions might be supplemented by dissenting opinions if judges disagree with the majority of the court. Precisely because a single decision might contain several rulings, in our research, decisions have been broken down into separate units (rulings).

Thus, in contrast to research of the judicial branch which generally considers one decision as the unit of observation, we take one ruling as our unit of observation. The following example justifies this decision. In decision 47/2009 (IV.21.) the Hungarian Constitutional Court first held that "in the application of Section 12 para. (3) of the Act XXIII of 1992 on the Legal Status of Public Servants, it is a constitutional requirement based on Article 59 and 60 of the Constitution that the deed of oath should not contain any data referring to the public servant's conviction of conscience or religion". This Ruling 1 is a constitutional requirement. As a second ruling of the same decision, the HCC rejected "the petitions aimed at establishing the unconstitutionality and the annulment of Section 12 and Section 13 para. (2) of Act XXIII of 1992 on the Legal Status of Public Servants". Consequently, Ruling 2 of this decision was a rejection. As a third ruling of that very same decision, the HCC terminated "the procedure aimed at the posterior review of the unconstitutionality of Sections 31/A–31/F of Act XXIII of 1992 on the Legal Status of Public Servants", which means that Ruling 3 of this decision was a suspension. As a fourth ruling, it refused in the same decision "the petition aimed at establishing the unconstitutionality and the annulment of Section 13 para. (1), Section 65 para. (2) item d) and Section 102 para. (8) of Act XXIII of 1992 on the Legal Status of Public Servants, and it refused other petitions as well". This means that Ruling 4 of this specific decision of the HCC was a rejection.

Certainly, constitutional courts do not always make unanimous decisions, and sometimes judges express their disagreement by formulating dissenting opinions. However, while dissenting opinions are linked to certain decisions of the court, the substantive content of dissent relates to one or more rulings of the same decisions. Consequently, not only decisions need to be broken down into rulings, but dissenting opinions can be accounted for only by disaggregating them into the same meaningful and distinct units. That is, in our research, dissenting opinions are also disaggregated into separate units referring to a specific ruling of the court decision. Disaggregating majority decisions and dissenting opinions into rulings implies that the judges' dissenting opinions can be directly linked to rulings of the majority decisions. This allows for avoiding the pitfalls of a simplified analysis that would link whole judicial decisions to dissenting opinions without taking into consideration that various rulings in dissenting opinions might refer to different parts of a majority decision. This means that dissenting opinions are analysed according to the same components and elements as the majority decisions themselves, and it becomes possible to investigate even individual judicial behaviour.

1.5.1 Components of rulings

Disaggregating decisions into rulings allows for identifying the most specific and meaningful units that describes the behaviour of the majority of the court

Table 1.1 Components and elements of rulings

I. Provision	*II. Completeness*	*III. Temporal effect*	*IV. Prescription*
(Ia) rejection or refusal (Ib) unconstitutionality by legislative omission	(IIa) qualitative partial annulment	(IIIa) pro futuro	(IVa) no prescription
(Ic) procedural unconstitutionality (Id) constitutional requirement	(IIb) quantitative partial annulment	(IIIb) ex nunc	(IVb) non-binding prescription (IVc) directive
(Ie) substantive unconstitutionality (If) constitutional interpretation in abstracto	(IIc) complete annulment	(IIIc) ex tunc	(IVd) binding prescription

or dissenting judges. However, as our aim is to go beyond the constitutional/unconstitutional binarity, rulings should not only be understood as the meaningful units within a decision but also as composites of various elements that account for the diversity of judicial behaviour and for the extent of the constrain imposed by the court on the legislature. Considering the complexity of judicial decisions, we aimed to elaborate a methodological framework that offers a sophisticated tool for mapping the diversity of rulings and measuring their strength. To be able to do this, one has to identify the elements in the ruling which affect the diversity and the extent of constraint (see Table 1.1). Thus, rulings are understood as consisting of four elements: a type of provision (e.g. declaring substantive unconstitutionality), a degree of completeness (e.g. partial annulment), a temporal effect (e.g. *pro futuro*), and a prescription for the legislature (e.g. binding or non-binding prescription), all of which might have different varieties that result in stronger or weaker constraint of the legislature.

The four elements – namely provision, completeness, temporal effect, and prescription – that are in the focus of our research project might be considered as options from which a judge or the constitutional court makes up a ruling. A ruling results from a mixture of the elements chosen. We have checked the presence/absence of all four elements rigorously in each relevant ruling, since even the absence of an element is an indicator of the strength or weakness of a ruling.

Obviously, the most important element of the ruling is the provision, which declares a law constitutional or unconstitutional. However, it is also important whether the court annuls only a part of the law or the whole act (or only a certain interpretation of it). This will be referred to as the completeness of a ruling. Furthermore, the temporal effect of the annulment can vary, which also influences the diversity and strength of the ruling. These three components (provision, completeness, and temporal effect) are always located in the operative part of a judicial decision. Finally, rulings may contain a prescription, which declares how unconstitutionality might or should be corrected – it formulates guidelines or directives which legislatures should transform into a law. A prescription might be found either in the operative part or in the justification of the decision. Although the present research primarily focuses on the operative part (since this contains the directly binding elements), justifications are also considered when they contain prescriptions.

Let us describe the elements of judicial rulings in more detail:

(I) Provision

Rulings of the constitutional court always contain a provision which might differ on the grounds on which the law has been found (un)constitutional: it might declare a refusal or rejection, unconstitutionality by legislative omission, procedural unconstitutionality, interpretation in harmony with the constitution (or constitutional requirements), substantive unconstitutionality, or constitutional interpretation in abstracto.

(Ia) Refusal/Rejection (Ref/ReJ)

Motions might be rejected on the grounds that the legal regulation under review is completely in accordance with the constitution. They might be refused, however, also without substantive court investigation, due to inadmissibility or by referring to the political question doctrine. The process of the court might be suspended, which, for the sake of our research project, might be considered as equal to a refusal except when the court determines some constitutional requirements to be respected by the legislature.

(Ib) Unconstitutionality by legislative omission (Om)

Unconstitutionality might emerge not only by the proactive operation of the legislature but also by legislative omissions. Legislative omissions might be caused not only by total inactivity of legislature but also by imperfect or insufficient legislation. Declaring unconstitutionality on these grounds is, however, a mild form of provision, since the constitutional court does not annul any acts of parliament but only calls upon the legislature to regulate something which is not regulated at all or is regulated in an imperfect or insufficient manner.

(Ic) Procedural unconstitutionality (PROC)

By procedural unconstitutionality, we mean all court provisions which abrogate a law due to the failures of the legislative process. Procedural unconstitutionality refers only to the legislative process and not to the substance of legislation. In this case, it is possible for the legislature to pass the bill a second time with the same or highly similar substance. Unconstitutionality means, in this sense, the violation of procedural rules but not the violation of the formal principles of rule of law. This category includes cases of inaccurate processes of legislation (like violation of the procedural rules of legislation, violation of the principle of the hierarchy of legal sources, omission of the prescribed consultation in the legislative process, omission of a substantive debate in the legislative process).

(Id) Constitutional requirements (CR)

While formally upholding a law, judges might have considerable room to manoeuvre in constraining the legislature by two means: first by judicial interpretation in harmony with the constitution, and second by determining constitutional requirements for either the courts or the legislature. To some extent, constitutional requirements in the operative part of a decision substantially broaden the regulation under constitutional review without the annulment of any of its parts. By giving guidance or directives for the legislature, the court is expanding the text of the law under review; consequently, it turns into a positive legislator. Constitutional requirement or interpretation in harmony with the constitution is suitable, however, for declaring both a particularly weak or a particularly strong provision which constrains the legislative branch seriously or just barely. This means that the court might be a mild or a very rigorous positive legislator.

(Ie) Substantive unconstitutionality (SUBST)

Substantive unconstitutionality constrains legislature more significantly than any previous forms of provisions since it imposes some substantive barrier on the legislature. Declaring a law unconstitutional based on its content and disharmony with some paragraphs of the constitution is a very strong provision which implies high levels of constraints on the legislature. Consequently, the legislature's room to manoeuvre will be considerably narrowed.

(If) Constitutional interpretation *in abstracto* (CIIA)

An even stronger way to constrain the legislative branch (and the constituent power) is constitutional interpretation *in abstracto*.[3] Constitutional interpretation *in abstracto* means that the court has been asked to explain and, consequently, to expand the text of the constitution in the operative part of its decision. Since the operative part of a decision usually contains only provisions

3 Beyond the German Federal Constitutional Court, no court in Western Europe has the competence to declare an abstract and binding interpretation of constitution without reviewing a law filed to the court. By contrast, this kind of constitutional adjudication is not unknown in Central Europe although even courts in CEE have rarely been asked to exercise it (for this see Hönnige (2007, 132) and Sadurski (2014, 23). Binding constitutional interpretations are not only advisory notes in the justifications of a decision but they are included into the operative part of judicial decisions, and they shouldn't be confounded with preliminary reference procedure of the ECJ. For an example see decision 21/1996 of the HCC (http://hunconcourt.hu/letoltesek/en_0021_1996.pdf).

like rejecting, refusing, suspending, or annulling, all other forms of provisions which do not rule but explain and thereby extend the text of the constitution are equal to a constitution writing process. Constitutional interpretation *in abstracto* means the expanding of the text of the constitution; therefore, the constitutional court becomes not merely a positive legislator but a constituent power (*pouvoir constituant*). The court undertakes constitution-making even if it is an implicit rather than an explicit process. Since legislative majorities are usually not equal to supermajorities, and in this case the constitutional court fulfils the role of the constituent assembly or the *pouvoir constituant*, these decisions might be regarded as meaning the strongest constraints of the legislative.[4] Constitution-making means that the legislature's room to manoeuvre is heavily limited, since amending the constitution usually requires a supermajority that only rarely coincides with the legislative majority.

(II) Completeness

Judicial decisions pertain to legal regulations or legal norms. Although it might be uncertain whether a legal norm is contained in one sentence, in an article or in several interconnected articles of a statute (or even of several statutes), we embrace the position of the legislator and assume that the legislator either included all relevant norms concerning a policy issue in a statute or that it referred to other statutes which are interconnected. By assuming this position, we argue that complete annulment means that all paragraphs of a statute have been quashed. Nevertheless, a judicial decision very rarely annuls all sections of a statute; it is more common that only certain parts of it will be quashed. Furthermore, we distinguish between qualitative and quantitative

4 At first glance it might be not obvious why we are arguing that constitutional interpretation in abstracto corresponds to constitution-making or writing. The idea (and problem) that constitutional courts might be not only positive legislators but actors of constitution writing processes have been developed in the legal scholarship in connection to the heavily discussed problem of unconstitutional constitutional amendments. Constraining the constituent power by judicial decisions means certainly that the court vindicates the right to be an integrative part of a composite body assumed as *pouvoir constituant*. Also, the concept of post-sovereign constitution-making, as presented by Andrew Arato, hints to the constitutional courts emerged as powerful actors to fill in the gaps and deficiencies of a transitory constitution. In several countries (and especially in Hungary and in South Africa), prominent actors of these post-sovereign constitution making processes were constitutional courts. Both of these directions of constitutional theories consider, however, either all forms of the activity of constitutional courts in general, or they narrow down the problem to the concept of unconstitutional constitutional amendment. In contrast to these trends, we argue that including lengthy and detailed interpretation of constitutional norms and concepts into the operative part of a judicial decision is clearly an expansion of the text of the constitution. Since the operative part of a decision is undoubtedly legally binding, while the status of justifications is contested in this regard, we argue that binding interpretation of the constitution included into the operative part is equivalent to constitution-making. To this question see: Arato (2016); Sweet (2012, 826); Vorländer (2006, 20).

partial annulment. Qualitative partial annulment of the norm might be best grasped perhaps as a negative constitutional requirement.

Determining a negative constitutional requirement, in practice, means that the court found the law (or a paragraph/section/some words of a law) unconstitutional as far as the norm (or legislative act) might have an interpretation which is unconstitutional. However, there might be some other interpretation of the same norm (or legislative act) that is in harmony with the constitution. Consequently, though the court annulled the norm (law or any part of the law), the legislature might find a solution by adopting the same law (part of the law) by explicitly excluding its unconstitutional interpretation. This is why this kind of ruling is only partial: the ruling of the court intends to exclude only some kinds of interpretation of the law (or part of the law), some part of the possible meanings of the law but no other kinds of interpretation of the law. In contrast to qualitative partial annulment, quantitative partial annulment means that not only a certain interpretation of some parts of the law but also all possible interpretations and meanings of that part of the law are unconstitutional, while the constitutional court annuls only one or some part(s) (paragraph, section, some words) of the law. In this sense, quantitative partial annulment is "more complete" than qualitative partial annulment since the law might remain in effect, given the possibility that its unconstitutional interpretation is excluded from the text of the law. Quantitative partial annulment thus means that the constitutional court annulled a part of the law – but only a part of it. Complete annulment, in turn, means that all paragraphs of the law have been annulled.

(III) Temporal effect

The temporal effect of the annulment is a further element of all judicial decisions, which affects the strength of rulings and consequently the room for manoeuvre of the legislature. Since *pro futuro* rulings may grant a transitional period, in which the goals of the legislative body might have temporarily been effectuated, this type of ruling seems to be a compromise and has a less dramatic effect on the legislature. This is not the case with *ex nunc* rulings, and even less in the most radical form of rulings (*ex tunc*). While an *ex nunc* ruling comes into effect immediately, leaving no room for the legislator, an *ex tunc* ruling annuls a law retroactively, which creates an especially strong encroachment on the legislative.

(IV) Prescription

As for the prescription determined by the courts, judges have quite a wide range of options: they can formulate recommendations, directives, or constitutional requirements, or they can even anticipate what kind of legislative acts might prove to be unconstitutional in the future. They can also prescribe detailed regulation as to how unconstitutionality might be remedied. Since prescriptions vary according to their legal force (or binding effect), it is reasonable to discern four categories reflecting the variegation of prescriptions. Prescriptions which are placed in the operative part of a judicial decision have a clear-cut, legally binding effect (binding prescription) and are functionally equivalent to a constitutional requirement in the operative part of the decision. Both prescriptions (or directives) in the operative part and constitutional requirements expand the text of the law under review; consequently, the court becomes a positive legislator by giving a prescription or a constitutional requirement. By contrast, prescriptions in the justification (or reasoning) have a less clear-cut status concerning their legal effect (non-binding). Prescriptions in the headnotes (*Leitsatz*) of the decision have an ambiguous legal effect: they are more constraining than prescriptions in the justification but less so than prescriptions in the operative part of the decision (directive). Furthermore, several decisions contain no prescription at all (no prescription).

1.5.2 Diversity and frequency

As already noted, our research starts from the assumption that the decisions of the constitutional courts should be considered more diverse than merely declaring constitutionality or unconstitutionality. The components we identified earlier allow judges to select from a wide range of measures to constrain the legislature.

Analysing the combinations and the diversity of rulings involves a significant advance compared to the earlier dichotomous approach, which allowed only for the distinction between the constitutional/unconstitutional categories. The diversity approach sheds light on the frequency of the specific combinations of the different parts of the rulings, as well as their temporal changes. This level of the analysis involves a nominal approach, which simply determines the different ruling combinations and their frequency. Since a specific ruling consists of different parts constraining the legislative power to a different extent, it is important to differentiate between weaker and stronger combinations. Whereas specific combinations imply a stronger constraint on the legislature, other combinations consisting of weaker parts suggest that the court intended a tempered intervention in the legislature's room for manoeuvre.

As mentioned earlier, the four elements – namely provision, completeness, temporal effect, and prescription – might be considered as options from which a judge or the constitutional court makes up a ruling. Based on the methodological framework, there are 79 possible combinations of the elements (different types of provision, completeness, temporal effect, and prescription) (Table 1.2). We are, however, aware that certain combinations of these elements are not applicable at all: in the case of unconstitutionality by legislative omission (Ib), completeness (II) and temporal effect (III) are not applicable since no legal norm has been annulled, which is a precondition for referring to the completeness or temporal effect of the annulment. Also, declaring a constitutional requirement in the operative part of the decision (Id) or declaring

Table 1.2 Possible combination of the elements of judicial rulings

Provision	*Completeness*	*Temporal effect*	*Prescription*
Rejection or refusal (REJ or REF)	NA	NA	NA
Omission (OM)	NA	NA	no prescription non-binding prescription directive binding prescription
Procedural unconstitutionality (PROC)	qualitative partial annulment quantitative partial annulment complete annulment	*pro futuro* *ex nunc* *ex tunc*	no prescription non-binding prescription directive binding prescription
Constitutional requirement (CR)	NA	NA	Constitutional requirement
Substantive unconstitutionality (SUBST)	qualitative partial annulment quantitative partial annulment complete annulment	*pro futuro* *ex nunc* *ex tunc*	no prescription non-binding prescription directive binding prescription
Constitutional interpretation *in abstracto* (CIIA)	NA	NA	Constitutional requirement

NA: Combination is not possible.

a constitutional interpretation *in abstracto* (If) both imply that completeness (II) and temporal effect (III) are not applicable, since no sections of the law have been annulled. Annulment is required in order to be able to check for the completeness and temporal effect of the annulment. Constitutional requirement in the operative part of the decision (Id) and constitutional interpretation *in abstracto* (If) imply that we cannot consider prescription (IV) at all. This is because constitutional requirements are functionally equivalent to prescriptions that expand the text of the law under review – as explained previously. Constitutional interpretation *in abstracto* (If), by contrast, expands the text of the constitution; thus, we cannot consider it as a prescription. Beyond these specific cases, in the coding process all four elements of a ruling listed here were checked one by one in four steps.

1.5.3 *Strength and weighting*

Beyond the dimensions of diversity and frequency of certain types of rulings, the main goal of the research is to determine the strength of the decisions of constitutional courts. More specifically, the aim is to measure the extent by which a ruling of the court might constrain the legislature. Measuring the strength of constitutional court rulings requires weighting the elements described in the previous section. Determining or predefining the relationship of the elements to each other is not unconceivable by formulating clear and plausible principles of weighting the elements (see Table 1.3). In order to determine the strength of a ruling, it is necessary to weight the elements by comparing the four criteria and ranking the decision options. The weighting assumes that the provision is the most important and decisive element of the decision, and the weight of the other elements in relation to the strength of the decision was determined in relation to this.

Two principles were used to determine the value of each element or option. According to the first principle, the weakest combination of substantive unconstitutionality (1e + 2a + 3a + 4a = 6) is always stronger than the strongest case of procedural unconstitutionality (1c + 2c + 3c + 4d = 5). According to the second principle, constitutional interpretation in abstracto (1f) is at least as strong as the strongest case of substantive unconstitutionality (1e + 2c + 3c + 4d = 10). Following these principles, the weighting of each element of the decisions has been developed, the exact values of which are shown in Table 1.3. By identifying the elements and giving them the appropriate weight, it is possible to determine the extent to which a given majority decision or dissenting opinion represents a constraint on the legislature. Furthermore, the decisional strength allows us to draw conclusions not only about the functioning of the Constitutional Court but also about the individual behaviour of judges, which will be crucial to account for dissenting opinions and their relation to majority rulings.

(I) Provision

The most important part of a judicial decision is its provision. The range of the scale extends from decisions that refuse the motion (without deciding on the merit of the case) or simply find the law constitutional, on the one end of the scale, and decisions in which the constitutional court becomes constituent power (constitutional interpretation *in abstracto*), on the other. There are different types of decisions between these two extremes. The relative weight might be determined according to the following relations.

- (Ia) Rejection does not constrain the legislature at all. [0.00]
- (Ib) Unconstitutionality by legislative omission merely declares that the legislature must adopt a new regulation but does not constrain the legislature regarding the substance of regulation. [+0.50]
- (Ic) Declaring the procedural unconstitutionality of a legal regulation implies that the regulation will be annulled but only due to some procedural mistakes in the legislative process. [+1.00]
- (Id) Constitutional requirements constrain the legislature more than the declaration of procedural unconstitutionality since the court becomes a positive legislator and the substance of the regulation will be altered while upholding the law under review. [+2.00]

Table 1.3 Weighting of the elements of rulings

I. Provision	(Ia) rejection or refusal [**0**]	(Ib) unconstitutionality by legislative omission [**0.5**]	(Ic) procedural unconstitutionality [**1**]	(Id) constitutional requirement [**2**]	(Ie) substantive unconstitutionality [**6**]	(If) constitutional interpretation *in abstracto* [**10**]
II. Completeness	(IIa) qualitative partial annulment [**0**]		(IIb) quantitative partial annulment [**0.5**]		(IIc) complete annulment [**1**]	
III. Temporal effect	(IIIa) *pro futuro* [**0**]		(IIIb) *ex nunc* [**0.5**]		(IIIc) *ex tunc* [**1**]	
IV. Prescription	(IVa) no prescription [**0**]	(IVb) non-binding prescription [**1**]		(IVc) directive [**1.5**]		(IVd) binding prescription [**2**]

- (Ie) Declaring substantive unconstitutionality implies that the substance of the legal regulation has been flawed to a degree that the court could not rectify unconstitutionality by stretching the text of the law under review (i.e. determining a constitutional requirement) but has to abrogate the legal regulation. The guiding principle is that any form of substantive unconstitutionality should be regarded as a stronger decision than any other decision based on procedural unconstitutionality or constitutional requirement. Therefore, the weakest combination of substantive unconstitutionality should always be regarded as stronger than the strongest form of procedural unconstitutionality. [+6.00]
- (If) Constitutional interpretation *in abstracto* is regarded as the strongest constraint on the legislator. This is why CIIA must be at least as strong as the strongest decision declaring substantive unconstitutionality [+10.00]. It is, however, of utmost importance to remark that CIIA does not always constrain the legislature. CIIA might sometimes rather extend the room of the national legislator to manoeuvre vis-à-vis other political actors. In this case, the constitution will be expanded in a way highly favourable for the legislature. This is why we have to make a clear difference between highly constraining CIIA, on the one hand, and highly permissive CIIA on the other. Consequently, CIIAs should also be evaluated case by case. [either +10.00 or 0.00]

(II) Completeness

The question of whether the court annulled the legal regulation totally (complete annulment), partially (quantitative partial annulment), or merely excluded some meanings of a legal term (qualitative partial annulment) is certainly not as important as the provision or a prescription. Thus, we had to add less weight for the strongest form of completeness than for the strongest form of prescription and the provision. This is how qualitative partial annulment is weighted as the weakest form [0.00], quantitative partial annulment as a middle-range [0.50], and complete annulment as the strongest form [+1.00].

(III) Temporal effect

Temporal effect should be considered as important as completeness if we compare the four elements of rulings. Temporal effect is certainly less important than the prescription and even less than the provision. Hence the weight of the three categories are as follows: *pro futuro* [0], *ex nunc* [0.50], and *ex tunc* [+1.00].

(IV) Prescription

Since courts might to some extent replace legislature by determining binding prescriptions, this fourth element (along with its functional equivalent constitutional requirement) must be the second-most important and weightiest element of a ruling after declaring the substantive unconstitutionality of a legal regulation. Weights of prescriptions vary according to their placement in the decision: non-binding is placed in the justification, which has a rather uncertain legal effect [+1.00]; directive is placed in the headnote (if there is such a thing in the decision), the legal status of which is still uncertain but might clearly be regarded as a stronger element [+1.50] than prescriptions in the justification. The strongest prescription is placed in the operative part, which has a legal binding effect [+2.00].

1.5.4 Dissenting opinions, dissenting coalitions, and networks

Constitutional courts do not always make unanimous decisions, and judges might express their disagreement by formulating dissenting opinions. Consequently, we have examined not only majority rulings but also dissenting opinions. We have, however, neglected all concurring opinions since they do not concern the tenor, i.e. the operative part of the judicial decisions, which is in the focus of our research project. Disaggregating majority decisions and dissenting opinions into rulings implies that the judges' dissenting opinions can be directly linked to rulings of the majority decisions. This allows us to avoid the pitfalls of a simplified analysis that would link entire judicial decisions to dissenting opinions without taking into consideration the fact that various rulings in dissenting opinions might refer to different rulings of a majority decision. This means that dissenting opinions are disaggregated into rulings and analysed according to the same components and elements as the majority decisions themselves, and it becomes possible to investigate even individual judicial behaviour.

Dissenting opinions are sometimes formulated by one judge without having any other judges aligning with the dissent. Several times, however, judges make a coalition when publishing dissenting opinions. A coalition of dissenting judges means that a dissenting opinion written by a judge might also be supported and signed by further judges. A coalition might involve a single case of agreement, but in the practice of the courts some coalitions of two or more judges are lasting, extending to several cases. Dissenter coalitions are considered here in a very restrictive sense: judges form a dissenter coalition only if their dissent has the same strength value and it is an outcome of the same composition of the elements of judicial decisions. This means that they selected the same components in all four aspects of the ruling (provision, completeness, temporal effect, and prescription). The same strength of two or more dissenting opinions is not a sufficient condition for a dissenting coalition since it could be an outcome of a different composition of their dissenting opinions. Two dissenting opinions with the same value [7] are not considered as a basis of judicial coalition if they differ, for example, in their temporal effect and completeness. To put it simply: a dissenting opinion declaring substantive unconstitutionality [6], with qualitative partial annulment [0] ex tunc [1] and without any prescription [0] is not considered as a basis of judicial coalition if another judge declared in his/her dissenting opinion a substantive unconstitutionality [6] with complete annulment [1] but *pro futuro* [0] and without any prescription [0], since they differ in temporal effect and completeness.

Dissenting opinions have been conjugated, and each interaction of judge "A" with any other judge has been counted in a matrix. Of course, there have been decisions where dissenting opinions were formulated by only one judge, without any other judges aligning with it. These cases have been neglected since we were interested in dissenting coalitions. The number of interactions between judge "A" and judge "B" shows the strength of the coalition: if the uniformity of their dissenting opinions occurred several times (even if the components of their dissenting opinion differed from time to time), it is considered a strong coalition. This framework of analysis will be applied consequently in all country studies.

Judges with identical dissenting opinions can be considered as coalitions that allow for a network analysis of the practice of the courts. Coalitions might be formed explicitly when a judge signs a dissenting opinion written by another judge, or implicitly when two or more judges form the same dissenting opinion. Identical dissents are determined by their specific composition of the elements described previously. That is, dissenting coalitions constrain the legislature not only by the same strength, but the strength of their dissent consists of the selection of the same elements (the same type of provision, completeness, temporal effect, and prescription). Coalitions were first arranged into a matrix of the pairs of dissenting judges to draw a map of the intensity of interaction between judges. The map identifies the judges' various clusters, actors in the centre or on the periphery of the network, as well as judges who act as links between separate parts of the network. On the next level of the network analysis, we intended to determine how polarized the network is. By using the edge betweenness algorithm, we managed to identify not only the groups separated within the network but also the degree of their separation, or in other words, their modularity which shows how far the clusters are from each other. Although the literature does not offer an uncontested view about a specific level of modularity to account for a significantly fragmented community, in practice, a network with modularity above 0.3 is usually considered meaningfully separated (Clauset, Newman, and Moore 2004).

1.6 Structure of the chapters

The country studies (Chapters 3 through 11) in this volume present the results of the coding process and the analysis of the data sets of the countries in question. Although the chapters are all structured in the same way, they differ slightly because we conducted a pilot project with six European countries. Consequently, the structure of the studies on the Czech Republic, Hungary, Poland, Romania, and Slovakia takes into account that the first results of the pilot project have already been published (Pócza 2019). These chapters find a balance between giving a short summary of the previous findings and including essential new findings on the courts' performance in five Central European countries. On the other hand, the chapters on Croatia, Estonia, Latvia, Lithuania, and Slovenia (countries not included in the pilot project) follow the predetermined chapter structure used also in the pilot project.

Keeping in mind this difference between the two groups of country studies, each chapter introduces the respective constitutional court by outlining its historical origins, the court's position within the constitutional system, its main competencies, and institutional peculiarities or special processes unknown elsewhere in the region. Secondly, the chapters present a general impression of the court's activity based on the evaluation of the JUDICON-EU dataset of the respective countries and, at the same time, clarify whether there was any kind of country-specific phenomenon concerning case selection, coding process, dissenting opinions, decision-making processes of the court, or other phenomena deviating from the consistent coding rules. Thirdly, the chapters assess the trends in majority decisions: preferred or missing ruling types or trends in ruling types, and explanations of these trends. The authors also determine whether changes in ruling types and strengths are linked to changes in political circumstances or changes in the court's composition. Some chapters used statistical analysis, while others more advanced quantitative methodologies in evaluating the data and looking for explanations. Nevertheless, in some countries, trends were not discernible; consequently, we asked the authors to find an answer to the absence of any trends.

Since the courts' presidents have usually a special influence on the court's activity, where relevant, the chapters discuss the president's performance and influence on the decision-making process. Subsequently, the analysis of dissenting opinions follows. In some courts the number of dissenting opinions is rather negligible, consequently, they cannot be analysed quantitatively. In other courts, however, trends in publishing or not publishing dissenting opinions are clearly recognizable, and the authors could assess individual judges' performance concerning the frequency and strength of their dissenting opinions, as well as their relative difference from the majority decisions' strength. Since we also prepared a network analysis of dissenting opinions, the country studies touch upon the question of dissenting coalitions, i.e. identifying the judges who were willing to join each other for a dissent. A qualitative evaluation of selected cases closes the country studies with a special focus on cases of utmost importance from the perspective of the research questions or on cases challenging the quantitative methodology of the project.

References

Arato, Andrew. 2016. *Post Sovereign Constitution Making: Learning and Legitimacy*. Oxford: Oxford University Press.

Bagashka, Tanya, and Lydia Brashear Tiede. 2021. "The Influence of Procurator Generals in Constitutional Review: The Case of Bulgaria." *Journal of Law and Courts* 9 (1): 189–214.

Benz, Arthur. 2017. "The Federal Constitutional Court of Germany: Guardian of Unitarism and Federalism." In *Courts in Federal Countries*, edited by Nicholas Theodore Aroney and John Kincaid, 193–222. Toronto: University of Toronto Press.

Bickel, Alexander. 1962. *The Least Dangerous Branch: The Supreme Court at the Bar of Politics*. New York: The Bobbs-Merrill Co.

Brewer-Carías, Allan R. 2011. *Constitutional Courts as Positive Legislators: A Comparative Law Study*. Cambridge: Cambridge University Press.

Bricker, Benjamin. 2017 "Breaking the Principle of Secrecy: An Examination of Judicial Dissent in the European Constitutional Courts: Breaking the Principle of Secrecy." *Law & Policy* 39 (2): 170–191.

———, and Jakub Wondreys. 2018. "Public Opinion and Opposition Party Success: Evidence from the European Constitutional Courts." *Justice System Journal* 39 (2): 123–138. https://doi.org/10.1080/0098261X.2018.1438217.

Brouard, Sylvain, and Christoph Hönnige. 2017. "Constitutional Courts as Veto Players: Lessons from the United States, France and Germany: Constitutional Courts as Veto Players." *European Journal of Political Research* 56 (3): 529–552.

Brunner, Georg. 1992. "Development of a Constitutional Judiciary in Eastern Europe." *Review of Central and East European Law* 18 (6): 535–553.

Bumin, Kirill M. 2017. "Judicial Institutionalization and Judicial Activism of the Post-Communist Constitutional Courts." *Journal of Politics and Law* 10 (2): 54–72.

Castillo-Ortiz, Pablo. 2019. "The Illiberal Abuse of Constitutional Courts in Europe." *European Constitutional Law Review* 15 (1): 48–72.

Clauset, Aaron, Mark Newman, and Christopher Moore, 2004. "Finding Community Structure in Very Large Networks." *Physical Review E* 70: 066111.

Dalla Pellegrina, Lucia, Jef De Mot, Michael Faure, and Nuno Garoupa. 2017. "Litigating Federalism: An Empirical Analysis of Decisions of the Belgian Constitutional Court." *European Constitutional Law Review* 13 (2): 305–346.

Daly, Tom Gerald. 2017. *The Alchemists: Questioning our Faith in Courts as Democracy-Builders*. Cambridge: Cambridge University Press.

De Visser, Maartje. 2014. *Constitutional Review in Europe: A Comparative Analysis*. Oxford: Hart Publishing.

Dixon, Rosalind, and David E. Landau. 2021. *Abusive Constitutional Borrowing: Legal Globalization and the Subversion of Liberal Democracy*. Oxford: Oxford University Press.

Drinóczi, Tímea, and Agnieszka Bień-Kacała. 2019. "Illiberal Constitutionalism: The Case of Hungary and Poland." *German Law Journal* 20 (8): 1140–1166.

Epstein, Lee, Jack Knight, and Olga Shvetsova. 2001. "The Role of Constitutional Courts in the Establishment and Maintenance of Democratic Systems of Government." *Law & Society Review* 35 (1): 117–164.

Ernits, Madis, Jolita Miliuvienė, Jānis Pleps, and Vytautas Sinkevičius. 2022. "Models of Constitutional Adjudication in the Baltic States." *International Social Science Journal* 72 (246): 1217–1235.

Feld, Lars P., and Stefan Voigt. 2003. "Economic Growth and Judicial Independence: Cross-country Evidence Using a New Set of Indicators." *European Journal of Political Economy* 19 (3): 497–527.

Florczak-Wątor, Monika. 2020. *Judicial Law-Making in European Constitutional Courts*. London and New York: Taylor & Francis.

Forejohn, John, and Pasquale Pasquino. 2004. "Constitutional Adjudication: Lessons from Europe." *Texas Law Review* 82: 1671–1704.

Garlicki, Lech. 2007. "Constitutional Courts Versus Supreme Courts." *International Journal of Constitutional Law* 5 (1): 44–68.

Garoupa, Nuno. 2015. *Judicial Reputation: A Comparative Theory.* Chicago and London: The University of Chicago Press.

———. 2019. "Constitutional Review." In *The Oxford Handbook of Public Choice, Volume 2*, edited by Roger D. Congleton, Bernard Grofman, and Stefan Voigt, 133–155. Oxford: Oxford University Press.

———. 2020. "Constitutional Courts in Civil-Law Western Europe: Quantitative Approaches." *George Mason University Law and Economics Research Paper Series No. 20–05* [Preprint].

———, and Tanya Bagashka. 2021. "Constitutional courts in Europe – Quantitative approaches." In *High Courts in Global Perspective: Evidence, Methodologies and Findings*, edited by Nuno Garoupa, Robert D. Gill, and Lydia Tiede. Charlottesville and London: University of Virginia Press.

———, and Tom Ginsburg. 2011. "Building Reputation in Constitutional Courts: Political and Judicial Audiences." *Arizona Journal of International & Comparative Law* 28 (3): 539–568.

Groppi, Tania, and Marie-Claire Ponthoreau, eds. 2013. *The Use of Foreign Precedents by Constitutional Judges.* Oxford: Hart Publishing.

Hein, Michael, and Stefan Ewert. 2016. "How Do Types of Procedure Affect the Degree of Politicization of European Constitutional Courts? A Comparative Study of Germany, Bulgaria, and Portugal." *European Journal of Legal Studies* 9 (1): 62–102.

Herron, Erik S., and Kirk A. Randazzo. 2003. "The Relationship between Independence and Judicial Review in Post-Communist Courts." *The Journal of Politics* 65 (2): 422–438.

Hirschl, Ran. 2008. "The Judicialization of Mega-Politics and the Rise of Political Courts." *Annual Review of Political Science* 11: 93–118.

Hönnige, Christoph. 2009. "The Electoral Connection: How the Pivotal Judge Affects Oppositional Success at European Constitutional Courts." *West European Politics* 32 (5): 963–984.

Jakab, András, Arthur Dyevre, and Giulio Itzcovich, eds. 2017. *Comparative Constitutional Reasoning.* Cambridge: Cambridge University Press.

Jovanović, Miodrag A., ed. 2015. *Constitutional Review and Democracy.* The Hague: Eleven International Publishing.

Kelemen, Katalin. 2013. "Dissenting Opinions in Constitutional Courts." *German Law Journal* 14 (8): 1345–1371.

———. 2018. *Judicial Dissent in European Constitutional Courts: A Comparative and Legal Perspective.* Abingdon: Routledge.

Kovalčík, Michal. 2022. "The Instrumental Abuse of Constitutional Courts: How Populists Can Use Constitutional Courts against the Opposition." *The International Journal of Human Rights* 26 (7): 1160–1180.

Lijphart, Arend. 2012. *Patterns of Democracy: Government Forms and Performance in Thirty-six Countries.* New Haven: Yale University Press.

Madsen, Mikael Rask, Pola Cebulak, and Micha Wiebusch. 2018. "Backlash against International Courts: Explaining the Forms and Patterns of Resistance to International Courts." *International Journal of Law in Context* 14: 197–220.

Magalhães, Pedro C. 1999. "The Politics of Judicial Reform in Eastern Europe." *Comparative Politics* 32 (1): 43–62.

Parau, Cristina E. 2018. *Transnational Networking and Elite Self-empowerment: The Making of the Judiciary in Contemporary Europe and beyond.* Oxford: Oxford University Press.

Pócza, Kálmán, ed. 2019. *Constitutional Politics and the Judiciary. Decision-making in Central and Eastern Europe.* London: Routledge.

Popelier, Patricia, and Samantha Bielen. 2019. "How Courts Decide Federalism Disputes: Legal Merit, Attitudinal Effects, and Strategic Considerations in the Jurisprudence of the Belgian Constitutional Court." *Publius: The Journal of Federalism* 49 (4): 587–616.

———, Sarah Verstraelen, Dirk Vanheule, and Beatrix Vanlerberghe, eds. 2013. *The Effects of Judicial Decisions in Time.* Cambridge: Instersentia Publishing.

Procházka, Radoslav. 2002. *Mission Accomplished: On Founding Constitutional Adjudication in Central Europe.* Budapest: Central European University Press.

Sadurski, Wojciech, ed. 2002. *Constitutional Justice, East and West: Democratic Legitimacy and Constitutional Courts in Post-communist Europe in a Comparative Perspective.* The Hague: Kluwer Law International.

———. 2014. *Rights Before Courts: A Study of Constitutional Courts in Postcommunist States of Central and Eastern Europe.* Dordrecht: Springer.

Scheppele, Kim Lane. 2003. "Constitutional Negotiations: Political Contexts of Judicial Activism in Post-Soviet Europe." *International Sociology* 18 (1): 219–238.

Schwartz, Herman. 1992. "The New East European Constitutional Courts." *Michigan Journal of International Law* 13 (4): 741–785.

———. 1998. "'Eastern Europe's Constitutional Courts." *Journal of Democracy* 9 (4): 100–114.

———. 2000. *The Struggle for Constitutional Justice in Post-Communist Europe.* Chicago: The University of Chicago Press.

Shapiro, Martin, and Alec Stone. 1994. "The New Constitutional Politics of Europe." *Comparative Political Studies* 26 (4): 397–420.

Smithey, Shannon Ishiyama, and John Ishiyama. 2000. "Judicious Choices: Designing Courts in Post-Communist Politics." *Communist and Post-Communist Studies* 33 (2): 163–182.

Stone Sweet, Alec. 1990 "The Birth and Development of Abstract Review: Constitutional Courts and Policymaking in Western Europe." *Policy Studies Journal* 19 (1): 81–95.

———. 2002. *Governing with Judges: Constitutional Politics in Europe.* Oxford: Oxford University Press.

———. 2012. "Constitutional Courts." In *The Oxford Handbook of Comparative Constitutional Law*, edited by Michael Rosenfeld and András Sajó, 816–830. Oxford: Oxford University Press.

Tsebelis, George. 2002. *Veto Players: How Political Institutions Work.* Princeton: Princeton University Press.

Utter, Robert F., and David C. Lundsgaard. 1993. "Judicial Review in the New Nations of Central and Eastern Europe: Some Thoughts from a Comparative Perspective." *Ohio State Law Journal* 54 (3): 559–606.

Vanberg, Georg. 1998. "Abstract Judicial Review, Legislative Bargaining, and Policy Compromise." *Journal of Theoretical Politics* 10 (3): 299–326.

———. 2004. *The Politics of Constitutional Review in Germany.* Cambridge: Cambridge University Press.

———. 2015. "Constitutional Courts in Comparative Perspective: A Theoretical Assessment." *Annual Review of Political Science* 18 (1): 167–185.

Vaubel, Roland. 2009. "Constitutional Courts as Promoters of Political Centralization: Lessons for the European Court of Justice." *European Journal of Law and Economics* 28 (3): 203–222.

Volcansek, Mary L. 2001. "Constitutional Courts as Veto Players: Divorce and Decrees in Italy." *European Journal of Political Research* 39 (3): 347–372.

Vorländer, Hans. 2006. "Deutungsmacht. Die Macht der Verfassungsgerichtsbarkeit." In *Die Deutungsmacht der Verfassungsgerichtsbarkeit*, edited by Hans Vorländer, 9–36. Wiesbaden: VS Verlag.

2 The Croatian Constitutional Court

From a potentially powerful court to a court of rejections

Monika Glavina

2.1 Introduction

In the words of Judge Siniša Rodin, one of the most important aspects of the creation of the 1991 Croatian Constitutional Court (CrCC) was the "establishment of an independent and potentially powerful" court (Rodin 1995, 783). This quote is interesting mainly because of seeing the CrCC for the first time as "potentially powerful". While it is true that Croatia, as part of the former Socialist Federal Republic of Yugoslavia (SFRY), had its own constitutional court (the Constitutional Court of the Socialist Republic of Croatia), the powers of the "socialist" Constitutional Court were much weaker than those provided for the new Court by the 1990 Constitution of the Republic of Croatia. The former "socialist" Constitutional Court's power of constitutional review was subject to state control both institutionally and politically: institutionally, it was subordinate to the Parliament of Yugoslavia, the so-called Federal Assembly (*Savezna skupština*), while politically, it was under the supervision of the Communist Party. In other words, in practice the doctrine of the primacy of the Federal Assembly prevented the Court from striking down government legislation as unconstitutional. Instead, the Court could only propose that the Assembly makes amendments to laws it deemed unconstitutional. Politically, the activity of the "socialist" Constitutional Court was severely limited by the informal but politically strong guidelines of the League of Communists of Croatia (the Croatian branch of the League of Communists of Yugoslavia), the Communist Party in power that played an important role in the appointment and dismissal of judges. This, too, constrained constitutional review or even blocked its initiation (Rodin 1995).

This relationship between the legislature and the Court changed with the adoption of the 1990 Constitution of the Republic of Croatia, which gave the newly created Constitutional Court the power to, among other things, rule on the compatibility of laws and other regulations with the Constitution and to annul them if they violated the Constitution or other laws/regulations (Constitution of the Republic of Croatia 1990, Article 129). The adoption of the 1990 Constitution and the establishment of the new CrCC marked a new path to democratization and opened a new phase of

DOI: 10.4324/9781003399483-2

constitutional review in Croatia. But how does this description of a new powerful Court compare to reality?

Not much has been written about the CrCC, especially from a political science perspective. With the exception of Barić's report, which is part of the project entitled "Courts as Policy-Makers? Examining the Role of Constitutional Courts as Agents of Change in the Western Balkans" (Barić 2016), the study of the CrCC remains the privileged domain of law professors (Rodin 1995, 1997; Crnić 2001; Podolnjak 2007) and Constitutional Court judges themselves (Omejec 2002; Arlović 2013, 2014; Omejec and Barić 2012). Moreover, most works on the CrCC can only be found in the Croatian language. Only a few scholarly articles or reports have been published in English on the topic (Rodin 1995, 1997; Omejec 2004; Barić 2016). This chapter attempts, among other things, to address these shortcomings.

This chapter will focus on the practice of the CrCC and empirically and systematically examine the decisions of the Court from its establishment in 1990 until 2020. The aim of this chapter is to investigate the extent to which the practice of the CrCC has constrained the room for manoeuvre of the legislature in Croatia and how the strength of the CrCC's decisions vis-à-vis the legislature has changed over time. In this way, I will attempt to critically assess whether the CrCC has fulfilled the expectation of becoming a "potentially powerful court" (Rodin 1995, 783).

This chapter is organized as follows. Section 2.2 explains the origin of the CrCC and discusses the political and constitutional framework in which the Court was created. This section analyses the powers and composition of the CrCC, the procedure for selecting judges, and some institutional features of the Court. Section 2.3 provides some general impressions of the Court's workload and the types of cases that the CrCC decides. I will also address the diversity of the Court's decisions, or rather the lack thereof since the Court's workload is heavily dominated by refusals and rejections. Section 2.4 presents and discusses general trends in CrCC decision-making based on an analysis of majority decisions on the constitutional review of laws passed by the Parliament. In this section, I will attempt to explain these trends by distinguishing between four different periods in Croatia's constitutional history and outlining how they relate to changes in government, the composition of the Court, and other factors. My analysis shows that while the first period of Croatia's constitutional history (1991–1999) was the CrCC's most powerful period, the Court was very cautious about finding unconstitutionality. While the CrCC did not shy away from challenging parliamentary legislation as unconstitutional, it generally refrained from taking an activist approach.

At the beginning of the new millennium, the number of the Court's rulings vis-à-vis the legislature declined and remained at a low level during the remaining three periods, largely due to the high number of rejections. Section 2.5 discusses a relatively recent trend of dissenting opinions in CrCC decisions that began in 2016 with the appointment of new opposition judges to the Court. Network analysis shows that this trend is due to a coalition of centre-left judges voting against the predominantly centre-right majority. Building on the literature on the judges' dissenting behaviour, I also analyse the extent to which the likelihood of writing a dissenting opinion in the CrCC is associated with various factors reported in the literature, such as party affiliation, academic career, gender, and age. I conclude that while the CrCC was established as a potentially powerful court, its level of influence on the legislature is still only average, as the Court generally prefers not to limit the power of the legislature and leaves it considerable room for manoeuvre. With the increasing trend of dissenting opinions in recent years and the greater ideological differences among the Court's judges, this may change in the years to come. Nevertheless, it is unlikely that a handful of left-wing, activist judges will fundamentally change the rules of the game.

2.2 A potentially powerful court

2.2.1 Origins of the Croatian Constitutional Court

The origins of the CrCC can be traced back to the 1960s, when Croatia was one of the six federal entities of the Socialist Federal Republic of Yugoslavia (SFRY). Constitutional courts were established in the former SFRY at both the federal and federal unit levels. The Croatian Constitutional Court was established by the 1963 Constitution, which gave it limited powers. This "socialist" Court had a jurisdiction to, among other things, rule on the compatibility of the laws of the Croatian federal entity with the Constitution (abstract constitutional review) and could rule on the compatibility of regulations, laws, and other general legal acts with the Constitution, federal laws, and other regulations of the Republic. The Constitution of the Socialist Republic of Croatia of 1974 also gave the CrCC the power to rule on the conformity of laws and other legal acts that have ceased to be valid and to suspend the execution of individual acts or measures taken on the basis of a law whose conformity is being examined. If the Court found that a law violated the Constitution, it could not annul it, however. Instead, due to the socialist primacy of the Federal Assembly (the Parliament of Yugoslavia), the Court could only rule on the nonconformity of the law, and it was left to the Federal Assembly to decide whether it would amend it or enact new legislation (Barić 2016; Rodin 1995).

The powers of the CrCC changed after the first multiparty elections in Croatia, which took place on 22 and 23 April 1990 – at a time when Croatia was still one of the six federal entities of the SFRY and the 1974 Constitution was still in force. Two months after the elections, on 25 July 1990, the Parliament decided to adopt the Constitution of the Republic of Croatia and promulgated amendments to the Constitution of SR Croatia, deleting the word *socialist* from the name of the country, the title of its Constitution, and from its provisions. On the same day, the Constitutional Court of the Socialist Republic of Croatia was renamed the Constitutional Court of the Republic of Croatia (CrCC).

On 22 December 1990, the Parliament adopted the new Constitution of the Republic of Croatia that gave the Court new competences beyond those provided for by the "socialist" Constitutional Court in the 1963 and 1974 constitutions. For the first time, the Constitutional Court was given the power of constitutional review, that is, the power to decide on the constitutionality of laws and other legal acts and to annul them if they are found to be unconstitutional. The newly created Court was no longer subordinated to the Parliament but followed the continental tradition and was designed to function as an intermediate body that supervises all three branches of government. The Constitutional Court does not stand hierarchically above any of the aforementioned branches, nor is it organizationally or functionally a part of them (Barić 2016). For this reason, and due to the fact that the Court is based exclusively on the provisions of the Constitution and the Constitutional Law on the Constitutional Court (the Constitutional Law),[1] the CrCC is often considered the fourth branch of the government in Croatia (Omejec 2004). The Court was established one year after the entry into force of the 1990 Constitution, when on 5 December 1991, the Croatian Parliament adopted the Decision on the election of the judges of the Constitutional Court of the Republic of Croatia and elected the first 9 of 11 judges of the Constitutional Court, who took office two days later, on 7 December 1991.[2] Although 11 judges were nominated, 2 judges did not receive the majority of votes in Parliament required to be elected (Croatian Parliament 1991). With only 9 judges holding office and the country focused on the Croatian War of Independence, the CrCC operated for a full three years with 9 judges instead of 11 until 1994, when the two remaining judges took office. Judge Jadranko Crnić, who had served as a constitutional judge since 1984 and as President of the Constitutional Court of SR Croatia since 1990, became the first President of the CrCC. As I will show in Section 2.4, his presidency was marked by the strongest decisions taken by the Court, and during this period the Court found unconstitutionality in almost three-quarters of its rulings, suggesting that the President's experience at the former "socialist" court did not influence the new Court's willingness to use its newly gained powers.

Thus, the establishment of the Croatian Constitutional Court in 1990 was strongly influenced by the turbulent times of the Croatian War of Independence (1991–1995), which followed the proclamation of Croatian independence on 8 October 1991. The first decade of the Court's activity is considered the most burdensome period in Croatian constitutional history, hampered by the severe consequences of the war and the post-war reparations (Omejec 2004).

1 A Constitutional Law is a legislative act that is defined as such by the Constitution and is adopted following the procedure for the adoption and change of the Constitution itself. There are only three Constitutional Laws in Croatia: the Constitutional Law for the Implementation of the Constitution of the Republic of Croatia, the Constitutional Law on the Constitutional Court of the Republic of Croatia, and the Constitutional Law on National Minorities' Rights.

2 Note: the term of the previous judges of the Constitutional Court of the Socialist Republic of Croatia expired on 5 December 1991.

2.2.2 *Composition and structure of the Croatian Constitutional Court*

The composition of the Court was established in the 1990 Constitution and further clarified by the 1991 Constitutional Law on the Constitutional Court (Constitutional Law). In its original format, the CrCC consisted of 11 judges. Two chambers of the Croatian Parliament were responsible for selecting the judges: the House of Counties proposed the candidates, while the House of Representatives made the final decision by absolute majority. However, following a constitutional amendment in 2001, the House of Counties was abolished, and the House of Representatives became the sole chamber of the Croatian Parliament. Consequently, the procedure for selecting judges also changed. The 2001 constitutional amendment introduced a new body – the Committee on the Constitution, Rules of Procedure and Political System of the Croatian Parliament – that was responsible for nominating candidates for CrCC judges, although the actual procedure for electing constitutional judges of the Court is still based on a majority vote of the members of Parliament. Although this change made the selection process more democratic and transparent, a comparative study by Podolnjak (2007, 572) suggested that at the time Croatia was one of the few countries where "the election of constitutional judges is left to the simple majority in the Parliament and no other branch of government participate[s] in the election." As I will show later in this section, although simple majority voting was revisited in 2011, Croatia remains one of the few countries where parliament is the only body responsible for electing constitutional judges.

The 2001 constitutional amendment brought another change regarding the number of judges, which was increased to 13. Judges are appointed for a period of eight years (Constitution of the Republic of Croatia 2014, art. 122), which can be renewed, although it is unclear whether the renewal is one-time or indefinite (see Barić 2016). While there is no official rule on the number of possible renewals, the scandal surrounding Judge Omejec in 2016 makes it clear that the public does not appreciate judges running for a third term (Jutarnji list 2016b).

A judge of the Constitutional Court must be a Croatian citizen and a graduate lawyer with at least 15 years of professional experience (12 years if they hold a doctorate in law) who has pursued an outstanding professional career of scientific or professional work or public activity (Constitutional Law 2002, Art.5). Since the establishment of the Court in 1991, there have been a total of 38 judges of the Court, 10 of whom were university professors.[3] A constitutional judge may not belong to any political party and may not publicly express support for a political party (Constitutional Law 2002, Art. 16). Yet, as Barić

3 Judges who also worked in academia as assistant or full professor or as quest lecturers at the universities are Velimir Belajec, Nikola Filipović, Davor Krapac, Željko Potočnjak, Aldo Radolović, Petar Klarić, Smiljko Sokol (former judges), Mato Arlović, Mario Jelušić, and Goran Selenec (current judges). See Ustavni Sud Republike Hrvatske n.d.

(2016) points out, at least one-third of all the judges who have served in the Court were publicly known members or supporters of active political parties in Croatia before their appointment. Indeed, the judges' biographies on the Court's official website generally do not hide their previous political affiliations (see Ustavni Sud Republike Hrvatske n.d.).

The most important constitutional amendment regarding the procedure for selecting judges was passed in 2011. The 2011 constitutional amendment was the result of more than a decade of criticism of the Court based on the fact that the majority of elected judges, with only a few exceptions, were chosen by the Croatian Democratic Union (HDZ), a conservative centre-right party that had a majority in Parliament from 1990 to 2000, from 2003 to 2011, and since 2016. Criticism, which began in the run-up to the 1999 Court election, escalated when only representatives of the ruling party voted for the candidates and the opposition boycotted them (see Podolnjak 2007; after Vjesnik 1999). The criticism continued after the election, when the ruling party was criticised by the media for "filling the Court with candidates of questionable quality" (Jutarnji list 2016c).

Following such criticism that started in the 1990s, the 2010 constitutional amendment introduced a change in the procedure for electing judges, requiring a two-thirds majority of all parliamentarians (instead of a simple majority) to elect them. It also introduced a new constitutional mechanism that provides for a judge's term to be extended for a maximum of six months until a new judge is elected, in order to prevent a deadlock in the work of the CrCC. This change in the method of election of judges led to new problems, however, as the Parliament was unable to achieve a two-thirds majority for the appointment of new judges for a full six years. As a result, for a time the Court operated with 10 judges instead of 13, raising fears that the Court would effectively be "euthanized" due to the constant non-appointments (Barić 2016). This period was marked by verbal disputes between the ruling party (the centre-right HDZ) and the opposition (the centre-left SDP), during which the Court was "often caught between two fires" (Barić 2016, 34). The Court was also subjected to a series of "uncensored verbal attacks from the left" (Barić 2016, 34) and even from Supreme Court justices. Perhaps one of the most famous descriptions of the CrCC from this period was that of Supreme Court President Krunislav Olujić, who said that "the Constitutional Court is like a punctured ship tilted to the right" (Barić 2016, 92).

A consensus between the ruling party and the opposition on the election of CrCC judges was finally reached in 2016, when eight new judges took office, with one additional appointment made in 2017 (IUS-INFO 2016). As reported by the media, the opposition party objected to two of the centre-right candidates but relented "to avoid a constitutional crisis" (Jutarnji list 2016a). It seems that securing five seats for their own candidates was sufficient. Moreover, both parties wanted to avoid a crisis over an empty chair at all costs. Although it is thought-provoking that the ruling centre-left party would give up its power over the election of judges, it seems that more than a decade of criticism from the media and the public has forced the ruling party to make a necessary compromise. Even so, most of the current judges continue to be nominated by the ruling party.

2.2.3 Voting

The number of judges sitting on the CrCC bench depends on the nature of the proceedings before the Court. Decisions on the constitutionality of laws and on the constitutionality and legality of other regulations are made at a separate session of the CrCC, which can be held only if a majority of the total number of judges is present at the session. Constitutional review cases are generally decided *en banc*, i.e. before the full Court (Constitutional Law 2002, Art. 53). The decisions of the Court in constitutional review cases are made by majority vote, and votes are always published together with a decision. The publication of votes is stipulated in Article 52 of the Constitutional Law (2002), which states that the minutes of the Court's session "shall contain information about the case, the manner in which the case was decided, and the vote (who voted for and who voted against)" (Constitutional Law 2002, Art. 51(3)). Decisions based on a constitutional complaint made by private individuals, on the other hand, are made anonymously in a Council of six judges by unanimous decision. If the Council does not reach a unanimous decision or considers that the matter is of greater importance, the decision is taken by a session of the Court *en banc* (Constitutional Law 2002, Art. 69).

2.2.4 Institutional peculiarities

There are several institutional features, or rather constitutional limitations, of the CrCC that are worth mentioning. I distinguish between two types of limitations: first, formal constitutional limitations, which are formally prescribed in the Constitution or in the Constitutional Law, and second, self-restrictions, which the Court has imposed on itself. If one peruses the text of the Croatian Constitution and the Constitutional Law, one formally prescribed restriction stands out. This is the stipulation that the Court can only exercise *ex post* constitutional review. In other words, the Court does not have the power to review laws and regulations before they are passed by the Parliament. The Court may conduct a constitutional review of laws and regulations that have expired, but only if no more than one year has elapsed between the filing of a petition for constitutional review and the date of its expiration (Constitutional Law 2002, Article 56). Other limitations are self-imposed, that is, the Court has imposed them on itself by adopting a certain position in its case law. As a result of the self-imposed limitations, the Court cannot review cases on the mutual harmonization of laws or regulations with the same legal force (e.g. of two ordinary laws).[4]

4 This was the position the Court took in its case law. See e.g. U-I-904/1995, U-I-3201/2005, U-I-1656/2011.

Furthermore, the Court is not empowered to decide cases of legislative omission, i.e. to judge the compatibility of laws with the Constitution from the point of view that the legislature failed to prescribe something in the law. Although this position is explicitly stated in the Court's case law,[5] in four cases, the Court has assessed the compatibility of laws with the Constitution from the point of view that the legislature failed to prescribe something in the law.[6] This suggests that the CrCC has decided to circumvent the restriction it has imposed on itself. Occasionally, the CrCC also issues a directive to instruct Parliament to enact or amend a law,[7] although such directives are always part of unconstitutionality rulings and never stand alone. However, a more common practice of the Court when determining unconstitutionality is to issue a non-binding opinion to guide or initiate legislative action in a certain direction (see also Section 2.3).[8] Moreover, in the procedure of abstract review of the constitutionality of laws, the Court does not have the power to assess the application of procedures before courts and other state bodies against which individuals have the right of constitutional complaint.[9] These four self-imposed limitations have been used as grounds for a number of rejections of complaints by the Court (see Section 2.3).

While there is an agreement between the judges on the Court's lack of jurisdiction in these situations, there is disagreement when it comes to the jurisdiction of the Court in cases of alleged incompatibility between international agreements and the Constitution or national laws and regulations (Barić 2016). This kind of jurisdiction, or the lack thereof, is not explicitly stated in the Constitution or the Constitutional Law. However, based on Article 140 of the Constitution, which states that international agreements have a higher legal force than domestic laws, the Court has declined jurisdiction to assess the compatibility of international agreements with the Constitution.[10] As of 2017, several judges took a different view, arguing that international agreements are below the Constitution in the hierarchy and can therefore be subject to constitutional review by the Court.[11]

Another institutional peculiarity of the CrCC lies in the practice of constitutional interpretation, which is not applied in Croatia (Rodin 1997). Unlike in Germany, for example, where a constitutional complaint against a law is admissible and where the establishment of a violation of fundamental rights by that law leads to the repeal of the law, the CrCC has not yet gone that far. However, in the absence of a constitutional or self-imposed limitation

5 See e.g. U-I-709/1995, U-I-709/1995.

6 See U-I-60/1991, U-I-4463/2013, U-I-60/1991, and U-I-378/2016.

7 See U-I-60/1991, U-I-673/1996.

8 E.g. U-I-1152/2000, U-I-5612/2011.

9 This was the position the Court took in its case law. See e.g U-I-6651/2010, U-I-2056/2001.

10 See, e.g., U-I-671/2001, U-I-1596/2012, U-I-35/2016.

11 See dissenting opinions of judge Andrej Abranovic and judge Branko Brkic in U-I-1596/2012, dissenting opinion of judge Andrej Abramovic in U-I-35/2016, U-I-6290/2016, U-I-2234/2017, U-I-2235/2017, and U-I-2236/2017.

preventing the Court from doing so, it may address this issue in the future. In Croatia, a constitutional complaint cannot be used to assess the compatibility of ordinary laws with the Constitution. Instead, a party to proceedings who claims that his rights have been violated by an unconstitutional law would have to initiate separate proceedings in the form of an abstract constitutional review (Rodin 1997). The constitutional complaint itself may not serve this purpose. In practice, however, the Court has not faced such a problem to date.

There are three ways of initiating abstract constitutional review: first, on request of a limited number of bodies enumerated in the Constitutional Law (one-fifth of the MP's, the President, the Supreme Court or another lower court, and the Ombudsman; Constitutional Law 2002, Art. 35). Second, on a proposal of the representative body of local and regional government and every individual or legal person, but it is up to the Court to decide whether the allegations are sufficient to initiate the proceedings (Constitutional Law 2002, Art.38(1)). Finally, the Court can also initiate proceedings ex officio. I return to this in Section 2.3.

2.2.5 *The most important periods*

Scholars writing about the CrCC (Omejec 2004; Barić 2016) usually distinguish between three periods of Croatian constitutional activity: (1) from 1991 to the end of 1999; (2) from 2000 to mid-2013; and (3) from 1 July 2013 (the accession of RC to the EU) to 2016. Added to this is the fourth period from 2016 (7 July 2016, when eight new judges, five from the centre-left opposition, took office) to the present, which is characterized by an increasing number of dissenting opinions and polarization between judges nominated by the ruling party and the opposition.

The first period was heavily burdened by the events of the war, post-war reconstruction, and the transition to democracy after communism (Omejec 2004). This period is often referred to as the "emergency period" because the CrCC's activities were primarily focused on preserving the constitutional core, i.e. preserving the principle of the separation of powers, the principle of representative government, supervising free elections, and retaining the essence of the multiparty democratic system (Omejec 2004). After 1989 and the fall of the communist regime, constitutional courts in CEE countries developed varying degrees of judicial activism. While some constitutional courts (such as the Hungarian one for example) were immediately labelled "activist", others developed this activism gradually and in accordance with the context in which they were operating at the time. The CrCC, Croatian scholars argue, falls into the second category (Barić 2016).

In this first phase, the CrCC generally refrained from taking an activist approach (see Omejec 2004; Barić 2016). Although the Court was not shy about using its power of constitutional review to strike down laws for substantive unconstitutionality (see Section 2.4), the literature shows that the Court was far less willing to engage in judicial law-making. The CrCC also exercised deference to the executive branch by upholding 11 presidential decrees with the force of law, even though none of the official requirements had been met.

Moreover, the style of the CrCC's jurisprudence during this period was often criticized as formalistic and uncreative. Arsen Bačić, one of the most prominent critics of the time, wrote that the Court's approach, by a mere reference to a legal provision and a complete lack of elaboration of constitutional principles, was "nothing but the Court's self-restraint and a formal style of interpretation of constitutional provisions" (Bačić 1998; Banić 2016, 189). There are several explanations for it taking such a moderate approach to judicial activism: the Croatian War of Independence, "during which national political leaders did not expect any challenge to the principle of unity of state power from other institutions" (Barić 2016, 59), the relationship between the legislature and the judiciary, which was characterized by the principle of the "unchallengeable authority of the head of state", and the "uncritical attitude of the judges of the Constitutional Court" (Barić 2016; Barić and Bačić 2011).

The Court's attitude toward the legislature in this early period was thus characterized by "the traditional concept of the judiciary which prevails in Croatian legal theory, according to which the courts play only a limited law-making role" (Rodin 1997, 75). Other scholars portrayed the role of the Court as a "regular appellate court", dealing primarily with clear cases of substantive and procedural unconstitutionality rather than interpretive methods common in constitutional adjudication, and whose decisions follow a standard jurisdictional scheme common at the appellate and Supreme Court levels (Barić 2016, 14). In this early phase, the CrCC rarely referred to international agreements such as the European Convention on Human Rights (ECHR) in its jurisprudence.

The beginning of the second period was marked by the election of a new left-wing government and the passing of a second constitutional amendment in 2000, which gave more powers to the Court by expanding its competences and increasing the number of judges from 11 to 13 (Amendments to the Constitution of the Republic of Croatia 2000). This period was also marked by preparations for European integration. After another constitutional amendment in 2001 aimed at integrating European standards into Croatian constitutional law, the harmonization of national legislation with the EU *acquis communautaire* began. During the period from 2003 to 2013, no less than 683 Croatian laws and regulations were harmonized with EU law (Barić 2016). However, the speed of harmonization led to some problematic translations: literal translations from English, incomprehensible provisions, and the introduction of legal principles that did not exist in Croatian law (Omejec 2004, 14; Glavina 2021). In parallel with this process, the CrCC began to rely more on the case law of the European Court of Human Rights (ECtHR) and to go beyond traditional methods of interpretation (see also Banić 2016). After the fourth constitutional amendment in 2010, Croatia was formally ready to join the EU. The 2010 amendment also introduced a two-thirds majority in Parliament for the election of constitutional judges.

The third and final transitional period of the CrCC began with Croatia's accession to the EU in 2013, a period which was also characterized by the well-established and accepted practice of constitutional review (Barić 2016). However, this period also saw growing criticism of the Court, which had been more or less absent in the earlier periods due to the constitutional definition of the Court's powers and its practice of using conservative methods of interpretation, i.e. grammatical interpretation or textualism, as Rodin (1997) points out.[12] In the period since 2013, the CrCC has been confronted with the economic crisis, growing ideological polarization on the political scene, an increasing tendency of the political elites to blame the Court for shortcomings or constitutional problems, and public criticism related to two scandals in which CrCC justices were involved (Barić 2016).[13]

Finally, I would add to this classification a fourth period of Croatian constitutional reality, which began in the summer of 2016, more precisely on 7 July 2016, when eight new judges were elected to the CrCC. This election had been severely delayed due to the 2010 constitutional amendment on the election of judges (which requires a two-thirds majority in the Parliament), until a consensus was finally reached in 2016. Of the eight newly elected judges, five judges were nominated by the centre-left opposition party. Until then, the majority of constitutional judges had been appointed by the ruling conservative centre-right party. The only exception was three judges appointed between 2000 and 2003, when the centre-left coalition had a majority in Parliament (see Appendix). As a result of the 2010 constitutional amendment, the fourth period witnessed an increase in the number of dissenting opinions, stated predominantly by the dissenting coalition appointed by the left-wing opposition in the Parliament.

2.3 General impressions

2.3.1 Court's statistics and judicial rulings

The CrCC is a "busy" Court, especially considering that Croatia is a country with less than 4 million inhabitants. The Court's workload has grown exponentially since its establishment in 1990, reaching a peak of 8,195 incoming cases in 2014, followed by a slow decline in the number of cases reaching the Court each year. However, cases involving the compatibility of laws with

12 *Textualism* refers to a type of decision-making where judges rely on a narrow and limited set of arguments, the earlier case-law of the same court, accepted and well-established legal doctrines and on the traditional methods of interpretation (see Bobek 2015).

13 The first scandal in this period revolved around the involvement of one of the judges in alleged attempt to annul parts of the Sport law and a second one involved the discovery of plagiarism in one of the judges' published works. Both scandals ended in a public apology as the Court was already operating with 10 instead of 13 judges (see Section 2.2) and could not afford to lose more judges (see Barić 2016).

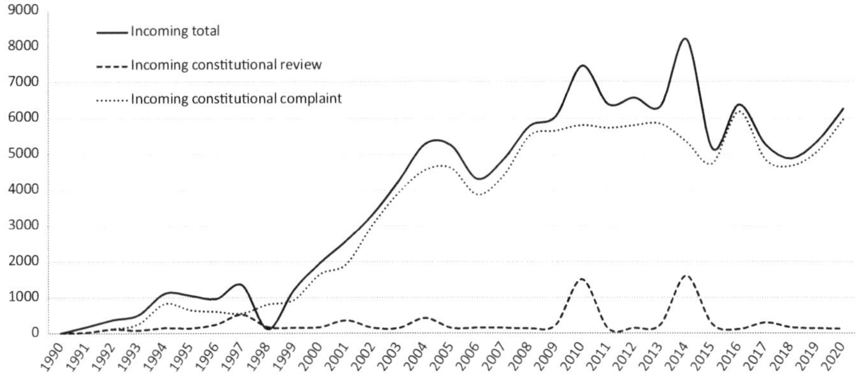

Figure 2.1 Caseload of the Croatian Constitutional Court (1993–2020)

the Constitution represent only a fraction of the total cases that come before the Court. Over the entire period studied (1990–2020) cases examining the constitutionality of laws account for only 7% of the Court's workload, while cases examining the constitutionality and legality of other legal acts (including presidential decrees) account for 3.8% of the Court's workload. In comparison, constitutional complaints account for nearly 90% of the Court's workload (see Figure 2.1).

Figure 2.1 illustrates all the incoming cases per year and the two most common types of procedure: proceedings initiated by a constitutional complaint (dotted line) and procedures for assessing the conformity of laws with the Constitution (dashed line). Other cases that the CrCC decides on are not presented in this figure.[14] Other cases account for 1.5% of the Court's workload (Ustavni Sud Republike Hrvatske 2022).

This discrepancy between the number of constitutional complaints and petitions for the constitutional review of laws can be explained by the fact that only a limited (and privileged) number of bodies can initiate a constitutional

14 Other cases that the CrCC decides are those concerned with: (1) resolving conflicts of jurisdiction, (2) deciding on the responsibility of the President, (2) oversight of the constitutionality of the programs and activities of political parties, (3) oversight of the constitutionality of elections and a state referendum, (4) resolution of electoral disputes that are not within the scope of the courts, (5) the procedure of temporary suspension of the execution of individual acts or actions undertaken on the basis of a law or other regulation under constitutional review procedure, (6–7) appeal against decisions of the State Judicial Council – dismissal of judges and disciplinary proceedings, (8) monitoring the implementation of constitutionality and legality and reporting to the President of the Croatian Parliament, (9) supervision over the adoption of regulations for the implementation of the Constitution, laws, and other regulations, and (10) the announcement of the people's constitutional referendum.

review: one-fifth of the parliamentarians, the working body of Parliament,[15] the President, the Supreme Court, another ordinary court (if the question of constitutionality arises in the proceedings before that court),[16] and the Ombudsman (Constitutional Law 2002, Art. 35) are authorized to do so. The review of constitutionality may also be initiated on the proposal of local and regional councils and by any natural or legal person, but it is for the Court to decide whether the reasons are sufficient to initiate the proceedings in such cases (Constitutional Law 2002, Art. 38(1)).

The Court also has the power to initiate procedures for examining the compatibility of laws with the Constitution on its own, based on Article 38(2) of the Constitutional Law (2002). The Court has so far initiated constitutional review *ex officio* in only three cases,[17] which again indicates that the Court interprets its new power of constitutional review very restrictively and prefers those proceedings be initiated by the bodies mentioned previously. All three cases ended with a partial annulment of the law (substantive unconstitutionality). When the possibility to initiate constitutional review proceedings *ex officio* was introduced in 2002 (Constitutional Law 2002, Art. 38(2)), there were some fears that the Court would use this power to assume the role of legislator and decide on policy issues reserved for the Parliament (see Arlović 2014), but as the statistics show, this has not been the case.

This section highlights some important elements specific to the CrCC that inform the research design of this chapter. In line with the methodology of the JUDICON project, which focuses on rulings as the units of analysis, the analysis in this chapter is based on 869 rulings in 808 Court decisions in which the Court assessed the constitutionality of laws. It is already clear from these two figures that the majority of the Court's decisions contain only one ruling.

Unlike some other courts in the CEE region, the CrCC does not have the authority to make a constitutional interpretation *in abstracto*, nor can it declare a legislative omission. This position has been explicitly expressed in the Court's case law. However, an analysis of the Court's rulings reveals that in four cases the Court declared the compatibility of laws with the Constitution from the point of view that the legislator failed to prescribe something in the law. This happened in cases U-I-60/1991 and U-I-4463/2013, where the Court asked the Parliament to enact new laws based on the Court's findings, and in cases U-I-60/1991 and U-I-378/2016, where the Court itself ended up regulating something that the legislature had not regulated.

15 The working bodies of the Croatian Parliament are committees established by the Rules of Procedure of the Croatian Parliament. These are: the Delegation of the Croatian Parliament in the Parliamentary Assembly of the Council of Europe, the Delegation of the Croatian Parliament in the NATO Parliamentary Assembly, and the Delegation of the Croatian Parliament in the Parliamentary Assembly of the Organization for Security and Co-operation in Europe (OSCE).

16 Introduced by the 2002 Constitutional amendment.

17 See U-I-4220/2020, U-I-5735/2014, U-I-4113/2008.

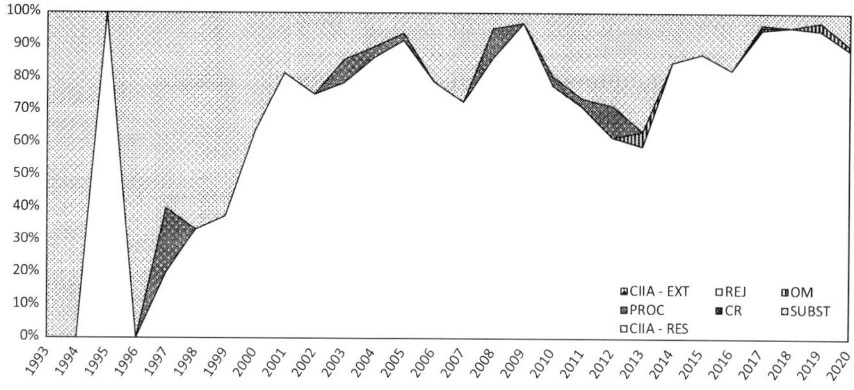

Figure 2.2 Frequency of the ruling types (1993–2020) (CrCC)

Note: REJ – Rejection/refusal, OM – Omission, PROC – Procedural unconstitutionality, SUBST – Substantive unconstitutionality

While constitutional requirements and constitutional interpretation *in abstracto* are completely absent from the Courts' practice, refusals/rejections and cases of substantive unconstitutionality are clearly favoured by the CrCC. In fact, during the period between 1990 and 2020, 82% of the rulings were rejected by the Court (see Figure 2.2). With a rejection rate of 82%, Croatia (with Ireland and Belgium) ranks in the top three compared to other countries covered by the JUDICON project (see Chapter 12).

The second most common type of rulings are cases of substantive unconstitutionality. These occurred in 16.3% of the cases decided by the Court. The Court first declared a law (or a legal norm) unconstitutional in 1993 and issued this type of ruling on average five times per year between 1993 and 2020. While it is true that the CrCC, especially in its early days, did not shy away from reviewing and overturning laws for unconstitutionality (Rodin 1997), this happens only very sporadically. When the Court reviews a law for constitutionality, it is highly likely to uphold the challenged law or its norm(s).

Based on the analysis, the CrCC declared substantive unconstitutionality in 16.3% of its rulings. However, the Court is more likely to resort to partial annulment of a legal norm than to order its complete annulment. Only in a total of 14 cases (6.2%) did the Court annul the entire law under review. This is not unusual. In all the countries covered by the JUDICON project, partial annulment is preferred to annulment of the entire law (see Chapter 12). Finally, in 1.2% of the cases, the Court declared unconstitutionality due to defects in the legislative process. In contrast to the cases of substantive unconstitutionality, the cases in which the Parliament violated the procedural rules when adopting the law are the most likely to result in the Court's decision to annul the entire law. This was the case in 80% of all cases of procedural unconstitutionality.

As far as temporal effect is concerned, CrCC decisions are enforceable immediately after their publication. This means that if the Court declares a law or provision unconstitutional, that law or provision ceases to have effect on the date of publication of the Court's decision in the Official Gazette, unless the Court specifies a different date (Constitutional Law 2002, Article 55). However, this exception to the *ex nunc* temporal effect is only available *pro futuro*, i.e. when the Court's decision takes effect at a later date. The Court seems to take the *pro futuro* exception seriously, because in only 16.3% of the unconstitutionality cases does the Court put the effect of the annulment in the future. As mentioned earlier, the Court does not have the power to declare a law unconstitutional with *ex tunc* effect (retroactively). Based on the wording of the Constitution and the Constitutional Law, the Croatian legislator does not recognize the retroactive effect (*ex tunc*) of declaring legal acts unconstitutional (see Arlović 2014; Omejec 2002). The CrCC may annul a law or its legislative act(s), but annulment (with *ex tunc* temporal effect) is reserved for other regulations (called "other acts" in Croatian law), which Parliament has limited to applying in only two situations: when the regulation violates the human rights and fundamental freedoms guaranteed by the Constitution, and when it unfairly discriminates against individuals, groups, or associations. However, the Court has the discretion to decide whether to annul (*ex tunc*) or simply repeal (*ex nunc*) a law.

Finally, prescriptions are not very common in CrCC jurisdiction. Only occasionally, and only in the context of rulings of substantive unconstitutionality (in a total of eight cases), did the CrCC issue a directive to instruct the Parliament to enact or amend a law.[18] Directives are much more urgent than simple recommendations because they are included in the headnote of the Court's decision. However, a more common practice of the Court when declaring a law unconstitutional is to issue a recommendation to the Parliament in order to guide or initiate legislative action in a certain direction.[19] This was done in a total of 13 cases.

2.3.2 Mapping the diversity of judicial rulings

This section will address the diversity of the Court's rulings, or rather, the lack thereof. The most common types of CrCC decisions are rejections. They account for the outcome of 82% of all constitutional review cases decided by the Court.

Substantive unconstitutionality with quantitative partial annulment, with *pro futuro* temporal effect and without any prescription (26 rulings in total) is also considered weak, as it gives the legislature time to solve the problems revealed by the Court (Pócza 2019). This is also true for rulings of procedural

18 See U-I-60/1991, U-I-673/1996.
19 E.g. U-I-1152/2000, U-I-5612/2011

unconstitutionality stipulating partial annulment and *pro futuro* effect (two rulings), although this combination of elements is very rare in the CrCC jurisprudence. Most rulings of procedural unconstitutionality end with a complete annulment of the law with *ex nunc* effect (16 rulings). These rulings can be considered medium-impact rulings, as they force the legislature to enact a new law. Medium-impact rulings also include cases of substantive unconstitutionality with quantitative partial annulment and *ex nunc* temporal effect and no prescription (167 rulings) or non-binding prescription (one ruling)

Only a handful of rulings of the CrCC can be considered strict. These include rulings of substantive unconstitutionality with quantitative partial annulment and *ex nunc* temporal effect and a binding prescription (three rulings) or a directive (three rulings), rulings of substantive unconstitutionality with complete annulment and *ex nunc* temporal effect (12 rulings) and a non-binding prescription (one ruling), and two rulings of substantive unconstitutionality with quantitative partial annulment and *ex tunc* temporal effect (which I already discussed).

Looking at the data, it can be concluded that the CrCC did not utilize a very broad range of measures to constrain the legislature. While the Court has the power to strike down laws for being inconsistent with the Constitution, it does so rarely (16.3% of rulings) and only with limited constraint on the legislature.

2.4 Trends in majority rulings

This section will examine majority rulings, with a particular focus on the strengths of majority rulings. Figure 2.3 reveals two tendencies. First, there were almost no cases of constitutional review in the early years of the CrCC's operation. Such a low workload after the establishment of a new court is not a peculiarity of the CrCC, but it occurs with any new judicial body (see Dyevre, Glavina, and Ovádek 2021). It took until the end of 1993, a full two years after its creation, for the Court to decide its first case on the compatibility of a law with the Constitution. There are two possible explanations for this development. First, according to the wording of the Constitutional Law (1991, 2002), constitutional review can only be initiated by a limited and privileged group of entities (see Section 2.2). Second, the possibility for the Court to repeal laws was still very new and unusual in Croatian constitutional history. Until 1990, this power was reserved exclusively for the legislature. It is therefore not surprising that it took until the early 2000s for constitutional review petitions to really get off the ground.

The early years of the Court's operation were also the Court's strongest years (see Figure 2.3). However, the peaks in 1993, 1994, and 1996 can be explained by what were in fact a small number of Court rulings. In these three years, the Court reviewed seven laws, and all seven were quashed as unconstitutional. The strength of the Court rulings went from seven in 1993 and 1994 to zero in 1995 because the Court upheld the constitutionality of a reviewed

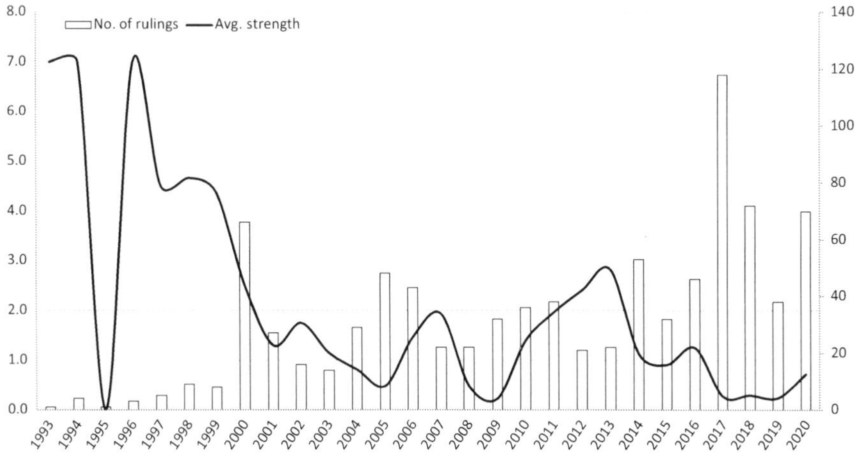

Figure 2.3 Number and average strength of rulings (1993–2020) (CrCC)

law in only one case in 1995. Despite the small number of rulings, in these early years the Court was more likely to strike down a law under review than to uphold it. In nearly three-quarters of the constitutional review cases decided from 1993 to 1999, the Court declared the challenged law unconstitutional (in 21 of 29 rulings). It is not surprising, then, that this piqued the interest of legal scholars such as Rodin, who wrote that the CrCC "has demonstrated its willingness to exercise its constitutional powers to strike down laws" (Rodin 1997, 75).

Looking at the four periods of Croatian constitutional history discussed in Section 2.2, the first period undoubtedly stands out as the strongest. However, this was also the period of the "state of emergency", during which the court focused primarily on preserving core constitutional values such as the rule of law, separation of powers, free elections, and a democratic multiparty system (see Omejec 2004). During this period, the CrCC found unconstitutionality in 72% of its rulings, although it actually proceeded very cautiously. Looking at the different elements of the judicial rulings, they were consistently cases of quantitative partial unconstitutionality, with *ex nunc* or *pro futuro* temporal effect and no prescription for the legislature. This is consistent with the picture painted by Barić (2016), according to which this early period of Croatian constitutional history was characterized by a cautious court that did not readily resort to the interpretive methods common in constitutional adjudication and whose decisions followed a standard legal scheme common at the appellate and Supreme Court levels (Barić 2016). This cautious approach of the Court in the first period of its operation can undoubtedly be attributed to the state of war in that period, when the legislature "expected no contestation of the unity of state power principle" (Barić 2016; Barić and Bačić 2011) and the Court met this expectation.

After the first period, a decline in the Court's average ruling strength can be observed, which can be explained by an increasing number of rejections and refusals. Since 2000, the number of rulings that ended in refusal or rejection has exceeded the rulings of substantive and procedural unconstitutionality. Although the early 2000s were marked by the election of a new left-wing government and by constitutional amendments that gave the Court more powers by expanding its competencies and increasing the number of judges from 11 to 13, this did not affect the strength of the Court's rulings vis-à-vis the legislature, which remained low throughout the second period (with the exception of 2007, when the Court issued proportionately more rulings of substantive unconstitutionality).

Although one would expect the change of government to trigger a conflict between the new centre-left majority and the centre-right Court, this did not happen. One explanation for the absence of conflict is that the victorious centre-left party (SDP) only won 43 seats and thus had to form a coalition to form a government.[20] This was also the first time since the country's independence that power had been shared between parties in a coalition. The centre-right party (HDZ), which held the majority in Parliament until the 2000 elections, still managed to secure 46 seats. Passing a new law requires a majority in the Parliament, while enacting and/or amending the Constitution and/or the Constitutional Act requires a two-thirds majority (Constitution 1990, Article 83(3)), which the new centre-left coalition, as a minority government (71 seats out of 151), did not have. Passing new legislation thus required a consensus between the centre-left and the centre-right, making the CrCC less likely to strike it down.

The average strength of the Court's rulings remained the same over the third period, although, as shown in Figure 2.3, it peaked in 2013, when the Court started using more prescriptions.[21] Finally, the period after 2016 is characterized by the Court's weakest stance yet toward the legislature. This period is also characterized by the highest percentage of rejections of cases by the Court since it was constituted (see Figure 2.2). It should be stressed, at the same time, that the fourth period has also seen an exceptionally high number of dissenting opinions, following the election of eight new constitutional judges, five of whom were nominated by the opposition. Thus, one possible explanation for the high percentage of rejections in the fourth period is the growing polarization at the Court, where the centre-right majority in the Court refrains from striking down the centre-right government's legislation due to the already existing attacks from the dissenting coalition of centre-left judges.

20 SDP (49 seats) formed a coalition with the Croatian Social Liberal Party (HSLS) (22 seats), Primorje Goranski Federation (PGS) (2 seats) and Slavonski-Baranja Croatian Party (SBHS) (one seat). See Državno izborno povjerenstvo Republike Hrvatske n.d.

21 The number of prescriptions are, however, not that high. The Court used them four times in 2013 and 2014, two times in 2015, and five times in 2016.

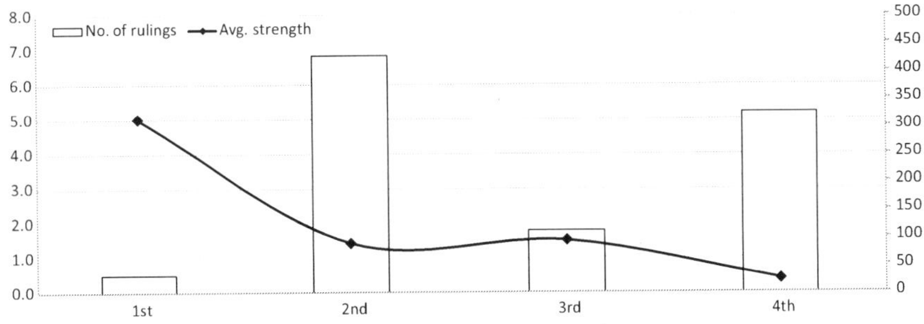

Figure 2.4 Average strength of rulings by courts (CrCC)

2.4.1 *The role of presidents*

The CrCC has had a total of six presidents, with Judge Željko Potočnjak serving only as interim president between December 2007 and June 2008. This occurred because neither of the candidates (Potočnjak and Omejec) received a majority of votes, which at the time was seven (Constitutional Law 2002, Article 6(7)). The judges agreed that Judge Željko Potočnjak would serve as interim president until all the judicial positions were filled (Jutarnji list 2007). His opponent, Judge Jasna Omejec, received a majority of votes in June 2008, becoming the first female President of the CrCC.

The average strength of rulings of the Presidents of the Court largely corresponds to the average strength of the rulings of the Court as a whole (compare Figures 2.5 and 2.3). Judge Jadranko Crnić was the most "powerful" of the presidents to date, having served during the Court's first constitutional period (1991–1999), when it exercised its powers the most.

Interestingly, before becoming the first President of CrCC, Crnić had been a judge of the Constitutional Court and President of the Constitutional Court of SR Croatia since 1984. One might think that the President's previous experience at the "socialist" Court would have informed the work of the CrCC in its early years, but this was not the case. The findings show that the CrCC, under the leadership of Crnić, was not afraid to use its newly gained powers to strike down parliamentary legislation as unconstitutional.

President Smiljko Sokol, Petar Klarić, and Željko Potočnjak entered office when the strength of the Court's ruling vis-à-vis the legislature was beginning to wane and the Court was more inclined to uphold the constitutionality of a challenged law. The strength of the Court's rulings rose again with President Omejec, who held the office the longest from 2008 to 2016. This was also the period when the Court moved beyond its cautious approach and began to issue more nuanced rulings, such as finding substantive unconstitutionality with *ex tunc* temporal effect (see U-I-3541/2015) and issuing prescriptions for the legislature. Although the Court's performance under President Omejec was, according to experts, the best since its establishment, she did not run

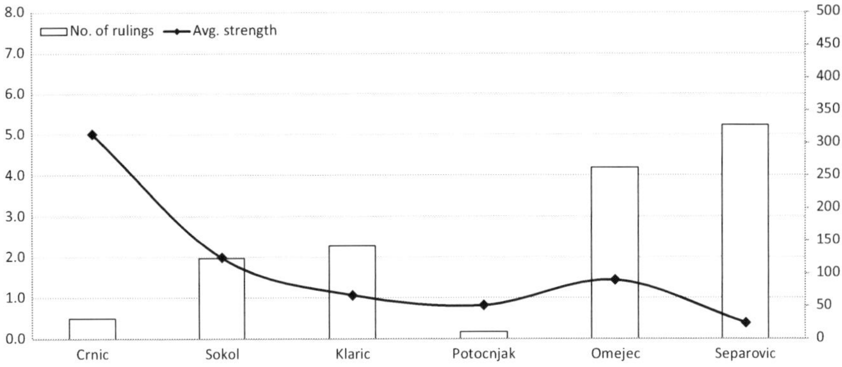

Figure 2.5 Average strength of rulings by presidents (CrCC)

for a third mandate following criticism by the media and the independent MOST political party (Jutarnji list 2016b). This suggests that the public or the opposition do not appreciate having a judge appointed by the centre-right political camp for too long as the President of the Court. Although the Constitutional Law does not contain a provision on the maximum number of mandates that the President of the Court may hold (see Constitutional Law 2002, Article 17), Judge Omejec was replaced as President of the Court by Judge Miroslav Šeparović in December 2016.

Another interesting observation is that none of the Presidents of the Court ever issued a dissenting opinion during their tenure.[22]

2.5 Trends in dissenting opinions

Although the possibility of writing a separate opinion was established in 1991 (Constitutional Act of 1991, Article 27 of 2000), the first three terms of the CrCC are characterized by an almost complete absence of both concurring and dissenting opinions. Even in cases involving high-stake constitutional issues, such as Case U-I-1397/2015 on the application of quotas for gender equality in the election of members of the Parliament (see Barić 2016), separate opinions were absent. This lack of separate opinions has been frequently criticized by scholars, who have argued that this is a result of the Court's internal agenda to provide a single voice that "ignores the very purpose of dissenting opinions in a constitutional democracy" (Barić 2016, 33). In Barić's words, it appears that the Court subscribes to the "passive virtues" of Chief Justice Roberts, who believes it is better to "speak with one voice by deciding

22 Judge Željko Potočnjak was the only Court president who has ever dissented from a majority vote, although that occurred one year prior to his appointment as an interim president.

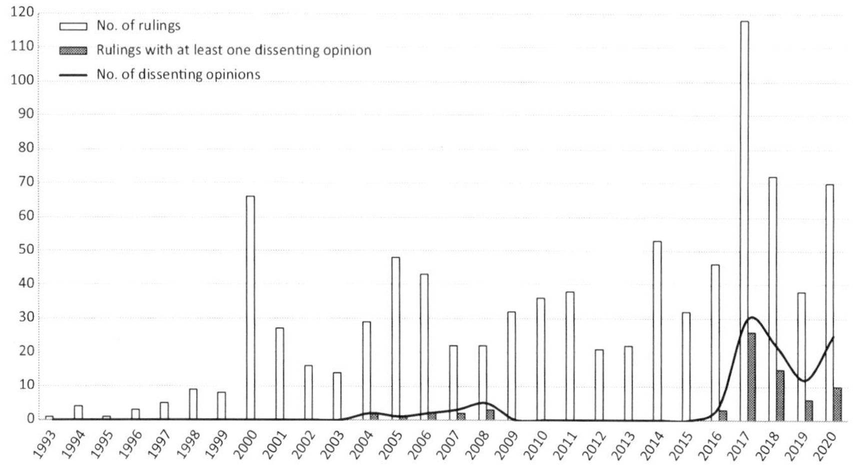

Figure 2.6 Number of rulings with at least one dissenting opinion (1993–2020) (CrCC)

cases 'on a narrow basis' than to issue bold opinions that conclusively resolve large legal issues" (Barić 2016, 33; Dorf 2006).

Looking at the data in Figure 2.6, it is clear that dissenting opinions emerged only from 2004 onwards, after the election of the new centre-left government in 2000 and nomination of three judges by it: Mario Kos, Agata Račan, and Nevenka Šernhorst. This was the first time that constitutional judges were not nominated by the centre-right government, which had held the majority in the Parliament since 1990. This led to a political polarization of the Court and several new developments in its decision making. Although most judges dissented only once during this period,[23] this was not true of the centre-left nominee, Agata Račan, whose dissenting opinions accounted for more than a third of all those written during the whole period of 2004–2008.

Moreover, two dissenting coalitions groups developed between centre-right nominated judges during this period: the first between Radolović, Krapac, and Babić, and the second between Klarić and Rajić (see Figure 2.7). However, it is important to emphasize that these judges formed a coalition only once: in the first case regarding the privatization law (U-I-834/2004) and in the second case in connection with investments (U-I-4120/2003). In contrast to the dissenting opinions of the nominated centre-left judge Agata Račan, who frequently criticized the Court for failing to recognise unconstitutionality[24] or denounced the Court for overstepping its constitutional limits and acting as

23 Mario Kos, Željko Potočnjak, Milan Vuković, Petar Klarić, Emilija Rajić, Aldo Radolović, Davor Krapac, and Marko Babić.

24 See U-I-2788/2003, U-I-3851/2004, U-I-1201/2006.

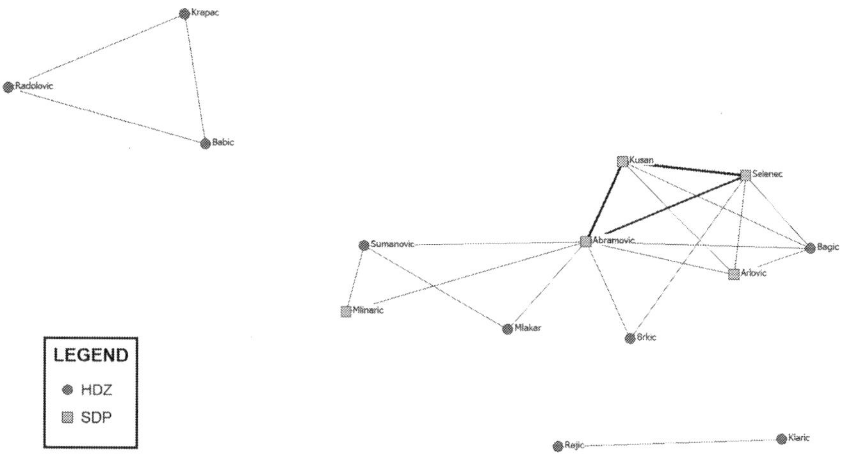

Figure 2.7 Dissenting coalitions (1993–2020) (CrCC)

a legislator (see U-I-928/2000), the dissenting opinions of the centre-right judges did not pose a serious threat to the centre-right majority in the Court.

The real surge in dissenting opinions occurred after 2016, more specifically after 7 July 2016, when eight new judges took office after a politically arduous six-year process (see Section 2.2.2). As a result of five judges being appointed by the centre-left opposition, the period between 2016 and today has witnessed an increase in the number of dissenting opinions, led predominantly by a coalition of left-wing judges: Andrej Abramović, Goran Selenec, and Lovorka Kušan (see Figure 2.7). These three judges formed a dissenting coalition a total of 11 times. Based on Figure 2.7, it can be seen that Judge Andrej Abramović is the most involved judge of the CrCC. He dissented a total of 51 times – accounting for 19% of his rulings (see Table 2.1) – and formed dissenting coalitions with both centre-left (Selenec, Kušan, Arlović, Mlinarić) and centre-right judges (Šumanović, Mlakar, Brkić, Bagić).[25]

Does party affiliation matter when it comes to expressing a different opinion? I used a one-way analysis of variance (ANOVA) to test the effect of the judge's nominating party on the likelihood of them holding a dissenting opinion. A one-sided ANOVA test was used for groups of data to examine the relationship between the dependent and independent variables. I used two

25 The coalitions between centre-left and centre right judges are, in general, diverse and have no common theme. For example, Left- and right-wing nominated judges formed a coalition on the issues such as arguing that the Court has the competence to assess the constitutionality of international agreements (U-I-1596/2012), that the Court has no competences in other areas (U-I-252/1996), that there is no legal basis for the constitutionality review (U-I-2854/2018), or arguing in favour of substantive unconstitutionality (U-I-4613/2015).

Table 2.1 Number of dissenting opinions per judges

Judge name	*Number of dissents*	*Number of rulings*	*Dissents percentage*	*Nominating party*
Andrej Abramović	51	269	19%	SDP
Lovorka Kušan	15	307	4.9%	SDP
Goran Selenec	12	176	6.8%	SDP
Agata Račan	5	200	2.5%	SDP
Miroslav Šumanović	5	289	1.7%	HDZ
Branko Brkić	4	306	1.3%	HDZ
Mato Arlović	2	524	0.4%	SDP
Rajko Mlinarić	2	306	0.6%	SDP
Aldo Radolović	1	189	0.5%	HDZ
Davor Krapac	1	222	0.4%	HDZ
Davorin Mlakar	1	85	1.2%	HDZ
Emilija Rajić	1	236	0.4%	HDZ
Mario Kos	1	205	0.5 %	SDP
Marko Babić	1	249	0.4 %	HDZ
Milan Vuković	1	255	0.4 %	HDZ
Petar Klarić	1	259	0.4 %	HDZ
Snježana Bagić	1	571	0.2 %	HDZ
Željko Potočnjak	1	210	0.5 %	HDZ

different dependent variables. The first one is whether the judge has ever expressed a dissenting opinion (dummy variable, where 1 represents judges who have expressed a dissenting opinion and 0 represents judges who have never expressed a dissenting opinion), and the second one is the number of dissenting opinions (numeric variable), which indicates how often a judge has expressed a dissenting opinion. As an independent variable, I used a judge's party affiliation based on the party nominations or newspaper articles about the judges' political preferences.[26] For more details see Table 2.1.

The results of the ANOVA test show that judges appointed or nominated by the left-wing party (SDP) are more likely to dissent. This finding is statistically significant at a 0.05 level.[27] When the number of dissenting opinions is used as an outcome variable, this result becomes statistically significant at the 0.001 level.[28] The difference between the number of dissenting opinions written by judges appointed by the centre-right (HDZ) and those appointed by the centre-left (SDP) is illustrated in Figure 2.8.

26 Note that, although CrCC judges may not belong to a political party and may not publicly express his support for a political party (Constitutional Law 2002, Art.16), at least one-third of all the judges who sat in the Court were, prior to their appointments, publicly known members or supporters of active political parties in Croatia (see Barić 2016, and the website of the CrCC).

27 One-way ANOVA test $p < 0.048$ **

28 One-way ANOVA test $p < 0.0044$ ***

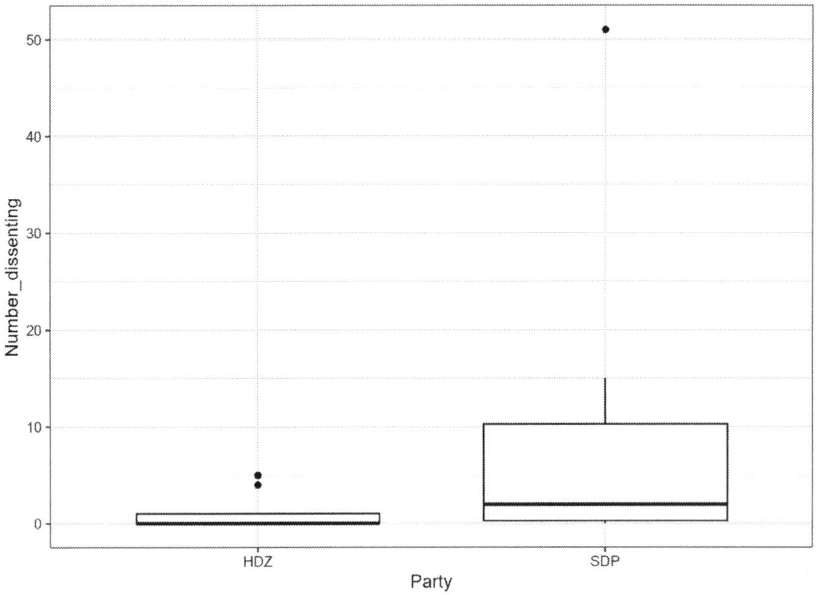

Figure 2.8 Number of dissenting opinions and party affiliation (1993–2020) (CrCC)

The academic literature on judicial politics has generally confirmed the role of ideology, attitudes, and policy preferences in constitutional courts' voting behaviour (Hanretty 2012; Hanretty 2013; Pellegrina and Garoupa 2013; Hönnige 2007; Bricker 2017). While the judicial decision-making process cannot be reduced to politics alone (Epstein and Knight 2013; Epstein, Landes, and Posner 2013; Glavina 2020), it is clear that ideology and politics play a role in the CrCC. This finding also supports the thesis in the literature that dissenting opinions are more likely when there are greater ideological differences between the judges in a court (Bricker 2017).

I also examined the role of other variables. The literature suggests that judges disagree somewhat infrequently because doing so comes at a cost to collegiality for the other judges sitting on the same panel and entails harder work (Posner 2008). Dissent also comes at a cost to one's reputation because dissenting judges are less popular with their colleagues, which ultimately affects internal job satisfaction (Epstein, Landes, and Posner 2013). For this reason, risk- and conflict-averse judges are less likely to dissent (Dumas 2010). Because women tend to be more risk-averse than men (Jianakoplos and Bernasek 1998), gender may play a role in the likelihood of dissent. In addition, research shows that age is also a potentially important variable: judges appointed at younger ages have less experience and training (Choi et al. 2011). They are also more likely to use the court as a springboard for their future careers and not to want to agitate the ruling party, in order to secure another appointment (Kerby and Banfield 2014). Research also suggests that judges appointed to the court from academic positions are more likely to write a dissenting opinion because they play a more important role in influencing legal developments (Lasser 2004; Caenegem 1993). On this basis, I examined the role of gender (dummy variable), age at the time of appointment (numeric variable), and whether a judge had pursued an academic career prior to appointment (dummy variable). In addition, to test whether presidents of the Court are less likely to dissent (Barić 2016), I tested whether a judge has served as President of the Court (dummy variable). Finally, I analysed whether judges who have had an international education are more likely to dissent. This is because judges who have received part of their education abroad are more likely to be exposed to different practises of constitutional courts. The result of the ANOVA test shows that gender[29] and age[30] have no bearing on the probability of dissenting. Furthermore, in line with the results reported by Bricker (2017), I found no support for the role of an academic career:[31] judges with academic backgrounds are no more likely to dissent than judges with legal or political backgrounds. I also found no evidence to suggest that court presidents are less likely to dissent. However, international training does seem to play a role. Judges who carried out part of their training abroad are more likely to write a dissenting opinion than judges who received all of their education in Croatia, although this effect is significant only at the 0.5 level.[32] Based on this, I can conclude that ideological differences among the judges are the most important driver of the dissenting behaviour in the CrCC.

2.6 Conclusion

In this chapter, I have examined the extent to which the CrCC has limited the legislature's room for manoeuvre in Croatia and whether the CrCC lived up to expectations of becoming a potentially powerful court, as Rodin predicted in 1995.

Several conclusions can be drawn from the results of my analysis. First, unlike several other CEE constitutional courts that developed a strongly activist approach after the fall of the communist regime, the CrCC's approach in the 1990s was very moderate. Faced with an imminent war in which the political leadership expected no challenge from other branches of government, the Court held back from adopting a very activist approach. Characteristic of the Court's practice in the first period were self-restraint, the formal style of interpretation of constitutional provisions, and an uncritical attitude on the part of the judges.

29 One-way ANOVA test $p < 0.974$
30 One-way ANOVA test $p < 0.962$
31 One-way ANOVA test $p < 0.374$
32 One-way ANOVA test $p < 0.0307$*

Second, the strength of the Court's rulings declined significantly around the turn of the millennium and remained at a low level during the remaining three periods. This trend, however, is due to a high number of rejections. In no less than 82% of the cases, the Court rejected the constitutional review request, mainly because it considered the challenged law or provision(s) to be fully constitutional. This casts doubt on the description of the potentially powerful court and may indicate that the remnants of the socialist legacy are still visible in terms of the dominance of the legislature in Croatia, even after the democratic transition.

Third, I concluded that the CrCC did not use a very broad range of measures to constrain the legislature. Notwithstanding its newly acquired power to strike down laws for being inconsistent with the Constitution, the Court has done so only rarely (in 16.3% of the rulings) and only with limited constraint on the legislature (e.g. partial annulment, *ex nunc* or *pro futuro* temporal effect, and no prescriptions).

In sum, while the CrCC was established as a potentially powerful court, its influence on the legislature is only average in strength. Given that three-quarters of all rulings in the 1990–2020 period were rejections, I argue that the Court has failed to live up to expectations and, instead of becoming a "potentially powerful court," has become a "court of rejection." With the increasing trend of dissenting judges arguing against the refusal of the petitions and in favour of substantive or procedural unconstitutionality, together with greater ideological differences in the Court, this may change in the future. However, it is unlikely that only a handful of activist judges will change the rules of the game.

References

Arlović, Mato. 2013. "O Nezavisnosti Ustavnog Suda i Njegovih Sudaca [On the Independence of the Constitutional Court and Its Judges]." *Pravni Vjesnik: Časopis Za Pravne i Društvene Znanosti Pravnog Fakulteta Sveučilišta JJ Strossmayera u Osijeku* 29 (3–4): 7–27.

———. 2014. "Ocjena Ustavnosti Zakona i Drugih Propisa [Assessment of the Constitutionality of Laws and Other Regulations]." *Pravni Vjesnik: Časopis Za Pravne i Društvene Znanosti Pravnog Fakulteta Sveučilišta JJ Strossmayera u Osijeku* 30 (3–4): 9–48.

Bačić, Arsen. 1998. "Zahtjevi Konstitucionalizma, Pitanje Interpretacije i Ustavni Sud Republike Hrvatske [Requirements of Constitutionalism, the Question of Interpretation and the Constitutional Court of the Republic of Croatia.]." *Zbornik Radova Pravnog Fakulteta u Splitu*, 1–2.

Banić, Slavica. 2016. "Activism and Self-Restraint of the Croatian Constitutional Court in the Constitutionalization of the Legal Order." *Constitutional Jurisprudence: Function, Impact and Challenges* 3: 179.

Barić, Sanja. 2016. "The Transformative Role of the Constitutional Court of the Republic of Croatia: From the Ex-Yu to the EU." *Analitika-Center for Social Research, Sarajevo*, Working Paper 6/2016.

———, and Petar Bačić. 2011. "Constitutional Courts as Positive Legislators: National Report – Croatia." In *Constitutional Courts as Positive Legislators*, edited by Allan R. Brewer-Carías, 407–444. Cambridge: Cambridge University Press.

Bobek, Michal, ed. 2015. *Central European Judges Under the European Influence: The Transformative Power of the EU Revisited*. London: Bloomsbury Publishing.

Bricker, Benjamin. 2017. "Breaking the Principle of Secrecy: An Examination of Judicial Dissent in the European Constitutional Courts." *Law & Policy* 39 (2): 170–191.

Caenegem, Raoul Charles van. 1993. *Judges, Legislators and Professors: Chapters in European Legal History*. Cambridge: Cambridge University Press.

Choi, Stephen J., Mitu Gulati, Mirya Holman, and Eric A. Posner. 2011. "Judging Women." *Journal of Empirical Legal Studies* 8 (3): 504–532.

Croatian Parliament. 1991. "Minutes of the 21st joint session of all Members of the Parliament of the Republic of Croatia held on 5 December 1991." 6702–91–21. Zagreb.

Crnić, Jadranko. 2001. "Ustavni Sud Republike Hrvatske: Iskustva i Perspektive [The Constitutional Court of the Republic of Croatia: Experiences and Perspectives]." *Politička Misao* 38 (4): 126–145.

Dorf, Michael C. 2006. "Chief Justice Roberts Advocates the Passive Virtues, Even as the Supreme Court's Docket Reveals Their Subtle Vices." *Findlaw* (blog), November 20. https://supreme.findlaw.com/legal-commentary/chief-justice-roberts-advocates-the-passive-virtues-even-as-the-supreme-courts-docket-reveals-their-subtle-vices.html.

Državno izborno povjerenstvo Republike Hrvatske. n.d. www.izbori.hr/arhiva-izbora/index.html#/app/home.

Dumas, Tao. 2010. "Gender and State Supreme Courts: Explaining Male and Female Judges' Concurring and Dissenting Behavior." In *Western Political Science Association 2010 Annual Meeting Paper*. https://ssrn.com/abstract=1580487.

Dyevre, Arthur, Monika Glavina, and Michal Ovádek. 2021. "Raising the Bar: The Development of Docket Control on the Court of Justice." *Zeitschrift Für Öffentliches Recht* 76 (2): 523–548.

Epstein, Lee, and Jack Knight. 2013. "Reconsidering Judicial Preferences." *Annual Review of Political Science* 16 (1): 11–31.

———, William M. Landes, and Richard A. Posner. 2013. *The Behavior of Federal Judges: A Theoretical and Empirical Study of Rational Choice*. Cambridge: Harvard University Press.

Glavina, Monika. 2020. "To Refer or Not to Refer, That Is the (Preliminary) Question." *Croatian Yearbook of European Law and Policy* 16: 25–59.

———. 2021. "The Reality of National Judges as EU Law Judges: Knowledge, Experiences and Attitudes of Lower Court Judges in Slovenia and Croatia." *Croatian Yearbook of European Law and Policy* 17 (1): 1–40.

Hanretty, Chris. 2012. "Dissent in Iberia: The Ideal Points of Justices on the Spanish and Portuguese Constitutional Tribunals." *European Journal of Political Research* 51 (5): 671–692.

———. 2013. "The Decisions and Ideal Points of British Law Lords." *British Journal of Political Science* 43 (3): 703–716.

Hönnige, Christoph. 2007. *Verfassungsgericht, Regierung, Und Opposition – Die Vergleichende Analyse Eines Spannungsdreiecks*. Wiesbaden: VS Verlag.

IUS-INFO. 2016. "HDZ i SDP postigli dogovor o imenovanju 10 ustavnih sudaca – neslužbeno [HDZ and SDP reached an agreement on the appointment of 10 constitutional judges].” *IUS-INFO*, March 6. www.iusinfo.hr/aktualno/u-sredistu/26455.

Jianakoplos, Nancy Ammon, and Alexandra Bernasek. 1998. “Are Women More Risk Averse?” *Economic Inquiry* 36 (4): 620–630.

Jutarnji list. 2007. “Potočnjak Temporary on the Head of the Constitutional Court.” July 12.

———. 2016a. “HDZ i SDP se dogovorili oko ustavnih sudaca” [HDZ and SDP agreed on constitutional judges] February 6. www.vecernji.hr/vijesti/hdz-i-sdp-se-dogovorili-oko-ustavnih-sudaca-1089302.

———. 2016b. “Most against Jasna Omejec,” March 11. https://www.jutarnji.hr/globus/most-protiv-jasne-omejec-quottreci-mandat-ne-to-ne-dolazi-u-obzir.-cak-i-da-je-radila-besprijekorno-potreban-nam-je-novi-predsjednik-ustavnog-sudquot-30370.

———. 2016c. “HDZ i SDP se dogovorili, donosimo popis kandidata koji idu u Ustavni sud!” [HDZ and SDP have agreed, we bring a list of candidates who will go to the Constitutional Court!] April 18.

Kerby, Matthew, and Andrew C. Banfield. 2014. “The Determinants of Voluntary Judicial Resignation in Australia, Canada, and New Zealand.” *Commonwealth & Comparative Politics* 52 (3): 335–357.

Lasser, M. de S. 2004. *Judicial Deliberations. A Comparative Analysis of Judicial Transparency and Legitimacy*. Oxford: Oxford University Press.

Omejec, Jasna. 2002. “Pravni učinci ustavnosudske kontrole zakona i drugih propisa [Legal effects of constitutional court control of laws and other regulations].” *Ustav kao jamac načela pravne države* 95.

———. 2004. “Fundamental Rights in Croatia.” In *Handbuch Der Grundrechte in Deutschland Und Europa*, edited by Detlef Merten and Hans-Jürgen Papier, 3–39. Heidelberg, Zürich/St. Gallen: C.F. Müller; Dike.

———, and Slavica Banić. 2012. “Diferencijacija propisa i općih akata u budućoj praksi Ustavnog suda i Upravnog suda u povodu Zakona o upravnim sporovima [Differentiation of regulations and general acts in the future practice of the Constitutional Court and the Administrative Court in connection with the Law on Administrative Disputes (2010)].” *Zbornik radova Pravnog fakulteta u Splitu* 49 (2): 309–324.

Pellegrina, Lucia Dalla, and Nuno Garoupa. 2013. “Choosing between the Government and the Regions: An Empirical Analysis of the Italian Constitutional Court Decisions.” *European Journal of Political Research* 52 (4): 558–580.

Pócza, Kálmán. 2019. *Constitutional Politics and the Judiciary: Decision-Making in Central and Eastern Europe*. Abingdon and Oxfordshire: Routledge.

Podolnjak, Robert. 2007. “Izbor Sudaca Ustavnog Suda Republike Hrvatske u Komparativnoj Perspektivi [Selection of Judges of the Constitutional Court of the Republic of Croatia in a Comparative Perspective].” *Zbornik Pravnog Fakulteta u Zagrebu* 57 (3): 547–575.

Posner, Richard A. 2008. *How Judges Think*. Cambridge: Harvard University Press.

Rodin, Siniša. 1995. “The Constitutional Court of the Republic of Croatia and International Law.” *Zeitschrift Fur Auslandisches Offentliches Recht Und Volkerrecht (Za6RV)/Heidelberg Journal of International Law (HJIL), Max-Planck-Institut Fur Auslandisches Offentliches Recht Und Volkerrecht* 3 (55): 788.

———. 1997. “Judicial Review and Separation of Powers in Croatia in Light of German Experience.” *Journal of Constitutional Law in Eastern and Central Europe* 3 (1): 75–107.

Ustavni Sud Republike Hrvatske. 2022. "Statistics." www.usud.hr/hr/statistika.
———. n.d. "Suci Ustavnog suda Republike Hrvatske [Judges of the Constitutional Court of the Republic of Croatia]". www.usud.hr/suci.
Vjesnik. 1999." Neuspješno oporbeno pranje ruku od izbora ustavnih sudaca razotkrilo odnose u oporbi" [The opposition's unsuccessful washing of hands since the election of constitutional judges exposed relations in the opposition], October 26. http://www.monitor.hr/clanci/neuspjesno-oporbeno-pranje-ruku-od-izbora-ustavnih-sudaca-razotkrilo-odnose-u-oporbi/4241.

List of legal acts

Act on Maternity Leave for Self-Employed Mothers and Unemployed Mothers Act, 1997, Official Gazette 109/97
Amendments to the Constitution of the Republic of Croatia, 2000, Official Gazette 113/00
Amendments to the Constitution of the Republic of Croatia, 2001, Official Gazette 28/01
Amendments to the Constitution of the Republic of Croatia, 2010, Official Gazette 76/10
Constitution of the Republic of Croatia, 1990, Official Gazette 56/1990, 135/1997, 8/1998, 113/2000, 124/2000, 28/2001, 41/2001, 55/2001, 76/2010, 85/2010, 5/2014
Constitution of the Socialist Republic of Croatia, 1963, Official Gazette 15/1963
Constitutional Law for the implementation of the Constitution of the Republic of Croatia (Official Gazette, No. 121/10)
Constitutional Law on Amendments to the Constitution of the Republic of Croatia, 1997, Official Gazette 135/97
Constitutional Law on National Minorities' Rights (Official Gazette 155/02, 47/10)
Constitutional Law on the Constitutional Court of the Republic of Croatia (Official Gazette 99/99, 29/02, 49/02)
Judiciary Act, 2005, Official Gazette 150/2005
Law on Croatian Citizenship, Official Gazette 53/91, 28/92
Law on the State Judicial Council, Official Gazette 8/93, 49/99

3 The Czech Constitutional Court

The inconspicuous constrainer

Katarína Šipulová and Alžbeta Králová

3.1 Introduction

The judicialization of mega-politics (Hirschl 2008), i.e. the engagement and active shaping of crucial and politically salient issues by the decision-making activity of constitutional and apex courts, has been drawing the attention of both lawyers and political scientists for several decades (Hirschl 2008; Ginsburg and Moustafa 2008; Sadurski 2014; Lustig and Weiler 2018).[1] Despite the increased interest in the topic since the early 2000s, the concept of judicial activism remains very much contested (Kmiec 2004). Scholars typically disagree on what behaviour amounts to activism, using the term to describe: (a) any judicial (constitutional) review leading to the court quashing a piece of legislation (Hirsch 2008; Graglia 1996); (b) courts actively engaging in borderline cases; (c) courts stretching the interpretation of their competence or the Constitution in order to disallow legislation (Cross and Lindquist 2007); and (d) courts actively creating new rules and appropriating the role of an active legislator (Kmiec 2004). The label "activist courts" has been typically associated with the US Supreme Court, the South African Constitutional Court, the German *Bundesverfassungsgericht*, the Polish Constitutional Tribunal, (particularly during Kaczynski's government in 2007), or the Hungarian Constitutional Court in the 1990s (Ginsburg 2003; Mathebe 2021; Sadurski 2014; Scheppele 2003).

However, as Pócza et al. have argued (Pócza 2019), constitutional courts differ quite profoundly both in their competences and in their willingness to become involved in mega-politics or politics with significant budgetary impacts. While in some countries, constitutional courts exhibit a significant level of self-restraint (King 2012; Ragnarsson 2019), in others, they do not shy away from constraining other political branches of power (Brown and Waller 2016). The conceptual disagreement is reflected in the simplified binary logic which political science scholarship traditionally applies when exploring the

1 The authors are grateful to Jaroslav Benák, Hubert Smekal and Ondřej Kadlec for insightful comments and consultations provided during the work on this chapter.

DOI: 10.4324/9781003399483-3

relationship between constitutional courts and parliaments. Given the lack of agreement on the meaning of the term *judicial activism*, political scientists traditionally equate any invalidation of contested legislation with an act of judicial activism. Such simplified logic is very much contested by legal scholars – and rightly so.

This chapter builds on the scholarship on judicial activism, while extending the conceptualization of the relationship between constitutional courts and parliaments beyond the binary logic mentioned earlier. Using the dataset and methodology developed under the JUDICON-EU project, the chapter will offer a more nuanced view of the interaction between these two actors. It argues that the overall picture is much more vibrant: sometimes constitutional courts invalidate legislation yet leave the parliaments broad room for manoeuvre as to how to proceed with new regulation. In other cases, decisions confirming the constitutionality of a legal rule can in fact significantly constrain the legislator by imposing an interpretation which far exceeds the original intent.

Constitutional courts in Central and Eastern Europe (CEE) occupy a particularly important place among the CEE political actors. They have shaped regimes changes, overseen processes of democratization, and installed new paradigms of individual human rights protection. Nevertheless, some of them proved inefficient as bulwarks against illiberal regime changes since the 2010s (Kosař and Šipulová 2018; Von Bogdandy and Sonnevend 2015). In this respect, the Czech Constitutional Court (CzCC) is notable as one of the very few fully independent constitutional courts in the region, despite several historical attempts to hijack it (Kosař and Vyhnánek 2020). This has led some scholars to portray the CzCC as an institution that has successfully withstood populist illiberal pressure (Smekal, Benák, and Vyhnánek 2022). However, the government of Andrej Babiš (2017–2021), a wealthy businessman and the leader of catch-all centrist party ANO (Hájek 2017), represented a different type of populism, leaning closely towards a traditional catch-all party using populist narratives for electoral gains. In terms of ideology, Babiš's government leaned to the centre, with a rather technocratic style of governance. Neither Babiš himself, nor his party, substantially challenged the legitimacy of core constitutional or international organizations. On the contrary, he remained rhetorically committed to Western Europe and the EU.[2]

2 The only exception being Babiš's book *What I Dream of When I Happen to Sleep* (in Czech original "O čem sním, když náhodou spím" (2017)), where Babiš pondered on a potential abolition of the upper chamber of the Parliament. This has never been translated into his practical policies or political aims, however, and, apart from a couple of speeches questioning the independence of the judiciary, mostly in relation to his own criminal prosecution related to misuse of EU funds, he did not attempt serious interference in the legitimacy of the political system and its institutional actors. It is worth noting that Babiš's rhetoric in 2023 presidential elections changed and shifted closer to the traditional rhetoric of illiberal populism.

On the other hand, the CzCC has faced periods of increased political pressure, often in retaliation for its decision-making. In 2006, President Klaus criticized the Court for undue activism (Klaus and Loužek 2006). In 2011, Prime Minister Nečas also criticized the negative effects of judicial activism after the CzCC issued a judgment on the *Building Savings* case (Smekal, Benák, and Vyhnánek 2022), where it found the use of a state of legislative emergency to push through a new regulation decreasing the state subsidy and increasing its taxation to be unconstitutional (Pl. ÚS 53/10). In 2021, the CzCC faced its most serious criticism thus far, after it annulled the electoral law a mere eight months before the parliamentary elections. Since the petition originally reached the CzCC in 2017, the judgment, which put additional pressure on the lower chamber of the Parliament, triggered questions over whether its timing was not strategic or politicized (Pl. ÚS 44/17).

Drawing on the categorization of different types of contestation faced by courts developed by Madsen, Cebulak, and Wiebusch (2018), the review of electoral laws has proved to be one of the rare areas where political actors not only normatively pushed back against the CzCC, but also questioned its legitimacy. However, historically the greatest source of pressure exerted on the CzCC came from presidents of the republic, who occasionally attempted to disempower the Court through the appointment process. None of these attempts, however, generated long-term pressure that would significantly endanger the court.

In the last decade, law and political science scholarship have extensively explored various legal (Kosař et al. 2020; Petrov 2018) and extra-legal factors (Chmel 2021; Smekal, Benák, and Vyhnánek 2022; Wintr 2022) affecting the results of the CzCC decision-making. Less attention has been paid to the relationship between the CzCC and the Czech Parliament (cf. Kopeček and Petrov 2016), particularly regarding the extent to which the CzCC constraints the Czech legislator and how this practice reflects its overall position on the political map. This chapter thus aims to contribute to the global debate on constitutional courts and judicial activism and show that even self-restrained constitutional courts can indirectly limit the discretion of parliament. In contrast to annulments, which may have significant consequences for democratic legitimacy, constitutional courts can tie the hands of elected political actors without risking such ramifications by offering a specific interpretation of the law under review. In other words, they can reinvent the applicability of the legislation in question in a way that actually changes the effect of the adopted legislation beyond the legislator's original intent.

The chapter proceeds as follows. Section 3.2 offers a bird's eye view of the competences of the CzCC and its overall position in the political arena. Section 3.3 summarizes the methodology used to evaluate the CzCC's relationship with the legislator and discusses the most important characteristics of the CzCC. Section 3.4 begins the analysis with a quantitative overview of the core trends in the 1993–2020 era. Section 3.5 explores these trends with a qualitative discussion of the most important cases. Section 3.6 shifts the attention from the CzCC as a unitary actor to the voting behaviour of individual judges. It explains how a combination of procedural constraints (a high voting quorum and the requirement of supermajority in constitutional review) have made frequent strongly constraining rulings on politically and socially salient topics unlikely. Instead, activist judges started relying on a less direct method of constitutional requirement (binding interpretation of reviewed legislation) both in constitutional review and in individual petition cases. In hindsight, this technique might have helped to shield the CzCC from a strong political backlash.

3.2 The position of the Czech Constitutional Court within the constitutional setting

The CzCC operates in a political system typically described as a parliamentary democracy (Kopeček and Strmiska 2005) with some elements of semi-presidentialism, a situation introduced after the direct election of the President of the Republic in 2012. Its core political institution is the bicameral Parliament consisting of the Chamber of Deputies (lower chamber, 200 members) and the Senate (upper chamber, 81 senators, formally established only in 1996). The Senate plays an important role in the selection of constitutional judges.

The Czech political system has been marked by chronic inefficiency and the instability of its cabinets, caused by unclear and inconsistent parliamentary majorities and shaky coalitions (Brunclík and Kubát 2016a, 2016b). Since 1993, there have been 16 cabinets, which have lasted on average less than two years. While the Czech Republic has not remained completely immune to the illiberal populist tendencies that have emerged in the CEE region, its character differed from conservative national populism of Hungary and Poland, leaning more closely toward centrist and technocratic populism (Havlík 2019). The 2021 elections ended the government of the populist party ANO. The Czech Republic hence remains the only country in the region that did not experience a significant erosion of the institutional system or grave democratic excesses (Smekal, Benák, and Vyhnánek 2022).

The Constitutional Court, with its concentrated model of constitutional review, is definitely one of the most influential political actors in the Czech Republic, having shaped the democratic transition (Šipulová and Smekal 2021; Kühn 2021a, 2021b), ensured individual human rights and compliance with international human rights norms (Kosař et al. 2020), and secured the legitimacy of the Czech judiciary, which underwent only very limited purging after 1989 (Kosař and Šipulová 2023; Wagnerová 2003). The CzCC has traditionally been among the public institutions enjoying the highest levels of public trust (STEM 2022).

The high legitimacy of the CzCC builds on its stability (juxtaposed with the Chamber of Deputies), as well as the strong legacy of the Czech and Slovak Federal Constitutional Court (CSFCC), one of the symbols of the 1989 transition and the break from the Communist regime (Kopeček 2017). The CSFCC defined the normative character and values underlying the new democracy, engaging with its identity and nationhood and shaping key elements of transitional justice policies, while often significantly departing from the original intent of the young federal Parliament (Šipulová and Smekal 2021). It laid down some of the fundamental principles that were further developed by its successor, including the doctrine of the substantive core of the constitution (Kosař and Vyhnánek 2021).

The CzCC, established in 1993, has taken up this legacy, retaining the institutional structure and some of the (Czech) federal judges. Its scope of jurisdiction is quite broad, including both abstract and concrete constitutional review, review of individual complaints, review of complaints on the results and process of presidential and parliamentary elections, and competence disputes between other constitutional bodies, as well as deciding on the compatibility of international treaties with the Czech Constitution.[3] In practice, 98% of its caseload consists of review of individual complaints (Kosař and Vyhnánek 2020).

The Court is composed of 15 judges selected and appointed by the President of the Republic upon the approval of the Senate.[4] The length of their term of office is 10 years, and their mandate can be renewed once. The renewal of mandates has been criticized by some Czech academics (Procházková 2023) as leading to an increased politicization of judges shortly before the end of their first term (Kühn and Kysela 2003; Kosař and Vyhnánek 2016). Even more controversially, the system of selection is not staggered (meaning that the whole bench is changed within a short timeframe) and overlaps with presidential elections. As all Czech presidents so far have served two consecutive five-year terms, this creates quite a conundrum. Each president of the republic has thus so far been able to determine "his own" composition of the CzCC (Kosař and Šipulová 2020, 2023; Kosař and Vyhnánek 2021) in his first years in office. This is very much visible at the time of writing (2023) when the new President, Petr Pavel, elected in February 2023, will have the chance to appoint 13 of out 15 constitutional judges within the first two years of his term. The President also gains informal leverage since (s)he also unilaterally selects the President of the CzCC from among the sitting judges.

Accordingly, the individual generations of the CzCC's bench are sometimes familiarly labelled after the respective presidents who appointed them: the first being Havel's Court (1993–2002); the second, Klaus's Court (2003–2012); and the third, Zeman's Court (2013–2022). Nevertheless, thanks to a combination of the Senate's gatekeeping role, and initial underestimation of CzCC's impact,

3 Art. 87 of the Constitutional Act No. 1/1993 Coll.

4 Although the Constitution presumes unconditional approval of the Senate (Art. 84/2), the Act on the Czech Constitutional Court No. 182/1993 Coll. stipulates that if the Senate does not approve the nominee within the 60 days from nomination due to its inactivity, there is a presumption of its approval, and the nominee becomes a judge.

none of the Presidents have so far succeeded in fully utilizing this power, and instead they created a relatively balanced Court (Kosař and Vyhnánek 2021). However, as we demonstrate later on, the CzCC also experienced isolated incidents when both President Klaus and President Zeman attempted to paralyze it by refusing to propose new candidates after the Senate rejected several of their nominees in a row (Šimíček 2016).[5]

The CzCC decides in chambers of three judges or in a plenary session of all judges. Constitutional review cases are always decided in plenary sessions. The key factor that shapes its dynamics is the combination of a voting quorum (10 judges)[6] and a supermajority (i.e. 9 out of 15 votes) requirement in certain types of proceedings – including the constitutional review of legislation.[7] The wording of the relevant provision does not provide a clear answer to the question of whether the requirement for a qualified majority applies both to rulings granting a petition or rejecting one. The CzCC resolved this issue in Pl. ÚS 36/93 by leaning towards the need for a qualified majority only for cases of substantive unconstitutionality, while requiring a simple majority for rejections. Although this conclusion provoked a vivid debate among judges (Kosař and Vyhnánek 2021), it was eventually accepted as a pragmatic safeguard against a deadlock in decision-making.

3.3 Methodological particularities of the Czech case

Drawing on the methodology adopted by the JUDICON-EU project, this section offers a quick overview of the core research design and discusses the elements unique to the CzCC. The quantitative research on the relationship between the CzCC and the Czech Parliament covers the period from 1993 to 2020, analysing altogether 361 decisions containing a total of 437 individual rulings. Except for the constitutional interpretation *in abstracto*, the CzCC is endowed with quite a wide range of competences (Šipulová 2019), and it significantly increased its influence on the political scene in the Czech Republic by appropriating the competence to review constitutional acts (see Section 3.5 for more details on case *Melčák*). The majority of cases in our dataset arose from abstract constitutional review that can be initiated only by a privileged group of actors: the President of the Republic, a group of MPs or senators, or the government. In the relevant period, the majority of decisions originated from petitions initiated by the members of the Parliament (Kosař and Vyhnánek 2020). This is an interesting observation, suggesting that the

5 It is worth mentioning that the Senate did not approve only two of Havel's nominations, although the number of rejected nominees was significantly higher for President Klaus (with eight nominees rejected, one of them rejected even twice) and for Zeman (with five rejections, one of them unsuccessfully nominated by Klaus).

6 The CzCC refuses, however, to hold plenary sessions if there are less than 12 judges on the bench. See more in Section 3.6.

7 Section 13 of the Constitutional Act No. 182/1993 Coll., on the Constitutional Court.

Parliament is a Janus-faced arena of constitutional review: on the one hand, it is mostly the lower chamber which bears the impact of constitutional review. On the other hand, the majority of proceedings have been initiated by members of the Senate, allowing for a fragile dynamic between the Parliament and the CzCC. Although JUDICON-EU focuses mostly on constitutional review cases, Czech scholars typically argue that the majority of CzCC's judicial activism stems from individual petitions, in the area of human and fundamental rights protection.

Before beginning the overview of the general patterns of the case law and its relationship with the Parliament, we need to note four caveats which slightly adjust the project's methodology. First, the *ex tunc* temporal effect of prescriptions is a concept highly contested among Czech scholars and generally perceived as contravening the principle of non-retroactivity (Filip, Holländer, and Šimíček 2007). The CzCC does not use *ex tunc* prescriptions. A vast majority of rulings have *ex nunc* effect and become binding immediately after their publication in the Collection. From time to time, the CzCC authorizes *pro futuro* effect of its decisions,[8] although such rulings are limited to occasions when the immediate application would further increase the existing violation of constitutional principles. It is worth noting that, informally, we can sometimes find binding *pro futuro* prescriptions outside the operative part of the ruling, i.e. in the reasoning of the decision. A typical example would be a prescription as to how the parliament should legislate or what should be done if it remains inactive (Kühn 2011).[9] These situations are very rare, however.

Second, this unique feature of the CzCC's reasonings relates to the formal structure of its decisions. The rulings in the CzCC's decisions are very formalized. They usually follow the wording of the petition and merely state whether the contested legislation violates the relevant constitutional provisions. The effect as well as the binding prescription of the Court might therefore appear in the reasoning and not in the operative part (Kühn 2011). As we later demonstrate in Section 3.5, this is particularly the case for decisions which declare a constitutional requirement or which reject the petitions.

Third, the scope of ruling types issued by the CzCC is narrower than the general categorization developed by the JUDICON-EU project (see Chapter 1). The CzCC might be considered weak compared to some of its European counterparts since it does not use some of the more stringent instruments described in the JUDICON methodology. Apart from the constitutional interpretation *in abstracto*, the CzCC is quite hesitant to push against the Parliament with "unconstitutionality by legislative omission". Historically, the Czech doctrine has perceived this category as contradictory to the principle of

8 E.g. Pl. ÚS 28/13. The CzCC can postpone the effect in a situation where the *ex nunc*, immediate effect of annulment of the norm would lead to even graver interference and violation of constitutional rules.

9 E. g. Pl. ÚS 8/02; Pl. ÚS 16/09 and Pl. ÚS 24/11.

the separation of powers: the Constitution does not allow an unelected body to issue a prescription to the directly elected Parliament to act or to pass a particular norm (Malíř 2008). The CzCC has mostly respected this principle and abandoned this position only twice, both times in cases related to the economic and democratic transition.[10] It is worth noting that while the CzCC interfered with the legislator's unique competence, it nevertheless limited itself by declaring inaction unconstitutional, but it did not prescribe any particular remedy to the legislator.

Fourth, as we already mentioned, the legislator constrained the CzCC by setting a higher quorum and requiring a supermajority for voting in constitutional review proceedings. According to the CzCC's own interpretation, the nine-vote supermajority is required only in cases where the CzCC finds substantive unconstitutionality. In contrast, cases leading to a rejection of petitions or to a constitutional requirement will still be decided by a simple majority of the judges present at the sitting. The CzCC justified this reduction of consensual deliberation as a pragmatic step, which still respects constrains imposed by the legislator, while it also avoids the risk of decision-making deadlock (Wagnerová et al. 2007). Nevertheless, as a consequence, it is significantly more difficult to achieve a vote of substantive unconstitutionality than to reject a case or to decide by constitutional requirement. We expect to see this inequality of voting pattern reflected in the lower strength of rulings.

All in all, these four caveats suggest that the Court would typically act as a self-constrained actor, mostly respecting the Parliament's legislative authority. This is well demonstrated also by the variability of different rulings used by the CzCC, which has evolved only marginally over time (Figure 3.1).

Shortly after its establishment, the CzCC operated in a binary fashion of either rejecting the petition or finding a substantive unconstitutionality (1993–1995). Proportionally, these two types of rulings have dominated the case law in all three decades. Since 2006, the variability has somewhat increased, although the use of other types has still been limited, as the number of different ruling types has remained quite low.

Since 2012 we can observe two interesting trends: (1) procedural unconstitutionality has disappeared completely; (2) the use of constitutional requirement has increased. The disappearance of procedural unconstitutionality might be explained by the increasing auto-limitation of the Parliament (Petrov 2018), which started incorporating a pre-emptive review of constitutional and international law compliance as an integral part of the legislative process. Although there have only been five cases of procedural unconstitutionality, their effect on the legislative practice of the Parliament was immense. These

10 See Pl. ÚS 20/05 on the non-activity of the Parliament in the question of regulated rents in apartments and Pl. ÚS 9/07, on the non-activity of parliament concerning legislation on the church restitution – the return of church property that was nationalized by the Communist Party.

Figure 3.1 Frequency of the ruling types (CzCC)

Source: JUDICON-EU.

Note: [REJ – rejection, in white; OM – legislative omission, in stripes; PROC – procedural requirement, in grid; CR – constitutional requirement, dotted; SUBST – substantive unconstitutionality, in grey].

cases reshaped the role of the actors in the legislative process[11] and established strict lines for the Parliament to follow. In particular, the CzCC rejected various forms of abuse and shortening of legislative debate on the pretext of legislative emergency (fast-track legislative procedure in case when fundamental rights are at risk, Pl. ÚS 53/10), or the random addition of partial amendments of provisions of acts unrelated to the given legislative proceedings at the very end of the last reading (Pl. ÚS 77/06, so-called legislative riders).

The second visible trend is the increasing use of the constitutional requirement, starting from the era of the second Court, before becoming a fully established practice in the third CzCC. The starting point correlates with the accession of the Czech Republic to the EU, an era when, due to various training programmes, general knowledge of and interest in international law increased among both judges and lawyers in general (Kosař et al. 2020). The increasing imposition of constitutional requirement to the detriment of finding substantive unconstitutionality might therefore be seen as a result of better pre-emptive control of constitutionality in the legislative process on the one hand, and more leverage in creative interpretation and inspiration from the European Court of Human Rights' case law on the other hand. It was during this period that the CzCC accepted the European Convention of Human Rights as a part of the framework for constitutionality review. The significant increase in its use in the CzCC's case law (Smekal and Vyhnánek 2018) may have allowed the Court more scope for creative interpretation and given it

11 For example, case Pl. ÚS 33/97, related to the calculation of time-limits for the application of the presidential veto.

more leverage. However, the increasing use of constitutional requirement rulings might also suggest an internal split among the judges of the CzCC. While judges typically characterize constitutional requirement as being in line with the principle of minimalist intervention, we argue that it might pose as a hidden finding of unconstitutionality with even stronger repercussions on the legislator – masking the lacking momentum of the Court, or actively shielding it from political backlash (Section 3.6).

3.4 General observations: selective constraints on the Czech Parliament

This section offers a bird's eye view of the general patterns present in the CzCC's performance between 1993 and 2020, and it explains its behaviour towards the Parliament in line with the concept of the inconspicuous constrainer (Šipulová 2019). In comparison to other constitutional courts in the CEE region (Chapter 12), the CzCC's overall performance can be characterized as average. Apart from two peaks in 2004 and 2009, and an abrupt drop in 2007, the strength of the CzCC's rulings oscillated around 2.5–3.5, with a median value of 2.5, suggesting consistency in the CzCC's reluctance to significantly constrain the legislator. Since 2009, the strength of the CzCC's rulings has demonstrated a decreasing trend, dropping to 1.71 in 2020 (Figure 3.2).

This decreasing tendency needs to be analysed against the background of the growing caseload of the Court (and the growing number of rejections in mundane cases), which essentially dilutes the longitudinal effect of politically salient rulings. This is well demonstrated by Table 3.1. The caseload of the

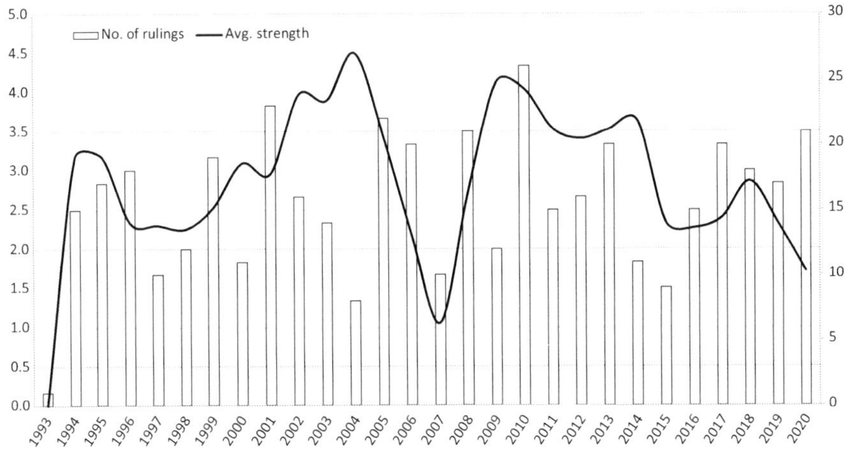

Figure 3.2 Number and average strength of rulings (1993–2020) (CzCC)

Source: JUDICON-EU.

Note: The right axis suggests the number of judgments and decisions examined in every year, portrayed in the figure by bars. The left axis suggests the strength of the decision (the black line).

Table 3.1 Caseload of the Czech Constitutional Court (1993–2020)

YEAR	*The number of petitions to be decided in panels*	*The number of petitions to be decided in a plenary session (constitutional review)*	*All (various) petitions*
1993	476	47	523
1994	829	33	862
1995	1,224	47	1,271
1996	1,462	41	1,503
1997	1,975	46	2,021
1998	2,169	29	2,198
1999	2,543	24	2,567
2000	3,077	60	3,137
2001	3,006	38	4
2002	3,140	44	3,184
2003	2,496	52	2,548
2004	2,713	75	2,788
2005	2,982	58	3,040
2006	3,455	94	3,549
2007	3,302	29	3,331
2008	3,208	42	3,250
2009	3,394	38	3,432
2010	3,726	60	3,786
2011	3,967	38	4,005
2012	4,915	31	4,946
2013	4,022	56	4,078
2014	4,057	27	4,084
2015	3,858	34	3,892
2016	4,256	36	4,292
2017	4,133	47	4,180
2018	4,331	48	4,379
2019	4,172	28	4,200
2020	3,605	113	3,718

Source: Czech Constitutional Court, https://concourt.cz/

CzCC has gradually increased from 523 petitions in 1993 to 4,915 petitions in 2012. Between 2013 and 2019 the number of petitions remained around 4,100 per year, dropping to 3,718 during the COVID-19 pandemic of 2020. Turning to petitions for constitutional review cases, the overall development is much more even. Starting at 47 petitions in 1993, we can observe significant increases in 2006 (94) and in 2020 (113). The increase in the number of cases roughly corresponds to the decrease in the average strength of rulings. The same logic, however, does not apply to the drops in 1996, 2007, or 2015. Interestingly, since 2015, the CzCC has decided on 76 constitutional review cases, delivering 91 rulings – which is a higher number than the overall average.

As we explain further along, these changes (the gradual increase until 2002, then a steep drop in 2005–2007 and a gradual decrease from 2010 onwards) correlate with: (a) the changing agenda of the CzCC (i.e. mainly the changing character of the contested legislative acts); (b) the political and economic background; and (c) the different composition of the Court and the change in the coalition potential among the judges.

3.4.1 Key trends and critical junctures

The first era of the CzCC in the 1990s was characterized by a rather low, even decreasing strength of rulings, with the average strength oscillating between 2.5 and 3 points. The low values from the 1990s are somewhat surprising given that the existing literature identifies the first CzCC as a powerful actor in mega-politics (Hirschl 2004), particularly in issues related to the democratic transition, transitional justice, and electoral law (Kopeček and Petrov 2016; Kühn 2010). Although the CzCC annulled several key legislative acts in the 1990s (Šipulová 2019), it did not bind the legislator with a particular form of prescription. Instead, the CzCC actually "concealed" part of its strength in proceedings on individual petitions. The weak rulings of the early CzCC also correlate with the evolving style of its reasonings, which, in the 1990s were still rather short, lacking broader elaboration or guidelines for the legislator. The first CzCC mostly acted as a partner, respecting the political legitimacy and accountability of the young Parliament.

The second era of the CzCC (2002–2012) brought a high volatility of ruling strength, reaching both the absolute peak (4.5) in 2004, then dropping to its lowest level (1) in 2007, before gradually regaining the strength of rulings back to values from the beginning of 2000s. The initial growth in strength from 2002 to 2006 correlated with the period of EU law approximation before the 2004 accession. The trend of Europeanization was also reflected in the CzCC's case law (Kosař et al. 2020), which delivered several strong rulings that can be interpreted as activist decisions. The emancipation of the CzCC is particularly visible in its relationship towards the EU law. Inspired by the German tradition, the CzCC carefully analysed what position the EU law should play within the Czech constitutional order, going to considerable lengths to show that it cannot have primacy over the material core of the Czech Constitution (Komárek 2012; Bobić 2017). On the other hand, it did not shy away from a pro-active approach when it came to the effects of the EU law on the legislator, urging the Parliament to incorporate the requirements of EU law months before they became formally binding (e. g. Pl. ÚS 39/01). The leading example of these controversial and highly debated decisions was the case Pl. ÚS 36/01, which addressed the effects of the so-called Euro-amendment of the Czech Constitution. The Euro-amendment, adopted in 2001 as part of the preparation for EU integration, inserted two new principles into the Czech Constitution. First, it recognized the conferral of sovereignty on an international organization. Second, it formalized a shift from the dualistic tradition to a monistic incorporation of ratified international treaties, which were to become an integral part of the Czech (constitutional) legal order. In a seminal case, the CzCC attempted to mitigate the effect of the monistic shift, appropriating the sole authority to review the compatibility of Czech legislative acts with ratified international human rights treaties. In other words, the CzCC conditioned the direct applicability of these treaties on its own judicial review. It is worth noting that in practice this ruling was poorly followed by general (and in particular apex) courts, and later more or less abandoned as too centralized and impractical (Kühn and Kysela 2002; Filip 2002; Petrov and Šipulová 2016; Kosař and Petrov 2019).

Interestingly, the peak of the strength of rulings in 2004 also correlated with a lower number of decisions delivered that year. The drop was most probably influenced by controversies linked to the appointment of new judges by President Václav Klaus, who was elected in 2003. As we indicated earlier, the Czech President typically appoints almost the full bench of the constitutional court within one or two years of entering into office. Klaus openly criticized the CzCC as too activist and wished to change this trend by appointing judges who were more aligned to his political preferences. After the Senate rejected several of his nominees as politicized or not competent, he attempted to starve the Court by not providing any new candidates for the Senate's confirmation. By the end of 2004, 4 out of 15 seats had been left vacant and were filled only at the end of 2005. This put the constitutional review competence of the CzCC in great danger. The combination of a requirement of a quorum of 10 judges and a supermajority of nine votes posed a risk that the CzCC would be unable to achieve a ruling on substantive unconstitutionality by default. Court President Rychetský therefore introduced an informal rule that the plenary session would be held only if the CzCC has more than 12 sitting judges.

The strength of rulings achieved its peak around the year 2004. Substantively however, most of those cases did not touch upon any politically salient issues and targeted mostly formal requirements of judicial proceedings, the breadth and length of judicial reasonings (Pl. ÚS 1/03), the judicial review of classified information (Pl. ÚS 11/04), or the right to be heard in criminal proceedings (Pl. ÚS 45/04). The only exception was the series of decisions related to the restrictions put on judicial salaries,[12] where the CzCC found freezing the salaries of public officials (a measure meant to reduce public expenses during an economic crisis) to be in violation of the principle of judi cial independence.

The strength of the court's rulings reached its lowest value in 2007. The steep drop needs to be interpreted in the context of the Court – which, by 2007, sat in a largely new composition, after facing several years of criticism for being overly activist.[13] After 2008, the strength of the CzCC's ruling rose again until 2010 and remained at the same level as it had been at the turn of the 1990s/2000s. Even though the average strength of its rulings did not

12 Pl. ÚS 34/04, Pl. ÚS 43/04, Pl. ÚS 9/05.

13 The CzCC triggered criticism for shifting towards judicialization and juristocracy mostly from President Klaus (Klaus and Loužek 2006), but the debate related to the "judgeocracy" became a part of broader discourse (see for example Smekal and Pospíšil 2013).

radically differ from the first CzCC, it was the second CzCC that triggered a critical debate on the judicialization of politics. The prime and most controversial example was the case *Melčák*, Pl. ÚS 27/09, in which the CzCC annulled a Constitutional Act[14] shortening the electoral term of the current Chamber of Deputies as a preparation for pre-emptive elections. The impact of *Melčák* is multi-layered, and we discuss it in more detail in Section 3.5 of this chapter. From the longitudinal perspective, *Melčák* redefined the position of the CzCC among Czech political actors since the CzCC controversially awarded itself the competence to review constitutional acts, pushing its role of negative legislator to another dimension.

Since 2011 the strength of the CzCC's rulings have gradually decreased, approaching the minimum value of 1.71 in 2020. This extreme drop correlated with a sudden jump in the court's caseload, which almost doubled in 2020, partly due to an increase of COVID-19 related cases, where the CzCC adopted a self-constrained attitude (Chvojka and Kovalčík 2022). In 2020, 5 out of 11 rejections were related to COVID-19 emergency measures. The overall decrease since 2011, however, calls for several more complex interpretations. First, the trend might suggest that the auto-limitation of the Czech Parliament was indeed successful (Kokeš 2015; Petrov 2018). Second, the scope of the CzCC's agenda shifted. While the first Court dealt with fundamental aspects of the democratization process and transitional justice, and the second CzCC decided on cases related to electoral issues, judicial independence, and fundamental human rights, the third CzCC focused more on social issues. There might be a correlation between the increasing number of social issues and the decreasing strength of its rulings due to the implementation of the "reasonability test". Compared to the standard proportionality test, well known also from the ECtHR's case law, the reasonability test weighs the severity of interference in social rights against the reasonable competing interest and grants the legislator much greater deference (Kratochvíl 2015). In other words, the social rights agenda allowed the Court to be less constraining vis-á-vis the Parliament. Third, the decreasing strength of the rulings at this time might correlate with the increasing diversity (particularly in terms of career background) and cleavages existing among the judges of "Zeman's Court", as well as the approaching end of the mandate of constitutional judges, which could be reflected in decision-making that is more responsive to the current political climate.

Overall, the longitudinal trends paint a portrait that contrasts with the traditional scholarship depicting the CzCC as a strong and relatively activist constitutional actor (Kosař and Vyhnánek 2020; Smekal, Benák, and Vyhnánek

14 In Czech legal doctrine, constitutional acts are considered to be a part of the Constitution in a wider sense. They need to be approved by 3/5th of all MPs and 3/5th of present senators. The Constitution does not explicitly give the CzCC a competence to review constitutional acts.

2022). Compared to its CEE counterparts, the CzCC leaves the Parliament considerable room for manoeuvre and does not issue particularly constraining rulings. We address this anomaly later, in Sections 3.5 and 3.6, arguing that due to a combination of procedural and ideological factors, the CzCC judges developed more indirect methods of shaping the interpretation of legislation and binding the legislator to follow it.

3.5 Outliers and most interesting cases

When looking at the role of the CzCC and its influence on the formation of Czech legislation, the scholarship typically identifies three areas where the CzCC has exerted intense pressure on the Parliament: transitional justice, electoral cases, and social rights.

As previously mentioned, the first CzCC built its legitimacy on an agenda related to transitional justice, the regulation of rents, a transformation of the economy and private ownership. While there were some landmark constitutional review cases, much of the substantive change in the transitional legislation also happened via individual petition cases, particularly those addressing reparations and damages paid to victims of the communist regime, or the privatization and restitution of property (Šipulová and Smekal 2021). The transitional jurisprudence has, however, already almost entirely been concluded, with crucial restitution of church property cases finished at the end of the second CzCC (Šipulová 2019).

The second group of cases where the CzCC particularly strongly interfered in the autonomy of the Parliament concerned electoral matters. The Czech Constitution prescribes the proportional electoral system for the Chamber of Deputies[15] and leaves its precise form to be determined by the legislator. Nevertheless, the CzCC has repeatedly used the proportionality principle to intervene and to set boundaries for the Parliament. The first opportunity arrived in 1997 with a constitutional complaint related to the 5% electoral threshold (Pl. ÚS 25/96). The CzCC, however, remained self-constrained. It emphasized that absolute proportionality is unachievable and rejected the case, arguing that the distortion of proportionality due to the existence of an electoral threshold does not contravene the principle of democratic representation.

In 2000, a significant change to the electoral system occurred as a consequence of "the Opposition Agreement", an informal pact between the two biggest political parties, the Social Democrats and Civic Democratic Party, which allowed the Social Democrats to assume power as a single-party minority government with the support of the Civic Democratic Party. In return for its support, the opposition Civic Democratic Party was promised far-reaching

15 Art. 18 of the Constitutional Act No. 1/1993 Coll.: "Elections to the Chamber of Deputies shall be held by secret ballot on the basis of a universal, equal, and direct right to vote, according to the principle of proportional representation".

electoral reforms, which were meant to reinforce the position of both major parties by raising the electoral threshold for partisan coalitions, changing the formula for allocations of votes to seats, and creating 35 relatively small constituencies. In 2001, in a closely scrutinized *Grand Electoral Judgment I*, Pl. ÚS 42/2000,[16] the CzCC found these elements unconstitutional. Despite several harsh dissenting opinions, the CzCC argued that the cumulative effect of the amendments breached the principle of proportional representation required by the Constitution. It upheld only the higher electoral threshold for coalitions, referring to the margin of appreciation left to the legislator. Given the extensive impact of the judgment on the political system, it spurred intense reactions, mostly from the representatives of the leading actors behind the reform, future presidents Václav Klaus and Miloš Zeman. According to some authors, the decision shaped the attitudes of both upcoming presidents and deepened their animosity towards the CzCC (Smekal, Benák, and Vyhnánek 2022).[17]

The electoral system created as a reaction to the *Grand electoral Judgment I* became the subject of several individual constitutional complaints. However, until the complaint of a group of senators in 2017, none of them was successful (due to the lack of interference with the complainant's individual fundamental rights or manifest unfoundedness).[18] It is worth mentioning that a group of senators challenged the electoral system as early as 2006, but the CzCC (deciding by refusal in three-judge panel) considered their complaint as manifestly ill-founded (Pl. ÚS 57/06). In the meantime, the CzCC delivered another ground-breaking judgment, in *Melčák* (Pl. ÚS 27/09). The case arose from a petition by an MP against a Constitutional Act that was meant to shorten the electoral term of the Chamber of Deputies and trigger an early election (which would favour the governing parties). Melčák argued that shortening the term violated his political rights and legitimate expectations. While the CzCC did not endorse this interpretation, it annulled the Act due to procedural and formal mistakes in the legislative process. The decision triggered a heated public debate and sparked criticisms of the CzCC, partly strengthening and partly damaging its reputation and relationship with the Chamber of Deputies (Roznai 2014).

Almost 12 years after *Grand electoral judgment I*, the CzCC returned to a review of the proportional representativeness of the electoral system and delivered another important judgment that reshaped the distribution of powers in the political arena. Although *Grand electoral judgment II* (Pl. ÚS 44/17)

16 Interestingly, the petition was brought to the CzCC by President Havel.

17 However, it should be stressed that Zeman respected the CzCC at the beginning of his term, mostly thanks to the presidency of Pavel Rychetský, whom he respected and trusted. Prior to joining the CzCC, Rychetský served as a Minister of Justice in Zeman's government.

18 See cases Pl. ÚS 76/06, I. ÚS 537/06, Pl. ÚS 57/06, III. ÚS 663/06, Pl. ÚS 2/14 or Pl. ÚS 42/17.

falls outside the timeframe of the JUDICON-EU project, as the CzCC finally decided on the case in February 2021, it is without doubt a clear demonstration of the Court's willingness to interfere in the realm of mega-politics. It confirms that the court's first intervention in the electoral system was not related to specific circumstances, nor was it an example of isolated activism. The Court seems to take its role as protector of the principle of proportional representation very seriously and does not perceive particular elements of the electoral system as the legislator's discretionary space. The CzCC has repeatedly emphasized that it is not its role to present alternatives to the current system or to deliver precise instructions to the legislator, even if the claimant explicitly asked the Court to do so.[19] It therefore "merely" annulled the threshold for coalitions (i.e. the feature that survived the first election judgment) and the combination of the D'Hondt formula used for allocation of seats with their division into 14 constituencies. According to the CzCC, these two mechanisms operating together caused unequal and disproportionate effects and possible disadvantages for smaller political parties. The decision provoked emotional reactions across the political spectrum, with Prime Minister Babiš accusing the Court of overstepping all boundaries and not acting impartially. The reason for the controversies lay in the combination of both the result and its timing. The decision was issued three years after the senators had lodged the complaint, but more importantly, only eight months before upcoming elections planned for October 2021. It therefore left the Parliament with little time to enact the necessary amendments to the electoral system. Despite the initially intense reactions, the political scene seemed to calm down relatively quickly, and the legislator managed to adopt an amendment in due time before the planned elections. In the end, the decision did not manifest in a backlash against the Court.

The third group of cases which are often on the agenda of the CzCC are a mix of social rights that represent very diverse areas but have a common denominator in the form of a ruling delivered by the CzCC. Particularly in the third era of the CzCC, a clear increase can be observed in the use of constitutional requirements. Although we provided some explanations for their emergence in Section 3.3, the impact of constitutional requirements deserves a deeper qualitative analysis.

Constitutional requirements found their way into the CzCC adjudication rather gradually (Figure 3.1). The first case prioritizing the conforming interpretation appeared in 1996. It took another seven years until the CzCC came to another milestone which turned the constitutional requirement into a commonly used technique. According to the CzCC case law, the binding part of the decision is represented not only by the ruling itself but also by the reasoning, more precisely by the parts of it containing substantial reasons.[20]

19 See for example par. 52, 175, or 204.

20 See cases Pl. ÚS 2/03 or III. ÚS 200/2000.

Although legal theory disagreed on the binding effect of the *ratio decidendi* (Kühn 2000), the CzCC reversed this in case Pl. ÚS 2/03 related to regulated rents. It openly criticized the government for disrespecting the substantial reasoning of its previous decisions, arguing that they have a binding effect. This interpretation was repeatedly confirmed. The CzCC argued that any other interpretation (i.e. narrowing down the binding effect to the operative parts only) would force it to abandon its previous self-restraint towards the legislator and annul legal provisions at the slightest sign of unconstitutional interpretation. In the CzCC's own interpretation, it is the binding effect of its legal interpretation that allows the CzCC to prioritize interpretations that are in harmony with the constitution over the annulment of potentially problematic provisions.[21] Compared to the core methodology of the JUDICON-EU project, the constitutional requirement (i.e. binding constitutionally conforming interpretation) is therefore not limited to the operative part of judgments but frequently also appears in the reasoning as an *obiter dictum*. If the CzCC includes constitutionally conforming interpretation in a ruling, it uses the label "interpretative ruling", i.e. a ruling equal to a legal norm.[22] Although the CzCC considers the reasoning to be the binding part, this is probably because it has reflected on the controversies of its approach and wants to reinforce the binding effect by including the substantial reasons directly into a ruling (i.e. it creates an interpretative ruling). The CzCC used interpretative rulings especially in the second half of the second CzCC era and at the beginning of the third CzCC era. Without any explicit explanation, it later abandoned this practice, replacing it with placing constitutional requirements in the decision's reasonings. Both variations are, however, considered binding by Czech legal doctrine.

Although the CzCC portrays its use of interpretative rulings as a self-constraining step, the practice is not without controversy and, on the contrary, it is instead criticized for being overly activist, if not *ultra vires*.[23] In fact, setting constitutional requirements might restrain the legislator far more than finding substantive unconstitutionality, as it provides a legally binding interpretation addressed to all public bodies and individuals,[24] without giving the Parliament any opportunity to legislate on the matter. In the end, the CzCC itself indirectly admits this when tying the constitutional requirement to its own

21 Pl. ÚS 41/02.

22 As explicitly explained by the CzCC for example in Pl. ÚS 45/04 or Pl. ÚS 39/13.

23 The mixed views were present also within the CzCC, as demonstrated i.e. by a dissenting opinion of judge Güttler in Pl. ÚS 41/02.

24 One of the examples is case Pl. ÚS 15/16 dealing with an accountability of a driver, where CzCC found a discrepancy between the constitutional protection of individual rights and the administrative ordinance regulating traffic offences. The CzCC put forward a conforming interpretation but addressed it directly to administrative courts dealing with this and similar cases.

authoritative interpretation of the Constitution, and not to the intent of the legislator.

Looking back at the frequency of use of the constitutional requirements, in general, the presence of constitutional requirements increased from 2015 to 2020. For a long time, the CzCC did not apply constitutional requirements in the politically salient cases. This somehow changed in 2017, when the CzCC applied a constitutional requirement to address more controversial issues, such as blocking illegal online gambling (Pl. ÚS 28/16), the financing of political parties (Pl. ÚS 11/17), or debt brakes on self-governing regions (Pl. ÚS 6/17). The changing character of constitutional requirements and their increasing use might signal various things. The CzCC might use this strategy deliberately, in order to shield itself from potential political backlash. That would allow it to consciously avoid making constraining rulings too frequent that might trigger a reaction from political actors. However, the constitutional requirement might also indicate that the CzCC prefers fast-track rectification of justice, without further relying on often lengthy legislative process. Or, as we argue in the following section, it might simply follow from the procedural constraints inherent in constitutional review proceedings and the increasing inability of CzCC judges to receive a supermajority of votes.

3.6 Voting coalitions, supermajority, and indirect constraints of the Parliament

How does a constitutional court arrive at a decision? Does the court act as a unilateral actor vis-à-vis parliament? What motivates its judges to opt for a more or less constraining approach towards the legislature? Bearing in mind the significantly high threshold needed to annul legislation (a supermajority of 9 judges out of at least 10 judges present), this section shifts the attention from the CzCC as a unitary actor to the voting behaviour of its individual judges. Here, we therefore refocus on the extra-legal factors affecting the CzCC's decision-making, searching mostly for the differences between individual judges and their abilities to form voting coalitions: based on ideology, partisanship, gender, or professional background.

Information on the ideological or partisan preferences of constitutional judges is inaccessible in the Czech Republic. As we previously explained, judges are nominated and appointed by the President and approved by the Senate, which plays a gatekeeping role and safeguards the quality of candidates. Neither the President nor the Senate are directly involved in party politics, although all three presidents were initially party leaders. Although the majority of the CzCC's judges come from the judiciary, some judges had also had previous political experience, particularly in the eras of the first and second CzCC. Nevertheless, the dominance of judges from the pool of the general judiciary with a strict career model prevents any open connection or ideological alignment with political parties, as this is perceived as suspicious and detrimental to judicial independence (Kosař 2017; Kosař and Spáč 2021).

This does not, of course, mean that sitting judges do not differ in their left-right preferences or that we do not have at least indirect indicators of which position they will be leaning towards once they join the Court. Transparency in this regard is traditionally higher in the case of judges nominated from academia or apex courts. However, the ideology judges ascribe to is almost never directly linked to partisan preferences, and the evidence of their ideological distribution is too fuzzy to deliver a clear conclusion.

The low mediatization of constitutional judges' selection in past further complicated predictions of their political ideologies. In fact, even some presidents underestimated the power and impact of their selection. President Zeman initially completely relied on the advice of the CzCC's own President Rychetský. Pavel Rychetský, a former dissident, started his career in 1990s as a politician and was the Deputy Prime Minister. Coincidentally, he also served as a Deputy Prime Minister and Minister of Justice in Miloš Zeman's government in 1998–2002. Rychetský capitalized on his past political experience, since Zeman initially trusted his advice on the majority of nominations to the third CzCC. Their cooperation only ended in 2015 when they fell out over disputes on the appointment of a new President of the Supreme Court. Since then, Zeman has purposefully selected three new judges who were ideologically further away from Rychetský's preferences (Kosař and Vyhnánek 2021).

It is also worth noting that considerations of proportional composition played a very minor role in the selection of Czech constitutional judges during the first three generations, perhaps apart from their professional background. This changed only with the arrival of a new President Pavel, who nominates the fourth Constitutional Court, which is outside of the scope of this chapter. For example, when it comes to gender, the first democratic CzCC had only two women on its bench. Overall, of 19 judges appointed by Havel, only 3 were women (Iva Brožová, Eva Zarembová, Eliška Wagnerová). The majority of the first CzCC judges were recruited from among dissidents and people close to Havel personally. The second CzCC was a little better balanced in terms of gender (5 female judges, 1 appointed by Havel, 4 by Klaus). The third CzCC had only one female judge, after the second one, Kateřina Šimáčková, was appointed to the European Court of Human Rights in 2021. The lack of women in the CzCC results from a combination of the phenomena of glass ceilings and of sticky ladders (Havelková, Kosař, and Urbaníková 2022). Like other post-communist countries of CEE, the Czech Republic has a decent representation of female judges at lower instances (Havelková, Kosař, and Urbaníková 2022), although the vast majority of these female judges never advance to appeal or apex courts, effectively limiting their chances to be appointed to the CzCC.

Similar observations could be raised in respect of other extra-legal factors such as age (the CzCC is progressively getting "older"), educational experience abroad (mostly lacking), or the representation of minorities (there has been no judge who could have been openly associated with any minority). Regarding professional background, the majority of the judges advanced to the CzCC from the general courts (Table 3.2). The rest were selected from the pools of academia, politics, or legal professional groups (mostly from attorneys). Particularly

Table 3.2 Professional background of the judges (CzCC)

GENERATION	*Judge*	*Politician*	*Academic*	*Lawyer*
I.	7	7	4	2
II.	3	5	3	3
III.	6	2	7	3
SUM	**16**	**14**	**14**	**8**

Source: authors.

Note: The sum of rows is higher than 15 due to some judges having a background in two disciplines, or due to the small fluctuation at the Court.

surprising might be the number of judges who pursued a career in politics (here we mean active MPs, not experts sitting in the legislative body; otherwise, the number would be even higher). As Table 3.2 demonstrates, this practice was common in the first and second CzCC. However, while the first CzCC comprised mostly former dissidents who briefly joined newly formed movements or Parliament before being appointed to the CzCC, the judges selected from the ranks of politicians by Klaus had already had extensive political careers. Outsiders are clearly in minority, represented almost solely by attorneys. Other groups and sectors (lawyers engaged in the NGO sector) are completely missing.

In sum, while some determinants of the CzCC portray it as a rather monolithic institution, the members' allegiance to professional groups (and related informal networks surrounding these groups) is the most visible line dividing the court. How is this composition reflected in the court's decision-making and, given the high procedural threshold for constitutional review, its ability to form voting coalitions? To answer this question, we looked deeper at the dissenting practice of judges.

The CzCC does not have public records of individual judges' votes. The only data we have at our disposal are dissenting opinions, which are facultative. It is important to stress the findings of existing scholarship, which suggests that there are also a lot of "silent" instances of dissent, as some judges use dissent strategically, or for internal purposes only, and do not perceive the need to publish it as a mandatory part of the decisions (Smekal et al. 2021). In the following figures, we tried to dissect the practice in the formation of dissenting coalitions and their correlation with the behaviour of the CzCC in constitutional review cases.

Figure 3.3 juxtaposes the average strength of the rulings against the ratio of those rulings with at least one dissenting opinion and offers four compelling observations.

First, we can observe a very clear trend of an increasing ratio of rulings with at least one dissent, which demonstrates an increasing dissonance between the judges, particularly from the second half of Klaus' CzCC onwards. Two caveats have to be, however, mentioned here: both the scope of constitutional review cases and the composition of the CzCC have significantly diversified over the years. While the first CzCC was a court composed of former dissidents adjudicating mostly on the character of the democratic regime, its

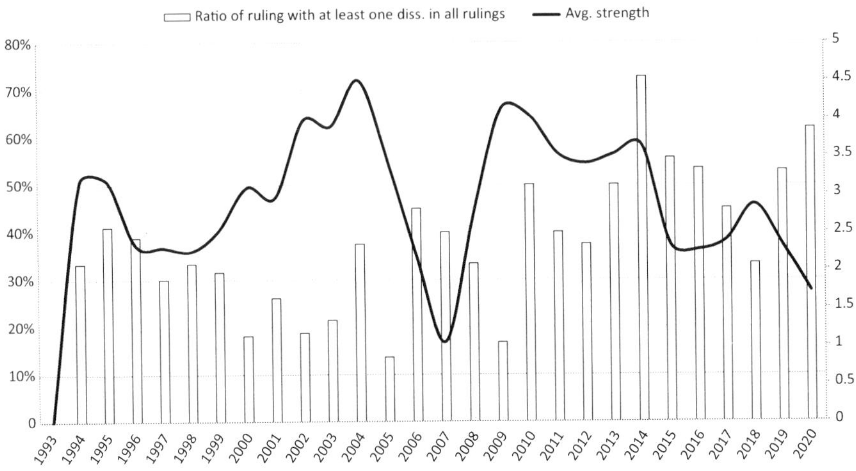

Figure 3.3 Proportion of rulings with at least one dissenting opinion (CzCC)

Source: JUDICON-EU.

Note: The columns (left axis) show the ratio of rulings with at least one ruling. The line (right axis) shows the average strength of rulings.

value embeddedness, or the implementation of transitional justice, the second CzCC faced issues related mostly to the economic and social transformation of the country and attempts to manipulate the electoral and party system. It was towards the end of this era that the CzCC fell behind in terms of internal communication and deliberation. The third CzCC was the most diversified, both in terms of topics, the range of actors petitioning the court, and the profiles and ideological distance between the judges (particularly after Rychetský and Zeman fell out).

Second, it seems that in the years 1998–2004 and 2008–2009 the CzCC was able to achieve a more unanimous voice, while the lower number of dissents interestingly correlates with a higher strength of constraining rulings issued in these years. Third, in contrast, in 2005–2007, the lower strength correlates with an increase in the proportion of dissents, which adds yet another interpretation to the most significant period of CzCC's self-constraining behaviour (see also Sections 3.3 and 3.4).

Similar observations can be made about Figure 3.4, which shows the complex network of all the CzCC judges and their dissenting coalitions. The right side of the network is the first CzCC. The judges of this era interacted intensively across the whole court, with only a few stable coalitions typically replicating the compositions of small panels. The visualization of the network corresponds with the existing narrative according to which the first CzCC held very open deliberations across the whole bench. The middle of the network represents the second CzCC and demonstrates a significant increase in the interactions between judges. As we discuss further in relation to

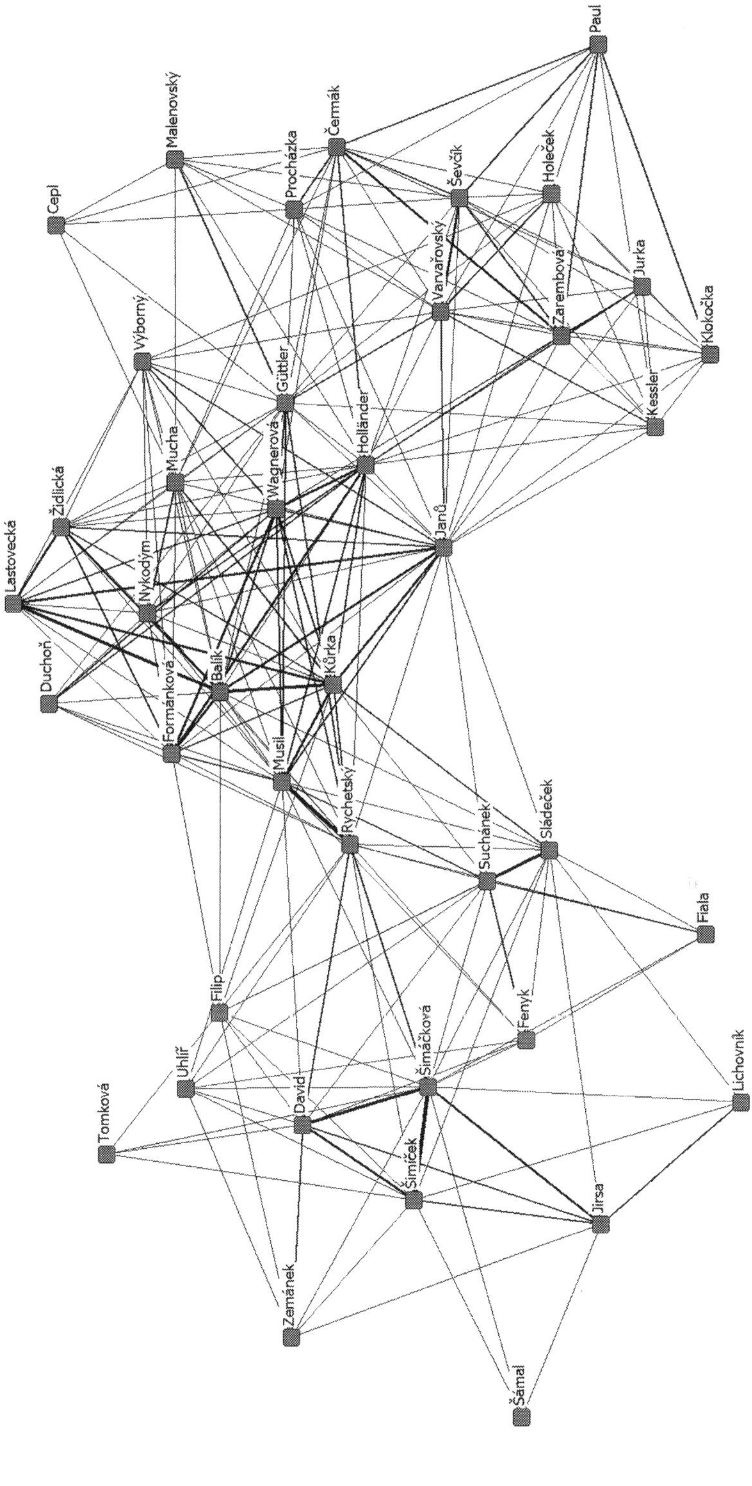

Figure 3.4 Dissenting coalitions (1993–2020) (CzCC)

Figure 3.4, this also correlates with the increasing trend of issuing dissenting opinions. The second CzCC, particularly in the second half of its term, is often described as having been rather polarized, with deep cleavages and problems in communication (Kmec 2010). The strongest coalitions within the triangle Balík-Kůrka-Lastovecká, or Wagnerová-Holländer-Formánková-Kůrka, copied both small chambers[25] as well as the left-right alignment and activist-self-constraint positions of the individual judges (with Holländer and Wagnerová representing the activist wing). The left part of the Figure 3.4 represents the dissenting network among the judges of the third CzCC. Although the number of dissenting opinions increased from 2013 to 2020, the coalitions became more stratified (possibly also partly impacted by the new system of rotations, changing the compositions of the small chambers every two years), typically around judges with the same background (judges coming from apex courts, the Law Faculty, etc.). Interestingly, the highest coalition potential can be identified with Court President Rychetský and with Kateřina Šimáčková, who is generally seen as one of the most liberal judges. Compared to the first CzCC, coalitions rarely copy the patterns of the small chambers. Generally, the network calls for more in-depth research on the judicial leadership and ability of judges who are either perceived as jurisprudential authorities (Filip, Holländer, Čermák, Klokočka), judges who strongly lean towards liberal or conservative ideology (Balík vs. Wagnerová, or Šimáčková) and judges who enjoy high political legitimacy (Rychetský, Wagnerová, Varvařovský, Klokočka) to attract large coalition potential.

Finally, the interaction between the average strength and dissenting behaviour of the CzCC changes from 2010 onwards. The overall usage of dissents is on the rise (despite the isolated drop in 2018). Incidentally, in the very same period, the CzCC started to hold back more often and to issue what our data identifies as less-constraining rulings. On the other hand, in the very same era, we also identified a gradual increase in constitutional requirements, used to the detriment of substantive unconstitutionality (Figure 3.1). These factors tell us the following: dissenting opinions are a good indicator of coalition potential inside the CzCC for cases of substantive unconstitutionality. Moreover, they strengthen our hypothesis that once the internal dissonance among judges increased (by the end of the second CzCC and during the third CzCC), the CzCC judges who could not reach the required supermajority for the annulment of the reviewed legislation started to strategically rely on constitutional requirement as a means of altering the binding constitutional interpretation of reviewed provisions, eventually indirectly binding the legislator.

25 Up until 2016, the composition of small chambers was stable. Since 2016, the CzCC has had a system of rotation, which also might have led to more variability and less stable coalitions at the end of the third CzCC.

3.7 Concluding remarks

The Czech scholarship traditionally categorizes the CzCC as one of the strong constitutional courts in the region (Kosař and Vyhnánek 2020), having made several formative interventions in partisan competition or on the separation of powers, but only rarely engaging in direct social transformation and human rights review (Smekal, Benák, and Vyhnánek 2022). Smekal et al. argued that such a selective judicial activism made the Court an unlikely target of political interventions. Yet, as the authors admit, the CzCC, on the other hand, was particularly strong in intervening on human rights violations in individual petitions, frequently forcing administrative bodies to adopt a new progressive approach allowing for higher human rights protection.

This chapter, while analysing the relationship of the CzCC with the Parliament through the optic of constraining rulings, attempted to explain this interesting phenomenon. We argued that while the CzCC remained formally self-restrained in its relationship with the Parliament and allowed it considerable room for manoeuvre, this position was largely dependent on procedural constraints which the legislator imposed on the ability of the CzCC to achieve supermajorities in constitutional review decisions. The combination of procedural constraints and increasing polarization inside the Court made frequent constraining rulings on politically and socially salient topics unlikely. Instead, activist judges started relying on a less-direct method of constitutional requirement (binding interpretation of reviewed legislation) both in constitutional review and in individual petition cases. In hindsight, this technique might have helped to shield the CzCC from strong political backlash and delegitimization. The Czech case adds important nuance to scholarship, suggesting that the success of democratic transition correlates with the constitutional courts constraining the legislator (Smith 2017) – as we have argued, constraint might take different forms and does not necessarily involve active prescription of the precise future form of legislation.

References

Babiš, Andrej. 2017. *O čem sním, když náhodou spím [What I dream of when I happen to sleep]*. Praha: Andrej Babiš.

Bobić, Ana. 2017. "Constitutional Pluralism is Not Dead: An Analysis of Interactions between Constitutional Courts of Member States and the European Court of Justice." *German Law Journal* 18 (6): 1395–1428.

Brown, Nathan J., and Julian G. Waller. 2016. "Constitutional Courts and Political Uncertainty: Constitutional Ruptures and the Rule of Judges." *International Journal of Constitutional Law* 14 (1): 817–850.

Brunclík, Miloš, and Michal Kubát. 2016a. "Český demokratický režim po roce 2012: přechod k poloprezidencialismu? [The Czech Democratic Regime after 2012: A Transition to Semi-Presidentialism?]." *Sociologický časopis/Czech Sociological Review* 52 (5): 625–646.

———, and Michal Kubát. 2016b. "The Czech Parliamentary Regime After 1989: Origins, Developments and Challenges." *Acta Politologica* 8 (2): 5–29.

Chmel, Jan. 2021. *Co ovlivňuje Ústavní soud a jeho soudce? [What does influence the Constitutional Court and its Justices?].* Praha: Leges.
Chvojka, Šimon, and Michal Kovalčík. 2022. "Judicial Review of COVID-19 Restrictive Measures in the Czech Republic." *Institutiones Administrationis – Journal of Administrative Sciences* 2 (2): 112–131.
Cross, Frank B., and Stefanie A. Lindquist. 2007. "The Scientific Study of Judicial Activism." *Minnesota Law Review* 91: 1752–1784.
Filip, Jan. 2002. "Nález č. 403/2002 Sb. Jako rukavice hozená ústavodárci Ústavním soudem [Ruling No. 403/2002 Coll. as a gauntlet thrown down to the Constitutionmaker by the Constitutional Court]." *Právní zpravodaj [Legal Reporter]* 11: 9–11.
———, Pavol Holländer, and Vojtěch Šimíček. 2007. *Zákon o Ústavním soudu. Komentář. [Commentary on the Constitutional Court Act].* 2nd ed. Praha: C. H. Beck.
Ginsburg, Tom. 2003. *Judicial Review in New Democracies: Constitutional Courts in Asian Constitutionalism.* Cambridge: Cambridge University Press.
———, and Tamir Moustafa, eds. 2008. *Rule By Law: The Politics of Courts in Authoritarian Regimes.* Cambridge: Cambridge University Press.
Graglia, Lino A. 1996. "It's Not Constitutionalism, It's Judicial Activism." *Harvard Journal of Law & Public Policy* 19 (2): 293–300.
Hájek, Lukáš. 2017. "Left, Right, Left, Right . . . Centre: Ideological Position of Andrej Babiš's ANO." *Politologický časopis – Czech Journal of Political Science* 26 (3): 275–301.
Havelková, Barbara, David Kosař, and Marína Urbániková. 2022. "The Family Friendliness That Wasn't: Access, But Not Progress, for Women in the Czech Judiciary". *Law & Social Inquiry* 47 (4): 1106–1136.
Havlík, Vlastimil. 2019. "Technocratic Populism and Political Illiberalism in Central Europe." *Problems of Post-Communism* 66 (6): 369–384.
Hirschl, Ran. 2004. *Towards Juristocracy.* Harvard: Harvard University Press.
———. 2008. "The Judicialization of Mega-politics and the Rise of Political Courts." *Annual Review of Political Science* 11: 93–118.
King, Jeff. 2012. *Judging Social Rights.* Cambridge: Cambridge University Press.
Klaus, Václav, and Marek Loužek, eds. 2006. *Soudcokracie v ČR: fikce, nebo realita?: sborník textů [The Judgeocracy in the Czech Republic: Fiction or Reality?:Collection of Papers].* Praha: CEP Centrum pro ekonomiku a politiku.
Kmec, Jiří. 2010. "Ústavní soudci, mluvíte spolu? ["Constitutional Judges, Do You Speak to Each Other?"]." *Jiné právo*, May 2. http://jinepravo.blogspot.cz/2010/05/ustavni-soudci-mluvite-spolu.html.
Kmiec, Keenan D. 2004. "The Origin and Current Meanings of 'Judicial Activism'." *California Law Review* 92 (5): 1441–1447.
Kokeš, Marián. 2015. "Pojistky ústavní konformity zákonodárného procesu – funkční nástroje či zmetky? [Fuses of the constitutionality of the legislative process – functional tools or wasters?]." In *Dny práva 2014 [Days of Law 2014]*, edited by Pavel Molek, Pavel Kandalec, and Jiří Valdhans, 161–176. Brno: Masarykova univerzita.
Komárek, Jan. 2012. "Czech Constitutional Court Playing with Matches: the Czech Constitutional Court Declares a Judgment of the Court of Justice of the EU Ultra Vires; Judgment of 31 January 2012, Pl. ÚS 5/12, Slovak Pensions XVII." *European Constitutional Law Review* 8 (2): 323–337.
Kopeček, Lubomír. 2017. "Czech political institutions and the problems of parliamentary democracy." In *Czech Politics: From West to East and Back Again*, edited

by Stanislav Balík, Vít Hloušek, Lubomír Kopeček, Jan Holzer, Pavel Pšeja, and Andrew Lawrence Roberts, 115–146. Opladen: Barbara Budrich Publishers.

———, and Jan Petrov. 2016. "From Parliament to Courtroom: Judicial Review of Legislation as a Political Tool in the Czech Republic." *East European Politics and Societies and Cultures* 30 (1): 120–146.

———, and Max Strmiska. 2005. *Politické strany a stranické systémy ve srovnávací perspektivě [Political parties and party systems in comparative perspective]*. Praha: Portál.

Kosař, David. 2017. "Politics of Judicial Independence and Judicial Accountability in Czechia: Bargaining in the Shadow of the Law between Court Presidents and the Ministry of Justice." *European Constitutional Law Review* 13 (1): 96–123.

———, and Ladislav Vyhnánek. 2020. "The Constitutional Court of Czechia." In *The Max Planck Handbooks in European Public Law Volume III: Constitutional Adjudication: Institutions*, edited by Armin von Bogdandy, Peter Huer, and Cristoph Grabenwarter, 1119–1179. Oxford: Oxford University Press.

———, and Ladislav Vyhnánek. 2021. *The Constitution of Czechia. A Contextual Analysis*. Oxford: Hart Publishing.

———. 2023. "Comparative Court-Packing." *International Journal of Constitutional Law* 21 (1).

———, and Jan Petrov. 2019. "The Domestic Judiciary in the Architecture of the Strasbourg System of Human Rights." In *How International Law Works in Times of Crisis*, edited by George Ulrich and Ineta Ziemele, 255–271. Oxford: Oxford University Press.

———, Jan Petrov, Katarína Šipulová, Hubert Smekal, Ladislav Vyhnánek, and Jozef Janovský. 2020. *Domestic Judicial Treatment of European Court of Human Rights Case Law: Beyond Compliance*. London: Routledge.

———, and Katarína Šipulová. 2018. "The Strasbourg Court Meets Abusive Constitutionalism: Baka v. Hungary and the Rule of Law." *Hague Journal on the Rule of Law* 2 (1): 83–110.

———, and Katarína Šipulová. 2020. "How to Fight Court-Packing." *Constitutional Studies* 6 (1): 133–164.

———, and Samuel Spáč. 2021. "Post-communist Chief Justices in Slovakia: From Transmission Belts to Semi-autonomous Actors?" *Hague Journal on the Rule of Law* 13 (1): 107–142.

———, and Ladislav Vyhnánek. 2016. "Senát a výběr soudců Ústavního soudu [Senate and Selection of Constitutional Court Judges.]." In *Dvacet let Senátu Parlamentu České republiky v souvislostech [20 Years of the Senate of the Parliament of the Czech Republic]*, edited by Jan Kysela, 2–16. Prague: Leges.

Kratochvíl, Jan. 2015. "Test racionality: skutečně vhodný test pro sociální práva? [The Reasonability Test: Really a Suitable Test for Social Rights?]." *Právník [The Lawyer]* 154 (12): 1052–1074.

Kühn, Zdeněk. 2000. "Je Parlament ČR vázán odůvodněním nálezů Ústavního soudu ČR? [Is the Parliament of the Czech Republic Bound by the Reasoning of the Constitutional Court Decisions?]." *Právník [The Lawyer]* 139: 721–736.

———. 2003. "Kreace ústavních soudů ze srovnávací perspektivy." [Creation of Constitutional Courts from a Comparative Perspective.]." *Časopis pro právní vědu a praxu [Journal of Jurisprudence and Legal Practice]* 11 (1):1–16.

———. 2010. "The Democratization and Modernization of Post-communist Judiciaries." In *Central and Eastern Europe After Transition*, edited by Alberto Febbrajo and Wojciech Sadurski, 177–200. London: Routledge.

———. 2011. *The Judiciary in Central and Eastern Europe: Mechanical Jurisprudence in Transformation?* Leiden: Martinus Nijhoff Publishers.

———. 2021a. "The Czech Constitutional Court in Times of Populism from Judicial Activism to Judicial Self-Restraint." In *Populist Challenges to Constitutional Interpretation in Europe and Beyond*, edited by Fruzsina Gárdos-Orosz and Zoltán Szente, 95–108. New York: Routledge.

———. 2021b. "The Judiciary in Illiberal States." *German Law Journal* 22 (7): 1231–1246.

———, and Jan Kysela. 2002. "Je Ústavou vždy to, co Ústavní soud řekne, že Ústava je? [Is the Constitution always what the Constitutional Court says that it is?]." *Časopis pro právní vědu a praxu [Journal of Jurisprudence and Legal Practice]* 10 (3): 199–214.

Lustig, Doreen, and J. H. H Weiler. 2018. "Judicial Review in the Contemporary World – Retrospective and Prospective." *International Journal of Constitutional Law* 16 (2): 315–372.

Madsen, Mikael Rask, Pola Cebulak, and Micha Wiebusch. 2018. "Backlash against International Courts: Explaining the Forms and Patterns of Resistance to International Courts." *International Journal of Law in Context* 14 (2): 197–220.

Malíř, Jan. 2008. *Odpovědnost členských států za škodu v právu Evropské unie: Studie ze soudcovské tvorby práva [State Liability for the Violation of EU Law: Studies of Judicial Decision Making]*. Prague: Charles University, Law Faculty.

Mathebe, Lucky. 2021. "The Constitutional Court of South Africa: Thoughts on its 25-Year-Long Legacy of Judicial Activism." *Journal of Asian and African Studies* 56 (1): 18–33.

Petrov, Jan. 2018. "Legislativní reakce ČR na judikaturu ESLP [Legislative reaction of the Czech Republic on the ECHR case law.]." In *Beyond Compliance – Implementace rozhodnutí mezinárodních lidskoprávních těles na národní úrovni [Beyond Compliance – Domestic judicial implementation of the international human rights case law]*, edited by Smekal Hubert and Ladislav Vyhnánek, 137–158. Prague: Wolters Kluwer.

———, and Katarína Šipulová. 2016. "International Human Rights Treaties in the Case Law of Domestic Courts" Supreme Court and Supreme Administrative Court." In *Making Sense of Human Rights Commitments: A Study of Two Emerging European Democracies*, edited by Hubert Smekal, Katarína Šipulová, Ivo Pospíšil, Jozef Janovský, and Petr Kilian, 183–212. Brno: MUNI Press.

Pócza, Kálmán, ed. 2019. *Constitutional Politics and the Judiciary: Decision-making in Central and Eastern Europe*. London: Routledge.

Procházková, Andrea. 2023. "Rozmanitost, přesah, víc žen. Nevybírat ústavní soudce jako králíky z klobouku [Diversity, overlap, more women. Not to select the constitutional judges like rabbits out of a hat.]." *Respekt [Respect]*, February 20. www.respekt.cz/newsletter/rozmanitost-presah-vic-zen-nevybirat-ustavni-soudce-jako-kraliky-z-klobouku.

Ragnarsson, Kári Hólmar. 2019. "The Counter-majoritarian Difficulty in a Neoliberal World: Socio-economic Rights and Deference in Post-2008 Austerity Cases." *Global Constitutionalism* 8 (3): 605–638.

Roznai, Yaniv. 2014. "Legisprudence Limitations on Constitutional Amendments? Reflections on the Czech Constitutional Court's Declaration of Unconstitutional Constitutional Act." *ICL Journal* 8 (1): 29–57.

Sadurski, Wojciech. 2014. *A Study of Constitutional Courts in Postcommunist States of Central and Eastern Europe*. 2nd ed. Dordrecht: Springer.

Scheppele, Kim Lane. 2003. "Constitutional Negotiations: Political Contexts of Judicial Activism in Post-Soviet Europe." *International Sociology* 18 (1): 219–238.

Šimíček, Vojtěch. 2016. "Výběr kandidátů na soudce Ústavního soudu a jejich schvalování Senátem [The selection of nominees for Constitutional Court judges and their approval by the Senate.]." In *Dvacet let Senátu Parlamentu České republiky v souvislostech [20 Years of the Senate of Parliament of the Czech Republic]*, edited by Jan Kysela, 225–240. Praha: Leges.

Šipulová, Katarína. 2019. "The Czech Constitutional Court: Far away from political influence." In *Constitutional Politics and the Judiciary Decision-making in Central and Eastern Europe*, edited by Kálmán Pócza, 32–60. New York: Routledge.

———, and Hubert Smekal. 2021. "Between Human Rights and Transitional Justice: The Dilemma of Constitutional Courts in Post-Communist Central Europe." *Europe-Asia Studies* 73 (1): 101–130.

Smekal, Hubert, Jaroslav Benák, and Ladislav Vyhnánek. 2022. "Through Selective Activism Towards Greater Resilience: The Czech Constitutional Court's Interventions into High Politics in the Age of Populism." *The International Journal of Human Rights* 26 (7): 1230–1251.

———, Jaroslav Benák, Ladislav Vyhnánek, Monika Hanych, and Štěpán Janků. 2021. *Mimoprávní vlivy na rozhodování českého Ústavního soudu [Extralegal Influences on the Decision-Making of the Czech Constitutional Court]*. Brno: Masarykova univerzita.

———, and Ivo Pospíšil. 2013. *Soudcokracie, nebo judicializace politiky? Vztah práva a politiky (nejen) v časech krize [Juristocracy, or judicialization of politics? Relationship of law and politics (not only) in time of crisis]*. Brno: Masarykova univerzita.

———, and Ladislav Vyhnánek. 2018. *Beyond Compliance – Implementace rozhodnutí mezinárodních lidskoprávních těles na národní úrovni [Beyond Compliance – Domestic Judicial Implementation of the International Human Rights Case Law]*. Prague: Wolters Kluwer.

Smith, Brian Clive. 2017. *Judges and Democratization. Judicial Independence in New Democracies.* Oxford: Routledge.

STEM. 2022. "Důvěra v instituce v červnu 2022." [Trust in institutions in June 2022], July 11. www.stem.cz/category/instituce/.

Von Bogdandy, Armin, and Pál Sonnevend, eds. 2015. *Constitutional Crisis in the European Constitutional Area: Theory, Law and Politics in Hungary and Romania.* Oxford: Hart Publishing.

Wagnerová, Eliška. 2003. "Position of Czech Judges in the Czech Republic." In *Systems of Justice in Transition: Central European Experience since 1989*, edited by Jiří Přibáň, Pauline Roberts, and James Young, 163–169. Aldershot: Ashgate Publishing Limited.

———, Martin Dostál, Tomáš Langášek, and Ivo Pospíšil. 2007. *Zákon o Ústavním soudu s komentářem [Commentary on the Constitutional Court Act]*. Praha: ASPI.

Wintr, Jan. 2022. *Třetí Ústavní soud [Third Constitutional Court]*. Praha: Leges.

4 The Estonian Supreme Court

Strength by pragmatic collegiality

Paloma Krõõt Tupay

4.1 Introduction

Estonia regained its independence in 1991, ending more than 50 years of Soviet occupation.[1] At the time of this new beginning, the Estonian economy was on its knees and the state had to be reinvented from scratch. After 30 years of independence, Estonia can look back on a successful journey back to freedom. In comparison to other EU states, the Estonian judicial system is a leader in terms of efficiency and speed of proceedings (European Commission 2021), and 71% of Estonian residents rate Estonian courts as trustworthy, an increase of up to 10% compared to previous years (ESC 2021b). Nevertheless, there has also been criticism of the court system in Estonia in recent years. For example, in 2017, the Minister of the Interior and leader of the national conservative EKRE party stated that "heads should roll" when referring to judges in a ruling that strengthened the rights of same-sex couples (Mõttus-Leppik 2019). It is therefore appropriate at this point to take a closer look at how the legal system of constitutional review in Estonia is structured and how "strong" it is in comparison to the legislature.

The chapter first provides an overview of the organization and procedure of Estonian constitutional review by the Constitutional Chamber of the Estonian Supreme Court (ESC) (Section 4.2.). What stands out from the following analysis of the – admittedly small – number of Estonian rulings is that these are the most restrictive ones compared to the other countries in the study (Sections 4.3. and 4.4.). Although one clear reason for this is to be found in the formal regulation of the Estonian norm control procedure, the relatively broad freedom enjoyed by the court also plays a role in this (Sections 4.5. and 4.6.). Finally, the chapter outlines in more detail the characteristics and challenges associated with constitutional review in Estonia (Section 4.7.).

1 The author would like to thank Berit Aaviksoo, Kerdi Raud, and Sten Kapten for their considerable help and advice in writing this study. Responsibility for its content rests solely with the author.

DOI: 10.4324/9781003399483-4

4.2 The Estonian Supreme Court and its procedure of constitutional review

According to § 149(3) of the Constitution of the Republic of Estonia (hereinafter EC), the Supreme Court is the highest court in Estonia; it reviews court decisions by way of cassation proceedings and also serves as a constitutional review body, i.e. as a constitutional court. The Supreme Court of Estonia (hereinafter ESC) consists of 19 judges who administer justice in one of three chambers: the Civil Chamber, the Criminal Chamber, or the Administrative Law Chamber. The ESC also has a fourth chamber, the Constitutional Chamber, which is charged with constitutional review within the Estonian legal system.

4.2.1 Historical background

Estonia's first constitution was enacted on 15 June 1920, a little more than four months after the signing of the Treaty of Tartu between Estonia and Soviet Russia, which marked the end of the Estonian War of Independence and the first *de jure* independence of the state. Like the Weimar Constitution, the EC did not provide for the creation of a separate constitutional court. Consequently, the idea of a separate constitutional court was discussed in the interwar period but never realized (Vallikivi 2021, 100; Lõhmus 2020, 29–31). In 1927, the ESC took the position that the ordinary courts should deal with constitutional issues (Lõhmus and Vallikivi 2020, 451). However, the annexation and occupation of the Republic of Estonia in 1940 by Soviet troops led to the abolition of the independent judiciary and the Supreme Court for more than 50 years.

In 1992, a little under a year after regaining independence from the Soviet Union, the completely rewritten Estonian Constitution was put into effect, and in May 1993 the newly created Supreme Court convened for its first session. The independent Estonian state had decided to revive the historical links between Estonian and German law from before the war, and the new Estonian legal order relied heavily on these links (Ernits et al. 2019, 887). Germany had in the meantime created its well-known Federal Constitutional Court in 1951. Like other countries transitioning to democracy, Estonia decided to follow suit (Ginsburg 2002, 1; Schneider 2002, 6).

The 1992 EC explicitly provides that the declaration of the annulment of laws on grounds of unconstitutionality is the responsibility of the third judicial instance (Schneider 2002, 9–10) and delegates this task to the ESC. The reason for the decision not to establish a separate constitutional court, as provided for in most countries that restored the democratic rule of law with the collapse of the Soviet Union, was mainly practical. On the one hand, the authors of the EC simply followed the example of the earlier Estonian constitutions (Pikamäe 2021, 145), and, on the other hand, it was a not insignificant argument for a small state that an integrative solution could be implemented with less effort and less regulation (Maruste 2020, 468; Tschenscher 2014, 188). However, it should also be noted that the idea of judicial constitutional review was clearly contrary to the guidelines of Soviet law that had prevailed in Estonia for a long time and was therefore unknown in its details. This may also have been a reason why its design in the new Estonian constitution remained rudimentary.

The legislature passed the Constitutional Review Court Procedure Act (hereinafter CRCPA) by qualified majority in 1993, providing for the creation of a separate body within the ESC, the Constitutional Review Chamber (ESC CRC). Since then, this Chamber has been entrusted (together with the Supreme Court in its full composition, if necessary) with conducting constitutional review. Nevertheless, the introduction of a separate constitutional court has been a controversial question ever since (Bartole 1997).

The Constitution is not clear on the question of whether any Estonian court may declare a legal norm unconstitutional. However, it states *expressis verbis* that only the Supreme Court "may declare invalid any law or other legal act inconsistent with the letter and spirit of the Constitution". In turn, the practice of the ESC has granted any Estonian court the right to declare a law unconstitutional. However, if a lower court declares a norm unconstitutional, it forwards its decision to the ESC for constitutional review (CRCPA § 9). If the Supreme Court, in turn, leaves the dispute unresolved on formal grounds and no one appeals, a decision may be rendered in which a court of first or second instance has declared a legal norm unconstitutional (ESC CRC 16.03.2006, 3-4-1-1-06; Ernits 2017, 63). Therefore, the current Estonian system of constitutional review is actually a mixed system.

4.2.2 *Structure of the ESC Constitutional Review Chamber*

The President of ESC is appointed by the Parliament by a simple majority on the proposal of the Estonian President (Courts Act (CA) § 27(1)). The other judges of the ESC are proposed by the President of the Supreme Court and appointed by the Estonian Parliament (EC § 150(2)), each by a simple majority. Before submitting his proposal, the President of the ESC hears the opinions of the Supreme Court *en banc* and of the Council for the Administration of Courts on the candidate (§ 55(4)). All Estonian judges are appointed for life and may not belong to a political party or hold political office (EC § 147). Therefore, in practice, the judges of ESC are also appointed to their posts (on the Supreme Court) for life, without this being explicitly mentioned in the law. There are no specific additional requirements for Supreme Court judges, but according to CA § 52, Supreme Court judges must be experienced and recognized jurists.

The ESC CRC is presided *ex officio* by the President of the ESC, who is assisted by eight judges of the ESC (see CA § 29). According to the Rules of Procedure of the Supreme Court, the eight judges of the ESC CRC are appointed for a term of four years by the court *en banc* upon the proposal of the President of the Supreme Court, which shall take into account the opinion of the other chambers of the ESC while considering the most equal representation of these chambers in the Constitutional Review Chamber. However, according to the previous version of the Rules of Procedure that were in force until 2020, the composition of the ESC CRC was to be changed according to a rotation principle, whereby each year the two longest-serving members of the Constitutional Chamber were dismissed and two new members were appointed by the Supreme Court *en banc* on the proposal of the President of the ESC (ESC 2020, 12). Since the abolition of this rule, judges have generally left the ESC CRC at the end of their four-year term, at the earliest, and have been replaced by new judges. The duties of a member of the Constitutional Chamber are performed by each judge cumulatively with his other duties in the chamber assigned to him.

4.2.3 Competences and responsibilities

Pursuant to Section 2 of the CRCPA, the ESC CRC decides on the following matters, among others: requests for review of the constitutionality of an international treaty or a legislative act, complaints against decisions of Parliament, complaints against activities of the organizer of elections or the decisions and actions of the electoral committees, complaints against decisions of the President of the Republic or Parliament, and requests for opinions on the interpretation of the Constitution in connection with EU law (see also: ESC 2021a). On the other hand, the Supreme Court shall rule *en banc* on petitions to determine the permanent incapacity of a member of the *Riigikogu*, the President of the Republic, the Chancellor of Justice, or the Auditor General to perform his duties, as well as on the termination of the mandate of a member of the *Riigikogu* or the activities of a political party. The ESC also decides in full when a constitutional appeal is initiated by one of the other chambers of the Supreme Court and in cases where the Constitutional Review Chamber deems it necessary, i.e. in cases where the Chamber wishes to deviate from the previous legal practice of the Supreme Court. (CRCPA § 3).

The constitutional review process provided for in Chapter 2 of CRCPA involves the review of general acts enacted by the legislative, executive, or local branches of government. A distinction is made between abstract and concrete norm control. An abstract norm control procedure verifies the conformity of a legal act regardless of its applicability in a concrete case. Only three state institutions can initiate such an abstract norm control procedure before the Supreme Court: the President of the Republic, the Chancellor of Justice, and the local government in cases connected to their constitutional guarantees. The President of the Republic, who has the task of promulgating laws, may opt not to promulgate a law if he considers that the act is unconstitutional. If the *Riigikogu* returns the law unchanged to the President for promulgation, the president must promulgate it or ask the ESC to review its constitutionality (EC § 107). The Chancellor of Justice, whose establishment is provided for in Chapter 12 of EC, is an independent constitutional officer appointed by the *Riigikogu* by a simple majority vote for a seven-year term. The Chancellor has two main duties: first, he or she checks the conformity of Estonian legislation with the EC. Although the opinions of the Chancellor of Justice do not have the force of law, he or she has the right to request the ESC to review the constitutionality of a general legal act (EC § 142). On the other hand, the Chancellor has the function of an ombudsman, who monitors the compliance of state authorities and officials with the fundamental rights of citizens and the principle of good governance (CoJ 2021). In all other cases, constitutional review of legal acts may be requested only in the form of a concrete review of norms, initiated in the context of concrete court proceedings, if the challenged legal act is relevant to the court's decision. The referring court must be convinced of the unconstitutionality of the challenged norm (CRPD § 14).

Estonian law does not explicitly provide for the right of individual constitutional complaint against the state in the manner of the German individual constitutional complaint procedure (*Individualverfassungsbeschwerde*) (BVerfG 2021). Nor does it know the institution of organ disputes (*Organstreitverfahren*), i.e. the constitutional dispute between supreme state organs, in the context of which the limits of the organs' respective competences and responsibilities are usually clarified. It follows that, under the Estonian Constitution, only state organs can initiate the constitutional review procedure before the Supreme Court. This means that the circle of applicants is limited and the number of obviously futile applications to the court is kept small. Thus, no application in the abstract norm control procedure has yet been dismissed as inadmissible on formal grounds.

Even in specific norm control proceedings, lawsuits are rarely dismissed on formal grounds. The author of this contribution is aware of only one court ruling,[2] in which the complaint was rejected because the court had not substantiated which legal norm it considered unconstitutional. However, there are no statistical data on the percentage of specific norm control petitions that were decided on their merits compared to petitions that were rejected on formal grounds.

As to the effective date of judicial decisions on norm control, the CRCPA originally provided that all decisions of the court take effect on the date of their pronouncement (CRPA § 22, version of 05.05.1993). Although the legality of the provision had never been questioned, the adoption of a substantially renewed CRCPA recodification in 2002 introduced into the law the court's limited right to promulgate decisions with a *pro futuro* effect. Section 58(3) of the CRCPA provides the court with the right to delay the effective date of a judgment on norm control for up to six months. Separate reasons must be given for this decision (CRCPA § 58 (3)). The legislature justified the

2 ESC CRC 16.03.2006, 3-4-1-1-06

change on the grounds of practical necessity (explanatory memorandum to the CRCPA of 2002).

4.3 General impressions

4.3.1 Country-specific phenomena

In the period from 1993 to 2020, a total of 207 rulings are recorded for Estonia, which is the second-lowest number of decisions after Cyprus in a comparison of the states reviewed in the project. On the one hand, the small size of the country may certainly explain this to an extent. However, the number of coded rulings in other countries varies considerably and is not necessarily related to their size: while Germany, for example, had only 334 rulings, Austria issued 956 rulings in the same period. It should be borne in mind that in Estonia norm control proceedings can only be initiated by a limited group of state institutions. It can therefore be assumed that the number of proceedings initiated will be lower overall, as the initiators of the norm control thoroughly examine the prospects of success of such an application.

The small number of Estonian rulings should not be ignored when evaluating the results of the study. A limited number of rulings means that the fluctuations in the assessment of their average strength are relatively large, which in turn makes it difficult to identify consistent, concrete trends. For example, 2006, a year in which the ESC issued only two constitutional review decisions, each with one ruling, and in both cases found substantial unconstitutionality, is statistically recorded as a year in which the court's rulings were particularly strong. At the same time, 1993, when the court reviewed two decisions and found in one case the norm under review to be constitutional and in the other decision the norm to be unconstitutional on formal grounds, is recorded as the year with the lowest strength of rulings on constitutional review. This also explains why Estonia's standard deviation of 3.56 is above the average of 3.13.

Estonia's 207 rulings correspond to 190 coded decisions. Thus, most of the decisions of the constitutional review consist of one constitutionally relevant ruling. Although the number of decisions varies from year to year, ranging from zero (for 1997) to 18 (for 2011), it should be noted that in the first 10 years of its operation the ESC issued a total of 35 decisions, along with 38 rulings, while in the last 10 years it has already issued 105 decisions, to which 110 rulings corresponded (see Table 4.1). The reasons for this are that the newly constituted Supreme Court first had to familiarize itself with its role and that it had to be called upon by the other state organs, which also had to learn to make use of their powers or duties.

It is worth mentioning the relatively large number of decisions on constitutional review of parliamentary acts that, according to the study's methodology, had no impact on the Estonian legislature, but whose content had a not insignificant impact on the relationship between the legislature and the court. These include decisions in which the court determined the unconstitutionality

Table 4.1 Number of decisions and rulings (ESC)

Year	*No. of decisions*	*No. of rulings*	*Avg. strength*	*Standard deviation*
1993	2	2	1.25	1.25
1994	6	6	5.67	2.43
1995	3	3	2.33	3.30
1996	2	2	3.75	3.75
1997				
1998	6	8	5.88	2.10
1999	2	2	4.50	2.50
2000	4	4	3.50	3.50
2001	4	4	5.25	3.03
2002	6	7	4.07	3.54
2003	4	4	4.00	4.00
2004	10	12	2.17	3.06
2005	9	10	1.70	2.96
2006	2	2	6.75	0.25
2007	5	5	7.20	0.40
2008	8	8	4.06	3.52
2009	8	9	5.22	3.59
2010	4	9	2.00	3.00
2011	18	18	4.64	3.60
2012	14	15	5.10	3.48
2013	10	10	4.70	3.50
2014	16	17	5.41	3.32
2015	12	12	3.29	3.54
2016	7	7	4.43	3.44
2017	10	10	3.35	3.45
2018	5	8	1.75	3.04
2019	8	8	6.06	3.52
2020	5	5	3.00	3.67
SUM	**190**	**207**	**4.14**	**3.57**

of challenged norms that had already lost their legal effect by the time the ruling was handed down. Since such rulings do not have an actual blocking effect, they are not coded (Pócza 2019).

In addition, there are cases in which the ESC CRC establishes the constitutionality of a norm, but at the same time, in the sense of *obiter dicta*, makes statements about regulations that the legislature should adopt in the future to ensure the constitutionality of state action. In these cases, too, the court's instruction to the legislature is not reflected in the results of the Estonian dataset. According to the research methodology, court decisions in which the court rejects a claim of unconstitutionality are not restrictive to the legislature. Even in Estonia, in some cases a rejection is issued only because the court, according to the reasoning of the decision – which does not acquire the force of *res judicata* – interprets the challenged legal norm to be in conformity with the constitution. Although these types of court decisions do not affect the strength of court rulings *vis-à-vis* the legislature as measured in the research project, they are a good example of the ESC influencing the legislature by milder measures than the declaration of unconstitutionality of legal acts in force.

It can thus be stated that, although both the court's prescriptions and the guidelines for legal interpretation are not included in the operative part of the decision, and so-called *Leitsatz* (i.e. decisions including prescriptions in the headnotes) are unknown, in Estonian legal practice the decisions' justification may contain quasi-binding declarations *vis-à-vis* the legislator.

4.3.2 *Differentiation of judicial rulings*

As can be seen from the statistical results that in the vast majority of norm control cases, the ESC establishes the substantive unconstitutionality of a norm (in 111 cases out of a total of 134 non-zero decisions). Various developments in constitutional review jurisprudence can be deduced from the frequency of the ruling types. For example, the majority of formal unconstitutionality rulings fall into the period between 1993 and 2002 (6 of the total of 10 rulings) (see Figure 4.1).

This can be explained by the fact that after Estonia regained its independence, it had to implement the entire regulation of the newly emerging democratic rule of law in a very short period of time. There was a lack of legal regulations that could have guided this process, and at the same time the principles of parliamentary legislative process were not yet sufficiently familiar to the state apparatus.

The right to adjudicate cases of legislative omission was enacted into law in 2004 as part of an amendment to ensure state liability for omission (including failure of the legislature to implement binding EU law; explanatory memorandum to the State Liability Law and CRCPA Amendment Act of 2004). The first time the ESC CRC ruled on a case that qualified as an (explicit) legislative omission in the record was in 2009, and of the nine omissions ruled on between 1993 and 2020, all were made between 2009 and 2017.

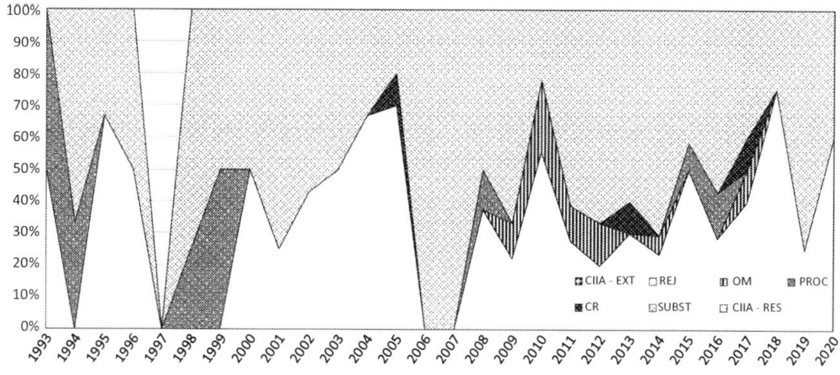

Figure 4.1 Frequency of the ruling types (ESC) (1993–2020)

The Court's practice emphasizes that it deliberately refrains from claiming policy-making powers that belong to the legislature. This explains why, although the court as a whole has a significantly above-average proportion of norms declared unconstitutional, the comparative figures show that ESC has issued prescriptions far less frequently than the average of the other courts compared. In 54.1% of the cases, the court issued no prescriptions at all, and in the provision the court did not articulate any constitutional requirements at all. However, the pattern of the Supreme Court's non-binding prescriptions to the legislature has evolved over time, suggesting that ESC has become more aware of its role and influence over the years. Until 2009, the ESC used the option to issue such a prescription only twice (in 2003). After 2009, the court added non-binding prescription to the legislature in at least one norm control decision each year except one (2016).

4.4 Overall trends

4.4.1 General remarks

In the period 1993–2020, the ESC CRC's decisions have become much more comprehensive and legally differentiated. This differentiation has taken place, in particular, through more comprehensive justifications of the decisions, but without the ESC CRC paying particular attention to the systematic elaboration of legal-theoretical approaches. A first look at the number and average strength of rulings does not reveal any clear trends; instead, the number and strength of rulings fluctuate over the period under review (see Figure 4.2). It should be borne in mind that the small number of decisions makes it difficult to identify clear trends.

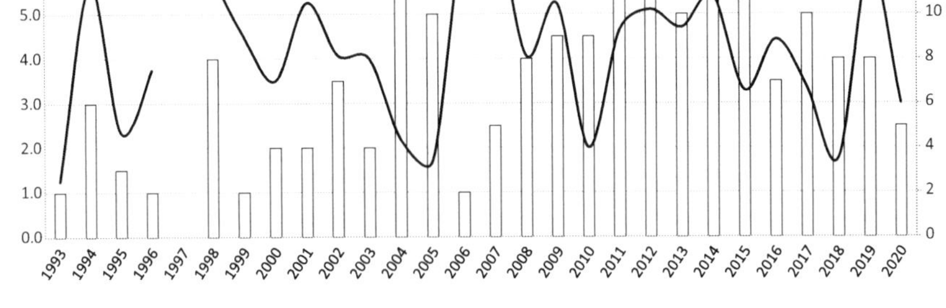

Figure 4.2 Average strength of rulings (1993–2020) (ESC)

Although no specific trend can be discerned, an overall increase in rulings is discernible in the 30-year retrospective, although this has occurred in waves. The largest number of decisions and rulings were declared between 2011 and 2014, although the number of cases has declined since then. One factor in this temporary increase was the large number of decisions on court fees that were found to be too high and therefore unconstitutional by the ESC. The former President of the ESC, Rait Maruste has also pointed out that when Estonia regained its independence in 1991, people had no idea that individuals could sue the state (Ristikivi and Sein 2022, 185f). Certainly, in this respect, people first had to become aware that they were able to assert their rights against the state.

It is striking that the proportion of Estonian rulings restricting the legislature is 32.1% higher than the average (71.6% versus 38.9%) of other states examined in the research project, with an average strength of 4.14, the most restrictive among the 19 other countries, whose average strength is 2.22, less than half as strong. Thus, the few Estonian decisions have considerable strength.

4.4.2 *Development of the legal practice on the temporal effect*

According to the consistent case law of the Court, rulings generally have *ex tunc* effect,[3] although this was not always the case. Prior to 2008, constitutional review decisions had *ex nunc* effect, according to the court. In its decisive ruling of 2008, the Supreme Court referred to earlier rulings[4] and argued that it was now legally provided that the rulings of the CRC could form the basis for the reopening of proceedings before the Administrative Court, and therefore the *ex tunc* effect of the rulings of the CRC could not be excluded.[5] This ruling marked a turning point after which, in the ESC's practice, constitutional review has been granted a generally retroactive effect.

However, according to the practice of the court, the possible retroactivity of rulings does not mean that they automatically have an *erga omnes* effect, which results in a full restoration of all legal relations in the context of which the unconstitutional norm was applied.[6] As in the previously mentioned case, where an administrative act was issued on the basis of a norm that was later declared unconstitutional, the corresponding laws of court procedure foresee the possibility of requesting the reopening of proceedings. The Administrative Procedure Act also provides that proceedings in which the administrative act was issued on the basis of an unconstitutional norm may be reopened.

3 See, e.g., CRC ESC 04/17/2012, 3-4-1-25-11, p. 55; ESC en banc 06/26/2014, 3-4-1-1-14, p. 130s.

4 ESC CRC 12.05.2000, 3-4-1-5-00, p. 37 and ESC en banc 22.12.2000, 3-4-1-10-00, p. 37

5 ESC CRC 10.03.2008, 3-3-2-1-07, p. 18

6 ESC CRC 10.03.2008, 3-3-2-1-07, p. 20

Therefore, in these cases, general and direct retroactivity cannot be assumed, and the retroactive annulment of these decisions depends on the consideration of the court or administrative authority.[7] Direct and general *ex tunc* effect may be assumed if the unconstitutional norm has a direct restrictive effect on individuals (Pilving 2020, 128 ff).

The ESC limits retroactive rulings, *inter alia*, on the principle of legal certainty and considering the conflicting fundamental rights of third parties.[8] It also takes into account the interests of the state and the administrative burden that the retroactivity of a decision may cause.[9] For example, in the case of the declaration of unconstitutionality of the ban on long-term visits for pre-trial detainees, it limited the retroactivity of the decisions on this to persons who, at the time of the entry into force of the decision, had challenged the denial of long-term visits or had requested compensation for the damage caused to them by that denial.[10] It should also be noted that the court has barely dogmatically explained its legal practice on the temporal effect of constitutional complaints, although Supreme Court Judge Ivo Pilving has written a relevant overview (Pilving 2020, 128 ff).

4.4.3 Correlations between constitutional review and political circumstances

When considering possible interaction between changes in the political context and constitutional jurisprudence, it should be noted that there were 14 changes of government during the reported period, over a total of 27 years. Because of this Estonian peculiarity of frequent changes of government (where all of these changes of government occurred through a change of coalition partners, but not through the calling of extraordinary elections), a connection between constitutional jurisprudence and political governance cannot be discerned.

However, correlations cannot be ruled out that arise from the very fact that, due to Estonia's small size, individuals tend to occupy several different, decisive positions during their careers. For example, Märt Rask, later President of the ESC, was previously Minister of Justice. His tenure also included the drafting and adoption of the law amending the Estonian Constitution (EC AA). As Minister of Justice, he defended the text of EC AA as "laconic, clear and unambiguous" (stenogram of the first reading of the draft law EC AA on 11.06.2002). Later, as President of the ESC, he participated in ESC decisions on the constitutionality of the EC.AA (ibid.).

7 ESC CRC 10.03.2008, 3-3-2-1-07, p. 20
8 ESC CRC 17.04.2012, 3-4-1-25-11, p. 55; see also: Pilving 2020, 128.
9 ESC CRC 3-3-1-35-15 p. 47
10 ESC en banc 1.06.2019, 5-18-8/19, p. 79

4.4.4 Non-zero rulings

Of the 207 coded rulings, 132 are non-zero rulings, i.e. rulings that are not rejections (or, in exceptional cases, refusals or rejections with dissenting opinions). Thus, 63.8% of the rulings are restrictive. Only Cyprus has more restrictive rulings. The average strength of all the rulings was 4.14, which is practically double the average strength of the rulings of all the other states studied in the JUDICON-EU project (2.22). The average strength of the ESC's non-zero rulings is even higher (6.49), which is again above the average strength of 5.70 of the non-zero rulings of all the states studied in the JUDICON-EU project.

One reason for the above-average strength and frequency of restrictive rulings, as compared to other states, can again be found in the small circle of persons entitled to file an application and the limited number of application options within the framework of the standard review. This ensures that the cases decided by the court are usually those that cannot be resolved by the state authorities by other means in accordance with the "ultima ratio" principle and which are classified by them as clearly unconstitutional. This assumption is confirmed by the fact that applications in the constitutional review are not usually rejected because of formal defects in the application or an obvious lack of reasoning.

4.5 Trends in dissenting opinions

Of the 207 total coded rulings in this report, 77 were rulings in which at least one judge dissented. Thus, on average, 37.2% of all rulings also contain corresponding dissenting opinions. If one considers that the judges of ESC also frequently issue concurring opinions that are not reflected in the present study, their willingness to deviate from the majority opinions can be assumed to be even higher. This is all the more likely since no judge issued a dissenting opinion in the first seven years of the court's operation. In the last 10 years of the reporting period, the number of rulings containing at least one dissenting opinion was at least 50%, over a total of five years (see Figure 4.3). These figures also reflect the evolution of the court, which only began its work in 1993. While in the first years after the democratic transformation the body responsible for constitutional control had to settle into its task, it has grown into a self-confident court over the years. In summary, it seems appropriate to state that the judges make their decisions freely and do not feel pressure to follow the majority view in their opinions.

The vast majority of dissenting opinions were made as decisions taken by the plenum (ESC *en banc*). In this case, the judges of all the chambers of the court jointly decide on the merits of the case. It is therefore understandable that dissenting opinions are more frequently formed in such cases.

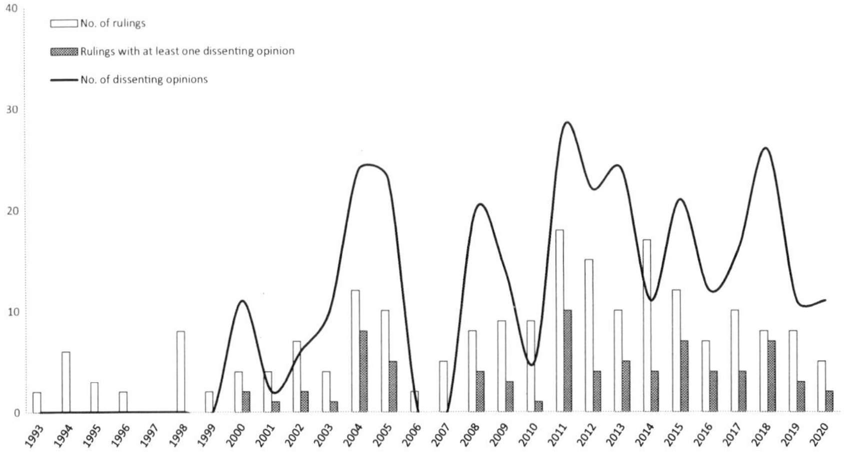

Figure 4.3 Number of rulings with at least one dissenting opinion (1993–2020) (ESC)

Looking at the network matrix of judges' dissenting opinions (Figure 4.4), it is not surprising that the judges with the strongest connections and the densest network all have tenures of at least 18 years (e.g. Peeter Jerovejev, Villu Kõve, Henn Jõks, Ants Kull, Tambet Tampuu). In addition, it is interesting to note that the vast majority of dissenting judges who have formed a strong network used to belong to the Civil Chamber of the ESC (e.g. Peeter Jerovejev, Henn Jõks, Villu Kõve, Ants Kull, Tambet Tampuu).

4.6 Qualitative evaluation

4.6.1 Formal requirements of concrete norm control

According to the EC § 15, second sentence, everyone has the right to request that the court declare any relevant law to be unconstitutional. Therefore, ordinary courts may submit a legal act for constitutional review only if the challenged act is relevant in resolving the case (see also CRCPA § 9 (1); 14). As stated earlier, the ESC in its jurisprudence understands this criterion to mean that the unconstitutionality and invalidity of the challenged act would require the court to decide the case differently than it would have to if it were constitutional.[11] Moreover, the ESC has emphasized that such a case should be decided only to the extent requested and that the court should not seek legal grounds for unconstitutionality.[12] While the ESC itself has not explicitly

11 ESC CRC 28.05.2008, 3-4-1-4-08, p. 18

12 ESC CRC 31.05.2004, 3-4-1-7-04, p 23; ESC CRC 12.12.2017, 5-17-10/10, p 52; see also: Aaviksoo 2007, 65.

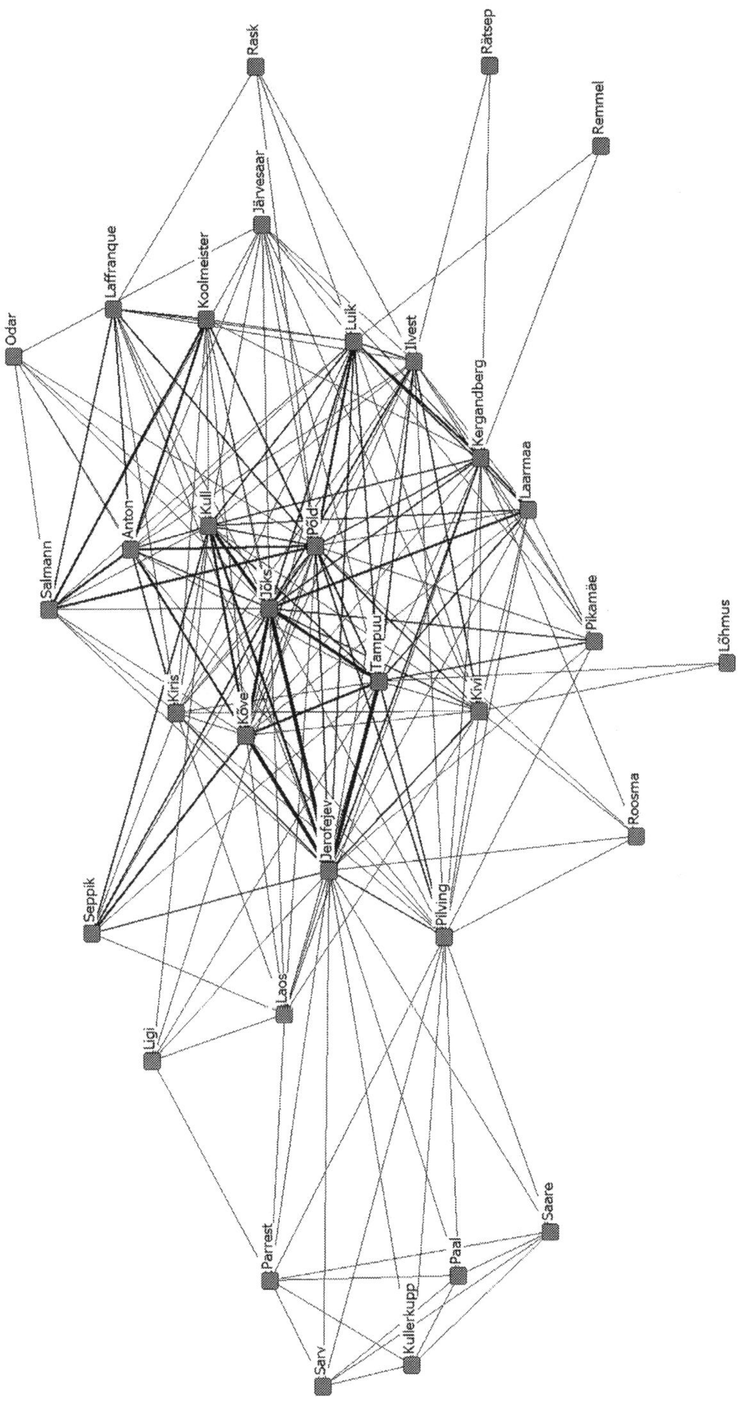

Figure 4.4 Dissenting coalitions (1993–2020) (ESC)

pointed it out, the reason for this self-restraint lies in the constitutionally enshrined division of duties, which is based on the principle of separation of powers. This prohibits the ESC from intervening "indiscriminately" in the legislature's area of responsibility (Ernits 2017, 53).

However, there are also cases in which the court has understood its authority in the context of norm control more broadly.[13] Pointing out that the specific norm control procedure is particularly intended to protect the rights of the plaintiff, the ESC has stated that, in order to maintain legal clarity, those provisions may also be considered relevant which are closely related to the contested provision and which, if maintained, could give rise to legal ambiguities.[14] The ESC CRC has also stated that it is for the ESC to decide on the extent to which it is necessary to depart from the reasoning or application in a particular case of concrete norm control.[15]

In some cases, the court dismissed the claim as such, but it addressed the legislature in an *obiter dictum*. In decision CRC 3-4-1-67-13 of ESC, a mother who received 70 euros of state support per month as a full-time caregiver for her adult severely disabled son had to add her son's disability pension of 268 euros to her declared income and was therefore not entitled to an additional subsistence allowance. The court held that the legal norm submitted for constitutional review by the referring administrative court, which was to be applied in the present case when assessing the amount of the subsistence allowance, did not violate the fundamental right to state assistance in case of need that is guaranteed by the Constitution. Since the referring court had not requested a constitutional review of the amount of the subsistence allowance as such, the ESC CRC subsequently stated in an *obiter dictum*[16] that:

> The Chamber . . . doubts the adequacy of the bases and the amount of subsistence allowance in the exceptional situations provided for in the Social Welfare Act. The obligation of the state to provide adequate support to its citizens in the event of material hardship also applies in exceptional situations, such as a situation in which a mother in material hardship is the guardian of her child.

These cases show that the court has interpreted the procedural requirement of "relevance" in different ways over the years (Pilving 2020, 37) and consequently has itself influenced the scope of its own jurisdiction. In addition to the fact that this practice has a direct impact on the right to be heard, the

13 ESC en banc 08.06.2009, 3–4–1–7–08, p. 23ff; ESC en banc 1.06.2019, 5–18–8/19, p. 71f; see also: Aaviksoo 2016, 24f.

14 ESC en banc 12.04.2011, 3–2–1–62–10 S 30; ESC CRC 1.10.2007, 3–4–1–14–07 S 12

15 ESC CRC 10.12.2004, 3–4–1–24–04, p. 12

16 ESC CRC 05.05.2014, 3–4–1–67–13, p. 51

question of the admissibility of norm control requests also has a direct effect on the strength of the court's position *vis-à-vis* the legislature. Considering that the composition of the ESC CRC – in contrast to the other chambers – is constantly changing and does not consist of constitutional lawyers per se, this can also be seen as a reason for such a changeable legal practice. Nevertheless, the ambiguities associated with assessing the relevance criterion can also be used by the court to limit its jurisdiction over politically charged or socially controversial issues.

4.6.2 The "margin of appreciation" of the legislator

Judicial practice in interpreting the legislature's "margin of appreciation" is an important indicator of the relationship between the judiciary and the legislature (Aaviksoo 2016, 65). In the early 2000s, the ESC CRC characterized the breadth of the legislature's discretion as follows:

> The second sentence of the second indent of § 28 of the Constitution, pursuant to which the categories and extent of and conditions and procedure for the receipt of assistance shall be provided by law, leaves it for the legislator to decide to what extent the state shall grant assistance to needy persons. . . . Nevertheless, an extended freedom of decision of the *Riigikogu* . . . does not mean that the legislator as the developer of economic and social policies may, using the argument of limited resources, freely decide to what extent and to whom the social rights established by § 28 of the Constitution shall be guaranteed. . . . The right to receive state assistance in the case of need is a subjective right, in the case of violation of which a person is entitled to go to court, and the courts have an obligation to review the constitutionality of an act granting a social right. But a court of constitutional review must avoid a situation where the development of budgetary policies goes, to a large extent, into the hands of court. That is why in implementing social policies the court cannot replace the legislative or executive powers.[17]

In addition to the areas of economic, social, and budgetary policy mentioned here, the court has also granted the legislature broad discretion in the area of penal policy[18] and the design of the system of local self-government.[19]

17 ESC CRC 21.01.2004, 3-4-1-7-03 p. 15f; see also: Administrative Law Chamber of ESC 10.11.2003, 3-3-1-65-03, p. 14
18 ESC CRC 25.11.2003, 3-4-1-9-03, p. 21
19 ESC en banc 20.12.2016, 3-4-1-3-16, p. 89; 91

Another criterion used by the court to evaluate its discretion is the extent to which the court is authorized to assess the possible unconstitutionality of the situation at the time of the decision. In this regard, the court argued that:

> As the legislator has exclusive competence to establish public financial obligations, and the extent of judicial review over it within constitutional review proceedings is limited, the Court *en banc* can assess the justifiability of the rates of support only in general terms. As arising from the purpose of establishing the renewable energy charge setting the rate of the charge requires complex calculations, taking account of various preconditions, including future estimates, within constitutional review proceedings the justifiability of rates of renewable energy support in the light of the aims of establishing the support can also be assessed only based on generic data.[20]

Because of their importance, most decisions on the separation of powers are made by the ESC in plenary. As a result, dissenting opinions have also quite frequently addressed the limits of the court's jurisdiction and the possible politicization of the court. As early as 2002, Judge Tõnu Anton stated in his dissenting opinion (joined by Judge Harri Salmann and Villu Kõve) that:

> The position of the Supreme Court *en banc* would be ultimately correct if the interpretation of the *Riigikogu* is in conflict with generally accepted legal principles or unreasonable or would lead to an unconstitutional result. The reasoning of the *en banc* does not allow (one) to draw any such conclusion. In the absence of clear and compelling arguments, I consider that the *en banc* has not sufficiently observed the principle of separation of powers.[21]

In his dissenting opinion on the court's decision on legal restrictions on the establishment of pharmacies, dissenting Judge Ivo Pilving stated: "I think that the question of whether to prefer establishment restrictions or, for example, a support fund as a means of solving the problem of rural pharmacies belongs to the political decision-making space of the legislator, and in this case the *Riigikogu* has not made any mistakes in choosing the measure."[22]

20 ESC en banc 15.12.2015, 3-2-1-71-14, p. 117
21 Dissenting Opinion of Judge Tõnu Anton, ESC en banc 17.03.2003, 3-1-3-10-02
22 Dissenting Opinion of Judge Ivo Pilving ESC en banc 9.12.2013, 3-4-1-2-13

On the other hand, in the dissenting opinion on the Court's decision on pension reform, the dissenting judges disagreed with the policy discretion that the *en banc* had granted to the legislature:

> The instrument used by the legislator cannot be an end in itself. The mere wish of the legislator, i.e. the so-called pure political will, is sufficient to organize a reform if the reform does not restrict the rights of individuals. There must be a justified need to establish a legislative solution if it is accompanied by violations of fundamental rights and freedoms (§ 11 of the Constitution).[23]

Based on these references, certain uniform legal developments can be identified. The ESC measures the boundary between political decision-making competence and judicial competence in particular by the subject matter of the regulation, granting the legislature broader discretion in certain matters compared to others. In addition, it emphasizes the importance of the temporal aspect of constitutional review, i.e. the extent to which case law can (already) concretely assess the effect of the disputed legislative amendment at the time the decision is rendered.

If one also considers that the ESC CRC is not staffed by judges specializing in constitutional law but is staffed on a rotating basis by judges from the other chambers, it can be assumed that such a composition contributes to the fact that uniform methodological approaches to constitutional law issues, including issues of the demarcation between legislative and judicial power, have emerged less frequently than in the other chambers/legal fields. This circumstance, in turn, is another reason for the high number of dissenting opinions. The low total number of decisions and the relatively young age of the court certainly also play a role here.

4.6.3 Compatibility with EU law

When the protracted negotiations on Estonia's accession to the EU were successful, Estonia had to bring itself into conformity with EU law within a short period of time. To meet this challenge, the legislature decided to draft a four-paragraph Amendment Act to the Estonian Constitution (EC AA), which was adopted by a referendum in 2003, instead of individual amendments to the law (Ernits et al. 2019, 887, 890 ff; Tupay 2013, 29, 32). According to the first paragraph of the law, Estonia can be a member of the EU as long as the fundamental principles of the EC are respected. As long as Estonia is a member of the EU, the EC is to be applied, considering its rights and obligations under the Accession Treaty (according to § 2 EC AA9). This broad formulation

23 Dissenting opinion of Judges Peeter Jerofejev, Kai Kullerkupp, Kaupo Paal, Nele Parrest, Ivo Pilving, Kalev Saare, and Juhan Sarv in ESC en banc 20.10.2020, decision 5-20-3/46, p. 11

gave the court a major role in assessing – i.e. interpreting – the conformity of Estonian law with EU law. The most important decisions of the court in this matter are briefly summarized in the following paragraphs.

In 2004, the Chancellor of Justice, within the framework of his right to conduct abstract norm control, applied to ESC CRC, among other things, to declare Section 5 I of the Political Parties Act unconstitutional. According to this provision, actually a repetition of the similarly worded constitutional provision § 48 EC, only Estonian citizens could be members of a party. The Chancellor argued that the provision constituted an unlawful violation of the principle of the right of EU citizens to vote and stand for election in local elections, and it violated the requirement of equal treatment of EU citizens arising from § 2 EC AA and EU law. With regard to § 48 EC, however, the Chancellor considered an interpretation in conformity with European law possible on the basis of § 2 EC AA. The court sitting *en banc* declared the application of the Chancellor inadmissible.[24] Although the latter had also raised the question of the possible scope for interpretation of § 48 EC, the court considered the content of the application to be justified under European law. However, the Chancellor is not authorized by law to examine whether national law conflicts with EU law. Moreover, since the primacy of EU law, according to the settled case law of the ECJ, is to be understood merely as primacy of application, there is no legal necessity for examining the compatibility of national law with EU law in the framework of constitutional review proceedings.[25] Thus, the Court did not, as the Chancellor had suggested, make use of the interpretative competence granted to it by the EC AA. Nor did it address issues of legal certainty and clarity, which are also among the principles protected by the EC. In their dissenting opinion, 6 of the 18 judges of the full court held that the Chancellor cannot be denied the power to review national legal acts for their conformity with the EC, which in turn must be interpreted in accordance with EU law, as required by § 2 EC AA.[26]

In another case, the ESC ruled for the first time, and unprecedentedly, on a legal basis granted to it by the legislature immediately beforehand.[27] According to this provision, the *Riigikogu* may ask the Supreme Court for an opinion on the interpretation of the Estonian Constitution in the light of EU law, if this is necessary in connection with the adoption of a national legal amendment based on European law (§ 71 CRCPA). Although the opinion is not listed in the Estonian JUDICON record due to its non-binding nature, this decision illustrates the cooperative approach of the court and the legislature to the issues of the compatibility of Estonian law with EU law. In their dissenting opinions, Judges Villu Kõve and Eerik Kergandberg questioned the

24 ESC en banc 19.04.2005, 3-4-1-1-05, p. 48ff
25 ESC en banc 19.04.2005, 3-4-1-1-05 p. 49
26 ESC en banc Apr. 19, 2005, 3-4-1-1-05 dissenting opinion of Julia Laffranque and others
27 Opinion of the ESC CRC 11.05.2006, 3-4-1-3-06

formal constitutionality of the regulation, which gives Parliament the right to ask the court for an opinion. The EC does not provide for the legal institution of non-binding court opinions, and their constitutionality and possible legal effect remains unclear – whether the issuance of such an "opinion" precludes, for example, an analogous abstract or concrete review of norms in the same case.[28] However, in its majority decision, the court did not address the issue of the constitutionality of the new type of procedure or its enactment as a *de facto* single act.

The court case concerned the question of whether § 111 EC, according to which the Estonian central bank has the sole right to issue Estonian money and is responsible for its stability, is compatible with the legal framework of the Monetary Union. The European Commission itself did not share the view expressed by the Estonian government but agreed to drop its concerns in this regard in the event of a positive ruling by the ESC. In its decision, the ESC stated that § 2 EC AA "means the substantial and continuous amendment of the Constitution insofar as it does not comply with European law. . . . The effect of those provisions of the Constitution which are not in conformity with European Union law and which therefore cannot be applied is halted".[29] On the basis of § 2 EC AA, § 111 EC was inapplicable and EU law, according to which the European Central Bank had the sole right to issue euro banknotes, must be applied.[30] As the two dissenting opinions by Kergandberg and Kõve emphasize, the court understood the right of interpretation granted to it by § 2 of EC AA without further explanation as a maxim of conformity with EU law, without explaining how § 1 EC AA is to be understood in this light, which, as a so-called safeguard clause, provides that the fundamental principles of the EC are to be upheld even in the context of membership of the EU. However, in its decision on the European Stability Mechanism, after establishing the constitutionality of the ESM as a treaty under international law on the merits, the ESC *en banc* stated in 2012 in an *obiter dictum*:

> The Supreme Court *en banc* is of the opinion that the [EC AA] does not authorize the integration process of the European Union . . . to be delegated to the European Union to an unlimited extent. Therefore, it is primarily the *Riigikogu* which must, upon a change in any founding treaty of the European Union and also upon entry into a new treaty, deliberate separately and decide whether the amendment to the founding treaty of the European Union or the new treaty leads to a deeper integration process . . . and thus also a more extensive interference with the principles of the Constitution. If it becomes evident that the new

28 Dissenting opinion of Judge Villu Kõve and dissenting opinion of Judge Eerik Kergandberg on the opinion of the ESC CRC 11.05.2006, 3-4-1-3-06, p. 1

29 ESC CRC 11.05.2006, 3-4-1-3-06, p. 16

30 ESC CRC 11.05.2006, 3-4-1-3-06, p. 18

> founding treaty of the European Union or the amendment to a founding treaty of the European Union gives rise to a more extensive delegation of the competence of Estonia to the European Union and a more extensive interference with the Constitution, it is necessary to seek the approval of the holder of supreme power, i.e. the people, and presumably amend the Constitution once again.[31]

The particular "EU-friendliness" of the legal practice of the ESC has been highlighted by many legal scholars in their publications (Ernits et al. 2019; Kerikmäe 2016; Albi and Kalmo 2022). A characteristic of the court's decisions in respect of the EU is their rather pragmatic approach and limited legal-theoretical reasoning. This, in turn, may also be seen as one of the reasons the court has been criticized by jurists for its lack of constitutional merit. Again, one reason for the court's pragmatic approach may be that the deciding judges do not specialize in constitutional law, so that certain constitutional aspects may remain in the background when they deal with complex legal issues.

However, this pragmatic view of the law is also a peculiarity of the Estonian legislator. As mentioned earlier, in order to make Estonia's accession to the EU domestically quick and straightforward, the legislator, instead of amending the EC, gave legal practice and the courts the right to interpret the entire Constitution in terms of EU law. However, several reasons can again be cited for these similarities in legal views. One is the aforementioned fact that, due simply to the country's small size, those lawyers who hold decisive government positions very often serve in both the legislative and judicial branches in the course of their careers. Moreover, it should be noted that the vast majority of these crucial positions are held by lawyers who have been educated at the law faculty of the same university (i.e. the University of Tartu).

4.6.4 *Development of case law concerning fundamental rights*

Particularly in recent years, the decisions of the ESC CRC give reason to believe that the court has become more aware of its power to shape the law in its decisions. In some rulings, the court has provided guidance on the application of a law until a constitutional basis comes into force. One such ruling concerned the law on registered civil partnerships (Registered Partnership Act, RPA). Here, in a first legal act the legislature had granted life partners of the same or different sex the right to a registered partnership. However, the adoption of the corresponding implementing legislation would have required an absolute majority in the *Riigikogu*, which did not exist at the time. As a result, several legal disputes subsequently arose in which the partners demanded the administrative implementation of the registered partnership granted to them.

31 EC en banc 12.07.2012, 3-4-1-6-12, p. 223

In an initial decision, the ESC CRC ruled that the lack of implementing legislation was not necessarily unconstitutional and that consideration should first be given to applying existing laws accordingly.[32] In 2019, however, the ESC *en banc* declared the Aliens Act unconstitutional and invalid because it conflicted with the fundamental right to family life to the extent that it precluded the issuance of a temporary residence permit to the registered partner of an Estonian citizen. In addition, the court noted that EC § 27 (1), which states that "the family, as the basis for the survival and development of the nation and society, is under the protection of the state" should also apply to same-sex couples in the future. The court also clarified how the Aliens Act applies to registered domestic partners until the legislature makes the necessary changes.[33]

The ESC also seems to want to avoid making substantive decisions on certain sensitive issues. For example, although the ESC recognized in its decision in an *obiter dictum* that an absolute prohibition of the right to vote for prisoners is incompatible with the established jurisprudence of the ECtHR, the court did not declare the relevant statutory prohibition unconstitutional because the plaintiffs in the specific case were accused of crimes that were too serious to grant them the right to vote.[34] In its decision, the court stated that the "*Riigikogu* has the power to replace unconstitutional provisions with constitutional ones on its own initiative".[35]

Similarly, in 2016, the ESC CRC ruled that an absolute ban on persons in pre-trial detention receiving long-term visits is already compatible with the Constitution due to the seriousness of the crime with which the complaining pre-trial detainee was charged.[36] This was decided even though the ban on receiving long-term visits – like the ban on prisoners voting – is absolute and therefore does not depend on the severity of the crime. However, the court indicated that it might consider the unconstitutionality of the norm in a case where the alleged crime is not as serious.[37]

Thus, in these two cases, the court exercised a form of discretion that the legislature had not provided for in the challenged acts in order to avoid declaring them unconstitutional (Soo 2021). In addition to the concrete review of norms, the court also examined the individual moral worthiness of the protection of the fundamental right-holder in the specific case, which is not provided for by law. In doing so, the court also approved the legislature's political decisions to restrict the voting rights of prisoners and the visitation rights of

32 ESC CRC 10.04.2018, 5–17–42, p. 37f
33 ESC en banc Jun. 21, 2019, 5–18–5 S 71
34 ESC en banc 01.07.2015, 3–4–1–2–15
35 ibid., p. 64
36 ESC CRC 16.11.2016, 3–4–1–2–16
37 ESC CRC 16.11.2016, 3–4–1–2–16, p. 136; It did indeed declare the regulation unconstitutional by decision ESC en banc 11.06.2019, 5–18–8/19.

pre-trial detainees. Although these rulings do not limit the legislature's discretion, but instead expand it, the rulings reflect the political power of the judges.

These examples show that the ESC is well aware of its power *vis-à-vis* the legislature. However, it does not always use this power to the detriment of the legislature. Rather, whether it uses this power also seems to depend on the issue on which the court has to rule. In this respect, the court's relatively weak legal methodological reasoning practice broadens its scope in deciding to what extent it intends to rule on filed lawsuits.

4.7 Conclusions

The results of the present analysis suggest the conclusion that the rulings of the ESC stand out for their strength compared to other countries. Among the 19 countries compared, the average strength of the rulings of the ESC is relatively high. At first glance, this result may seem somewhat unexpected, since both the ESC itself and the state institutions closely associated with the constitutional review process place particular emphasis on its apolitical orientation. It should be noted, however, that the strength of rulings cannot be equated with the "politicization" of the court. There is no necessary conditional relationship between an "activist court" and the strength of its decisions. The decisions of a strong court can be just as "activist" as "non-activist". It should also be borne in mind that the Estonian figures do not always reflect the actual relationship between the court and the legislature because of the small number of decisions.

Since both the types of proceedings and the group of possible applicants for a constitutional review of norms are narrowly limited, the probability of an unsuccessful review of norms is low. However, this also means that case numbers are kept low and that the scope of judicial practice for the constitutional review of norms is narrow, which in turn limits the development of certain legal approaches and rules. Moreover, the possible initiation of (abstract) norm control proceedings by the Chancellor of Justice and the President depends, in turn, on the personal attitude of the respective office holder. For this reason, the establishment of a separate constitutional court, including the expansion of the possibilities of constitutional review, has been a topic of discussion since the current order came into force (Bartole 1997). So far, however, such efforts have not been supported by the political majority.

The Chancellor of Justice, for example, who is often seen as a balancing counter-position to the German model of the constitutional complaint, reflects the criticism of such initiatives in the following statement on a draft law to introduce individual constitutional complaints:

> [The proposal] completely ignores the risk that the possibility of an individual appeal would be a first step in the politicization of the Supreme Court. The constitutional review procedure would essentially become a fourth reading of the bill. The protection of fundamental human rights,

> the separation and balance of powers and the rule of law are better served by a professional and independent judiciary. . . . Today, the risks of politization of the Supreme Court are mitigated by the filters of the judiciary, the Chancellor of Justice and the President of the Republic mentioned in the Constitution.[38]

Constitutional law is also not given separate attention in the composition of the ESC. The judges of the CRC are all members of the Chambers of Civil, Administrative or Criminal Law, depending on their specialization, and perform their duties in these Chambers in parallel with their membership in the CRC. Moreover, members of the CRC are not required to have a specialization in constitutional law. This may be one of the reasons why, in the last 30 years of Estonian judicial practice, a separate methodological approach to issues of constitutional law has emerged only to a modest extent. Bartole also noted as early as 1997 that in the Estonian model of constitutional review, the ESC's lack of constitutional expertise could pose a challenge to its development (Bartole 1997, 4f; Pikamaee 2021, 161f). In the long run, this methodological weakness may have had a negative impact on the line that the court has so far clearly taken, namely that of strictly separating law from politics. For example, the weak legal reasoning on which the court based its rulings on the interplay between EU law and Estonian constitutional law, as well as the rulings in which the court replaced statutory prohibitions with judicial discretion, raise questions about the soundness of its legal reasoning.

It is important to note the relative freedom that the legislature grants to the ESC (and its President) in designing and conducting the constitutional review. The law simply provides that the CRC is composed of nine judges, whose president is the President of the ESC and whose remaining eight members are elected by the Supreme Court in its full composition. The political independence of the constitutional review is preserved to the greatest extent possible through an election process in which the judges of the ESC are elected in a process that is relatively free of current party politics, and the judges of the CRC are in turn elected by the ESC itself. The fact that the judges of the CRC are appointed in rotation from among the judges of the other chambers of the ESC contributes not insignificantly to the public perception of the CRC as a politically independent institution.

The relative freedom to shape the content of reviews is another reason for the strength of Estonian constitutional review. For example, the court has, among other things, adjusted the temporal effect of judgments on constitutional review, influenced the framework of admissibility of norm control proceedings, and created the legal construct of the individual constitutional complaint (Aaviksoo 2007, 64f). Moreover, with the adoption of the EC AA, the legislature granted judges the right to shape the compatibility of domestic

38 The Chancellor of Justice's opinion no. 9–2/170305/1701102 from 10.03.2017, 3

law with EU law according to their ideas. In the context of constitutional review, the ESC has used this possibility to develop the application of the Estonian Constitution far beyond its wording. In interpreting the Estonian Constitution in accordance with EU law, the ESC has considered the possible limits of statutory interpretation, such as wording, clarity of norms, and certainty to be relevant. In the wording of the Supreme Court itself, it can therefore be confirmed that the application of EU law in Estonian law has led not only to a primacy of application, but also to an amendment of the Estonian Constitution through the interpretation of ESC.[39]

Although the quantitative data indicate that it is a strong court and the reasons for this can be found in the design of the constitutional review process, it is worth noting that a qualitative analysis suggests that the ESC can also be a rather modest court. For example, the court has used the discretion granted to it by the legislature in assessing the compatibility of national and EU law in a way that has, in practice, imposed few additional obligations on the legislature. Similarly, on issues of prison inmates' rights, the ESC for a long time saw no need to legally correct the legislature's political stance in this regard. The court's relationship with the legislature can thus be described as collegial and pragmatic rather than mutually competitive. In this sense, the ESC has found ways to influence the legislature by means of less restrictive measures than declaring a legal norm unconstitutional. On various issues over the years, the Court has initially indicated that it believes a particular legislative change is necessary for legal reasons. Only after the legislature repeatedly ignored the court's opinion did the court declare the norm in question unconstitutional. One example of this is the issue of long-term visitation rights for detainees.

One reason for this rather collegial relationship can certainly be found in the small size of the country, where people in the leading offices of the country basically know each other and the smooth functioning of the state is often perceived as a communal task. Moreover, given the small size of the country, it is not unlikely that Estonian lawyers who qualify for representative offices will themselves have to decide on significant state matters both from the perspective of the legislature – or at least the executive – and in the robes of a judge. Moreover, the vast majority of Estonian lawyers graduated from the same university. Therefore, at least as a rule, they know who is on "the other side". The results of this study also show, however, that the court has become more aware of its law-shaping power over time (see, for example, the increase in non-binding prescriptions and dissenting opinions over the years). In this context, it is certainly also worth mentioning that until 2002 the court, where there is no rotation of judges appointed for life, consisted of judges who had received their training while still under the Soviet regime. It was not until 2002 that a renewal of the judiciary of the ESC, due to the retirement of the older judges, began, a process which is practically complete today.

39 ESC CRC 11.05.2006, 3-4-1-3-06, p. 16

Another peculiarity of Estonian constitutional review is that not every significant constitutional issue is decided by the ESC CRC. The Chancellor of Justice often influences the legislature during the legislative procedure (Madise 2022). It is also not uncommon for the President to indicate even before a law is passed by Parliament whether he considers its promulgation to be problematic (Karis 2022). Similarly, if the President decides not to promulgate a law, he must give Parliament the opportunity to amend the legal norm/law challenged by the President (EC § 107(2)), which the *Riigikogu* has repeatedly done. However, such an effect is not reflected in the record. In particular, if the legislature amended the law after a lawsuit and the Supreme Court in its ruling determined the unconstitutionality of the previously applicable law, this ruling is not included in the present record, since the determination of the unconstitutionality of norms that are no longer valid does not limit the legislature's room for manoeuvre.[40]

In summary, the strength of the constitutional review of the ESC owes much to its procedural design, according to which the judicial review of norms is an "ultima ratio" measure that can be initiated only by a few institutions, all of which have special legal expertise. All the admissible applicants for constitutional review are institutions or representatives of institutions that are organizationally integrated into the system of public administration. As a result, both a limited number of applicants and alternative norm control procedures correspond to the rather broad freedom of decision in the Estonian constitutional review process and a rather weak methodological basis. This restrictive handling of constitutional review in Estonia has also had an inhibiting effect on the development of a strong constitutional law culture. In this respect, it must be considered that a court that is subject only to vague legal rules runs the risk of becoming politicized.

References

Aaviksoo, Berit. 2007. "Judicial Activism in Constitutional Review Decisions of the Supreme Court of Estonia." *Juridica International* 2007 (XIII): 60–69.

———. 2016. "Riigikohtu aktivism asjassepuutuvuse ja seadusandja otsustusruumi doktriinide valgel: Vingt ans après, dix ans plus tard (Activism of the Supreme Court in the light of the doctrines of relevance and legislative discretion: ing tans après, dix ans plus tard.)." *Kohtute aastaraamat* 2016: 61–79.

Albi, Anneli, and Hent Kalmo. 2022. "Estonia: From Rules to Pragmatism." In *National Constitutions and EU Integration*, edited by Griller, Stefan, Lina Papadopoulou and Roman Puff, 171–210. Oxford: Hart Bloomsbury.

Bartole, Sergio. 1997. "Konstitutsioonikohtu Reform Eestis (Reform of the Constitutional Court in Estonia)." *Põhiseaduse Juriidilise Ekspertiisi Komisjon/*

40 See e.g. ESC CRC 21.01.2004, 3-4-1-7-03, where the lawmaker had already before the court's judgment amended the law on the proposal of the Chancellor of Justice.

Venice Commission. www.just.ee/era-ja-avalik-oigus/pohiseadus-ja-pohioigused/pohiseadus#iv-osa-valisekspert.

BVerfG (Bundesverfassungsgericht). 2021. *Constitutional Complaints*. Accessed January 18, 2022. www.bundesverfassungsgericht.de/EN/Verfahren/Wichtige-Verfahrensarten/Verfassungsbeschwerde/verfassungsbeschwerde_node.html.

CoJ (Chancellor of Justice). 2021. *Constitutional Review*. Accessed November 8, 2021. www.oiguskantsler.ee/en/constitutional-review.

Ernits, Madis. 2017. "§ 15." In *Eesti Vabariigi Põhiseadus. Kommenteeritud väljaanne [The Constitution of the Republic of Estonia. Commentary]*, edited by Ülle Madise, Hent Kalmo, Lauri Mälksoo, Raul Narits, Peep Pruks, Jüri Raidla, and Priit Vinkel. 4th ed., 210–241. Tallinn: Juura.

———, Carri Ginter, Saale Laos, Marje Allikmets, Paloma Krõõt Tupay, René Värk, and Andra Laurand. 2019. "The Constitution of Estonia: The Unexpected Challenges of Unlimited Primacy of EU Law." In *National Constitutions in European and Global Governance: Democracy, Rights, the Rule of Law*, edited by Anneli Albi and Samo Bardutzky, 887–950. The Hague: T.M.C. Asser Press.

ESC 2020. *The Supreme Court of Estonia*. Accessed October 20, 2021. www.riigikohus.ee/sites/default/files/Tr%C3%BCkis/2019-Riigikohus-brozuur-2019-ENG.pdf.

———. 2021a. *Constitutional Review Chamber*. Accessed November 1, 2021. www.riigikohus.ee/en/chambers/constitutional-review-chamber.

———. 2021b. *Uuring: kohtuid usaldab 71 protsenti eestimaalastest (Survey: 71% of Estonians trust the courts)*, November 30. Accessed January 30, 2022. www.riigikohus.ee/et/uudiste-arhiiv/uuring-kohtuid-usaldab-71-protsenti-eestimaalastest.

European Commission. 2021. *The 2021 Justice Scoreboard*. Accessed June 15, 2023. https://commission.europa.eu/system/files/2021-07/eu_justice_scoreboard_2021.pdf.

Ginsburg, Tom. 2002. "Constitutional Courts in New Democracies: Understanding Variation in East Asia." *Global Jurist Advances* 2 (1): 1–24.

Karis, Alar. 2022. "Estonia Must Not Seem Arrogant When Talking about Russian Threat. Radio Interview with Estonian President Alar Karis." *Eesti Rahvusringhääling* (Estonian Public Broadcasting), October 11, 2022. https://news.err.ee/1608746944/karis-estonia-must-not-seem-arrogant-when-talking-about-russian-threat.

Kerikmäe, Tanel. 2016. "Estonia as an EU member state: Lack of pro-active constitutional dialogue." In *Constitutional Evolution in Central and Eastern Europe: Expansion and Integration in the EU*, edited by Alexander H.E. Morawa and Kyriaki Topidi, 11–41. London: Routledge.

Lõhmus, Uno. 2020. "Põhiseaduslikkuse kohtuliku kontrolli sünniloost (The genesis of constitutional judicial review)." In *Riigiõiguse aastaraamat 2020*, 7–31. Tallinn: Eesti Teaduste Akadeemia riigiõiguse sihtkapital.

———, and Hannes Vallikivi. 2020. "Lisandusi põhiseaduslikkuse järelevalve sünniloole Eestis (Additions to the genesis of constitutional review in Estonia)." *Juridica* 2020 (6): 451–464.

Madise, Ülle. 2022. "Revoking Right to Vote of Third Country Citizens Could Be Unconstitutional. Excerpts of a Written Comment of Chancellor of Justice Ülle Madise to the Riigikogu Constitutional Committee." *Eesti Rahvusringhääling (Estonian Public Broadcasting)*, August 23. https://news.err.ee/1608693025/revoking-right-to-vote-of-third-country-citizens-could-be-unconstitutional.

Maruste, Rait. 2020. "Mis oli, on ja võiks olla põhiseaduslikkuse kohtulikus järelevalves (What was, is and could be in constitutional judicial review)." *Juridica* 2020 (6): 465–473.

Mõttus-Leppik, Elo. 2019. "New Ministers Want Fresh Blood Interview with then Minister of Finance Martin Helme." *Postimees*, July 3. https://news.postimees.ee/6721301/new-ministers-want-fresh-blood.

Pikamäe, Priit. 2021. "Ääremärkusi Eesti põhiseaduslikkuse järelevalve korralduse ja menetluse kujunemisele ja võimalikule edasisele arengule (Comments on the evolution and possible future development of the organisation and procedure of constitutional review in Estonia)." *Riigiõiguse aastaraamat 2021*, 139–170. Tallinn: Eesti Teaduste Akadeemia riigiõiguse sihtkapital.

Pilving, Ivo. 2020. "§ 152." In *Eesti Vabariigi põhiseadus. Kommenteeritud väljaanne* (Constitution of the Republic of Estonia. Commented edition), edited by Ülle Madise, Hent Kalmo, Oliver Kask, and Peep Pruks, 127 ff. 5th ed. Tartu: Sihtasutus Iuridicum.

Pócza, Kálmán, ed. 2019. *Constitutional Politics and the Judiciary: Decision-making in Central and Eastern Europe*. London and New York: Routledge.

Ristikivi, Merike, and Karin Sein. 2022. *Õigusriigi taastamine: Eesti seaduste ja institutsioonide reformid 1992–2002 (Restoring the Rule of Law: Reforming Estonian Laws and Institutions 1992–2002)*. Tartu: Tartu Ülikooli Kirjastus.

Schneider, Heinrich. 2002. "Eesti põhiseadused ja nende järelevalve." *Riigikogu Toimetised*, nr 5, October 19. https://rito.Riigikogu.ee/wordpress/wp-content/uploads/2016/03/Eesti-p%C3%B5hiseadused-ja-nende-j%C3%A4relevalve.pdf.

Soo, Anneli. 2021. "Vahistatu pikaajalise kokkusaamise saaga: vangistusseaduse jõustumisest Riigikohtu üldkogu 11. juuni 2019. a otsuseni asjas 5–18–8. " (The Saga of a Person in Custody Receiving a Long-term Visit: From the Entry into Force of the Imprisonment Act to the Supreme Court Judgment en banc of 11 June 2019 in Case No 5–18–8). Juridica 2021 (1, 64 - 70).

Tschenscher, Axel. 2014. "Supreme Court und Schweizerisches Bundesgericht als Modelle Integrierter Verfassungsgerichtsbarkeit." In *Der Staat. Schutz der Verfassung: Normen, Institutionen, Höchst und Verfassungsgerichte*, edited by Thomas Simon Johannes Kalwoda, 187–212. Berlin: Duncker& Humblot.

Tupay, Paloma Krõõt. 2013. "Verfassungsinterpretation für Europa – Das Ende des estnischen Verfassungsrechts?" *Osteuropa-Recht* 2013 (1): 28–55.

Vallikivi, Hannes. 2021. "Õigusteaduslik arvamus põhiseaduslikkuse järelevalve küsimuses 1920–1940." In *Riigiõiguse aastaraamat*, edited by Ernits, Madis, Marju Luts-Sootak, Uno Lõhmus, and Lauri Mälksoo, 89–104. Tallin: Eesti Teaduste Akadeemia riigiõiguse sihtkapital

Court decisions, legal acts

Since 1 June 2010, the Estonian state gazette *Riigi Teataja* has been published online exclusively at https://www.riigiteataja.ee and contains the official Estonian legal acts along with English translations of several of them. English translations of Estonian legal acts are available at www.riigiteataja.ee/en/.

5 The Hungarian Constitutional Court

Dialogue in practice

Attila Gyulai, Kálmán Pócza and Gábor Dobos

5.1 Introduction

The Hungarian Constitutional Court (HCC) has been widely known as one of the most formative institutions of constitutional adjudication in Central and Eastern Europe. Established early during the 1989–1990 democratic transition, vested with significant competences, adopting an activist stance, the HCC was considered as a key player in the successful democratic transition of Hungary. The prominent role of the HCC stems, at least in part, from the legal continuity that characterized the transition in Hungary. Although as a result of the "negotiated revolution" (Tőkés 1996) the Communist constitution was changed in all details, legal provisions that did not run counter to the new democratic polity remained in force, while the HCC had to decide on many ambiguous cases, placing the institution at the centre of political conflicts (Gárdos-Orosz and Kinga 2022, 17–18). The same legal continuity may explain the early "activist" period of the HCC when, under the presidency of László Sólyom, the court established modern Hungarian constitutionalism and the practice of constitutional adjudication (Jakab and Fröhlich 2017, 394).

During the first decade of its existence, the HCC enjoyed an exceptional position in the Hungarian political context. Due to a number of features, the court developed into a prominent institution of the democratic transition. Compared to other courts in the region, it was granted particularly broad competences. In its formative years, the court pursued a rather expansive institutional strategy. Moreover, the strong court benefited from the political environment in which depoliticization was considered the default position, and the HCC enjoyed widespread respect as the final arbiter in everyday political battles. Since the late 1990s, however, all of these features have become less and less characteristic of the Court's functioning. Since recent years, polarization has slowly permeated the benches of the Court (as evidenced by the growing number of dissenting opinions). Activism has been replaced by a more restrained institutional strategy as the parties responsible for filling the benches of the Court adapted to the presence of such an institution. Finally, the Court has been significantly curtailed since 2010.

DOI: 10.4324/9781003399483-5

Two decades after its establishment, the HCC was one of the first institutions to be restricted after 2010, when Viktor Orbán's government, backed by its supermajority in Parliament, reshaped the country's institutional framework according to its political interests. Operating not as the highest level of the ordinary judicial system, but as an independent branch of power for several years after the transition (Jakab and Johanna 2017, 405) and being a potentially effective constraint on the legislature for decades after the transition, the court was subjected to parliamentary sovereignty not only due to institutional engineering but also following a reshuffled composition and the changes in the political environment. As of 2012, not only the functioning, composition, and the competences have been changed significantly but also the text (i.e. the constitution) the institution is meant to interpret.

This chapter analyses the Hungarian Constitutional Court not only in the context of two constitutional texts – the 1989 Constitution and the 2012 Fundamental Law – but also in terms of the trends describing the Court's relationship with the Hungarian legislature. Section 5.2 briefly outlines the institutional framework, composition, and the competences of the Court. Section 5.3 contextualizes the functioning of the Court by summarizing the changes in the composition of the HCC between 1990 and 2020. In Section 5.4, we then turn to an analysis of the overall evolution of the strength and diversity of rulings, while in Section 5.5 we analyze the evolution of dissenting opinions. Finally, in Section 5.6, we turn to the HCC's policy agenda.

The chapter traces the process of how the strength of the Court's decisions diminished over time and how both the political environment and the internal practice of the HCC became more polarized with respect to majority decisions, dissenting opinions, and policy areas. Like some other chapters in this volume, this chapter draws on an earlier work by the authors (Pócza, Dobos, and Gyulai 2019a), to which the reader is referred as needed.

5.2 Institutional setting: election of members, functioning, and competences

During the democratic transition, the Hungarian Constitutional Court was established as a new institution in the Hungarian polity. Unlike some other countries in the region, there was no precedent for constitutional adjudication in Hungary, nor was the institution established in the late years of communism, as it was in Poland. The HCC was the result of the roundtable talks between the ruling Communist party and the democratic opposition parties, and it was only during the negotiated transition in 1989 that constitutional adjudication was finally included in the National Round Table agreement that prepared the new Hungarian constitution (Sadurski 2002; Luchterhandt, Christian, and Albrecht, 2007; Sadurski [2008] 2014).

The HCC is a Kelsenian court established as separated from the judicial system and regulated by specific laws. The HCC was created by Article 32/A of Act XXXI of 1989, which amended – and practically replaced in almost all details – the old Communist Constitution (hereinafter "Constitution"). The Constitutional Court was regulated by Act XXXII of 1989 (hereinafter the "old HCC Act"). The HCC started its operation on 1 January 1990 and underwent a major transformation after 2010, when Fidesz, relying on its supermajority in the Parliament, made several changes, first by amending the existing regulation, then by replacing the Constitution with the new Fundamental Law, and finally by introducing the 2011 Law CLI on the Constitutional Court (hereinafter, Fundamental Law, new HCC Act). Both the old and the new Law on the HCC required a two-thirds majority in Parliament to amend them. Since the differences between the old and the new HCC are significant, this section will first briefly describe the changes in the composition of the court, the election of its members, and the functioning and the competences of the court.

Unlike with some of its counterparts in Europe, recruiting the members of the HCC has always been a single-logic procedure with parliamentary decision being the only source of the nomination and election of new judges. In the Hungarian case, formally, neither the government, nor the Head of State, and not even judicial or professional bodies are assigned with any role in filling the benches of the court. Members of the court are proposed by a nomination committee of the Parliament and elected by a secret vote of the two-thirds of the MPs. Under the old HCC Act, the committee consisted of one member from each party represented in the Parliament, practically resulting a need to compromise between the government and the opposition. That is, even if there existed a plenary supermajority to pass a successful vote, a more balanced committee could block the process by not nominating a judge. Nevertheless, election of the judges was a highly politicized process within the unicameral legislature (Körösényi, Tóth, and Török 2009, 34). Significantly modifying the election procedure, the nomination committee under the new HCC Act was redesigned to reflect the proportion of the mandates, meaning that a party with a supermajority could control both the nomination and the election procedure.

Elected by the two-thirds of MPs, according to the old HCC Act, members of the court served nine years with an option of re-election once, but their mandate ceased at the age of 70. Under the new arrangements, the term of the office of the judges has been increased to 12 years; however, re-election was abolished just as the age limit.

The President of the HCC has a formative role in determining the operations, agenda, and the distribution of the cases, and certain periods of the Court can be characterized according to the presidential terms. During the first decades of its functioning, it was an important contribution to the Court's standing that the President and the Vice President were elected by the judges of the HCC. The term lasted for three years while re-election was an option. The changes brought about by the introduction of the Fundamental Law and the new Act on the HCC placed the decision about the President in the hands of the MPs. A two-thirds majority is needed to elect a new President, whose term lasts until the termination of his or her mandate as a member of the HCC. Although the decisions of the Court are made by simple majority of the judges (without abstention), the President plays an influential role by appointing the rapporteur for the cases and presiding over the plenary sessions where the most important cases are dealt with. Less significant cases, however, are decided by one of the five-member panels composed upon the proposal of the president (before 2011, panels had three members). Filling the position of the Vice President and the Secretary General of the HCC is also decided by the plenary session following the proposal of the President. Apart from the performance of important operational tasks, in cases where the HCC rejects a petition without further consideration, the decision is made by a single judge on the proposal of the Secretary General.

The HCC has been given broad competences which – together with the fact that the court was not part of the judicial system – made the institution a strong player within the Hungarian polity. Although the changes introduced after 2010 maintained the wide competences, several of them have been significantly constrained parallel to the changes in the composition of the Court and the altered political environment. Both before and after 2010–2011, *a priori* and *a posteriori* forms of norm control were available to the Court, but with the introduction of the Fundamental Law and the new Act on the HCC, the scope of constitutional review have been curtailed by restricting the circle of petitioners and by the substantive requirements enumerated in the Fundamental Law. The new regulations, adopted after 2010, abolished the *actio popularis* which allowed anyone without personal interest to initiate *a posteriori* norm control. Nevertheless, it was meant to be replaced by a newly introduced and varied form of constitutional complaint. Let us see the competences in more detail by focusing on how the changes after 2010 modified the power of the HCC.

Under the Constitution, the HCC could review laws adopted but not yet promulgated, the rules of procedure of the Parliament, and international treaties. Besides these types of preliminary norm control, the Fundamental Law adds the review of the Fundamental Law and the amendments of the Fundamental Law but only with regard to the procedural requirements of their adoption. Preliminary norm control can be initiated by the Parliament or the Head of State (constitutional veto).

A posteriori norm control has been a competence of the HCC since the establishment of the HCC, allowing the judges to annul laws and normative orders even retroactively. Under the Constitution, *ex post* abstract review could be initiated by anyone. However, under the Fundamental Law, *a posteriori* norm control can be initiated by the government, a quarter of the members of Parliament, the President of the Curia (Supreme Court), the Prosecutor General, or the Commissioner for Fundamental Rights. The latter have been added later to the list, recognizing that the defined group proved to be too narrow. Furthermore, *a posteriori* norm control can be initiated as a judicial initiative in a concrete case of judicial proceeding by an ordinary judge.

As already mentioned, under the Fundamental Law and the new Act on the HCC, the *actio popularis* as a specific form of *a posteriori* abstract norm control of laws initiated by anyone without direct involvement was abolished, a step welcomed even by former judges of the HCC (Bragyova 2010, 59–61; Paczolay 2010, 44). At the same time, however, possibilities of norm control have been broadened by the introduction of the "genuine" constitutional complaint which can be initiated against a judicial decision by those who are affected by it in a concrete case.

The HCC has power to declare legislative omission if, due to a failure of the Parliament to legislate, unconstitutionality can be established. The HCC makes decisions in cases of conflict of competences between state organs (including local governments) and also examines conflicts between international treaties and domestic laws. It is also a competence of the HCC to examine the resolutions of the Parliament concerning referendums.

Finally, both before and after the changes in 2010–2011, the HCC had and has the competence to interpret constitutional norms. According to the new HCC Act, the abstract interpretation of the Fundamental Law can be initiated – with a reduction of the potential petitioners – by the Head of State, the government, or the Commissioner for Fundamental Rights.

Although the Court's powers remain broad and can potentially impose significant constraints on the legislature, the Fundamental Law has established limits and rules of interpretation that significantly restrict the HCC's scope of action. First, the HCC is bound in its interpretive activity to the content of the motion, and according to the Fundamental Law the provisions whose review have not been requested can only be reviewed if there is a close substantive connection with the provisions to be reviewed. Second, it is prescribed that in interpreting the Fundamental Law the HCC shall follow the *telos* of the Fundamental Law and shall take into consideration the content of its preamble (National Avowal) and that the interpretation should be in accordance with the achievements of the historical constitution (for the contemporary relevance of the historical constitution in Hungary, see Pócza 2019). Third, the competences of the Court have been significantly reduced concerning legislation on public finances, budgetary issues, and taxation, except for cases related to the fundamental rights (rights to life and human dignity; protection of personal data; freedom of thought, conscience, and religion; rights related to Hungarian citizenship). Fourth, the Fundamental Law declared that the decisions of the HCC under the previous Constitution were void and no longer bound the HCC as of the time the Fundamental Law came into force.

To sum up, the institutional setting that has characterized the HCC since its establishment demonstrates continuity and change at the same time. On the one hand, many of the competences of the court are still present even after the post-2010 changes, which makes the HCC a potentially strong player compared to its counterparts in the CEE region. On the other hand, however, the amendments to the regulation of the HCC brought about important shifts in practice. According to some legal scholars, the "new" HCC demonstrates what can be termed limited or restricted constitutional adjudication (Chronowski 2014, 4), while others argue that the HCC has been silenced (Halmai 2019), that the principles of "legal certainty and the protection of acquired rights often seem to be neglected" in the practice of the HCC (Chronowski 2021), that the HCC deferred uncritically to the government (Chronowski and Varju 2016), that an illusion of constitutional dialogue between the European courts and the HCC prevailed (Uitz 2015, 294), and that the HCC engaged in new judicial deference (Scheppele 2012a, 2012b). Other authors doubt whether the protection of constitutional norms is effective enough after the court-packing (Pozsár-Szentmiklósy 2020), arguing that the HCC became a fellow-traveller in establishing autocratic legalism after 2013 (Scheppele 2018), that the new judges became willing executors of party interests (Szente 2016), that the court was rendered absolutely ineffective (Tóth 2019), that the HCC opted for passivist strategies in order to survive (Lánczos 2019), that its powers were very limited (Halmai 2018), and some even argue that courts simply assist autocratic leaders in preserving their power (Dixon and Landau 2019). Gárdos-Orosz (2016, 449, 451) contend that the introduction of the "genuine" constitutional complaint, along with other changes, actually makes it its primary competence and shifts the court from the position of controlling legislation to that of controlling judicial practice, with the key relationship being not between the court and the legislature but between the court and the judicial system (Gárdos-Orosz and Kinga 2022, 29). In the literature, the alteration of the constitutional text and the transformation of the political climate are also mentioned to be responsible for the changes regarding the HCC (Jakab and Fröhlich 2017, 430). Finally, combining the relevance of the institutional setting, the political environment, as well as the parties in charge over the election of the judges of the HCC, the composition of the HCC should be mentioned as being responsible for the actual practice of constitutional adjudication *vis-à-vis* the legislature. It is to this latter question of composition that we turn next.

5.3 Changes in the composition of the HCC 1990–2020

The HCC, with five judges on its benches, began its work on 1 January 1990, four months before the first democratic elections were held and about six months before the first democratic Parliament was convened. The first five members of the Court were nominated partly by the Communist party and partly by the democratic opposition. In the summer of 1990, five more judges were elected by the new democratically elected Parliament, so that from then on, the Court sat with 9 or 10 judges. Originally, the last five judges should have been elected by the second Parliament after the democratic transformation process, but due to the lack of agreement about candidates, the missing members were never elected. Filling the empty chairs in the HCC caused serious problems later as well (the HCC was constantly on the verge of its quorum), as the double-nomination (a political deal about the election of one right-wing and one left-wing candidate) became the informal standard. Nevertheless, filling the vacant seats often took several months and sometimes directly jeopardized the functioning of the Court.

After the landslide victory of the Fidesz party in 2010, the Orbán government (supported by a two-thirds parliamentary majority) was able to abandon the practice of double-nomination and elected several new judges, backed exclusively by the right-wing majority. This reshuffling of the Court led to a thin majority of the judges nominated by the right-wing parties as early as the autumn of 2010 (four judges nominated by the left-wing parties, one by consensus and five judges nominated by the right-wing parties).

The introduction of the new Fundamental Law also affected the structure of the HCC: since 1 January 2012, the Court consists of 15 judges. With the election of the new judges, a clear right-wing majority dominated the Court (4 left-wing nominations, 1 consensus, and 10 right-wing judges), but the "old" judges, who were elected in pairs before 2010 (i.e. in a kind of compromise), were still in the majority (8 to 7). It was only after a new wave of judge elections in spring 2013 that new judges elected only by the post-2010 right-wing parliamentary majority formed the majority in the Court (8 to 7). It can be argued that this was a decisive point for the HCC: from 2010 to May 2013, the Court struggled with the constitutional majority of the Parliament in several ways, while after May 2013 deference (with several dissenting opinions) became the dominant pattern of behaviour of the Court's majority.

Finally, a notable change in the composition of the court occurred in November 2016, when four new judges were elected due to vacancies. As a result of losing two by-elections in 2015, Fidesz lost its supermajority in Parliament. This meant that the ruling party had to make a deal with the opposition to be able to elect new judges to the HCC. Thus, the four new judges were elected with the support of the small green opposition party (LMP, Politics Could be Different). Nevertheless, the majority of the court still consists of judges with a right-wing political background.

5.4 Strength and diversity of the HCC rulings

Turning to the strength of the rulings of the HCC on a yearly basis, the strong start is quite apparent (Figure 5.1). That is, understanding strength as the extent of the constraint the HCC aimed to level at the legislature, the opening strategy of the HCC becomes visible during the year shared by the outgoing Communist Parliament and its new, democratically elected successor. Certainly, if the HCC as a new organ in the separation of powers, wanted to establish its position *vis-à-vis* the legislature, irrespectively of the political composition of the latter, the message to be sent was exactly a series of decisions including declarations on substantive unconstitutionality and constitutional interpretations *in abstracto*. Without overrating the figures of the first year, it suffices to highlight that the record high level of strength in 1990 is the result of merely 13 rulings.

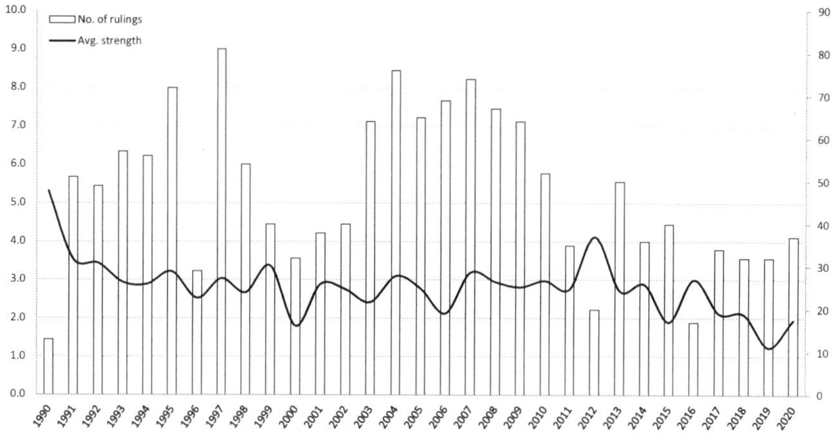

Figure 5.1 Number and average strength of rulings (1990–2020) (HCC)

After the first year of the HCC's existence, the strength of its rulings diminished somewhat and fluctuated at more moderate intervals. The average strength of the court's rulings has levelled off between 2.0 and 3.5 (compared to the maximum of 10), which in itself does not indicate a particularly stringent court. The performance of the HCC in this regard seems to be in accordance with the courts of other CEE countries (for a comparison, see Chapter 12). In average, during its 30 years of existence, the HCC took restraining steps against the decisions of the parliament in a bit more than 50% of all its rulings. It could be argued that in the first decade after the transition, the legislature, aware of the fact that the HCC tended to limit its scope of action, was in fact constrained by the separation of powers between the two institutions. Thus, it did not require particularly strict decisions by the HCC to keep Parliament within the limits that the Court had set for it in the early 1990s, since the former organ could anticipate the latter's potential decisions.

In the context of the mid-1990s, it is worth noting another year in which the Court became the focus of political debates. In 1995, the left-liberal government introduced a series of austerity measures, the so-called Bokros package, named after the finance minister, which restricted citizens' access to public health care. The HCC responded with a series of strong rulings, and it is equally significant that in that year the proportion of restraining rulings was the second highest (63.9%) in the entire three decades.

As it will be seen from the analysis of the dissenting opinions, from the late 1990s, the HCC started to become more polarized, not unrelated to the departure of László Sólyom, the Court's first President. As it was seen earlier, it is also the period when filling the banks of the court was mostly manageable by electing judges in pairs due to the lack of compromise between government and opposition. None of this, however, seems to have translated into a significant shift in the average strength of rulings, indicating that the Court has found its place within the polity, recognized by political and legislative actors as a potential arbiter even in political issues.

This chapter has already discussed how the institutional framework, competences, and composition of the HCC changed after 2010, when the government of Fidesz and Viktor Orbán, relying on its supermajority in Parliament, tried to prevent any counterweight that could hinder its political goals. Following conflicts over parliamentary jurisdiction to hold officials of the previous government accountable by introducing retroactive laws, the HCC was one of the first institutions affected by the changes. However, because the composition of the Court changed only gradually, the majority of its members decided, even in 2012, to make very restrictive decisions *vis-à-vis* the constitutional two-thirds majority that prevailed in Parliament. As shown in Figure 5.1, in 2012 the HCC averaged 4.13, its second strongest year since 1990. Even more revealing is that the number of rulings was relatively small (20) and that half of them established substantive unconstitutionality or adopted a restrictive form of constitutional interpretation *in abstracto*, indicating a serious dispute between the government and the HCC. Looking at the subject matter of the rulings in question, it is also clear that the HCC touched on the core issues of government. To name a few, the Court ruled on the provisional regulations of the new Fundamental Law, laws on labour strikes, ethnic minorities, local government authorities, and the personnel of the judicial system. It is worth noting that in the previous year, the Court had to deal with similarly important issues – media law, electoral law, regulation of churches – but the average strength of rulings for the year was significantly lower. The explanation for this difference is that the latter issues were dealt with in a series with many less-sensitive issues, where the Court's decisions were less-constraining. However, in the mid-2010s, changes in the institutional framework, the composition of the judiciary, and the political environment increasingly affected HCC. This is evident from the annual figures, which, with the exception of 2016, are below the overall average of the Court's three-decade performance.

The next step is to examine how the figures of average strength can be contextualized by the diversity of the rulings. As the methodology underlying this analysis suggests, there is more to constitutional adjudication than the constitutional/unconstitutional dichotomy, and courts can draw on a variety of measures and competences when reviewing acts of the legislature. In particular, the HCC has been vested with a highly diverse set of powers.

The diversity of available options is reflected in the three decades of the practice of the HCC (Figure 5.2). Compared to all other constitutional courts studied in the JUDICON-EU project, the HCC is the most diverse, with less than three-quarters of all decisions involving either rejection or substantive unconstitutionality. Beyond this dichotomous approach, the HCC developed a practice of constitutional adjudication that helped the Court secure an adaptive position within the Hungarian polity. Certainly, certain options were not chosen as frequently as others. Interestingly, only 2% of all rulings were

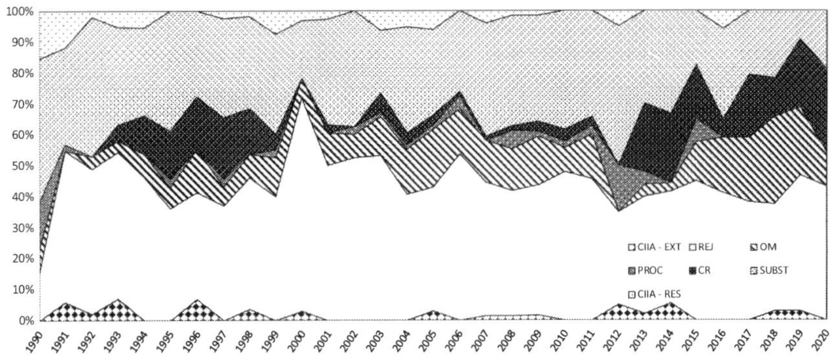

Figure 5.2 Frequency of the ruling types (HCC) (1990–2020)

declared as procedural unconstitutionality, this was not a preferred path for judges. Declarations of omission or constitutional requirement, on the other hand, were more common types of rulings that merit closer examination.

In the Hungarian context, declaring omission does not imply a particularly strong decision, since in these cases Parliament is not told how to remedy an unconstitutional situation, but the Court merely establishes the fact of unconstitutionality resulting from inadequate or missing legislation. That is, omissions do not usually imply any prescription, and if they do, it is limited to a non-binding prescription, without any sanction as to the time by which the omission should be remedied. Moreover, it is in some ways characteristic of the first era of the Court that omissions become more frequent after the presidency of László Sólyom.

Compared to omission, constitutional requirement is a stronger type of ruling where the Court becomes a mild or a rigorous positive legislator by giving guidance and directions for the legislators and the judiciary about what interpretations of a regulation under review are constitutional. In the Hungarian case, the constitutional requirement became an important instrument in two periods. Starting in 1994, the constitutional requirement became a frequently used tool of the Sólyom Court. While constitutional requirements almost disappeared after the Sólyom-era, a renaissance of this type of provision can be observed since 2013. Combined with the constant presence of omissions, the declaration of constitutional requirements means that 2013–2020 was the most diverse period of the HCC in terms of the type of provisions.

As for the most restrictive type of constitutional adjudication, the high ratio of constitutional interpretation in *abstracto* demonstrates the activism of the early Court on such important issues as privatization and land ownership. Although the HCC rarely used this highly restrictive instrument (only 2.8% of the Court's rulings are restrictive constitutional interpretations in *abstracto*), the HCC's activity is remarkable compared to other countries: more than 70%

of all restrictive constitutional interpretations in *abstracto* were found in the Hungarian case.

5.5 Dissenting opinions: from unity to polarization

Members of the HCC can formulate dissenting opinion if they do not agree with the majority opinion of the Court. Dissenting opinions might be issued by a single judge, or they can declare that they join to another judge's dissent. Disaggregating dissenting opinions into rulings the same way as decisions and link majority rulings to dissenting rulings allows one to have a more nuanced analysis of the practice of constitutional adjudication.

To begin with, while looking into majority decisions it was possible to ascertain some revealing general trends, an insightful periodization of the Court's practice during its 30 years of existence becomes possible through analysing dissenting opinions which exhibit a clear increasing trend (Figure 5.3). The number of rulings with at least one dissenting opinion is revealing: 1990–1998: 5.3 per year; 1999–2010: 15.1 per year; 2011–2020: 22.0 per year. The total number of dissenting opinions has also increased massively: while there was a total of 10 dissenting opinions per year on average during the Court's first eight years, this number increased to an average of 37 dissenting opinions per year between 1999 and 2010, and to an average of 62 per year between 2011 and 2020. The three periods designated by these numbers correspond to changes within the Court or its political environment; they are the first period under the Sólyom presidency; the second, which represents the "post-Sólyom era"; and a third, which begins immediately after Fidesz won a two-thirds parliamentary majority in 2010.

As mentioned, the HCC began its activity as a guarantor of democratic transition based on legal continuity. The potential need to review laws that

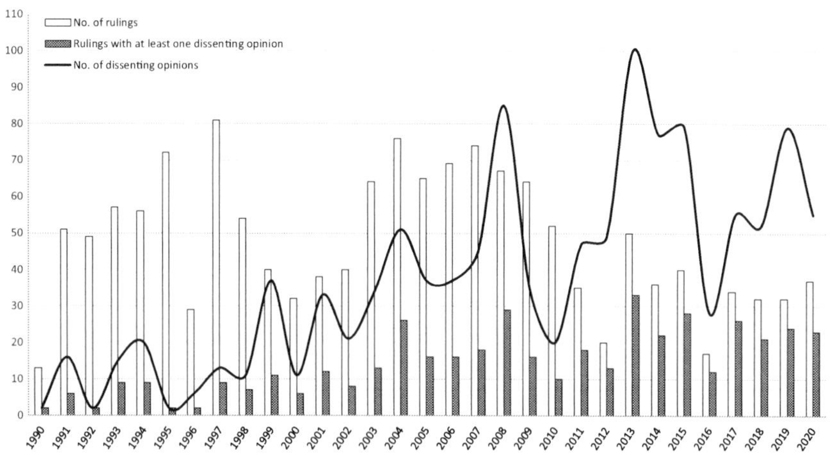

Figure 5.3 Number of rulings with at least one dissenting opinion (1990–2020) (HCC)

remained in force despite the fact that they were adopted by the Communist Parliament, as well as the newly established democratic institutional framework, placed the HCC in a position that was seen as, or expected to be, above polarized politics and institutional uncertainties. In this context, the low number of dissenting opinions during the first period might be explained as an attempt to follow an institutional strategy based on unified decision-making. In this period between 1990 and 1998 only 10% of the majority rulings were openly challenged by dissenting opinions. The combined trend of the average strength of majority rulings and the frequency of dissenting opinions is characteristic of the Sólyom court. During this period, the court was particularly strong in constraining the legislature by relying on the strongest possible type of rulings and exhibiting the lowest degree of internal polarization. Of course, all of this is true only in comparison to the further periods, and it would be an exaggeration to claim that the Court was solely responsible for the scope and content of legislation in the period immediately following the fall of Communism.

The differences become clear, however, when one turns to the later periods of the HCC. In the Court's second decade, an average of one-quarter of all rulings were supplemented by at least one dissenting opinion. This significant increase might be attributed to a general trend of consolidation: with the democratic polity established, it was natural that the HCC lost its role of guarantor, therefore, the institutional strategy that required unity became outdated. However, based on the data as well as the shifts in the political environment described earlier, polarization within the Court seems to be a more plausible explanation. Electing new judges became an openly politicized issue in parliamentary politics, where filling the empty seats to secure the necessary two-thirds majority, was often possible only in pairs when both the government and the opposition had their own preferred judge. Thus, the political leaning of the potential judges was no longer a problem since, instead of compromise, the parties "shared" the vacant seats. As a result, challenging the majority decisions of the HCC became more likely and a more reasonable outcome of the shifts regarding the nomination process (without any significant change of the formal procedure) taking place in a more polarized political environment. It should therefore come as little surprise that the share of rulings with at least one dissenting opinion peaked in 2008 (43.3%), when the political disputes that frequently affected decisions of the Court were at their most intense.

The third period, as indicated by the number of dissenting opinions, begins after the 2010 elections, when Fidesz won two-thirds of the seats in Parliament and thus had enough mandates to amend the constitution or laws for which supermajority is required. As Figure 5.3 shows, the proportion of rulings with at least one dissenting opinion increases sharply from the following year onward; on average, only one in three judgments is without a dissenting opinion. That is, despite the fact that the ruling party had the power to reshape the institutional framework, including the new Fundamental Law adopted in 2011, and to appoint the members of the Court without consulting or compromising with the opposition, the HCC become more polarized than ever before, while, with the exception of the particularly strong rulings in 2012, there has also been a steady decline in the strength of the rulings. Surprisingly, the increase in dissenting opinions continues after 2013, when, due to the gradual replacement of previously elected members of the Court with new judges appointed exclusively by government MPs, the latter group forms the majority in the HCC. For an explanation, one must turn to the individual level to see to what extent and how a member of the HCC voted with the majority or formulated a dissent proposing a different level of constraint toward the legislature.

We assume that individual judicial behaviour might be explained by the political leaning of the judges. With respect to the Hungarian case, trends in dissent become meaningful when they are attributed to the appointment and election of judges. That is, in this part of our analysis, we rely on a combination of the attitudinal model (Spaeth and Segal 1992; Segal and Spaeth 2002) and the external strategist model of judicial behaviour (Gillman and Clayton 1999) arguing that ideological attitudes, values, and political preferences determine the decisions of the members of the Court (Kantorowicz and Garoupa 2016). More precisely, due to the specificities of the institutional setting, as taking their election as a proxy, we turn to the appointment of the judges. The political affiliation of the members of the HCC cannot be ascertained as openly as in the case of the US Supreme Court, but it is more traceable than in the case of several constitutional courts where political parties have lesser role in the election of judges or where their political orientation is not disclosed. Given the limited and less explicit public information on the political orientation of judges, we relied on a cross-checked body of data set composed of parliamentary committee minutes, media sources, and expert interviews with HCC staff. As a result, five categories were formed: HCC members were classified as left-wing, left-wing consensual, consensual, right-wing consensual, and right-wing according to their appointment.

In our analysis, we consider the proportion of dissenting opinions relative to all of the Court's rulings. In other words, the proportion of dissenting opinions signed by an individual judge is measured against all rulings in which he or she participated. Since majority rulings can be linked to individual dissenting rulings in this way, it becomes possible to compare the strength of the majority ruling with the proposed strength contained in the dissent also disaggregated to the level of rulings. Using the two resulting indicators – the average frequency of dissenting opinions and the average relative strength of rulings – a detailed map of dissenting opinions can thus be constructed (Figure 5.4).

From a bird's-eye view, the figure shows that judges are found in the lower-left part of the map, suggesting that once they dissented, they wanted the HCC to be less restrictive toward the legislature than the majority decision. Thus, dissenting judges generally took a more moderate position, proposing less-severe rulings when they disagreed with the majority of the court.

As noted, the issue becomes particularly interesting after 2010, in the third period of the HCC, when the government had the sufficient majority in Parliament to overrule the Court, either by appointing more loyal judges or by

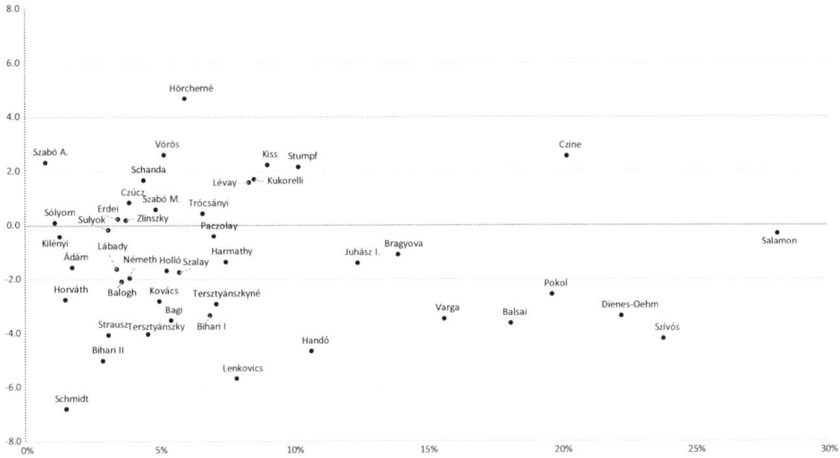

Figure 5.4 Relative strength and frequency of dissenting opinions (HCC)

changing the institutional framework or even by amending the constitutional provisions. Since July 2010, right-wing judges have held a majority on the court. Figures 5.3 and 5.4 show, however, that the differences of opinion, measured by dissenting opinions, within the HCC not only persist, but are actually increasing. The figures suggest that an additional explanation beyond the attitudinal model must be considered. Apart from the fact that right-leaning judges were in the majority on the Court, there appears to be another split with significant results. As far as constraining the legislature is concerned, there appears to be a difference between the behaviour of the old and the new judges. Among the old judges, who were appointed before 2010 and nominated by either the left or the right, some institutional socialization seems to be taking place (Pócza, Dobos, and Gyulai 2019b). That is, the old members of the HCC (even if they were nominated by right-wing parties) seem to behave more restrictively than most new judges, whose post-2010 right-wing political affiliation seems to be more determinative.

It is also worth noting that, in terms of dissent, the HCC has not become more unified since 2016, when no pre-2010 appointed judge remained on the Court. It seems to be a continuing trend that there is a group of judges who express their dissent quite frequently and consistently to argue for less constraint toward the legislature. Moreover, it should be added that there is a group of judges who were elected in 2016 when Fidesz, which temporarily lost its two-thirds majority in Parliament, compromised with a minor opposition party to elect new members to the HCC.

This is where looking at the coalitions of dissenting judges becomes insightful. Trends in dissenting opinions, combined with the political affiliation of the judges, allows one to map the networks among members of the HCC, revealing groups and coalitions either lasting or temporary. Figure 5.5 shows

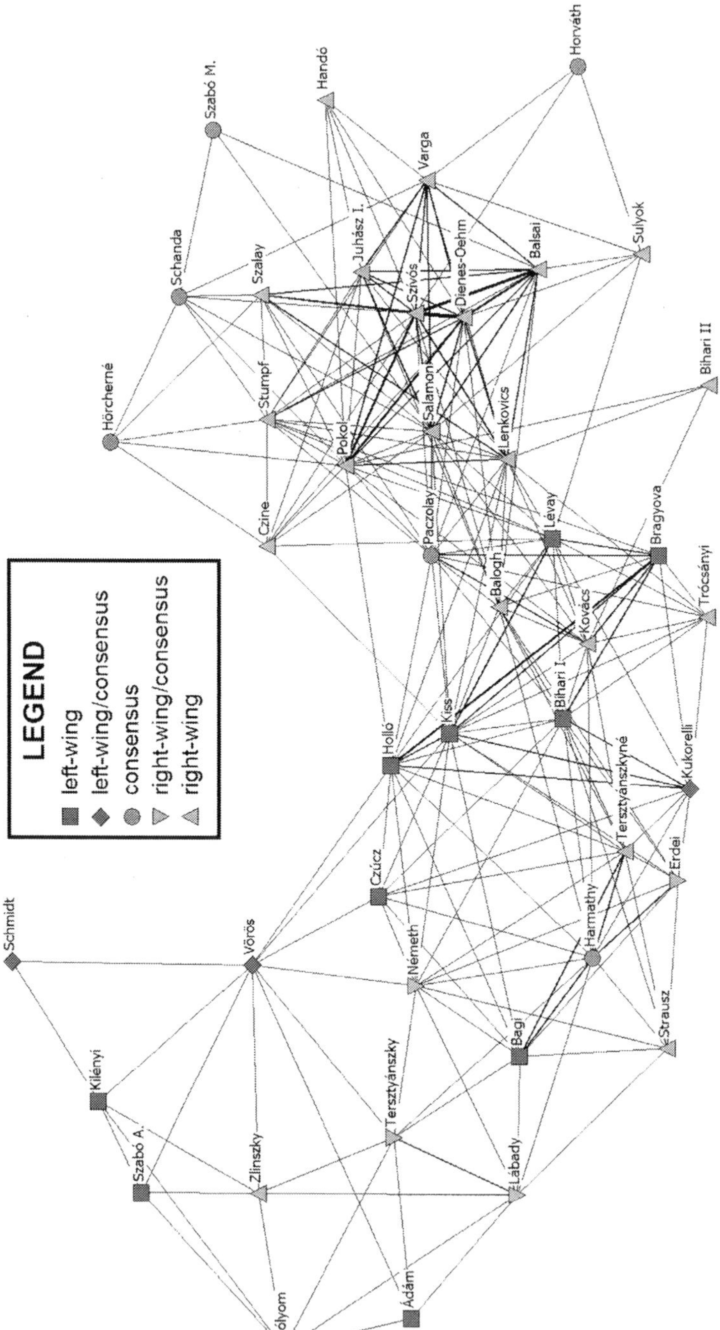

Figure 5.5 Dissenting coalitions 1990–2020 (HCC)

all members of the HCC with at least one dissenting opinion. The low interactions at the left pole between the judges from the first period of the HCC can be explained by the relatively small number of dissenting opinions under the Sólyom presidency.

At the right pole of the network map, there seems to be a core group that formulates a coherent network (Balsai, Szívós, Dienes-Ohm, Pokol), to which Lenkovics (appointed before 2010) and Varga joined. Around this core group of old and new right-wing judges, there is a circle of judges with similar political affiliation (Czine and Stumpf), but they sometimes form coalitions with left-wing judges. Those elected as a result of the 2016 compromise (Hörcherné, Szabó M., Horváth, Schanda) are more loosely connected to the core.

The judges elected between 1999 and 2010 are between these two poles. Four judges nominated by the left-wing parties (Holló, Lévay, Kiss, and Bragyova) seem to form a very strong and very cohesive group. They published dissenting opinions quite frequently and often joined each other. Based on the dataset, we can also say that this core group was formed long before 2010, which means that party affiliation played a crucial role in their case before they strengthened their cooperation after 2010 to resist pressure from outside (constitutional majority in Parliament and the government) and inside (new judges elected by the right-wing majority). Justices Bihari and Kukorelli also joined this core group several times (although they have somewhat looser ties to this inner circle).

5.6 Policy areas in constitutional adjudication

The previous sections have shown how the HCC can issue more or less restrictive rulings on legislation and how the strength and diversity of the rulings is related to the composition of the Court or the frequency of dissenting opinions. However, we know less about the substantive content of the cases under review. What policies dominate the Court's decision-making practice? What kinds of laws most often end up before the Court? To what extent is the strength of the rulings related to the policy area of the case under review?

In this part, we turn to a less-studied question of HCC activity by focusing on the relationship between the policy agendas of the Parliament and the HCC. While the performance of Kelsenian constitutional courts within the political system has become a popular research topic over the past two decades, we know little about their propensity for "judicial activism" in various policy areas. In contrast, scholars studying the US Supreme Court have written extensively not only about the court's precise function within the separation of powers system, but also about its agenda-setting practices in the policy-making process. (e.g. Black and Owens 2009; Lane and Black 2017).

By linking the policy agenda of the HCC and legislative majorities, we can assess the relationship between policies and trends in the strength of rulings. That is, analysing the agendas in light of the evidence obtained from examining the investigation of rulings reveals differences in the Court's adjudication depending on the various policy areas with which the Court is concerned. For example, one might ask whether the HCC reviewed macroeconomic legislation of the left-wing and right-wing majorities with the same intensity, or whether the Court has more frequently reviewed laws affecting government operations after the institutional changes of 1989–1990 and 2010–2012.

Surely, Kelsenian constitutional courts might have some room for manoeuvre to refuse discussing cases on their merit: judges can postpone cases and deal with them only months or even years later (if there is no legal prescription for deadlines), they might review laws which have not been challenged by the petitioners (by referring to direct connections between legal issues), they might even "share" the case with transnational courts (like several European courts do by the preliminary reference procedure of the European Court of Justice) and get rid of the burden of decision. Nevertheless, the default position of the Kelsenian constitutional courts is that they must decide the cases submitted by petitioners, and they cannot cherry-pick among them. Thus, the policy profile of these courts is mainly determined by external actors. In this respect, the courts' docket control and its agenda-setting ability are certainly limited. Even if we can have a general assessment on the policy area discussed by the Kelsenian courts, we have to admit that this profile will tell us more about the external political context and less about the court itself. Recognizing these limitations does not mean, however, that we cannot make a policy profile for the courts with different procedural rules as those of the US Supreme Court.

5.6.1 *Identification of policy fields in HCC's decisions*

In order to assess the policy agenda of the HCC, we use the research framework and outputs of the Comparative Agendas Project (CAP), which categorizes legislative acts according to 21 policy fields.[1] To be able to utilize the results of the CAP, we need to identify the specific legislative acts that are affected by the Court's decisions, which lets us connect the rulings of the HCC to policy fields. With this method, we can measure and analyze which policy issues implicated stronger or weaker decisions of Hungarian Constitutional Court. By doing this, we will be able to map the courts' impact on certain policy areas.

A ruling by the Court does not necessarily refer to a whole law but to one (or more) of its particular part (e.g. paragraph). That means that it is not necessarily the original law that is subjected to constitutional adjudication but its amendment possibly by a different law. This modifying or amending legislative activity is the one that needs to be paired to a specific court ruling. In the Hungarian practice, it occurs frequently that the part of a law under review was amended by several later pieces of legislation. In these cases, they need to

1 For the CAP project see: www.cap.tk.hu/.

be considered one by one. Obviously, the last version of a law that was never amended is its originally adopted variant. Thus, the database of the related laws could be paired to CAP's "Laws (1790–2018) dataset", which applies a major and a subtopic code to each item that were integrated into the list of the disaggregated decisions by the court.[2]

From all this it follows that laws and constitutional court decisions do not necessarily overlap, as a ruling might concern several laws and a law might be reviewed by several HCC rulings. Thus, in this case, the basic unit of observation is not the ruling but a pair of a single ruling and a single law, a ruling-law connection (RLC).

It is important to note that this method of identifying policy fields necessarily excludes some rulings from the analysis. First, some rulings of the court cannot be connected to concrete legislative acts: omissions (i.e. the absence of a legislative act), constitutional interpretations *in abstracto*, or even some non-specific constitutional requirements. Second, due to the legal continuity during the democratic transition of Hungary, the early decisions of the HCC concern the legislative acts of the Communist regime, so they cannot be connected to any policy agendas of the democratic regime. Excluding these two ruling types, we have to deal with 1,015 majority rulings (out of the 1,476) of the HCC that can be connected to specific legislative acts, which results in 1,247 ruling-law connections (RLCs).

5.6.2 *Policy agenda of the HCC*

Given that the constitutional court's extraordinary power is originated (beyond its wide competences) in the institution of *actio popularis* (i.e. in the legal regulation that anybody without any personal involvement in the law to be reviewed is entitled to submit a petition to the court), we can rightly argue that all important issues have been discussed by the HCC sooner or later. There was no preselection bias as far as the court's docket is concerned – at least until 2012, when the institution of *actio popularis* was abolished by the new Fundamental Law of Hungary (Gárdos-Orosz 2012). Consequently, until 2012 the HCC served as a potential access point to all citizens eager to set the agenda of the HCC and, by this, influencing the Hungarian policy-making process. In this respect, we can argue that the cases brought before the court and decided by it on its merit, reflect more or less the policy preferences of the citizens – at least until 2012.

2 It should be added, however, that as *a priori* review is one of the competences of the Hungarian Constitutional Court some rulings missed laws to determine major and subtopic codes therefore these cases – concerning laws adopted by the parliament but not yet promulgated – were coded separately but also according to the CAP codebook. The authors are grateful to Csaba Molnár, member of the Hungarian CAP who coded these cases.

Keeping in mind this highly responsive character of the HCC, we are interested in the policy agenda of the HCC as compared to the agenda of the Hungarian Parliament, exploring the differences or similarities between the two institutions' agenda as far as their policy profiles are concerned. Theoretically, two different assumptions can be drawn from the citizens/parliament/constitutional court relations. On one hand, we could assume that courts might function as an extra access point for citizens who are discontent with the *inactivity* of the parliament and use another political institution to influence indirectly the agenda of the legislature. In this case, the policy agenda of the HCC and the Hungarian Parliament differ significantly due to the citizens' discontent with the inactivity of the representative body. On the other hand, we could also assume that citizens are following and reacting to the policy agenda of the Parliament, thus petitions submitted to the HCC will reflect the agenda of the Parliament. Since citizens concern and react to the legislative activity, the HCC serves as a further access point for citizens discontent with the *activity* of the Parliament. In this case, the policy agenda of the HCC will be more or less in line with that of the representative body.

As a first step of our analysis, we disclose the distribution of RLCs according to their policy fields. Figure 5.6 shows the distribution of policy fields in the legislation's agenda and in the HCC's agenda. There is a clear deviation from the uniform distribution of cases concerning both institutions' activity, but the HCC's RLCs deviated more radically from the uniform distribution

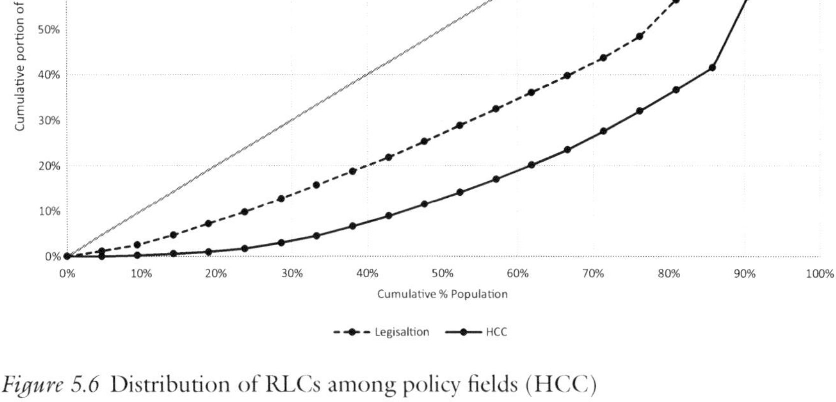

Figure 5.6 Distribution of RLCs among policy fields (HCC)

than the laws adopted by the Hungarian legislature. The Gini coefficient[3] is lower for the legislature's activity (0.35) than for the HCC (0.59) between the time period 1990 and 2020.

This means that the policy fields are not distributed equally in the legislation's agenda, but the inequality in the HCC's agenda is even higher. The Lorenz curve of the HCC suggests that there are three policy fields (out of the 21 policy areas) that consists of almost 60% of all RLCs.

Table 5.1 shows the distribution of RLCs among policy fields by electoral cycles.[4] Based on this data, the three top policy fields that are dominant in both the legislature's and HCC's agenda are *law and crime*, *macroeconomics*, and *government operations*.

The most surprising result is that the HCC reviewed a disproportionately high number of law- and crime-related laws in the 1998–2002 electoral cycle (49% of the examined laws were connected to this policy field). Based on the data, certain cyclical pattern of issue attention by the HCC can be detected, partly depending on whether left-wing or right-wing majorities adopted the legal regulation on this policy field. For example, the first Orbán government's (1998–2002) Criminal Procedural Code from 2000 became a central topic for the HCC even several years after its adoption, but laws of the second Orbán government (2010–2014) on this policy area shifted also into the focal point of the HCC's attention. Nevertheless, it is interesting that neither the new Criminal Code (Act C of 2012) nor the new Civil Code (Act V of 2013) adopted by the right-wing majority got much attention. Although both codes were heavily amended after 1990, they were originally adopted in the Communist era, thus experts agreed that adoption of a new Criminal Code and Civil Code was more or less a necessity. Perhaps this might also explain why these two significant codes have not been reviewed frequently by the HCC.

It is also striking that RLCs concerning macroeconomics of the right-wing government after 2010 almost disappeared from the cases, which means that the HCC reviewed only a handful of laws on the heavily debated, unorthodox economic measures of the Orbán government after 2010. This sudden drop in the number of RLCs concerning laws on macroeconomics is even more striking because macroeconomic was one of the most dominant topics of the HCC's agenda between 1990 and 2010. It seems to be logical that transformation from planned economics to capitalism required massive legislative activity, which has been several times challenged by citizens before the HCC. Table 5.1 shows, however, that macroeconomic laws of the right-wing governments (1998–2002 and cabinets since 2010) has been a significantly lower

3 The Gini coefficient is the ratio of the area that lies between the line of equal distribution and the Lorenz curve (see Figure 5.6.). A Gini coefficient of zero expresses perfect equality, while a Gini coefficient of 1 expresses maximal inequality among policy fields.

4 In our analysis, the RLCs are connected to electoral cycles according to the adoption of the law even if the court's decision was made under a following electoral cycle.

Table 5.1 Distribution of RLCs by electoral cycles (HCC)

Policy field	*Legislation (%)*	*HCC (%)*	*HCC (% by electoral cycles)*							
			1990–1994	*1994–1998*	*1998–2002*	*2002–2006*	*2006–2010*	*2010–2014*	*2014–2018*	*2018–2020*
Macroeconomics	**11%**	**16%**	16%	24%	11%	21%	23%	3%	8%	8%
Civil rights	**3%**	**5%**	9%	4%	2%	3%	3%	9%	0%	0%
Health	**3%**	**4%**	1%	6%	4%	7%	7%	2%	1%	4%
Agriculture	**4%**	**2%**	3%	1%	1%	2%	1%	4%	0%	19%
Labor	**4%**	**3%**	4%	2%	6%	3%	5%	2%	0%	4%
Education	**4%**	**2%**	2%	1%	0%	4%	7%	2%	1%	0%
Environment	**3%**	**2%**	0%	3%	2%	3%	2%	1%	1%	0%
Energy	**3%**	**0%**	0%	0%	1%	1%	0%	1%	0%	0%
Immigration	**1%**	**0%**	0%	0%	0%	0%	0%	0%	1%	8%
Transportation	**5%**	**1%**	0%	0%	0%	3%	3%	0%	0%	0%
Law and crime	**10%**	**22%**	15%	15%	49%	26%	12%	27%	16%	19%
Social welfare	**4%**	**4%**	2%	9%	2%	4%	1%	3%	10%	0%
Housing	**2%**	**3%**	5%	3%	2%	1%	0%	2%	8%	4%
Domestic commerce	**9%**	**5%**	0%	1%	5%	2%	5%	11%	17%	0%
Defence	**4%**	**3%**	2%	5%	4%	4%	3%	4%	0%	0%
Technology	**3%**	**3%**	1%	5%	0%	2%	1%	7%	0%	0%
Foreign trade	**3%**	**0%**	0%	0%	0%	0%	0%	0%	0%	0%
International affairs	**8%**	**1%**	1%	1%	0%	4%	2%	1%	0%	0%
Government operations	**13%**	**21%**	34%	18%	9%	7%	25%	21%	23%	31%
Public lands	**3%**	**3%**	3%	1%	2%	1%	1%	0%	15%	4%
Culture	**1%**	**0%**	0%	0%	0%	0%	0%	2%	0%	0%
Sum	**100%**	**100%**	**100%**	**100%**	**100%**	**100%**	**100%**	**100%**	**100%**	**100%**
N	**4,759**	**1,247**	**232**	**278**	**162**	**137**	**132**	**187**	**93**	**26**

share of the policy agenda of the HCC than those of the left-wing cabinets. One of the main policy areas which almost completely disappeared from the adjudicational practice of the HCC after 2010 was macroeconomics, which is all the more astonishing because the unorthodox economic policies of the second and third Orbán governments after 2010 have been heavily criticized by experts and economists. This radical transformation of the policy profile might be a consequence of at least three factors. By abolishing the unrestricted access to the court (*actio popularis*) in 2012, the number of potential applicants has been seriously limited, which might have functioned as a natural filter and led to a situation where crucial policy issues did not end up at the Court. Second, the shift in the dominant motion types from abstract review to individual constitutional complaints might also have an explanative power since the bulk of the cases after 2012 became reviews of ordinary courts' decisions (with less specific policy issues). Third, the transformation of the HCC from 2010 on which led to a Court almost exclusively packed with right-wing judges can also explain the changes.

It is less surprising that the first electoral cycle's laws (1990–1994) concerning the government operations dominated the policy agenda of both Parliament and HCC since the most fundamental issues of the democratic transition were related to the questions of how the government should work in a new democracy. The structural reforms of the left-wing Gyurcsány cabinet on government operation in 2006 and the reshuffle of the whole polity after 2010 are also reflected in the shift of the HCC's policy agenda, as Table 5.1 shows. Although the Parliament's activity on this policy field has not been increased after 2006, it concerned essential and politically highly salient issues. This saliency is reflected in the increasing attention of the HCC to the laws on government operation adopted in the electoral cycles from 2006 on.

As far as the laws of the 2014–2018 and 2018–2020 electoral cycles are concerned, we have to be careful with our conclusions, since the number of cases is significantly lower than in any other group of RLCs. One reason for this might be that these acts are the most recent laws, while another one reflects the institutional changes: once again the abolishment of the *actio popularis* and the shift in the main activity of the HCC from the abstract to the concrete norm control might played an important role in the decreasing number of RLCs of this time period.

If we compare the activity of the Hungarian Parliament with that of the HCC from the perspective of the policy agenda, the general picture is rather mixed. As the Lorenz curve showed, the distribution of policy fields is more uniform in the case of the Hungarian Parliament, but it is also evident that the main policy areas of the HCC's activity overlap with those of Parliament (law and crime, government operations, macroeconomics). There is a difference in proportion and accent although, as the three topics covered 59% of all cases of the HCC but only 34% of the Parliament. This means that the HCC rather followed the policy agenda of the Hungarian Parliament and focused on similar policy areas with slightly different accents. Consequently, we can argue

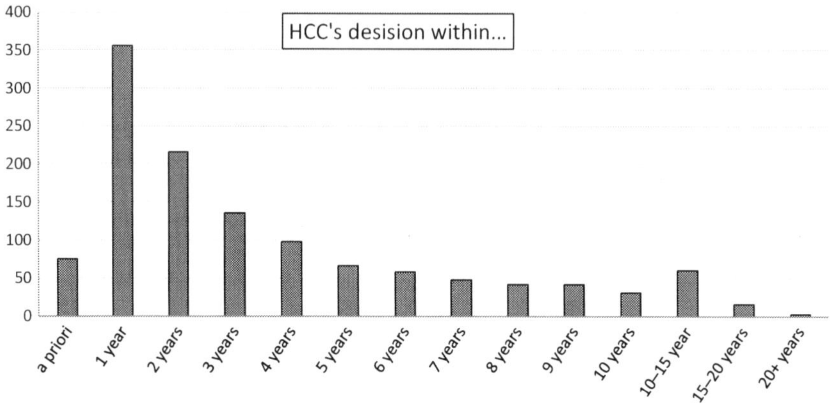

Figure 5.7 Time-leg between the promulgation of the law and the decision of the HCC

that citizens were more or less content with the policy agenda of the Parliament and have not used the HCC as an extra access point to fill some gaps in the policy agenda of the representative body. Citizens and, consequently, the HCC rather focused on the top three policy areas of the Parliament, which means that citizens were rather discontent with recent regulatory activities of the Parliament (and not with its inactivity).

Connecting the majority rulings of the HCC with adopted laws of the Parliament also highlights the asynchrony between the two institutions, due to the HCC's decision-making practice.[5] As Figure 5.7 shows, it is not unusual that the HCC decides on a case years after the law was adopted by the Parliament. The HCC decided more than one year after the adoption of the law in ca. two-thirds of the cases, and more than two years after the adoption of the law in ca. half of the cases. On average, it took 3.5 years for the HCC to take a decision on a law, which might have been caused by late-coming petitions as well as by the postponed decision-making of the HCC. This means that several times the time-leg between the parliamentary activity and the HCC's decision on the law was quite big, i.e. the asynchrony is significant.

5.6.3 *The political leaning of the court in case of the dominant policy fields*

While the analysis of the (somewhat diverging) policy agendas of the Court and the legislature showed that constitutional adjudication and party politics are to some extent and in an indirect way interrelated, this section goes one step

5 Although this asynchrony could be avoided by analysing the activities of both institutions in the same moment or time period, this would distort the picture, since both institutions might consider different laws (even from different electoral cycles) belonging to the same policy areas.

further and examines whether there are specific policy fields in which the political affiliation of the Court's majority have a crucial role in the judicial decision-making process. To answer this question, we apply the slightly modified version of the attitudinal model of judicial behaviour to the Hungarian case and combine it with the data of the policy agenda analysis.

According to the attitudinal model of judicial behaviour, judges will seek to include their policy preferences into their decisions (which is in line with the majority of the court) or, if they disagree with the majority, into their dissenting opinions. Although the original version of this attitudinal model was elaborated in American political science to analyze US Supreme Court justices (Segal and Spaeth 2002), a slightly modified version cross-fertilized with the external strategist model of judicial behaviour has already been applied to European constitutional courts as well (Kantorowicz and Garoupa 2016). Since we are able to determine the political affiliation of the Hungarian judges (i.e. we can disclose which parties nominated them), we can identify the "political" majority of the court in any given moment. Furthermore, we can clearly identify the parliamentary majority which adopted a law. Thus, combining the political affiliation of the court and the "affiliation" of laws under review, we can examine whether judges took into consideration their own political affiliation during the decision-making process.

Here we simply assume that there will be a pattern in the decisions of the HCC on the dominant policy fields: the Court's right-wing majority will take weaker decisions on laws adopted by right-wing parliamentary majorities and stronger decisions on laws adopted by left-wing parliamentary majorities, while the court's left-wing majority will take weaker decisions on laws adopted by left-wing parliamentary majorities and stronger decisions on laws adopted by right-wing parliamentary majorities.

Table 5.2 shows that our expectancy on political leaning has been mostly disproved by the data. It is astonishing that left-wing court majorities

Table 5.2 Modified attitudinal model of judicial behaviour by dominant policy fields (HCC)

		Right-wing majority (HCC)	*Left-wing majority (HCC)*	*No majority (HCC)*
Right-wing cabinet	Macroeconomics	1.88	2.50	3.08
	Law and crime	2.60	3.16	2.66
	Government operations	2.06	2.31	2.33
Left-wing cabinet	Macroeconomics	1.75	3.83	3.79
	Law and crime	2.25	3.27	4.20
	Government operations	4.05	2.44	2.55
Difference (RW-LW)	Macroeconomics	0.13	−1.33	
	Law and crime	0.35	−0.10	
	Government operations	−1.99*	−0.14	

constrained the *macroeconomic* policies of the left-wing cabinets (3.83) more heavily than right-wing cabinets' economic policies (2.50), and clearly more than right-wing Court majority in any cabinets. This result of judicial activism of the left-wing judges on the macroeconomic policy field also disapproves our assumption and shows that left-wing judges played a crucial role in obstructing the implementation of the economic policies of left-wing cabinets. Consequently, the modified version of the attitudinal model does not fit left-wing judges when it comes to macroeconomic issues. Furthermore, right-wing court majorities showed a completely different face of the Court on the same policy field: majorities dominated by right-wing judges were absolutely reserved if it came to economic issues and constrained very slightly any cabinets (1.88 and 1.75). This clear and consistent divergence between right-wing and left-wing majorities of the Court indicates that in macroeconomic issues, the political affiliation of the judges did not play a crucial role in their considerations and decisions.

This is, however, certainly not true when it comes to issues on *government operations*. Here, we have a different finding in so far as right-wing majorities of the HCC seemed to be sensitive to their political affiliations and constrained more the left-wing cabinets in this policy field than right-wing cabinets. Since left-wing court majorities' performance was more or less consistent in this policy field (2.31 and 2.44), and, furthermore, since we cannot detect huge differences in their rulings' strength depending on which cabinets' *law and crime* policies have been reviewed either, we can conclude that it was rather *exceptional* (but not unprecedented) that court majorities took their political affiliations into consideration.

5.7 Conclusions

The Hungarian Constitutional Court was established early during the democratic transition and began its work as a particularly strong institution within the system of separation of powers. The Court's judges were able to draw on broad competencies, but the role of the constitutional adjudication in Hungary cannot be explained solely in terms of formal powers and position within the institutional framework. Focusing on the relationship between the Court and the legislature through the strength of the HCC's rulings (and their relationship to dissenting opinions or policies) sheds light on the dynamic interaction that substantiates the formal framework. Of course, it is also important to see that the HCC was subject to changes in the political environment, which eventually affected the position of the institution within the polity.

As for the role of the HCC, there are two trends, two major changes to note in our analysis. The first concerns the changes in the constitutional status and the competences of the court. As discussed, while the Court's powers remained broad, the post-2010 restrictions resulted in a different institution. To be sure, the HCC is no longer the same counterweight to the legislature that it was in the 1990s. As it was seen, it may either exercise limited constitutional adjudication or engage in a shift in function that is more relevant to the judicial system than to the polity as a whole. Such a shift, however, cannot be attributed solely to a change in formal rules, competences, or even the replacement of the Constitution with the Fundamental Law.

The political environment also had a significant impact on the Court. As our analysis has shown, this began, at least in part, before 2010. First, the HCC gradually lost its image as a nonpartisan institution that could rise above highly politicized institutions such as the Parliament due of its position as a non-political arbitration body. Of course, the Court's members have always been appointed by the parties. Since the late 1990s, however, political actors have become accustomed to the existence of such an institution, and, paradoxically, they have contributed to the polarization of the Court precisely through a series of compromises with which they have chosen the new judges, more specifically through the way the seats seem to be divided among the parties. In addition, Fidesz has been able to appoint judges almost continuously since 2010 without compromising with the opposition, thus contributing to the politicization of the Court on another level. The result has been a decline in the ruling strength but, more tellingly, a surge in dissenting opinions.

Overall, constitutional adjudication has undergone a fundamental transformation. From an institution that was supposed to check parliamentary sovereignty, it has transformed into a politicized and polarized, but at the same time much less powerful, institution whose functioning depends directly on the political environment. Whatever conceptual framework one uses to compare the performance of the post-transition Hungarian polity with the trends from 2010 onward – populism, democratic backsliding, hybridization, autocratization, etc. – it is certain that the Hungarian Constitutional Court is engaged in a very different practice of constitutional adjudication, which is more dependent on direct political influences than in the early 1990s.

References

Black, Ryan C., and Ryan J. Owens. 2009. "Agenda Setting in the Supreme Court: The Collision of Policy and Jurisprudence." *Journal of Politics* 71 (3): 1062–1075.

Bragyova, András. 2010. "Az alkotmánybíráskodás jövője." *Fundamentum* 14 (1): 59–74.

Chronowski, Nóra. 2014. "Az alkotmánybíráskodás sarkalatos átalakítása." *MTA Law Working Papers*, 2014/08, Budapest: Hungarian Academy of Sciences.

———. 2021. "The Post-2010 'Democratic Rule of Law' Practice of the Hungarian Constitutional Court under a Rule by Law Governance (in: Hungarian Journal of Legal StudiesOnline First)." *Hungarian Journal of Legal Studies* 61 (2): 136–158.

———, and Márton Varju. 2016. "Two Eras of Hungarian Constitutionalism: From the Rule of Law to Rule by Law." *Hague Journal on the Rule of Law* 8 (2): 271–89.

Dixon, Rosalind, and David Landau. 2019. "1989–2019: From Democratic to Abusive Constitutional Borrowing." *International Journal of Constitutional Law* 17 (2): 489–96.

Gárdos-Orosz, Fruzsina. 2012. "The Hungarian Constitutional Court in Transition: From Action Popularis to Constitutional Complaint." *Acta Juridica* 53 (4): 302–315.

———. 2016. "Alkotmánybíróság 2010–2015." In *A magyar jogrendszer állapota*, edited by Jakab András and Gajduschek György, 442–479. Budapest: MTA Társadalomtudományi Kutatóközpont.

———, and Zakariás Kinga, eds. 2022. *The Main Lines of the Jurisprudence of the Hungarian Constitutional Court: 30 Case Studies from the 30 Years of the Constitutional Court (1990–2020)*. Baden-Baden: Nomos.

Gillman, Howard, and Clayton, Cornell W. 1999. "Beyond Judicial Attitudes: Institutional Approaches to Supreme Court Decision-Making." In *Supreme Court Decision-Making. New Institutionalist Approaches*, edited by Cornell W. Clayton and Howard Gillman, 1–12. Chicago: Chicago University Press.

Halmai, Gábor. 2018. "A Coup against Constitutional Democracy: The Case of Hungary." In *Constitutional Democracy in Crisis?*, edited by Mark A. Graber, Sanford Levinson, and Mark Tushnet. Oxford and New York: Oxford University Press.

———. 2019. "Dismantling Constitutional Review in Hungary." *Rivista di Diritti Comparati* 1: 31–47.

Jakab, András, and Fröhlich Johanna. 2017. "The Constitutional Court of Hungary." In *Comparative Constitutional Reasoning*, edited by Jakab András, Dyevre Arthur, and Itzcovich Giulio, 394–437. Cambridge: Cambridge University Press.

Kantorowicz, Jaroslaw, and Nuno Garoupa. 2016. "An Empirical Analysis of Constitutional Review Voting in the Polish Constitutional Tribunal 2003–2014." *Constitutional Political Economy* 27: 66–92.

Körösényi, András, Tóth, Csaba, and Török, Gábor. 2009. *The Hungarian Political System*. Budapest: Hungarian Center for Democracy Studies Foundation.

Lánczos, Petra. 2019. "Passivist Strategies Available to the Hungarian Constitutional Court." *Zeitschrift für ausländisches öffentliches Recht und Völkerrecht* 79 (3): 971–93.

Lane, Elizabeth A., and Ryan C. Black. 2017. "Agenda Setting and Case Selection on the U.S. Supreme Court." *Oxford Research Encyclopedia of Politics*, December 19. Accessed June 28, 2023. https://oxfordre.com/politics/view/10.1093/acrefore/9780190228637.001.0001/acrefore-9780190228637-e-91.

Luchterhandt, Otto, Starck Christian, and Weber Albrecht, eds. 2007. *Verfassungsgerichtsbarkeit in Mittel- und Osteuropa*. Baden-Baden: Nomos Verlag.

Paczolay, Péter. 2010. "Nekünk az a feladatunk, hogy az alapjogok pártját fogjuk, és ne a társadalomirányítás általános szempontjait vegyük figyelembe." *Fundamentum* 14 (1): 41–50.

Pócza, Kálmán. 2019. "Is a Revival Possible? Theoretical Reflections on the Historical Constitution." In *A History of the Hungarian Constitution. Law, Government and Political Culture in Central Europe*, edited by Hörcher Ferenc and Lorman Thomas, 211–236. New York: Bloomsbury Publishing.

———, Gábor Dobos, and Attila Gyulai. 2019a. "The Hungarian Constitutional Court: A constructive partner in constitutional dialogue." In *Constitutional Politics and the Judiciary: Decision-making in Central and Eastern Europe*, edited by Pócza Kálmán, 96–126. New York: Routledge.

———, Gábor Dobos, and Attila Gyulai. 2019b. "Dissenting Coalitions at the Hungarian Constitutional Court 1990–2018." In *The Role of Courts in Contemporary Legal Orders*, edited by Belov Martin, 359–370. The Hague: Eleven International Publishing.

Pozsár-Szentmiklósy, Zoltán. 2020. "The Hungarian Constitutional Court as a Lawmaker: Various Tools and Changing Roles." In *Judicial Law-Making in European Constitutional Courts*, edited by Florczak-Wątor, Monika. New York: Routledge.

Sadurski, Wojciech, ed. 2002. *Constitutional Justice East and West.* The Hague and London: Kluwer Law International.

———, ed. [2008] 2014. *Rights Before Courts. A Study of Constitutional Courts in Postcommunist States of Central and Eastern Europe.* Dordrecht and New York: Springer.

Scheppele, Kim L. 2012a. "How to Evade the Constitution: The Hungarian Constitutional Court's Decision on Judicial Retirement Age, Part I-II." *Verfassungsblog* (blog). https://verfassungsblog.de/evade-constitution-case-hungarian-constitutional-courts-decision-judicial-retirement-age/.

———. 2012b. "The New Judicial Deference." *Boston University Law Review* 92 (82): 89–190.

———. 2018. "Autocratic Legalism." *University of Chicago Law Review* 85 (2). https://chicagounbound.uchicago.edu/uclrev/vol85/iss2/2.

Segal, Jeffrey A., and Spaeth Harold J. 2002. *The Supreme Court and the Attitudinal Model Revisited.* Cambridge: Cambridge University Press.

Spaeth, Harold J., and J. Segal. 1992. *The Supreme Court and the Attitudinal Model.* Cambridge: Cambridge University Press.

Szente, Zoltán. 2016. "The Political Orientation of the Members of the Hungarian Constitutional Court between 2010 and 2014." *Constitutional Studies* 1 (1): 123–49.

Tőkés, Rudolf. 1996. *Hungary's Negotiated Revolution.* Cambridge: Cambridge University Press.

Tóth, Gábor A. 2019. "Constitutional Markers of Authoritarianism." *Hague Journal on the Rule of Law* 11 (1): 37–61.

Uitz, Renáta. 2015. "Can You Tell When an Illiberal Democracy is in the Making? An Appeal to Comparative Constitutional Scholarship from Hungary." *International Journal of Constitutional Law* 13 (1): 279–300.

6 The Latvian Constitutional Court

Dialogue and cooperation among constitutional bodies

Anita Rodiņa and Dita Plepa

6.1 Introduction

Judicial review, the power of courts to control the constitutionality of laws, plays an important role in most European countries (De Visser 2014, 55). It is widely held that constitutional supremacy, constitutional rights, and judicial review are fundamental elements of modern constitutional states (Weinrib 2016, 148). In Latvia, as in most EU countries (Komarek 2013, 423), constitutional review is centralized, and the Latvian Constitutional Court (hereinafter: LaCC or the Court) is entrusted by the constitution with reviewing legislative acts for their constitutionality.

The aim of this chapter is to characterize the relationship between the LaCC and the Latvian Parliament (hereinafter: *Saeima*) by analysing the decisions of the Court according to the methodology of the JUDICON-EU project. The analysis suggests that the average strength of rulings is not characterized by stability, but rather by frequent ups and downs. The data also reflect that the Court has had to rule on politically contested issues since 2015, which has led to some polarization on the benches of the Court. Nonetheless, the LaCC has always sought to engage in respectful dialogue with the legislator. While the case law shows that the Court has exercised self-restraint on certain issues (tax regulation and fundamental social rights), it has not shied away from taking strong decisions when necessary.

The chapter starts with a brief presentation of the history of the Court, its competences and composition. Next, the chapter explains some of the special features of the system of constitutional review in Latvia. Based on the data and an analysis of the case law, trends in majority decisions are described, focusing on the different periods of the Court's activity. The study shows that the strength of the rulings depended on the saliency of the issue to be decided, the limits of the legislature's discretion, and the how much "courage" the Court displayed when it came to creating new requirements and conditions for good legislation. As described in the following section, the frequency of dissenting opinions and dissenting coalitions is influenced by judges' careers, affiliation with one or another school of law, and academic background. Finally, some important cases will be qualitatively assessed.

DOI: 10.4324/9781003399483-6

6.2 Institutional design

6.2.1 Historical background

In Latvia, the idea of constitutional review was rather unpopular among legal scholars in the interwar period. In the Constituent Assembly, established on 1 May 1920 to draft the Latvian Constitution (hereinafter also: *Satversme*), the idea that an institution could "stand above" Parliament was almost unequivocally rejected during the debate on the text of the *Satversme*. The notion that the *Satversme* should be protected in some way from serious violations was first expressed in 1930 by a Member of the Parliament (MP), Pauls Šīmanis. On 8 May 1934, another MP, Helmuts Štegmanis, submitted a motion to amend the *Satversme* to establish a special court. This motion did not receive the required majority of votes (Ziemele, Spale, and Jurcēna 2020, 515), and therefore a constitutional court was not established during the first period of Latvian independence. Nevertheless, constitutional review was used as a method by the Supreme Court of Latvia, which, among other things, ruled on the validity of legal acts of the executive branch, i.e. their compliance with the *Satversme* (Krūma and Plepa 2016, 105). During the Soviet occupation, constitutional review was not implemented in the Latvian Soviet Socialist Republic.

After the collapse of the Soviet Union, constitutional courts were established in all Central and Eastern European democracies (Prochazka 2002, 33–73, Schwartz 2000, 5–21). The first decision providing for the establishment of a constitutional court in Latvia was the Declaration of the Supreme Council of the Latvian Soviet Socialist Republic of 4 May 1990. This Declaration in general played a significant role in the restoration of the Latvian statehood. The LaCC later ruled that this declaration is still in force with the same legal force as the *Satversme*. The second sentence of Article 6 of this Declaration provided that disputes on questions of the application of a legal act shall be decided by the Constitutional Court of the Republic of Latvia.[1] In spite of this, the 1992 Law on Judicial Power assigned the task of constitutional review to the Supreme Court.[2] While the idea that constitutional review should be performed by the Supreme Court was soon abandoned and legal scholars began to develop the concept of a court specialized in constitutional review, it took more than five years to establish this special court. In 1996, a constitutional amendment and the adoption of the Law on the Constitutional Court created the Latvian Constitutional Court. For this reason, the LaCC belongs to the "third generation" of constitutional courts (Sólyom 2015, 6).

1 Declaration of the Supreme Soviet of the Latvian SSR "On the Renewal of the Independence of the Republic of Latvia" on 4 May 4 1990.

2 Law on Judicial Power of 15 December 1992.

The LaCC, as the youngest constitutional institution, started its work on 9 December 1996 and issued its first decision on 7 May 1997.

6.2.2 Competences of the Latvian Constitutional Court

The LaCC is charged with examining: (1) the conformity of laws with the *Satversme*; (2) the conformity of international agreements with the *Satversme*; (3) the conformity of other laws and regulations with the norms (acts) of a higher legal force; (4) the conformity of other acts of the *Saeima*, the Cabinet, the President, the Speaker of the *Saeima* and the Prime Minister, except administrative acts, with the law; (5) the conformity of a ministerial order overruling a decision of a local council with the law; and (6) the conformity of Latvian national legal norms with international agreements not in conflict with the *Satversme*.

Apart from *a posteriori* constitutional review, *a priori* review is possible in exceptional cases and can only be initiated to review international treaties before their ratification. Petitions may be filed by the President of the Republic, the *Saeima* as a collegial body, or at least 20 members of the *Saeima*, the Cabinet, the Prosecutor General, the Council of the State Audit Office, the Judicial Council, and the Ombudsman (Rodiņa and Kārkliņa 2017, 202). An ordinary court has the right to challenge the conformity of a particular law with the *Satversme* if it raises doubts about the constitutionality of the applicable law.

If fundamental human rights are violated by a legal norm, any person who has an interest in the case may file a constitutional complaint (normative constitutional complaint), but there is no possibility for any individual or body to file a petition without having any interest in the case (*actio popularis*). Municipal councils may challenge a normative act if it violates the rights of the municipality concerned, and municipal councils may challenge compliance with a ministerial order that annuls a decision taken by the municipal council.

6.2.3 Composition of the court

The LaCC is composed of seven judges appointed by at least 51 votes out of 100 members of the *Saeima*. Three judges are appointed on the proposal of at least 10 members of the *Saeima*, two on the proposal of the Cabinet of Ministers, and two candidates must be ordinary judges proposed by the plenum of the Supreme Court. Their term of office is 10 years. It is not uncommon for the appointment of the judges to lead to political debates in the *Saeima*, which can delay the appointment process. Section 11 (3) of the Law on Constitutional Court provides a solution if the *Saeima*, for whatever reason, is unable to appoint the next judge: the mandate of the previous judge is extended until a new judge is appointed. However, this legal provision applies only to cases in which the mandate of the incumbent judge expires, and not to other cases, such as when a judge leaves office of his or her own volition. As of 2020, there had been no serious political debates about the appointment of the judges. However, after Ineta Ziemele left the LaCC to become a judge at the European Court of Justice, none of the five candidates received the required majority of votes in December 2020 (Rodiņa 2021, 129–145). Therefore, the Constitutional Court continued to operate with six judges until April 2021.

It should be emphasized that the normative regulation on the possible reappointment of judges is rather obscure and not very explicit. Article 7(3) of the Law on the Constitutional Court states that "the same person may not hold the office of constitutional judge for more than 10 consecutive years". In practice, however, at the end of 2020 a person who had been a judge for a full 10 years was re-nominated as a candidate, noting that there was an interruption between this period and a possible second term, and therefore the second term could not be considered as "consecutive". While some legal scholars argued that judges could be reappointed if there was a break between their two terms (Priekulis 2021), others contested this interpretation of the relevant rule (Neimanis 2021). Therefore, the question of whether a person can be reappointed to the bench for a second term is still open. In practice, not a single judge has yet been reappointed to this position.

The LaCC is one of the smallest constitutional courts in Europe. As a result, the Court has no chambers but always sits in full session. According to the Law on the Constitutional Court, the LaCC must sit with at least five judges. The plenary session is presided over by the President or the Vice-President of the LaCC. However, the LaCC has not always operated with its full composition of seven judges. For example, from 1997 to June 2000, the LaCC operated with only six judges, since the *Saeima*'s deputies could not agree on the seventh candidate, who was eventually confirmed in office on 11 May 2000 – almost four years after the court began its work.[3] Also, in the period from March 2008 to April 2011, only six judges sat on the benches because Judge Ķinis was serving as a judge at the International Criminal Tribunal for the former Yugoslavia.[4] The Law on the Constitutional Court allows for a judge to perform official duties at an international court while keeping his position at the LaCC at the same time.

The President of the Constitutional Court is elected by the judges themselves by secret ballot with an absolute majority of votes for a three-year term. The same applies to the Vice-President of the LaCC. The President of the LaCC usually performs three main functions: (a) representing the Court; (b) organizing the Court's work; and (c) presiding over the Court's sessions.

3 Judge and Vice-President of the Constitutional Court Mr. Juris Jelāgins (Constitutional Court of the Republic of Latvia, nda).

4 Judge and Vice-President of the Constitutional Court Mr. Uldis Ķinis (Constitutional Court of the Republic of Latvia, ndb).

6.3 General impressions

Constitutional review in Latvia has some peculiarities that should be considered when analysing the data provided by the JUDICON-EU project. First, it should be noted that in the period from 1997 to 1998, the LaCC mainly reviewed cases concerning the compatibility of Cabinet regulations with the force of law with the *Satversme*. Article 81 of the *Satversme* gave the government the right to exercise legislative functions in exceptional cases.[5] Since Cabinet regulations with the force of law are temporary, the rulings on this category of cases are not included in the report. This is the reason why the number of decisions on the compatibility of a law with the *Satversme* is low in certain periods. For example, in 1998, there was only one ruling on the constitutionality of a law.

Second, until 2001, the number of decisions was also low because the number of actors who had the right to appeal to the Court was limited. Until 2001, only the President of the Republic, at least one-third of all *Saeima* members (amendments to the Law on Constitutional Court later reduced it to 20 members of the *Saeima*), the Supreme Court, the Prosecutor General, and local governments had the right to appeal to the LaCC. Since 1 July 2001, when the constitutional complaint procedure was introduced, giving individuals the right to submit an application to the Court, the number of cases has increased significantly. Legal scholars have concluded that the introduction of the constitutional complaint procedure in 2001 marked a new phase in the development of the Constitutional Court (Spale 2016). The number of decisions issued in 2003 tripled as compared to 2001, and 11 out of the 15 decisions that year concerned constitutional complaints. The Constitutional Court dealt with the most cases in 2009–2011, when the legal acts adopted by the *Saeima* in response to the economic crisis were reviewed.

Third, laws cannot be declared incompatible with the *Satversme* in a decision where the proceedings end before reaching the Constitutional Court.[6] Termination of the proceedings means that the examination of the case is not possible for objective reasons. Fourth, the decisions of the LaCC have an *erga omnes* effect, i.e. the interpretation of the respective legal norm is binding on all persons in Latvia. The decision enters into force on the day of its

5 Article 81 of the *Satversme* allowed the Cabinet to adopt, between the *Saeima*'s sessions, regulations with the force of law. These regulations were hierarchically equal to laws. These regulations lost their force if they were not submitted to the *Saeima* within three days of the next session of the *Saeima*.

6 Adjudication of a case can be terminated (Section 29 of the Constitutional Court Law) following the written request of the applicant; if the disputed legal norm has ceased to be in force; if the Constitutional Court establishes that a decision regarding initiation of a case does not comply with the requirements set for application; if a legal norm, the compliance of which is being disputed, has ceased to be in force; if a judgment has been pronounced in another matter regarding the same subject matter of a claim; and in other cases when continuation of judicial proceedings in a case is impossible.

pronouncement, and it must be published in the Official Gazette. Pursuant to Section 32(3) of the Law on the Constitutional Court, a legal provision declared by the Constitutional Court to be incompatible with a higher-ranking legal norm shall be deemed not to have entered into force as of the day of the publication of the decision (*ex nunc*). This is the so-called general presumption, which is most frequently applied in the practice of the LaCC and which provides the opportunity to strike a fair balance between two values: legal certainty and legitimate expectations. Meanwhile, the Law on the Constitutional Court afforded the LaCC wide discretion to decide on the moment when the norm incompatible with *Satversme* becomes invalid. The Constitutional Court may decide that the unconstitutional norm becomes invalid as of the date of its adoption (*ex tunc*), or the date may be determined in the future (*pro futuro*). The case law indicates that a challenged legal norm was declared invalid *ex tunc* if it had been enacted *ultra vires* or if significant procedural violations had been committed.[7] The principle that "an unconstitutional law is not a law" (Field 1926) should be applied to such cases. In fact, such laws never really existed because they were enacted in an unlawful procedure. At the same time, the LaCC has recognized that it may depart from this presumption if important circumstances are established.[8] In deciding on the temporal effect of its rulings, the LaCC takes into account several principles: the principle of justice, the principle of legality, the principle of the separation of powers, legal expectations, and legal certainty.[9] The reason is that the law not only empowers the LaCC, but it also imposes responsibilities on it so that its decisions ensure legal stability, clarity, and peace in social reality.[10]

Another peculiarity that should be considered is related to the Court's discretion. If the LaCC considers a challenged piece of legislation to be unconstitutional, it may annul this legal norm *ex nunc*, but, for example, with respect to a person who filed the constitutional complaint, the Court may decide otherwise and annul this unconstitutional legal norm *ex tunc*. For example, in case no. 2014–09–01 the LaCC declared the challenged legal norm to be incompatible with the *Satversme ex nunc*, but with respect to the legal entity that filed the complaint, the norm became invalid *ex tunc*.[11] The *ex tunc* decision was crucial for the person because it offered the possibility of resolving the dispute by applying legal norms that were compatible with the *Satversme*,

7 Decision of the Constitutional Court of the Republic of Latvia of 17 January 2008 in case no. 2007–11–03, para. 29.

8 Decision of the Constitutional Court of the Republic of Latvia of 29 June 2017 in case no. 2016–23–03, para. 18.

9 Decision of the Constitutional Court of the Republic of Latvia of March 11 1998 in case no. 04–05(97), para. 5,

10 Decision of the Constitutional Court of the Republic of Latvia of January 18 2010 in case no. 2009–11–01, para. 30,

11 Decision of the Constitutional Court on 28 November 2014 in case no. 2014–09–01.

thus eliminating the violation. This is a very typical combination of decisions in cases reviewed in the constitutional complaint procedure.

Fifth, while dissenting opinions are allowed in general, the Law on the Constitutional Court does not provide the possibility to dissent if the Court decides to terminate the legal proceedings. Legislative omissions are also missing from the repertoire of actions available to the LaCC because it has not been granted jurisdiction to review the constitutionality of legal lacunae. Similarly, the LaCC does not have the competence of constitutional interpretation *in abstracto*.

6.4 Trends in majority decisions

6.4.1 Issue-related rigour: strength of the rulings and ruling types

As Figure 6.1 shows, the average strength of rulings proved to be relatively volatile over time. The ups and downs in ruling strength could partly be explained by the relatively small number of decisions (10.6 decisions on average and 14.6 rulings per year). The literature on the LaCC generally identifies four periods of Court: the first period from 1996 to 2001, the second period from 2001 to 2009, the third one from 2009 to 2014, and the fourth one from 2014 onwards. Each of these periods has some specific characteristics (Ziemele 2018, 13).

In the first phase, political actors and citizens had to familiarize themselves with the LaCC. As mentioned earlier, in the beginning only a small group of plaintiffs could bring cases before the LaCC, which did not review the compatibility of laws but rather the compatibility of Cabinet regulations with the Constitution. Although the number of cases it dealt with was quite small, this period was very important for the development of the organization of the

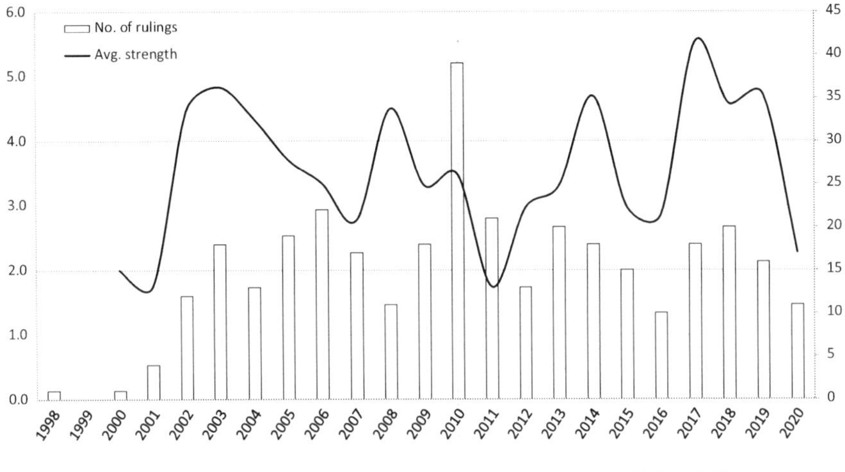

Figure 6.1 Number and average strength of rulings (1998–2020) (LaCC)

Court's work. The LaCC issued a total of only six rulings in this period (three of which were rejections), and the non-zero ruling strength varied between 2.50 and 1.75, while only one decision found substantive incompatibility with the *Satversme* (no. 2000–08–0109). In another case, the Court found procedural violations of the Constitution (no. 01–05 (98)), and it included a constitutional requirement into another ruling. Nevertheless, this latter case concerned the right to stand for election, an issue with a high political profile. Article 5 (6) of the contested Election Law provided that citizens who had been active members in the Communist Party of the Soviet Union, the International Front of Working People of the Latvian SSR, the United Council of Working People, the Organization of War and Labour Veterans, and the All-Latvian Salvation Council or its regional committees after 13 January 1991 could not be elected to the *Saeima*.[12] The LaCC accepted this restriction as necessary in a democratic society, but noted that "the legislature, which regularly evaluates the political situation and the necessity and validity of the restrictions, should decide on the determination of the duration of the restrictions, since such restrictions on the right to stand for election may only apply for a certain period of time".[13] This decision could be considered symbolic, since it concerned the right of the "KGB men" to be members of the *Saeima*, and since the LaCC assigned a clear task to the legislature, namely to review the legitimacy of these regulations from time to time.

After the amendment of the Law on the Constitutional Court in 2001, the scope of applicants was significantly expanded: the law gave both individuals and legal entities, as well as courts, the opportunity to apply to the LaCC. These changes were accompanied by a significant increase in the average strength of rulings in the Court's second period. Moreover, this new rigour of the LaCC was directed towards issues concerning fundamental rights. The number of applications to the LaCC increased significantly, resulting in a heavy workload for the Court. The legislator, being aware of these changes in its workload, modified the legal proceedings before the LaCC. The new regulation provided that panels consisting of three judges shall decide on admission of a case or it should refuse the petition. Decisions of the panel are final. Also, a written procedure for reviewing cases was introduced.

As EU accession became one of the most important goals of Latvia's political class and citizens, EU law and international law came to the forefront of constitutional interpretation. The LaCC has stated in several decisions that the state's obligation to respect international human rights derives from Article 89 of the *Satversme*, according to which the state must recognize and protect fundamental human rights in accordance with the *Satversme* and international agreements binding on Latvia. Moreover, the understanding of the sources

12 The Saeima Election Law.

13 Decision of the Constitutional Court of the Republic of Latvia of 30 August 2000 in case no. 2000–03–01, para. 7.

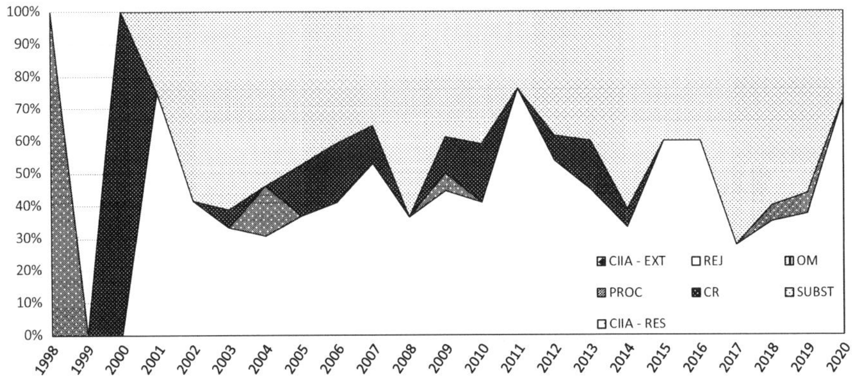

Figure 6.2 Frequency of the ruling types (1998–2020) (LaCC)

of law has also changed. For example, decision no. 2002–06–01 was of fundamental importance, as the LaCC declared the norm allowing the Supreme Court to issue binding legal declarations, which were considered to be a mandatory source of law, to be incompatible with the Constitution.[14]

The LaCC also declared several constitutional requirements in this period (Figure 6.2). The inclusion of these ruling types can be explained by the fact that, at that time, the LaCC gave the legislature time to decide on these issues, thus respecting the legislator's discretion to decide on necessary legal regulation and to preserve the stability of legal system. In addition, various provisions were included in the decisions that afforded the legislature some leeway. For example, the LaCC, in its decision no. 2003–05–01, found Article 271 of the Criminal Code incompatible with Article 100 of the *Satversme* and declared it null and void as of 1 February 2004 if the legislature had not defined by that date the group of civil servants who require the protection of the Criminal Code in order to perform the duties assigned to them. The LaCC obliged the legislator to revise the law and set a sufficient deadline (six months) for fulfilling this obligation.[15] While the introduction of constitutional complaints was accompanied by a sudden increase in ruling strength, the Court gradually became more restrained in the following years, and the ruling strength reached its low point in 2007.

In addition, in 2007 the LaCC reviewed cases (e.g. decision no. 2006–07–01 and no. 2006–04–01) assessing the compatibility of a legal norm with social rights (Article 109 of the *Satversme*). According to the case law of the LaCC, the nature of such social rights also determines the limits of its jurisdiction.

14 Decision of the Constitutional Court of the Republic of Latvia of 4 February 2003 in case no. 2002–06–01.

15 Decision of the Constitutional Court of the Republic of Latvia of 29 October 2003 in case no. 2003–05–01.

The Court argued that the legislature has a wide margin of appreciation in the substantive implementation of social rights, as long as it is proportionate to the economic situation of the state. The low ruling strengths in this year can therefore be explained by the particular nature of the cases examined. The Court was rather reluctant to restrict the legislature in matters of social rights, as this could have serious financial consequences.

In stark contrast to this deferential attitude on social rights issues, the following year saw some very strict rulings. In 2008, only 10 cases were reviewed, which means that the number of rulings was clearly lower than usual, but the Court found that most of the legal norms challenged were not compatible with the *Satversme*. A possible explanation for this severity could again lie in the nature of the cases examined, as the LaCC had to decide on cases related to individual human rights (decision no. 2008–42–01, no. 2008–48–01, and no. 2008–02–01). Another reason why these cases must be highlighted is the fact that at that time the Criminal Code from the Soviet era (1970) was still in force. In a way, it is remarkable that a legal regulation adopted in the Soviet era was still being applied after the dissolution of the Soviet Union. Considering that many provisions of this law were in sharp contrast to the modern understanding of fundamental human rights in the *Satversme*, it is not surprising that the court found most of the petitions to be justified and declared the challenged paragraphs to be essentially unconstitutional.[16] During this period, a group of prisoners who were subjected to significant restrictions actively used their right to submit constitutional complaints to the LaCC, as they had realized that the LaCC is an effective means of protecting their rights.

In its fourth term (2009–2014), the LaCC faced new challenges that were triggered by the financial and economic crisis of 2008–2009. In order to avoid economic collapse, the legislature took painful measures that had serious effects on the social and economic rights of the citizens. Unsurprisingly, many challenged the government's austerity measures before the LaCC. In this period, various forms of social benefits (including pensions) were cut, and the salaries of state employees, including judges, were reduced. The number of constitutional complaints increased, showing that despite the rather disappointing results of the Court's jurisprudence on social rights in recent times, people saw the LaCC as an institution that could protect their social rights even at critical moments (Balodis and Pleps 2013, 115–140). However, the Court once again showed a rather deferential attitude regarding social rights issues and, with few exceptions, decided not to impose serious constraints on the legislator that would have severe financial consequences. For this reason, the average strength of rulings at this time declined as compared to 2008, when fundamental rights issues dominated the Court's agenda (see also Figure 6.1).

By issuing *pro futuro* rulings, even when the LaCC has overturned a piece of legislation that had budgetary implications, the Court gives the legislature

16 Judgment of the Constitutional Court of the Republic of Latvia of 29 September 2009 in case no. 2008–48–01.

time and/or broad discretion in making legal regulations consistent with the findings of its decisions (decision no. 2009–111–01, no. 2010–39–01, and no. 2011–04–01). The Court generally gave the legislature six months leeway when it declared a legal regulation unconstitutional. The year 2010 marked a turning point in the Court's practice in this regard, as it declared certain norms of the Civil Law to be unconstitutional with a *pro futuro* temporal effect but gave the legislature more than one year to adopt a new regulation.[17]

Other aspects of the Court's jurisprudence show that it has sought to strengthen the role of the legislature *vis-à-vis* the executive. The "doctrine of substantiality", as elaborated in decision no. 2009–43–01, posits that when it comes to the restriction of fundamental rights, only the legislature (and not, for example, the executive branch) may devise a regulation on these issues. Moreover, it should be noted that the LaCC was even more lenient toward the legislature in other aspects during those critical years: for example, it accepted the legislature's practice of passing bills in an accelerated procedure as being consistent with constitutional principles, even though the accelerated procedure meant two readings of the bill on the same day and a 15-minute deadline for submitting proposals for the second reading (no. 2009–08–01). As the LaCC explained, under the conditions of a severe economic recession, the legislature must act as quickly, concertedly, and decisively as possible. In doing so, the legislature must be given a reasonable margin of appreciation.

The lowest average ruling strength in 2016 (2.85) can be explained partly by the topics of the petitions and partly by the fact that the previous year (2015) had the lowest number of initiated proceedings, which accordingly means that 2016 had the lowest number of decisions (8) and rulings (10). In that year, the LaCC recognized legal norms as incompatible with *Satversme* in only four rulings, three of which were decided with *pro futuro* and one with *ex nunc* temporal effect. The low ruling strength also resulted from the fact that the Court decided cases of tax law and banking where the legislator may enjoy broad discretion.

As far as the ruling strengths are concerned, 2017 was certainly an extreme year as it peaked with a value of 5.53 while the number of rulings was also quite high. Up until then, the LaCC significantly constrained the legislator's leeway only when it considered fundamental human rights issues or referred to the state's positive obligations. However, in its decision no. 2016–06–01 and no. 2016–12–01, in examining the compliance of the contested norms with Article 92 of the *Satversme*, the Court used a different test. The Court determined whether the impugned norms guaranteed the procedural rights compatible with the first sentence of Article 92 of the *Satversme* and whether the applicant had been denied access to the court and fair trial. Applying a different methodology allowed the Court to define a higher standard for the protection of fundamental rights and to constrain the *Saeima*'s leeway more heavily (Constitutional Court of the Republic of Latvia 2018).

17 Judgment of the Constitutional Court of the Republic of Latvia of 27 December 2010 in case no. 2010–38–01.

6.4.2 *The role of the president*

The LaCC has been presided over by six presidents since its foundation. Phrases like the "Endziņš Court" or "Kūtris Court" vividly illustrate the importance attributed to the role of the presidents in constitutional adjudication (Laviņš 2016, 234–256). The presidents' authority remains one of the most important factors in determining the social influence of the Court. It is a well-known fact that the higher the authority of the president and the Court, the greater its influence will be on politics and society. This conclusion also applies in full to the LaCC and its presidents.

Nevertheless, the presidents' impact might vary according to the challenges they had to face. For example, Endziņš (1996–2007) had to clarify the purpose and nature of constitutional adjudication. In its first decade, the Court played an important role in strengthening Latvian statehood and developing the interpretation of the *Satversme* in accordance with the principle of rule of law. Endziņš has always been one of the most renowned constitutional law professors in Latvia. The data analysis shows that, with the exception of one case when he dissented, Endziņš's will invariably prevailed or, at least, he was able to forge a coalition of judges who delivered the majority decisions. Furthermore, this majority was a quite monolithic one, which can once again be explained by his general authority inside and outside the Court. The presidency of Ineta Ziemele (2017–2020) seems to be outstanding from another perspective: under her presidency the LaCC increasingly engaged in respectful dialogue with the legislature. The LaCC focused more and more on the quality of the legislative process, reviewing whether a challenged norm had been adopted in due process.

6.5 Trends in dissenting opinions

According to the normative rule, the Constitutional Court's decision is adopted by a majority vote and judges can only vote "for" or "against".[18] The votes are never made public and are protected by secrecy in the courtroom. In general, however, it is possible to see who voted for and who voted against the decision. The reason for this is that a judge who is opposed to the majority decision is allowed to publish a dissenting opinion (Rodiņa 2019, 145–164). Dissents are published, but only two months after the decision has entered into force. This time difference is intended to prevent the Court from getting embroiled in serious political debates.

6.5.1 *Evaluation of the strength of dissenting opinions*

From 1997 to 2020, 337 rulings were rendered by the court, and judges added 81 dissenting opinions to the majority decisions. Figure 6.3 also shows

18 The dissenting opinions that are added to cases about conformity of law and not other normative acts and that have been published are analysed in the project.

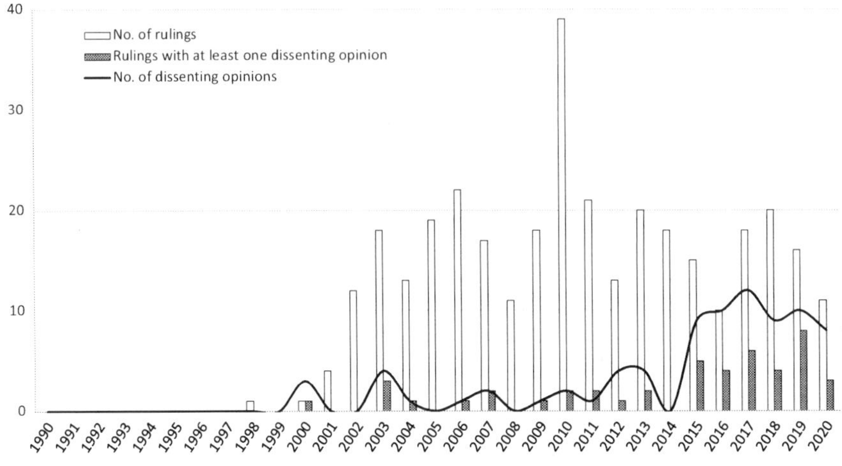

Figure 6.3 Number of rulings with at least one dissenting opinion (1998–2020) (LaCC)

that judges dissented quite infrequently until the mid-2010s, although the rate of dissent increased from 2015 on.

In the initial phase of the Constitutional Court's activity (from 1996 to 2001), dissenting opinions were written rather rarely. The first dissenting opinion was written four years after the Court started its work.[19] It is typical of the first Court that judges did not write their dissenting opinions individually. Interestingly, Judge Ilma Čepāne, Romāns Apsītis, and Ilze Skultāne did not attach a single dissenting opinion to a case.

The relatively low number of dissenting opinions during this period may be due to the fact that it was a kind of "exploratory period" during which the judges had to familiarize themselves with constitutional review in general. The number of cases examined during this period was also rather low, which gave the judges the opportunity to reach agreement. Most importantly, the cases heard in those years did not involve complex issues on fundamental human rights. Decisions were very brief, and no common methodology was used to assess the conformity of the challenged legal norm. It seems that there was more or less consensus on the basic principles of the application of the *Satversme*.

A certain paradox appears in Figure 6.4, which suggests that Judges Endziņš, Ušacka, Kūtris, and Ķinis published comparatively strong dissenting opinions, although these judges wrote only one or two dissenting opinions. Moreover, the strength of their dissenting opinions is higher than the strength of some more active judges in later years who dissented more frequently (e.g. Jānis

19 Dissenting opinion of the Constitutional Court Justices Aivars Endziņš, Juris Jelāgins, and Anita Ušacka in case no. 2000–03–01.

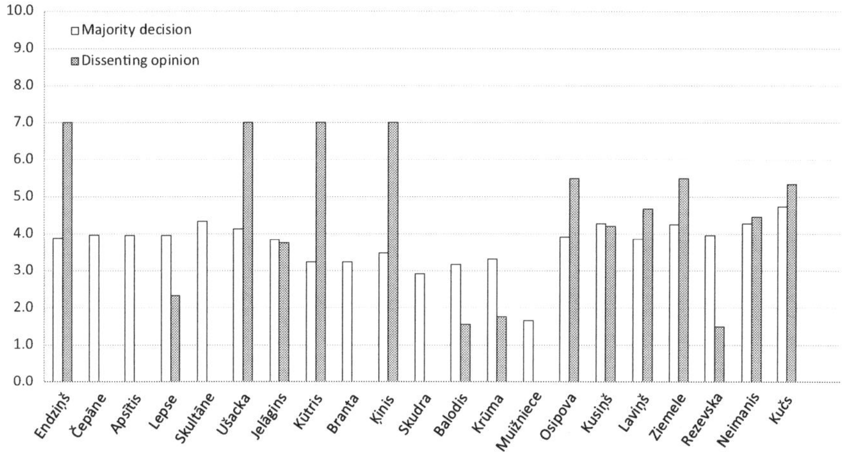

Figure 6.4 Average strength of dissenting opinions by judges (LaCC)

Neimanis). The analysis of the content of these dissenting opinions shows that the strength of the dissenting opinions of Endziņš (7.00) and Ušačka (7.00) as well as Gunārs Kūtris and Uldis Ķinis appears to be high because in their dissents they argue about substantive unconstitutionality of the challenged legal norm. In contrast, for example, the strength of the dissenting opinion of Judge Andrejs Lepse, who published three dissents, is lower (2.33) because his opinions deal more with procedural nuances (in two dissenting opinions Lepse argues that there is no violation of fundamental rights, and therefore court proceedings should have been terminated).

The number of dissenting opinions started to increase from 2007 onwards with the gradual replacement of the so-called first composition of the Court, when new judges joined the LaCC. Of the judges from this period, Judge Kaspars Balodis deserves special mention, as he became one of the most fervent dissenters. During his 10-year term, he wrote dissenting opinions to nine decisions. This was quite a high number compared to the previous practice. Notwithstanding the activism of Balodis, the average strength of his dissenting opinions is only (1.56), as he declared substantive unconstitutionality only twice. In the remaining dissenting opinions, Balodis expressed the view that the norm was compatible with the *Satversme*. Moreover, it should be emphasized that in his dissenting opinions (e.g. decision no. 2007–03–01), as well as criticising the majority opinion he also offered alternative arguments for the interpretation of the legal norm. Thus, Balodis was the first judge to cultivate the style and culture of writing dissenting opinions that offers a variety of arguments.

The issue of social rights seemingly polarized the LaCC and became one of the most important issues for triggering dissenting opinions. While President Kūtris (2007–2014) published only two dissenting opinions, both reached a strength value of 7.00, and both cases concerned social rights issues or fundamental questions of social benefits (decision no. 2009–44–01 and no. 2011–03–01). During his presidency he consistently pursued the idea of the social state, a state which should take care of vulnerable groups. Also, Judge Ķinis' dissenting opinion (would have) constrained the legislator more heavily concerning social rights issues: he only wrote one dissenting opinion, but he considered the challenged norm to be absolutely incompatible with the *Satversme* (decision no. 2011–03–01). This specific decision no. 2011–03–01 was decided by a narrow majority of four judges with three judges (Ķinis, Kūtris, Osipova) dissenting. All dissenters were against the liberal interpretation of state responsibility concerning social rights.

While in the early 2010s the issue of social rights still divided the LaCC to some extent, resulting in a few dissents, the number of dissenting opinions has significantly increased in recent years. Currently, there are some judges who have written more dissenting opinions than the pioneer Judge Balodis. This most recent increase in dissent can be explained by several factors. In recent years, the Court has had to rule on hot topics concerning the restriction of fundamental human rights and the legislative process. This has led once again to the polarization of opinions in the Court. In particular, it can be noted that references to natural law have emerged, inter alia, in relation to the assessment of the legislature's discretionary power.

The main differences between the judges concerned the understanding of the quality of the law. Some of the judges (followers of natural law) advocated a strict application of the principle of good legislation, which means that the legislator must observe various procedural and substantive requirements as well as the general principles of law during the legislative process. Moreover, this group of judges considered that the LaCC may also review whether the legislature has followed these principles. Another group argued that the Court cannot review the work of the legislature in such a strict manner. Different views were also expressed on the scope of human rights. One group of judges held that there can be an absolute limitation on fundamental human rights and that the constitutionality of such a limitation should be reviewed in different ways. Another group of judges rejected this idea, pointing out that the "normal" method should be applied even in cases where a legal norm restricts the rights of a group of people. Concerning the method of the interpretation of the constitution, Judge Jānis Neimanis' dissenting opinions should be mentioned. He published several dissenting opinions focusing on the method adopted by the Court to review the constitutionality of a legal act referred to it. This methodological focus of Neimanis can be explained by his solid academic training precisely in the field of legal theory and legal method.

6.5.2 Dissenting coalitions

The study of coalitions of judges is the first of its kind and thus represents a unique study of the cooperation between judges of the Latvian Constitutional Court. As the data show, coalitions are based on the judges' previous careers, common understanding of legal theory and law, and academic interests.

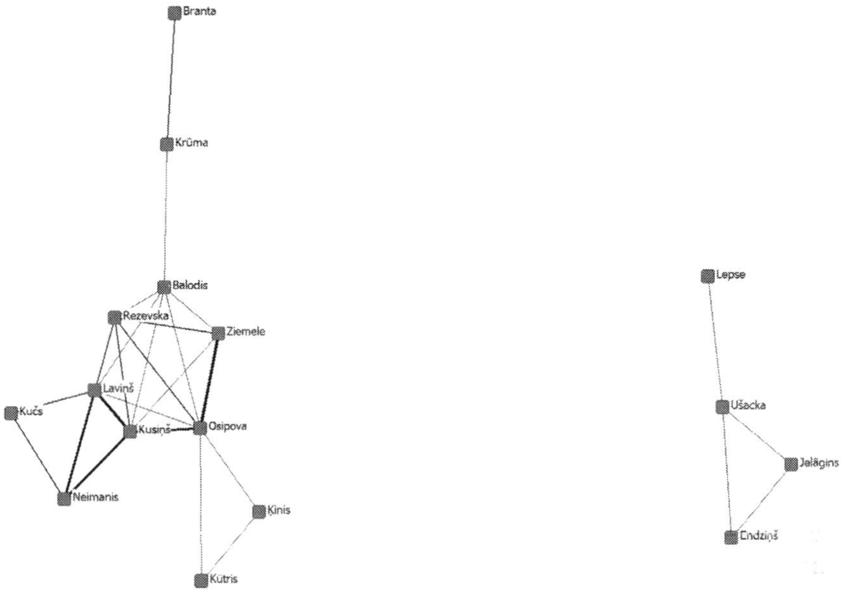

Figure 6.5 Dissenting coalitions 1998–2020 (LaCC)

A decidedly stable network has developed between two judges: Ineta Ziemele and Sanita Osipova. These two judges have issued joint dissenting opinions in six cases. Nevertheless, it should be noted that in three cases another judge with an academic background joined them. Judge Ziemele joined the bench in 2015 after completing her term as a judge at the European Court of Human Rights, an experience which is clearly reflected in her dissenting opinions based on arguments set out in ECtHR case law. Thus, in decision no. 2018–25–01 Judge Ziemele, referring to the case law of the ECtHR, emphasized that in a democratic state governed by the rule of law, the fact that a person is different from others cannot be the reason for disproportionate restrictions on his or her rights.[20] Also, both judges share similar views when it comes to the concept of human dignity.

A different kind of network has been formed between two other judges: Aldis Laviņš and Jānis Neimanis. These judges have repeatedly expressed their discontent with the methodology used to review a challenged legal norm. In their dissenting opinion to decision no. 2016–12–01, both judges raised the issue of the violation of several important procedural principles of the Constitutional Court, such as the principle of objective investigation or the principle of *iura novit curia*.[21] Laviņš and Neimanis noted in their dissent that the Court

20 Dissenting opinion of the Constitutional Court Justice Ineta Ziemele case no. 2018–25–01.
21 Dissenting opinion of the Constitutional Court Justice Aldis Lavins case no. 2016–12–01.

should review not only one aspect of the challenged norm, but it should take a broader perspective, thus ensuring the protection of fundamental human rights. As mentioned earlier, some judges argued that the Court should review legislative procedure in a very strict manner (in accordance with the principle of good legislation). Neimanis and Laviņš opposed this view, and in their dissenting opinion to decision no. 2017–17–01, they argued that the arguments presented by the majority were essentially a political desideratum that violated the principle of separation of powers and impermissibly interfered with the powers of the legislature.[22] This coalition of the two judges can be explained once again by their earlier careers. Both judges came from the Supreme Court and have worked as professional judges. Laviņš's career took him from the lower courts to the Supreme Court, while Neimanis was appointed directly to the Administrative Chamber of the Supreme Court. This could be the reason for these judges placing more emphasis on procedural issues. However, it is also true that both judges in any case share the view that the legislator should have a wide margin of discretion in legislative procedures.

While dissents do not have *per se erga omnes* effect, some dissenting opinions have been used as legal material worthy of study at universities. For example, in his dissenting opinion to decision no. 2004–01–06, concerning the compatibility of national legal norms with international treaties, Judge Jelāgins emphasized that the Court cannot review the conformity of a law with an international agreement which has the same legal force as the law.[23] Another example is Daiga Rezevska's dissent to decision no. 2016–14–01, in which her position is undeniably strengthened by compelling arguments that were later analysed once again by law students.

6.6 Qualitative evaluation

The principle of good legislation, mentioned several times in the previous sections, is currently one of the central research topics in Latvian legal studies. For several years now, the LaCC has been consistently developing the content of this principle. Therefore, this principle needs to be analysed in more detail.

6.6.1 Legislative process and the LaCC

As mentioned earlier, the Constitutional Court has been actively involved in assessing the quality of the legislative process over the last decade and has created a new level of requirements for the legislative process. In particular, the LaCC has developed the principle of good legislation. Rulings that found challenged norms to be unconstitutional because this principle had been violated

22 Dissenting opinion of the Constitutional Court Justices Aldis Lavins and Janis Neimanis in case no. 2017–17–01.

23 Dissenting opinion of the Constitutional Court Justice Juris Jelāgins in case no. 2004–01–06.

have at times astonished the legislators. Today, however, no one doubts that compliance with this principle gives society the certainty that the outcome of the legislation, even if a section of the society is dissatisfied with it, has been carefully examined and weighed (Letter No. 288).

Methodologically, the LaCC derived the principle of good legislation from the general principle of the rule of law (Rezevska 2020, 330–337). The LaCC explained the principle of good legislation for the first time in decision no. 2018-11-01. In this particular case, the Court considered the compatibility of an obligation arising from subsection 1 and subsection 2 of section 3 (92) of the Act On the Remuneration of Civil Servants and Employees of State and Local Government Agencies, to publish the remuneration of employees of state-funded higher education institutions, with Article 96 of the *Satversme*, which guarantees the right to private life.[24] The Court found the provisions challenged in this case to be incompatible with Article 96 of the *Satversme*, since the legislator had disregarded the obligation to comply with the provisions of European Union law when adopting the law. As the law had been adopted in violation of the principle of good legislation, the Court declared the norms as void as of the date of their adoption (*ex tunc*).

Another set of decisions marking deficiencies in compliance with the principle of good legislation is closely related to another aspect of constitutional adjudication, namely the understanding of the *erga omnes* effect and the enforcement of the decisions of the LaCC. In this particular case (decision no. 2017-17-01), a legal norm, the drafting of which had ignored the findings contained in the LaCC's decision, was adjudged to be incompatible with the constitution with a *pro futuro* effect. The petitioners considered that the *Saeima* had not taken into account the findings contained in the Court's decision when amending and adopting the new bill. In other words, the LaCC had to return to the issue that had already been decided several times (*res iudicata*) (decision no. 2008-34-01, no. 2008-36-01, and no. 2010-22-01). The repeated assessment of this case gave the Court the opportunity to point out that the principle of good legislation also requires ensuring a proper analysis of the constitutionality of the legal regulation, including the established case law of the LaCC.

It should be noted that the development of the content of the principle of good legislation represents a turning point in the understanding of the provisions of the *Satversme*, which also affects the relations between the LaCC and the legislature. Indeed, until the LaCC clarified the principle of good legislation, the dominant view had been that the review of the quality of legislation was the exclusive responsibility of the *Saeima* (Pleps 2012). Until 2017, the substantive aspects of the validity of a law predominated in the LaCC's practice of reviewing constitutionality. With the development of the principle of good

24 Judgment of the Constitutional Court of the Republic of Latvia on 6 March 2019 in case no. 2018-11-01.

legislation, however, the procedural aspects gained importance. Nevertheless, some argue that the control of the quality of the legislative process constitutes excessive interference by the LaCC in the competence of the *Saeima* (see the dissenting opinion of Laviņš and Neimanis to decision no. 2017–17–01). Others proposed the establishment of a special new constitutional body – the Council of State – which could perform the constitutional review of the procedural aspects of legislation.[25] Its aim would be to ensure the drafting of high-quality laws, i.e. those that correspond to the *Satversme*.[26]

6.6.2 Public finances and tax legislation

As a general tenet, it is accepted today among Latvian legal scholars that no legal act falling within the jurisdiction of the LaCC may avoid constitutional review.[27] Nevertheless, this principle does not mean that the LaCC cannot limit its own activity. When drafting tax regulations or the state budget, the legislature has a wide margin of appreciation, which is also respected by the Court.

It is recognized that the same restrictions cannot be placed on the legislature in the area of tax law as, for example, in the area of the protection and guarantee of civil or political rights.[28] This means that the legislature has greater discretion in determining and implementing tax policy.[29] In spite of this self-constrained mentality of the LaCC, some limits on the legislature remain. It is also true that the LaCC cannot review whether the measures chosen by the legislature are economically justified. The turning point in constitutional review in the field of taxation came in 2017, when the LaCC reviewed the compatibility of solidarity tax regulations with the *Satversme* in two cases (decision no. 2016–14–01 and no. 2016–16–01). Decision no. 2016–14–01 contains an innovative thesis, namely that the legislator must respect the principle of a sustainable economy.[30] With this decision, the LaCC set a new

25 Par un pret valsts padomes ideju Latvijā [For and against the idea of a state council in Latvia]. Jurista Vārds, Nr. 5 (11150), 04.02.2020, pp. 12–13.; Ziemele I. Likumdošanas procesa pilnveidošana: jauna konstitucionāla orgāna piedāvājums [Improving the legislative process: proposal for a new constitutional body]. Jurista Vārds, Nr. 10 (964), 07.03.207, pp. 10–13.

26 Kā uzlabot likumdošanu un ierobežot likumdevēja netikumus. Latvijas valsts prezidents Egils Levits intervijā žurnāla "Jurista Vārds" galvenajai redaktorei Dinai Gailītei [How to improve legislation and limit the lawmaker's vice. The President of Latvia Egils Levits in an interview with Dina Gailīte, Editor-in-Chief of the journal "Jurista Vārds"]. Jurista Vārds, Nr. 5 (1115), 04.02.2020, pp. 8–11.

27 Judgment of the Constitutional Court of the Republic of Latvia of 18 January 2010 in case no. 2009–11–01, para. 5.

28 Judgment of the Constitutional Court of the Republic of Latvia of 13 April 2011 in case no. 2010–59–01, para. 9.

29 Judgment of the Constitutional Court on 20 May 2011 in case no. 2010–70–01, para. 9.

30 Judgment of the Constitutional Court of the Republic of Latvia of 19 October 2017 in case no. 2016–14–01.

standard for the legislature, which led to tensions between the LaCC and the legislature since views on economic growth issues differed.

Another issue that affects the relationship between the LaCC and the legislature concerns the scope of constitutional control in relation to the state budget. In its decision no. 2010–06–01, for the first time the LaCC had to answer the question of whether the adoption of the State Budget Act was compatible with the constitution.[31] Even though the ruling did not establish the incompatibility of the challenged legal norm with the *Satversme*, the Court stated that in assessing whether there is a significant threat to the interests of society or the state, it is necessary to determine which interests in the specific case may have been affected by the adoption of the contested sub-chapter of the state budget. The LaCC showed self-restraint in this decision, stating that it would only examine the state budget in procedural terms. However, it also noted that the LaCC could also find the state budget to be incompatible with the *Satversme* based on substantial incompatibilities. For example, in its decision no. 2019–29–01 concerning the funding of higher education, the Court pointed out very clearly that while the state budget is an explicitly "political" issue, in a democratic state governed by the rule of law, the law must be respected in the drafting and adoption of the state budget.[32] The Court found the state budget, which did not provide funds for the enforcement of a law, to be compatible with the *Satversme*, but the norm, which provided specific funding for higher education, was considered incompatible with *Satversme*. This ruling triggered a wide debate as the LaCC reviewed the priorities set by the legislature for funding higher education and pointed out that there was no real and justified source for its funding.

6.6.3 *Enforcement of ex tunc decisions and constitutional requirements*

As mentioned, the LaCC may declare an unconstitutional norm null and void with an *ex tunc* temporal effect. It has also been mentioned that an *ex tunc* ruling may be the only way to safeguard a person's fundamental rights in some cases. If the Court takes an *ex tunc* decision, the question of enforcement of the decision may arise. In Latvia, there is no specific legal regulation providing for the enforcement of the Court's decisions and the mechanisms for their supervision. In some cases, the LaCC itself has defined how enforcement will occur and established the relevant constitutional requirements.[33] The LaCC has justified this practice by applying section 31(12) of the Law on the Constitutional Court, which provides for rights to secure the enforcement

31 Judgment of the Constitutional Court on 2 February 2012 in case no. 2011–11–01.

32 Judgment of the Constitutional Court of the Republic of Latvia of 29 October 2020 in case no. 2019–29–01.

33 Judgment of the Constitutional Court of the Republic of Latvia of 24 October 2013 in case no. 2012–23–01, para. 20.4.

of their decisions, namely the authorization of the LaCC to decide on important legal consequences of its decisions itself.[34] For example, in the case where the challenged norms restricting the payment of social pensions during the economic crisis were *ex tunc* annulled with respect to all pension beneficiaries as of the date of their adoption, the Court declared the enforcement of the decision regulating the restitution of the part of the pensions withheld from the persons concerned. The Court ruled that:

> The reimbursement of the withheld part of the pension must be made within a reasonable time and within certain limits, taking into account the different situation of the individuals. In view of the economic situation in Latvia and the state budget, the part of the pensions withheld on the basis of the contested provisions must be reimbursed in full by 1 July 2015 at the latest, in accordance with the procedure laid down by the *Saeima*.[35]

6.7 Politically sensitive issues

Over the last three decades several decisions of the LaCC have triggered huge interest in the media, sending a kind of shockwave through society and politicians, and starting discussions on various issues.

Interestingly, the LaCC's first decision turned directly into its first high-profile ruling. The LaCC delivered its first decision on 7 May 1997 with decision no. 04–01(97). Both the court hearing, with many journalists present, and the decision, which was impatiently awaited, attracted attention. The first decision caused a kind of a "shock" for the political elite because the LaCC declared the contested legal norms to be incompatible with legal norms of a higher legal force. The LaCC presented in this decision the general principles of law, the references to which evoked both incomprehension and appreciation. Some argued that "if the Constitutional Court is unable to substantiate the invalidity or validity of a certain norm by the *Satversme* and the laws, then 'general legal principles', known only to the Constitutional Court, are applied" (Radziņš 1998, 17). Although the decision was laconic and relatively short, its impact upon the legal system and the Constitutional Court was very significant. Moreover, this decision showed that the Constitutional Court has to reckon with criticism. Before and after its decision no. 04–03(99)[36] in 1999,

34 Judgment of the Constitutional Court of the Republic of Latvia of 21 December 2009 in case no. 2009–43–01, para. 35.

35 Judgment of the Constitutional Court of the Republic of Latvia of 21 December 2009 in case no. 2009–43–01, para. 35.3.

36 Judgment of the Constitutional Court of the Republic of Latvia of 9 July 1999 case no. 04–03(99).

even quite radical opinions were voiced that the LaCC should be abolished.[37] The idea of "reorganizing" the institution, however, did not succeed, and the LaCC became known as an institution to be reckoned with.

One of the politically most sensitive cases the Court has dealt with was the so-called Latvian-Russian border treaty case.[38] Members of the *Saeima*, who filed a petition to the Court, were of the opinion that the border treaty, concluded between Latvia and Russia and envisaging that part of the former Abrene district (territory of Latvia) would be part of the Russian Federation, and the law by which the *Saeima* had approved this border treaty, were incompatible with Article 3 of the *Satversme*. Likewise, it was held that the law, by which the *Saeima* authorized the Cabinet to sign the border treaty, was incompatible with the Preamble and paragraph 9 of the Declaration on Restoration of the Independence of the Republic of Latvia. Although the LaCC found incompatibility only with respect to the words "abiding by the principle of the unchangeability of borders adopted by the Organization for Security and Cooperation in Europe", this decision is to be deemed "historical". The decision includes not only a meticulous presentation of the history of the Latvian state but also explains the doctrine of the continuity of the state, outlines both a broader and narrower understanding of the *Satversme*, and provides a contemporary concept of constitutional-level legal acts. The LaCC found that losing the Abrene district did not affect the continuity of the Latvian state and also recognized that, after 1990, Latvia has consistently adhered to the opinion that it is the successor of the state occupied by the Soviet Union in 1940. Simultaneously, the LaCC's decision found that the USSR had treated Latvia unlawfully in 1940.

Another court decision that sparked a social debate was delivered recently, in late 2020. This case concerned the compatibility of Section 155(1) of the Labour Code, which provided for a 10-day leave for the father in connection with the birth of a child, with the first sentence of Article 110 of the *Satversme*. The plaintiff was not the father of a child, but the female partner of the child's mother, with whom a stable relationship had developed and who could not claim this leave on the basis of the challenged norm. The central question to be answered by the LaCC concerned what type of family is protected by Article 110 of the *Satversme* and whether a same-sex partner can claim paternity leave. The idea that prevails in this decision is the statement that the family is a social institution based on close personal ties and based on the understanding and respect observed in social reality. Another important aspect that influenced the content of the decision is the application of the principle of human dignity,

37 Lase I., Egle I. Nespēj pamatot ideju reorganizēt ST [Unable to justify the idea of reforming the ST]. Diena, 13.08.1999, p. 1.; see also Lase I. Aivars Endziņš neredz iemeslus likvidēt Satversmes tiesu [Aivars Endziņš sees no reason to liquidate the Constitutional Court]. Diena, 10.08.1999, p. 3.

38 Judgment of the Constitutional Court of the Republic of Latvia of 29 November 2007 case no. 2007–10–0102.

which is reflected in the preamble of the *Satversme* and which characterizes the human being as the supreme value in the state.[39] Based on this principle, the Constitutional Court stated that the state cannot deny fundamental rights to a particular person or group of persons and that the state must also respect those members of society who, by their nature, enter into personal relationships with persons of their own sex, and it must also respect the fact that a family may be formed on the basis of such relationships.[40] In other words, the LaCC, in interpreting the first sentence of Article 110 in conjunction with the principle of human dignity and the individual's right to the inviolability of privacy, came to the historical conclusion that the state is obliged to protect and support the families of same-sex partners as well as partners of the opposite sex.[41] It should be emphasized, however, that the LaCC did not deal with same-sex marriages because, according to Article 110 of the *Satversme*, marriage is a union between a man and a woman, and a different understanding of marriage would require the amendment of this provision of the *Satversme*. Based on its conclusions, the LaCC recognized the challenged legal norm in this case, insofar as it provides for the protection and support of the partner of the mother of the child in connection with the birth of the child, as being incompatible with the first sentence of Article 110 of the *Satversme*. This means that the regulation of the legal status of same-sex couples is in the hands of the legislator, but, according to the LaCC, it must be based on objective and valid criteria.

It is undeniable that the ruling the LaCC made at the end of 2020 "shook" society, including some of the political forces represented in the *Saeima*, and led to tensions between the LaCC and the legislator. During a confirmation hearing in the *Saeima*, the rhetorical question was raised as to whether such a court was needed at all and whether its functions could be transferred to the Supreme Court.[42] Also in response to the Court's decision, a bill was submitted to the *Saeima* to amend Article 110 of the *Satversme* and add to the definition so that "family" is based on marriage, consanguinity, or adoption, including the rights of the child to grow up in a family which is constituted by a mother (woman) and a father (man).[43]

39 Judgment of the Constitutional Court of the Republic of Latvia of March 2019 in case no. 2018–08–03.

40 Judgment of the Constitutional Court of the Republic of Latvia on 12 November 2020 in case no. 2019–33–01, para. 12.2.

41 Judgment of the Constitutional Court of the Republic of Latvia on 12 November 2020 in case no. 2019–33–01, para. 12.3.

42 13th Saeima of the Republic of Latvia 43rd (remote extraordinary) sitting of the autumn session 21 December 21 2020.

43 The draft law provides to express Article 110 of the *Satversme* in the following wording: "110. The State shall protect and support marriage – a union between a man and a woman, the family based on marriage, consanguinity or adoption, the rights of parents and rights of the child, including the right to grow up in the family, the foundation of which is formed by the mother (woman) and the father (man). The State shall provide special support to disabled children, children left without parental care or who have suffered from violence".

6.8 Conclusions

Based on the methodology of the JUDICON-EU project, the strength of the Court's decisions, the influence of individual judges, dissenting coalitions, and the position of presidents were analysed. Although the authors have had the opportunity to follow the activity of the LaCC from its beginning, the data showed some interesting aspects.

Over the years, a stability in the LaCC's jurisprudence can be observed. The statistics show that the ratio between declarations of constitutionality and unconstitutionality of the reviewed legal norms has remained the same. Predominantly, the Court finds substantive incompatibility with the *Satversme* in cases where the legislature has failed to strike an appropriate balance between the interests of a person and those of society when establishing a restriction on fundamental rights and has thus failed to observe the principle of proportionality.

The LaCC has always sought to engage in respectful dialogue with the legislature. Until 2017, the substantive aspects of a law's validity predominated in the constitutional review process, whereas since then, with the development of the principle of good legislation, the procedural aspects have become more important. The case law also shows the Court to be self-restrictive on specific issues (tax regulation, fundamental social rights). Nevertheless, when necessary, it even includes constitutional requirements that impose obligations on the legislature. Despite various misunderstandings, the Constitutional Court has been able to maintain a high reputation in society and among politicians in Latvia (Kučinskis 2019, 19).

References

Balodis, Ringolds, and Janis Pleps. 2013. "Financial Crisis and the Constitution in Latvia." In *Constitutions in the Global Financial Crisis. A Comparative Analysis*, edited by Xenophon Contiades, 115–141. Farnham and Burlington: Ashgate.

Constitutional Court of the Republic of Latvia. 2018. *Report on the Work of the Constitutional Court of the Republic of Latvia in 2017*. www.satv.tiesa.gov.lv/en/wp-content/uploads/sites/2/2018/02/Report-on-the-work-of-the-Constitutional-court-of-the-Republic-of-Latvia-in-2017.pdf

———. n.d.a "Juris Jelāgins." Accessed September 5, 2022. www.satv.tiesa.gov.lv/en/history/history-of-the-court/juris-jelagins/

———. n.d.b Uldis Ķinis. Accessed September 5, 2022. www.satv.tiesa.gov.lv/en/history/history-of-the-court/uldis-kinis/

De Visser, Maartje. 2014. *Constitutional Review in Europe. A Comparative Analysis*. Oxford and Portland, OR: Hart Publishing.

Field, Oliver. 1926. "Effect of an Unconstitutional Statute." *Indiana Law Journal* 1: 2–16.

Komarek, Jan. 2013. "The Place of Constitutional Courts in the EU." *European Constitutional Law Review* 9: 420–450.

Krūma, Krisnīne, and Dita Plepa. 2016. *Constitutional Law in Latvia*. Alpen aan den Rijn: Kluver Law International.

Kučinskis, Māris. 2019. "Speech at the Opening of the Conference." In *The Role of Constitutional Courts in the Globalised World of the 21st Century. Proceedings of the 2018 Conference of the Constitutional Court of the Republic of Latvia*. Riga: Constitutional Court of the Republic of Latvia, 19–23.

Laviņš, Aldis. 2016. "Discussion between the President of the Constitutional Court Mr Aldis Laviņš and the Former Presidents of the Constitutional Court Aivars Endziņš, Gunārs Kūtris and Aija Branta about the Constitutional Court through the Times." In *Judicial Activism of a Constitutional Court in a Democratic State. Proceedings of the 2016 Conference of the Constitutional Court of the Republic of Latvia*. Riga: Constitutional Court of the Republic of Latvia.

Letter No. 288 of 28 November 2019 from the President of the State to the Speaker of the Saeima I. Mūrniece and the Prime Minister A.K. Kariņš regarding the formation and discussion of the budget and the budget package in the Saeima. Accessed September 2, 2022. www.president.lv/storage/kcfinder/files/VP_281119_Nr.288.pdf

Neimanis, Jānis. 2021. *Tiesneša atkārtotas apstiprināšanas aizliegums Satversmes tiesā [Prohibition of re-appointment of a justice in the Constitutional Court, No. 4 (1166)]*. Rīga: Jurista Vārds.

Pleps, Janis. 2012. "The Principle of Good Legislation." In *The Quality of Legal Acts and its Importance in Contemporary Legal Space*, edited by Rozenfelds Jānis, Pleps Jānis, Kenny Mel, Osyka Igor, Burduli Irakli, Prokop Krzysztof, Mizaras Vytautas et al., 16–26. Rīga: University of Latvia Press.

Priekulis, Jānis. 2021. *Par tiesībām atkārtoti ieņemt Satversmes tiesas tiesneša amatu [On the right to re-hold the position of a justice of the Constitutional Court, No. 4 (1166)]*. Rīga: Jurista Vārds.

Prochazka, Radoslav. 2002. *Mission Accomplished. On Founding Constitutional Adjudication in Central Europe*. New York: Central European University Press.

Radziņš, Egils. 1998. "Karavāna -tuvojas – kam? *Satversmes* tiesas pirmais spriedums. Ko tas nozīmē Latvijas tiesību sistēmai? *Satversmes* tiesas pirmais spriedums." [The caravan approaching – to whom? The Constitutional Court's first judgement. What does it mean for the Latvian legal system? The first Constitutional Court judgement] In *Sprieduma teksts, atsauksmes, analīze, vērtējumi*. Rīga: LU žurnāla, Latvijas vēstures fonds'.

Rezevska, Daiga. 2020. "Deriving and Concretization of the Principle of Good Legislation." In *Legal Science: Functions, Significance and Future in Legal Systems II. Collection of Research Papers in Conjunction with the 7th International Scientific Conference of the Faculty of Law of the University of Latvia*, edited by Amatucci Carlo, Schafer Frank L., Rodiņa Anita, Oijama Kazunobu, Kull Irene, Sharkey Nolan, Oberman Steven et al., 330–338. Riga: University of Latvia.

Rodiņa, Anita. 2019. "Foreign Materials in the Judgments of the Constitutional Court of the Republic of Latvia." In *Judicial Cosmopolitanism. The Use of Foreign Law in Contemporary Constitutional Systems*, edited by Giuseppe Franco Ferrari, 476–500. Leiden and Boston: Brill Nijhoff.

———. 2021. *Appointment of the Constitutional Court Justice: Some Issues. No. 14*, 129–145. Rīga: Juridiskā zinātne.

———, and Annija Kārkliņa. 2017. "Constitutional Law and Constitutional Review." In *The Law of the Baltic States*, edited by Tanel Kerikmäe, Kristi Joamets, Jānis Pleps, Anita Rodiņa, Tomas Berkmanas, and Edita Gruodytė, 192–204. Leiden: Springer International Publishing.

Schwartz, Herman. 2000. *The Struggle for Constitutional Justice in Post-Communist Europe*. Chicago and London: The University of Chicago Press.

Sólyom, László. 2015. "The Rise and Decline of Constitutional Culture in Hungary." In *Constitutional Crisis in the European Constitutional Area. Theory, Law and Politics in Hungary and Romania*, edited by von Bogdandy Armin and Sonnevend Pál, 5–32. Oxford and Portland, OR: Hart Publishing.

Spale, Alla. 2016. *Satversmes tiesa divdesmit gados: no idejas līdz šodienai [Constitutional Court within twenty years: from the idea to nowadays, No. 49]*. Rīga: Jurista, Vārds.

Weinrib, Jacob. 2016. *Dimensions of Dignity. The Theory and Practice of Modern Constitutional Law*. Cambridge: Cambridge University Press.

Ziemele, Ineta. 2018. "Foreword." In *Selected Case-law of the Constitutional Court of the Republic of Latvia: 1996–2017*. Riga: The Constitutional Court of the Republic of Latvia.

———, Alla Spale, and Laila Jurcēna. 2020. "The Constitutional Court of the Republic of Latvia." In *The Max Planck Handbooks in European Public Law. Volume III. Constitutional Adjudication: Institutions*, edited by von Bogdandy Armin and Grabenwarter Peter Huber Christoph, 505–563. Oxford: Oxford University.

7 The Lithuanian Constitutional Court

The gradual emergence of a strong guardian

*Dovilė Pūraitė-Andrikienė**

7.1 Introduction

After the restoration of Lithuania's independence on 11 March 1990, the Constitution of the Republic of Lithuania (hereinafter LC), adopted by a referendum on 25 October 1992, created for the first time in the history of the Lithuanian state an institution devoted to constitutional review – the Constitutional Court of the Republic of Lithuania (hereinafter LiCC or Court). Constitutional review is the most important instrument in a legal system for ensuring the effectiveness of the constitution, especially in countries with a newly established constitutional order. For this reason, after the collapse of the totalitarian system, Central and Eastern European countries relied heavily on this new institution. The "constitutional renaissance" coincided with the "democratic renaissance", and legal thinking was easily overwhelmed by the idea of a special court reviewing the constitutionality of legal acts. Thus, constitutional courts were established in these states, including Lithuania, with the aim of ensuring constitutional stability in order to avoid the erosion of democratic values.

It can be confidently argued that the LiCC, established in 1993, has successfully performed this task in Lithuania for almost three decades. Not only has the establishment of the LiCC fulfilled its purpose, but its performance has exceeded the expectations of its creators and has gone far beyond their initial theoretical considerations in several ways. Constitutional review has changed the way the Lithuanian legal system is understood (Kūris 2003, 45–46).

The development of a country is inseparable from the development of its constitution. On the one hand, the constitution determines the development of the political system, establishing its directions, forms, and limits. On the other hand, the development of the political system and of society poses new challenges to the constitution as well as to the ever-changing legal reality, dictating its dynamics and progress. As guardians of the constitution, constitutional courts cannot avoid facing the challenges posed by the metamorphosis of the state and society. Thus, the performance of constitutional courts also depends significantly on the social, political, and legal environment they are situated in.

* Law Institute, Lithuanian Centre for Social Sciences

DOI: 10.4324/9781003399483-7

Considering these challenges, it is possible to distinguish three periods of the LiCC's activity.[1] The first period of the LiCC's activity (1993–2000) can be described as a period of the consolidation of the newly established institution of judicial review in the Lithuanian legal system. The second period (2001–2010) might be best understood as the years of the consolidation of its own role as a central and strong guardian of the Lithuanian Constitution. Then in the third period (2011–2020), the LC became an actual standard of constitutionality, with sufficiently clear and defined criteria that would be further developed by the case law of the LiCC. The last years of this decade were also marked by significant changes related to the powers of the LiCC. In 2019, amendments to the LC entered into force, introducing the mechanism of the constitutional complaint, which gives individuals and legal entities the right to appeal directly to the LiCC in the event of a violation of their constitutional rights or freedoms.

These developments show that the position of the LiCC in the Lithuanian legal and political system has gradually gained in strength. According to recent opinion polls, the LiCC is among the most trusted institutions in Lithuania.[2] However, this does not mean that this institution has not faced challenges caused by the political and economic crises of the last decade. Although the LiCC did not experience such drastic restrictions on its powers or activity as its Hungarian or Polish counterparts, it nevertheless came under pressure from the political authorities in times of social and economic turmoil and during the COVID-19 pandemic.

7.2 Structure and competences of the LiCC

Article 103 of the LC provides that the Lithuanian Constitutional Court shall consist of nine judges, each appointed for a single term of nine years. One-third of the LiCC is replaced every three years. The *Seimas* (Parliament) appoints three judges (by a simple majority) from among the candidates proposed by the President of the Republic, the Speaker of the *Seimas*, and the President of the Supreme Court (each of whom proposes one candidate). The *Seimas* appoints the President of the LiCC from among its judges upon the proposal of the President of the Republic. Thus, all the judges of LiCC and the President of the LiCC are appointed by the *Seimas* (Parliament). However, since the President of the Republic, the Speaker of the *Seimas*, and the President of the Supreme Court also contribute to deciding the composition of the LiCC

1 These periods will be discussed in more detail in the following parts of this chapter.

2 As of 2021, 46.7% of respondents have full confidence in the Constitutional Court. Confidence in the Constitutional Court is the highest among all the classical public authorities (legislative, executive, judicial) and twice as high as in other courts (Constitutional Court of the Republic of Lithuania 2021).

(by nominating the candidates), it can be concluded that all three branches of government participate in the formation of the Court.[3]

The LiCC hears all cases in its full composition. The Law on the Constitutional Court (hereinafter LCC) does not provide for the possibility of deciding cases in chambers or in reduced compositions. Article 19 of the LCC provides that the Court shall hear cases and adopt rulings, conclusions, or decisions collegially in the presence of at least two-thirds of the total number of judges, and that the judges shall not have the right to withhold their vote or abstain from voting.

Article 105 (1–2) of the Constitution determines the powers of the LiCC to review the constitutionality of laws and other legal acts. It stipulates that the LiCC shall examine and decide whether the laws of the Republic of Lithuania or other legal acts adopted by the *Seimas* are in conflict with the Lithuanian Constitution (Article 105 (1)) and whether the acts of the President of the Republic and the acts of the Government of the Republic are in conflict with the Constitution ***and laws*** (Article 105 (2)).[4] In addition, pursuant to Article 105 (3), the LiCC shall decide: (1) whether electoral laws were violated during the process of the election of the President of the Republic or the election of the members of the *Seimas*; (2) whether the state of health of the President of the Republic allows him to continue to hold office; (3) whether the international treaties of the Republic of Lithuania are in conflict with the LC; and (4) whether concrete actions of the members of the *Seimas* and state officials against whom impeachment proceedings have been initiated are in conflict with the LC. Pursuant to Article 102 (2), the status of the LiCC and the procedure for exercising its powers are determined by the Law on the Constitutional Court (LCC), adopted on 3 February 1993.

Constitutional review had never existed in Lithuania before 1992, a situation which led the creators of the current model of judicial review to take a cautious position concerning this institution. Both Lithuanian (Jarašiūnas 2003, 63) and foreign (Sadurski 2008, 6) constitutional law research emphasizes that Chapter VIII of the LC establishes a rather minimalist conception of the LiCC's jurisdiction. With regard to the powers to review the constitutionality of legal acts, it should be noted that the rather narrow scope of these powers was made even more evident in relation to the LiCC by the rather limited circle of legal entities that are entitled to appeal to the LiCC (a group of the members of the *Seimas*, the President of the Republic, the government, the courts, and the *Seimas in corpore*). However, the range of potential applicants was significantly expanded in 2019, when the *Seimas* adopted constitutional amendments establishing the mechanism for individual constitutional

3 In 2020–2021 the Constitutional Court faced an unprecedented challenge regarding the appointment of judges to the Constitutional Court. For more on this, see 7.4. of this chapter.

4 Interestingly, Article 105 stipulates that the Court should consider whether government orders or presidential orders conflict with the Constitution and *laws* adopted by the Parliament.

complaints. Lithuania introduced the so-called normative constitutional complaint[5]: a person may file an individual constitutional complaint against laws and other legal acts adopted by the *Seimas*, as well as against legal acts of the executive branch.

Up until March 2019, when the mechanism of individual constitutional complaints was introduced, the Lithuanian model of constitutional review had not undergone any significant changes. Notwithstanding some previous initiatives, the legal regime set forth in Chapter VIII of the Constitution was amended only recently. Although the Law on the LiCC had been amended and supplemented several times, these amendments, except for those allowing dissenting opinions in 2008, had not resulted in more profound changes to the original model of constitutional review adopted after the transition to democratic rule (Pūraitė-Andrikienė 2021, 225–243).

Furthermore, it is widely held that the lacuna of Article 102 (1) and Article 105 (1–2) of the Constitution has significantly expanded the possibilities of constitutional review (Kūris 2011, 83). These provisions of the Constitution do not specify which particular laws (other than ordinary laws) or other legal acts fall within the scope of constitutional review. Therefore, in its jurisprudence, the LiCC has been confronted with the need to interpret whether the scope of constitutional review it is authorized to exercise includes laws amending the Constitution, constitutional laws, laws adopted by referendum, laws adopted before the entry into force of the Constitution, the Standing Orders of the *Seimas*, or acts that are no longer in force (Pūraitė-Andrikienė 2020, 72–91). The Constitution and the LCC do not even mention *expressis verbis* that the LiCC has the power to interpret the Constitution, although the assessment of the constitutionality of legal acts undoubtedly involves the interpretation of the Constitution as an indispensable element of constitutional review. Consequently, the LiCC had to explicitly declare that it has the powers to interpret the Constitution itself, and it did so for the first time in its ruling of 30 May 2003.

As regards the temporal effect of its rulings, Article 107 of the Constitution stipulates that a legal act may not be applied from the moment of the official publication of the Court's decision, which declares the legal act in question unconstitutional. Nevertheless, in its decision of 30 December 2003, the LiCC stated that the general rule enshrined in Article 107 (1) of the Constitution stating that the temporal effect of the decisions of the LiCC are *ex nunc* is not absolute. Currently, there are four such exceptions in the case law of the LiCC

5 Under the Constitution, every person shall have the right to apply to the Constitutional Court concerning the acts specified in the first and second paragraphs of Article 105 if a decision adopted on the basis of these acts has violated the constitutional rights or freedoms of the person and the person has exhausted all legal remedies (Article 106 (4)).

(three of these are defined in the decision of 19 December 2012,[6] and one more is mentioned in the decision of 19 June 2018[7]). Thus, the LiCC elaborated in its case law certain elements of the *ex tunc* model of judicial review, despite the fact that there is no *expressis verbis* mention of *ex tunc* rulings in the Constitution (see Pūraitė -Andrikienė 2020, 70–90).[8] The same is true for *pro futuro* rulings, since the Court has found ways to postpone the temporal effect of its decisions. Considering the specific circumstances of a particular case, the LiCC may set a later date for the publication of its decisions declaring a particular act (or part thereof) unconstitutional (Article 84 (3) LCC). The delay in the publication of the Court's decisions means that the decision, although taken on a certain date, has legal effect only at a later date, i.e. after it has been published in the Register of legal acts (Pūraitė-Andrikienė 2020, 70–90).

7.3 General impressions

Section VIII of the LC, which sets forth the main features of the status of the LiCC, refers to decisions and conclusions of the LiCC. Article 105 (1) of the Constitution states that the LiCC shall consider and adopt a decision as to whether the laws of the Republic of Lithuania and other legal acts adopted by the *Seimas* are in conflict with the Constitution or not. Article 105 (3) of the Constitution lists the cases in which the LiCC shall submit its conclusions. However, the official constitutional doctrine stresses that the term *decisions* in the Constitution cannot be interpreted as meaning that the Constitutional Court, when deciding on matters falling within its competence, can only adopt a legal act which is called a decision.[9] Article 71 of the LCC provides for two types of rulings by the LiCC: (1) a finding that a legal act does not violate the Constitution or the law; and (2) a finding that a legal act does violate the Constitution or the law.

Nevertheless, in the literature the prevailing view is that the dichotomy of "upholding/striking down" does not accurately reflect the actual diversity of ruling types issued by the LiCC (Staugaitytė 2007, 256). Brewer-Carías argues convincingly that the role of the constitutional courts has changed significantly in the last decades and that it is no longer limited to examining the

6 The Constitutional Court of the Republic of Lithuania Decision of 19 December 2012 (Official Gazette Valstybės žinios, 2012, No. 152–7779).

7 The Constitutional Court of the Republic of Lithuania Ruling of 19 June 2018 (Register of Legal Acts, 2018, No. 10101).

8 By the ruling of Constitutional Court of 19 May 2021, for the first time, all the consequences of the application of an unconstitutional legal regulation were declared unconstitutional. It was stated that the consequences that arose on the basis of the impugned unconstitutional legal regulation before the date of the official publication of this ruling of the Constitutional Court must not be regarded as lawful.

9 The Constitutional Court of the Republic of Lithuania Ruling of 28 March 2006 (Official Gazette Valstybės žinios 2006, No. 49–1600).

constitutionality of laws: constitutional courts often choose not to determine the unconstitutionality of a law or regulation, but instead to *interpret* them in a way that is compatible with the constitution (Brewer-Carías 2011, 10). The same can be said of the LiCC.

Lithuanian legal scholars have identified and discussed the following types of rulings: rulings finding the reviewed legal act to be constitutional; rulings of substantive unconstitutionality; rulings of partial substantive unconstitutionality ("partial" rulings); rulings of procedural unconstitutionality; rulings of insufficient legal regulation; rulings of legislative omission; and interpretive rulings (Staugaitytė 2007, 257).

Clearly, the rulings of the LiCC which declare laws unconstitutional have the greatest impact on the legal system. However, it is important to recognize that even unconstitutionality rulings on substantive grounds are not uniform. Sometimes the Court has to clarify the specific legal consequences of these rulings. It should be noted that the power of the Court to set out these concrete legal consequences is not explicitly enshrined in the Constitution but has been developed in the case law of the Court. Two main types of specific legal consequences can be distinguished: the first type of legal consequence can be associated with the role of the LiCC as a "negative legislator" while the second one is connected with its role as a "positive legislator" (Žalimas 2019, 527–539). For example, one specific type of legal consequence associated with the role of the "negative legislator" is the provision of legislative guidance to the legislator.[10] The Court indicates the outlines of a specific legal regime to be established in the implementation of a particular decision of the LiCC. These guidelines can be both abstract and very specific. The specific legal effects of the decisions are related to the court's role as a "positive legislator", as they formulate binding rules derived from the Constitution (including in the justification of the LiCC decision) which are temporary, transitional, or preventive until the legislature establishes permanent legal rules in accordance with the provisions of the Constitution. It is important to emphasize, however, that while these so-called negative and positive roles are attributed to the LiCC in the constitutional law literature, they in no way imply the power of the LiCC to legislate. Indeed, according to the constitutional principle of separation of powers, the LiCC would not be permitted to do so. The need to establish certain legal consequences is not dictated by the desire to assume the functions of

10 It should be emphasized that the term *negative legislator* has a rather different meaning in the international literature than it does in Lithuanian legal discourse. *Negative legislator* in the international literature means that the constitutional court does not give the parliament any instruction on how to remedy the unconstitutionality, while the court becomes *positive legislator* when it includes either general (non-binding) prescriptions in the justification, or, more particularly, binding prescriptions in the operative part of its decision. This is in sharp contrast to how the terms *negative* and *positive legislator* are interpreted in Lithuanian legal scholarship.

the legislature, but by the interest to ensure that not only formal but substantive constitutional justice is established in the review process.

Regarding the other types of rulings that were predetermined by the JUDICON-EU project, it should be noted that some of them do not fall within the jurisdiction of the LiCC. For example, the LiCC does not interpret the constitution *in abstracto*; therefore, there are no examples of such rulings by the LiCC. The same applies to constitutional requirements as defined by the project's methodology. The situation is different concerning the procedural unconstitutionality of a law. Although finding a legal act unconstitutional on procedural grounds is not explicitly mentioned in the Constitution, it is enshrined in Article 64 (1) of the Law on the Constitutional Court, which provides that the LiCC shall examine the compatibility of a law or other legal acts with the Constitution on the basis of the following criteria: (1) the content of the norms; (2) the scope of the regulation; (3) the form of the regulation; and (4) the procedure of its adoption, signing, publication, or entry into force.

Furthermore, another ruling type has also emerged in the case law of the LiCC. While legislative gaps or omissions are not expressly mentioned in the provisions of the LC, the original position of the LiCC has changed considerably in this respect. At the beginning of its activity, the Court stated that it does not deal with gaps in the law (legislative omissions), as this is the prerogative of the legislature.[11] Nevertheless, later the LiCC did start to review legislative gaps and argued that it falls within its jurisdiction to declare instances of unconstitutionality by legislative omission (Kūris 2011, 100). Thus, according to the official doctrine of the LiCC, subjects listed in Article 106 of the Constitution may also bring the issue of assessment of legislative omissions before the LiCC. The doctrine states that in cases where laws (or parts thereof) do not provide for a certain legal regulation, the LiCC is empowered to examine the constitutionality of these laws (or parts of thereof) if the absence of legal regulations may violate constitutional principles and/or norms. In delimiting the scope of conflict of a legal norm with the Constitution in cases of legislative omission, the LiCC often uses the phrase "contradicts insofar as it is not provided for", as well as the phrases "contradicts insofar as it cannot be according to the legal regulation provided for in it", "contradicts insofar as it refers to it", or "contradicts insofar as it is restricted by it". Given that the position of the LiCC has evolved in relation to its own powers to declare legislative omissions, it can be concluded that the results of the coding of rulings in the first period of the LiCC's activity will not show any cases of legislative omission.

11 The Constitutional Court of the Republic of Lithuania Ruling of 21 April 1994 (Official Gazette Valstybės žinios 1994, No. 31–562) and The Constitutional Court of the Republic of Lithuania Ruling of 22 December 1995 (Official Gazette Valstybės žinios 1995, Nr. 106–2379).

Since the mechanism of individual constitutional complaints was introduced in Lithuania only in 2019, the first rulings issued under this procedure can be found in the coding material only in 2020. The same applies to dissenting opinions. The first dissenting opinions appeared only in 2009, as the possibility to issue dissenting opinions came into existence only with the amendments to the LC in 2008.

7.4 Trends in majority decisions

As mentioned in the introduction, the activity of the LiCC can be divided into three main periods. These periods are, of course, not strictly delimited from each other, but merely reflect certain sequential phases in the development of the jurisprudential activity of the LiCC.

7.4.1 The first period: 1993–2000

The first period of the LiCC's activity (1993–2000) can be described as a period of consolidation of the new model of constitutional review, which had never existed in Lithuania before. During this period, the LiCC not only had to review the constitutionality of laws, but also began to develop the protection of human rights. Nevertheless, the Court acted with a high degree of caution. The LiCC's prudent approach is also reflected in the coding results as compared to the later periods: a relatively low number of rulings were issued (144); the average strength of its rulings was relatively low (3.31); and there was a relatively low percentage of restraining rulings (47.2%). These indicators are significantly lower than in later periods (Figure 7.1 and Table 7.1).

The self-restraint of the first LiCC is also reflected in the fact that the Court issued only two types of rulings either: (1) the act was declared

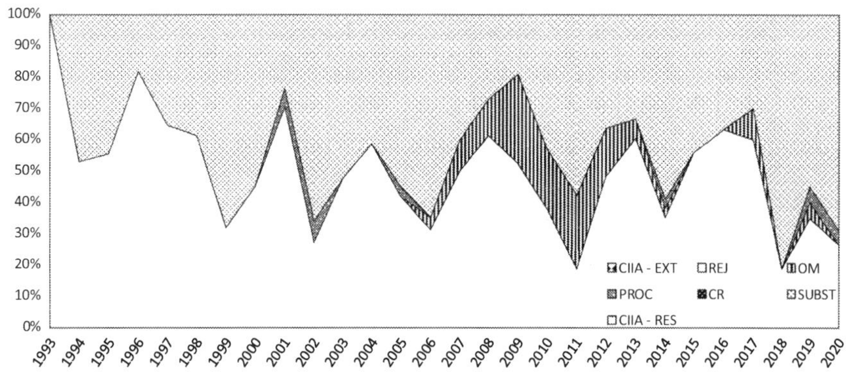

Figure 7.1 Frequency of the ruling types (1998–2020) (LiCC)

Table 7.1 Three periods of the LiCC

Period	*No. of decisions*	*No. of rulings*	*Avg. strength*	*Standard deviation*	*Ratio of restraining rulings*
1993–2000	61	144	3.31	3.49	47.2%
2001–2010	114	338	3.69	3.50	57.7%
2011–2020	130	390	3.50	3.51	57.4%
SUM	**305**	**872**	**3.54**	**3.51**	**55.8%**

constitutional (76); or (2) it was declared unconstitutional on substantive grounds (68) (Figure 7.1). The Court's cautious approach in the early years also meant (at least in part) that it was not subject to major pressure or criticism from the political authorities during this period.

Although, as mentioned, the LiCC was quite cautious in its first years, this does not mean that it did not have to deal with cases that were of particular importance for the legal and political development of the country. During this period, the LiCC had to rule on issues such as the death penalty and the form of government.

In its decision of 9 December 1998, the LiCC found that the death penalty provided for in the Criminal Code violated the Constitution. At that time, the death penalty was still supported not only by a large majority of the citizens (about 70–80%, according to opinion polls), but also by representatives of the state authorities. Thus, this particular decision had significant consequences since the death penalty was abolished at the national level despite the political context which favoured upholding the possibility of death penalty. The LiCC's decision cemented the concept of human rights and freedoms as irrevocable, inseparable rights of individuals who are not bound either to a territory or to a nation.[12]

Another important decision of 10 January 1998 underscores the Court's role as a legal arbiter in political disputes over the functioning of the supreme state authorities. The most important aspect of this case is that the LiCC clearly determined the form of government of the Lithuanian state. The LiCC found that Lithuania is a parliamentary republic, although it also has some features of the so-called semi-presidential form of government. The Court also noted that after the election of the President of the Republic, unlike after the election of the Parliament, the government is not obliged to resign, but it can continue the activities envisaged in its programme.[13]

12 The Constitutional Court of the Republic of Lithuania Ruling of 9 December 1998 (Official Gazette Valstybės žinios 1998, No. 109–3004).

13 The Constitutional Court of the Republic of Lithuania Ruling of 10 January 1998 (Official Gazette Valstybės žinios 1998, Nr. 5–99).

7.4.2 The second period: 2001–2010

The second period of the LiCC's activity (2001–2010) can be characterized as the years of the consolidation of its role as a strong guardian of the Constitution. In the first years of this period, the LiCC not only summarized the developments of the constitutional doctrine of the Constitution as a supreme law without gaps,[14] but it also officially clarified the disputes about the status of the LiCC in the system of separation of powers. The LiCC also developed a doctrine on the scope of its own powers and consolidated its role as the sole official interpreter of the Constitution: in 2003, it was established for the first time that, under the Constitution, only the LiCC has the power to formally interpret the Constitution[15] and that the LiCC also has the power to examine questions of legislative omission.[16] It was also established for the first time that the general rule established in the Constitution that the decisions of the LiCC are to be applied prospectively is not absolute.[17] Moreover, it was established that the LiCC may review the constitutionality not only of ordinary laws, but also of laws amending the Constitution, constitutional laws, laws adopted by referendum, laws adopted before the Constitution came into force, the Standing Order of the *Seimas*, and acts that are no longer in force (Pūraitė-Andrikienė 2020, 72–91).

The strengthening of the role of the LiCC as the main guardian of the Constitution is also reflected in our dataset, since the number of rulings issued has more than doubled (338), while the average strength of rulings (3.69) and the percentage of restrictive rulings (57.7%) have also increased (Table 7.1). This trend is also reflected in the greater diversity of the ruling types as compared to the first period: 19 rulings declared legislative omissions, and 5 found procedural unconstitutionality. In this period, the majority of rulings declared legislation to be unconstitutional (Figure 7.1 and Figure 7.2).

What are the reasons behind this phenomenon? First, this strengthening is related to the gradual consolidation of the LiCC as the central guardian of the Constitution, which began in the previous period. Of course, it is also related

14 According to the official constitutional doctrine formulated by the LiCC, the Constitution is the supreme law without gaps, and therefore no legislation can escape constitutional review. In other words, all laws and other legal acts must be consistent not only with the Constitution, but also with the official constitutional doctrine formulated by the Constitutional Court. Of particular relevance in this respect is the LiCC's ruling of 25 May 2004 (Official Gazette Valstybės žinios 2004, No. 85–3094).

15 The Constitutional Court of the Republic of Lithuania Ruling of 30 May 2003 (Official Gazette Valstybės žinios, 2003, No. 53–2361).

16 The Constitutional Court of the Republic of Lithuania Ruling of 4 March 2003 (Official Gazette Valstybės žinios 2003, No. 24–1004).

17 The Constitutional Court of the Republic of Lithuania Ruling of 30 December 2003 (Official Gazette Lietuvos žinios, 2003, No 124–5643).

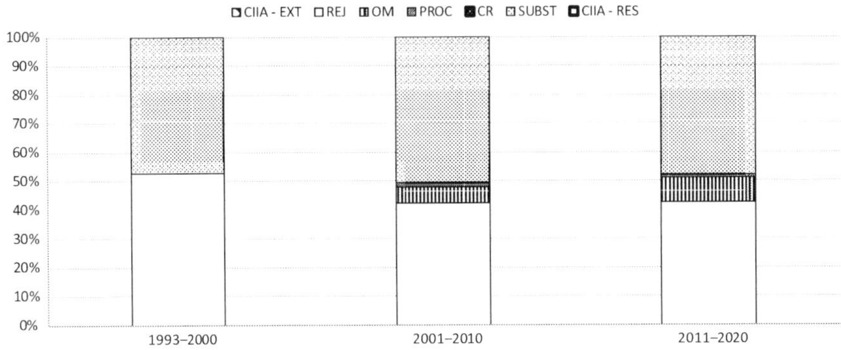

Figure 7.2 Frequency of ruling types by courts (LiCC)

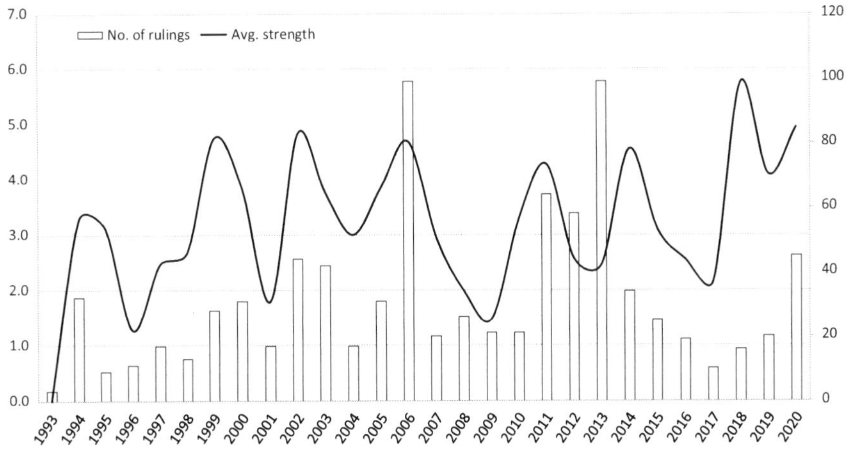

Figure 7.3 Number and average strength of rulings (1993–2020) (LiCC)

to the maturity of society and politicians and their willingness to accept the new concept of a constitution-centred law developed by the LiCC. Secondly, the LiCC in this period was composed of some of the most prominent scholars of Lithuanian constitutional law (E. Kūris, E. Jarašiūnas, V. Sinkevičius, T. Birmontienė) as well as specialists in other fields of law. The role of Judge Kūris, President of the LiCC in 2002–2008, who had a great influence on strengthening the Court, should also be highlighted. During his presidency, the average strength of rulings increased to 4.11 (Figure 7.3 and Figure 7.4). Kūris and other judges at that time enjoyed high respect both in society and in political circles. It is likely that (at least partly) for this reason the rulings

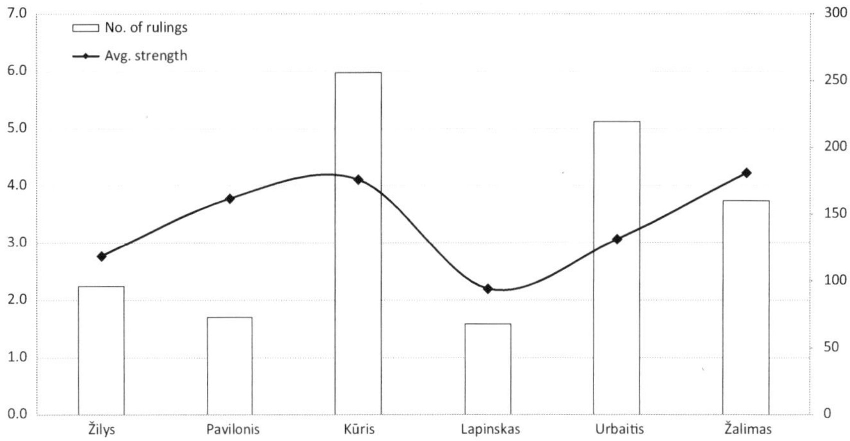

Figure 7.4 Average strength of rulings by presidents (1993–2020) (ESC)

of the LiCC were accepted by the general public as well as by political circles without much resistance.[18]

The strengthening of the role of the LiCC as the main guardian of the Constitution is also reflected by some decisions of the LiCC, which had a very strong political resonance and, in the interests of upholding the supremacy of the Constitution, restricted the legislator's room for manoeuvre quite significantly. In this context, it is worth mentioning the decision of 25 May 2004. After the LiCC concluded that President Paksas had broken his oath and seriously violated the LC, Parliament removed him from office in 2004 through an impeachment proceeding. However, this decision of the Parliament did not completely end the constitutional crisis, and the LiCC had to deal with other related cases preventing the constitutional crisis from continuing. The case was initiated by a group of members of Parliament who supported President Paksas' intention to stand in the presidential elections announced after his impeachment. The LiCC ruled that the amendment to the Law on Presidential Elections, according to which a person impeached by the *Seimas* and

18 Of course, this trend of strengthening of the role of the LiCC is not absolute. For example, the postponement of the introduction of the individual constitutional complaint can be evaluated as a reluctance to further strengthen the LiCC (although the necessary drafts to amend the Constitution and the relevant laws were prepared as early as 2007, it was decided in 2009 to postpone the introduction of this mechanism). Although official documents state that it was the economic crisis that led to the "freezing" of the introduction of this mechanism, the scholarly literature also suggests that political will, or rather, the lack of it, was the decisive factor that delayed the introduction of the possibility of constitutional complaints (Danėlienė 2019, 421).

removed from office through impeachment proceeding cannot be elected if less than five years have passed since his impeachment, does not violate the Constitution except for the clause "if less than five years have passed", which was declared unconstitutional. This decision is based on the principle that the Constitution does not provide a time limit within which a person removed from office by the *Seimas* may resume the same office. The judges argued that the purpose of impeachment proceedings is not only to remove from office a person who has committed a serious violation of the Constitution, but it is also much broader: to prevent that person from assuming another office that involves taking an oath under the Constitution.[19]

Another example is the Court's decision of 13 November 2006, which declared unconstitutional the contested provisions of the Citizenship Law, under which a very broad range of persons were authorized to hold dual citizenship. The Court found that this created the conditions for dual citizenship to become a widespread phenomenon rather than a particularly rare exception. The Court stated that, within the framework of the Constitution, the legislature may not be guided by the idea that there is no reason to limit cases of multiple citizenship. However, if the legislature does so, the relevant provisions of the Constitution must be amended. Thus, only a referendum to amend Article 12(2) of the Constitution could make it possible to make multiple citizenship a widespread rather than an exceptional case.[20] By formulating the constitutional doctrine that the Constitution must be amended by referendum to change the content of the prohibition on multiple citizenship, the LiCC completely limited the ability of the legislature to change the content of this prohibition.

Furthermore, in its decision of 6 June 2006, the Court had to deal with a unique case involving its own status. In this case, the Court considered whether the title of Article 1 of the Law on Constitutional Court as well as the provision that stipulated that the LiCC is an autonomous and independent court exercising judicial power in accordance with the procedure established by the Constitution and the LCC were contrary to the Constitution or not. In this ruling, any doubts as to whether the LiCC is a court were refuted, and it was emphasized that the body entrusted by the Constitution with the exercise of constitutional review is directly enshrined in the Constitution and that this body is called a court in the Constitution itself. This decision also stated that the LiCC is an autonomous and independent court that exercises constitutional review and guarantees the supremacy of the Constitution in the legal order and develops constitutional doctrine, which is the only binding, official interpretation of the Constitution. Therefore, the decisions of the LiCC that

19 The Constitutional Court of the Republic of Lithuania Ruling of 25 May 2004 (Official Gazette Valstybės žinios 2004, No. 85–3094).

20 The Constitutional Court of the Republic of Lithuania Ruling of 13 November 2006 (Official Gazette Valstybės žinios 2006, No. 123–4650).

constitute the official constitutional doctrine have the same force as the text of the Constitution.[21]

7.4.3 The third period: 2011–2020

Thanks to the concept of constitution-centred law established by the earlier case law of the LiCC, in the third period of the Court, the Constitution became an actual standard of constitutionality with sufficiently clear and defined criteria, which were further developed by the LiCC. The concept of the living constitution, inspired by the Court's jurisprudence, changed not only the concept of the Constitution but also the entire legal framework of the state.

These trends are confirmed by the coding results: in this period, the average strength of the LiCC's rulings remained similar to those in the second period (3.6), as did the proportion of restrictive rulings (57.4%). The Court's activist approach in this period is also reflected in the fact that the number of rulings declaring the unconstitutionality of legislation on substantive grounds was higher than the number of those which declared constitutionality of the reviewed legal act (187 as compared to 166) (Figure 7.2).

The number of rulings in which the Court found legislative omission almost doubled as compared to the previous period, while there were four rulings in which the LiCC declared laws unconstitutional on procedural grounds, including one ruling on a constitutional amendment. The Court's high level of activity during this period is at least partly due to the influence of Judge Žalimas, who was the President of the Court from 2014 to 2021. As the coding results show, during Žalimas' presidency the average strength of rulings (4.22) was the highest in comparison to other presidents of the Court.

Unlike in the previous periods, however, in the first half of the third period the LiCC faced a sharp increase in harsh criticism from some politicians, which was generally unfounded from a legal point of view (and which, moreover, was not particularly supported by the public). There was also a growing number of political initiatives aimed at limiting the powers of the LiCC or otherwise obstructing the Court's work. This backlash was due not only to the activist approach of the LiCC, but also to the effects of the economic and financial crisis that had hit the country. In 2011–2013, the Court's caseload was dominated by questions concerning the constitutionality of the austerity measures taken by the legislative and executive branches. This led to a significant increase in both the number of petitions received by the LiCC and the number of rulings it issued, as well as the number of provisions of legislative acts it declared unconstitutional.

The increase in the number of rulings was also due to the fact that the amendments to the Law on Constitutional Court in 2011 made it possible to

21 The Constitutional Court of the Republic of Lithuania Ruling of 6 June 2006 (Official Gazette Valstybės žinios 2006, No. 65–2400).

hear cases by written procedure. These amendments also abolished the legal rule according to which the LiCC was not allowed to hear several cases at the same time (which meant that once it started hearing a particular case, it could also take up a new case) (The 2011 Act).

The increase in the number of rulings by the Court declaring legislation unconstitutional and the rise in cases of legislative omissions can also be attributed to the economic crisis, when legislators often took measures which sidelined human rights and freedoms in order to stabilize the economy. The LiCC was faced with the challenge of preventing human rights from being violated by legislative decisions based on short-sighted motives of political expediency. On the other hand, this responsibility of the LiCC created some tensions between the LiCC and the political authorities.

After some of the austerity measures had been ruled unconstitutional, some subsequent LiCC decisions were received unfavourably by politicians. There were political calls for the LiCC to be abolished, for its powers to be limited, and for its activities to be made excessively difficult. At the time of the economic crisis, the LiCC was threatened by reducing its budget, while at the same time it had to face an increased workload and attempts to apply various forms of political pressures (see Masnevaitė, Pūraitė-Andrikienė, and Žalimas 2015, 484–491).

In this period the LiCC decided several other important cases in which it protected certain family groups from discrimination (see LiCC decisions from 28 September 2011 and 11 January 2019[22]). In these decisions, the LiCC held that the constitutional concept of the family may not be derived solely from the institute of marriage. Moreover, it established that the constitutional concept of family is based on mutual responsibility between family members, understanding, emotional affection, assistance, and similar bonds, as well as on the voluntary determination to take on certain rights and duties. This means that the crucial point is the content of relations, whereas the form of expression of these relations carries no essential significance for the constitutional concept of family. These decisions were the subject of widespread debates and focused on how the concept of family should be defined.

In the wake of the economic crisis, the LiCC also decided several important cases concerning the constitutionality of constitutional amendments. In its decisions of 24 January 2014 and 11 July 2014, the LiCC declared that amendments to the Constitution cannot be arbitrary and that those that attempt to override the eternity clauses of the Constitution cannot be adopted, even by referendum. The 24 January 2014 decision was the first time that a constitutional amendment (the Law Amending Article 125 of the Constitution) was declared unconstitutional on procedural grounds. In this

22 The Constitutional Court of the Republic of Lithuania Ruling of 28 September 2011 (Official Gazette Valstybės žinios 2011, No. 118-5564) and The Constitutional Court of the Republic of Lithuania Ruling of 11 January 2019 (Register of Legal Acts 2019, No. 439).

ruling, the court identified the substantive and procedural limits for amending the Constitution, non-compliance with which may result in such amendments being declared unconstitutional.[23] A further decision of 11 July 2014 elaborated on the limitations on amending the Constitution. The court declared that amendments to the Constitution may not erode the Constitution itself, nor may they be adopted by any procedure. Perhaps the most important of these limitations is the doctrine of eternal provisions. It states that it is absolutely forbidden to make amendments to the Constitution that would deny the inherent nature of human rights and freedoms, democracy, and the independence of the state. Since the denial of these constitutional values would undermine the very essence of the Constitution, constitutional amendments that would override them cannot be adopted at all, not even by referendum.[24]

Nevertheless, questions have sometimes been raised as to whether the LiCC has interpreted the limits of its powers too broadly in deciding the constitutionality not only of constitutional amendments adopted by Parliament, but also of amendments adopted by referendum. Although the LiCC has not been confronted with such drastic backlashes as those confronting the Hungarian or Polish courts, it should be noted that during this period the suggestion was repeatedly voiced that Lithuania should follow the Hungarian example. In this regard, there is reason to be pleased that similar initiatives in Lithuania, unlike in other states in the region, have not gone any further. Moreover, as noted already, in 2019 the competences of the LiCC were significantly expanded by introducing the mechanism for hearing individual constitutional complaints.[25] Since the introduction of the constitutional complaint, the LiCC has received most of its petitions from individuals and legal entities. These changes have further strengthened the role of the LiCC in the Lithuanian legal and political system.

However, at the end of the third period, the LiCC faced an unprecedented challenge in connection with the appointment of judges to its benches. At the start of the pandemic, the Parliament was approaching the deadline for appointing three new judges, who had to be approved by 19 March 2020. However, due to the lockdown restrictions, no new judges could be appointed in time. When the vote in the *Seimas* was finally held on 23 April 2020, none of the three proposed candidates were approved. The Law on Constitutional Court provides that in cases where a new judge is not appointed, a judge whose term has expired shall act in his place until the new judge is appointed and sworn in (Article 4). Therefore, some judges whose terms have expired have continued to

23 The Constitutional Court of the Republic of Lithuania Ruling of 24 January 2014 (Register of Legal Acts, 2014, No. 478).

24 The Constitutional Court of the Republic of Lithuania Ruling of 11 July 2014 (Register of Legal Acts, 2014, No. 10117).

25 Initiatives to introduce the mechanism of constitutional complaints were renewed when the *Seimas* approved the program of the new government in 2016. The program announced the government's intention to establish "the right of every citizen of the Republic of Lithuania to appeal to the Constitutional Court".

hold office. Even as of 14 January 2021, only two of the three candidates to the LiCC had been appointed,[26] thus the term of President Žalimas was extended by one year and two months, until his successor was appointed in May 2021.

These examples show that in times of radical social upheavals (economic crisis and pandemic), the Lithuanian Constitutional Court was exposed to greater pressure from the political authorities. It should also be noted, however, that the criticism of the LiCC voiced by some politicians, as well as the political initiatives to limit the LiCC's powers, have not been widely supported by Lithuanian society. As mentioned, according to the most recent opinion polls, the LiCC is among the institutions that are trusted the most.[27]

7.5 Trends in dissenting opinions

Nowadays, the publication of dissenting opinions is allowed everywhere in Central and Eastern Europe. However, Lithuania has long been an exception (but not the only one) among these countries. In the times when the court's authority was still weak, the publication of seemingly unanimous decisions was believed to help protect the newly established court. In Lithuania, the publication of dissenting opinions was not allowed in the early days because it might jeopardize the authority of the newly created court. It took about two decades before it was accepted that the authority of the LiCC was sufficiently established to publish dissenting opinions. Therefore, the institution of dissent in Lithuania has "grown up" along with the LiCC itself (Kelemen 2011, 1357).

Until 2008, the LCC did not provide for the possibility for judges to express dissenting opinions. The creators of the LCC considered it unfounded, given the division of Lithuanian society, the rather poor quality of its legal and political culture, and the fear that Lithuania would not find sufficient social, psychological, and other safeguards against classifying judges as "good" or "bad" based on whether they "agree with the majority" (Pūraitė-Andrikienė 2017, 238–250).

Nevertheless, amendments to the LCC adopted in 2008 eventually introduced the possibility for a judge to issue a dissenting opinion. Article 55 of the LCC was amended to provide that "a judge of the Constitutional Court who disagrees with an act adopted by the Court shall have the right to state in writing his or her dissenting opinion, stating his or her reasons in writing, not later than three working days after the pronouncement of the act in the court room".[28]

26 The candidates proposed by the President of the Republic and the President of the Supreme Court were appointed, while the candidate proposed by the Speaker of the Seimas was not.

27 As of 2021, 46.7% of respondents have full confidence in the Constitutional Court. Confidence in the Constitutional Court is the highest among all the classical public authorities (legislative, executive, judicial) and twice as high as in the other courts (Constitutional Court of the Republic of Lithuania 2021).

28 Motivations for introducing dissenting opinions included the prevalence of dissenting opinions in most European constitutional courts, but it was also argued that dissenting opinions would contribute to the advancement of constitutional doctrines and legal culture, thereby improving the work of the Constitutional Court.

Since these amendments, the situation regarding the principle of secrecy of the deliberation room has also changed significantly. Quite clearly, according to Article 53 of the Law on the Constitutional Court, neither the judges nor the officials who participated in the hearing have the right to disclose the opinions expressed in the courtroom or to reveal which way the justices voted. However, the amendments to this Article also stipulated that the expression of a separate opinion shall not be considered as a disclosure of the opinions voiced in the courtroom. But is this really the case? Although a dissenting opinion does not automatically mean that the judge actually voted against the majority decision, it is of course more likely that a dissenting judge voted against rather than for the Court's majority decision. It is also more likely that the judges who did not dissent voted in favour of the majority decision rather than against it (Kūris 2012, 1042).[29]

The fact that even dissenting opinions can make the outcome of a vote quite clear is well illustrated by a specific case. Following the LiCC's decision of 11 December 2013, no less than four judges issued a joint dissenting opinion.[30] In this context, it should be noted that at that time the LiCC consisted of only eight judges (the Lithuanian LiCC normally consists of nine judges), as no other judge had yet been appointed to fill the vacant seat of Judge Bieliūnas. It became obvious that the majority decision was adopted with four votes against and four votes in favour (including that of the President of the LiCC, whose vote was decisive). This case caused some resentment among the political authorities, which was reflected in some initiatives to amend the LCC to avoid such delicate situations in the future (Pūraitė-Andrikienė 2017, 238–250).[31]

After the introduction of dissenting opinions in 2008, legal scholars (Kūris 2011, 20) criticized Article 55(5) of the LCC, which provided for the possibility for judges who disagree with a majority position to submit a dissenting opinion within three working days. It was argued that the new regulation may give rise to reasonable doubt that the reasoning of the dissenting opinions may have been influenced by the debate or criticism that followed the Court's decision.

However, this criticism was not only related to the regulation in question, but also to the practice of using this option. In 2009, dissenting opinions were published to 11 out of 21 rulings (52.4%) (Figure 7.5). The number of dissenting opinions continued to increase in 2012 to 18, representing 31% of the rulings that year. It is important to note that the early practice of issuing dissenting opinions was the subject of considerable criticism in the Lithuanian

29 It should be noted that in Lithuania both types of separate opinions, i.e. concurring and dissenting opinions are called dissent.

30 Dissenting opinion of judges T. Birmontienė, G. Mesonis, A. Taminskas, D. Žalimas on the LiCC's ruling of 11 December 2013.

31 It was proposed that a quorum of two-thirds of the judges should be required to hear cases and the number needed to pass decisions be increased to eight judges.

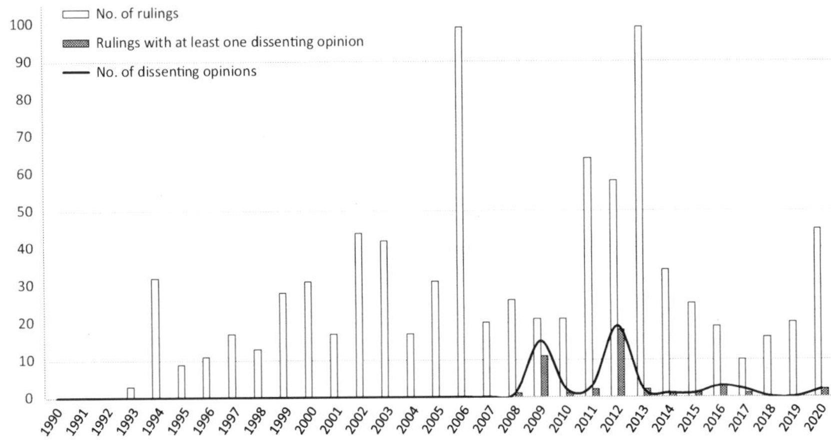

Figure 7.5 Number of rulings with at least one dissenting opinion (1993–2020) (LiCC)

legal scholarship not only for its quantity, but also for its quality. Partly due to this criticism, the number of dissenting opinions decreased significantly over time (Figure 7.5).

What were the reasons for the high number of dissents directly after its introduction? First, there was no established practice and tradition of using dissenting opinions, thus perhaps judges often issued dissenting opinions in haste and without considering whether they were necessary. Second, in 2009–2013, the LiCC issued a number of rulings on the constitutionality of government measures addressing the economic crisis, which created some tensions between the LiCC and the political authorities. The increasing number of LiCC cases, the complexity of the cases, and the pressure exerted by the political authorities on the Court during this period may also have led to some tensions between the judges. Third, the number of dissenting opinions was also influenced by the personalities that made up the LiCC during this period. From 2009 to 2020, there were a total of 51 dissenting opinions issued by seven judges, but the overwhelming majority of them were issued by Judge Šileikis, who issued 33 dissents, i.e. more than 50% of all dissents. Other dissenting judges followed with fewer dissents: Birmontienė (5); Ruškytė (5); Taminskas (4); Jočienė (3). Šileikis is a famous professor of constitutional law in Lithuania who has always been distinguished by his original writing style and distinctive approach.

In 2013, the procedure for issuing a dissenting opinion was amended so that judges may file a dissent within five working days of the pronouncement of the act, instead of within three working days (The 2013 Law). Evidently, however, this amendment has not improved the situation in any way. Therefore, the LiCC itself had to take the initiative to improve the legal regime for dissent. Although the LiCC was not empowered to change the legal regulation, in 2015 the requirements for the content and form of the dissenting opinion were established in the Rules of Procedure of the LiCC. It was stipulated that a dissenting opinion may be delivered only by a judge who had participated in the deliberations (Art. 144), that a dissent may present arguments only on the legal act adopted in the case in question, and that it may contain only information directly related to case under review (Art. 145). The Rules of Procedure also provide that: (1) the dissenting opinion shall clearly indicate the parts or provisions of the majority decision which the judge disagrees with (Art. 147); (2) the dissenting opinion may refer to the reasons and/or the operative part of majority decision (Art. 148); and (3) the dissenting opinion must be written in accordance with the norms of the Lithuanian common language, and it must be formalized in accordance with the requirements of the procedure for formalization of decisions of the LiCC (Art. 148).

These changes were triggered mainly by an unofficial dissenting opinion given by Judge Šileikis of 14 March 2014, which was published on the Internet (Račas 2014; Chochrin 2014). This opinion was not officially published by the court, since judges are not entitled to issue a dissenting opinion on a decision which rejects an application. Judge Šileikis did not participate in the adoption of the majority decision on 20 March 2014, thus the provision that "a dissenting opinion may be expressed by a judge who participated in the deliberation of a constitutional case" was included in the Rules of Procedure based on this precedent (Pūraitė-Andrikienė 2017, 238–250).

It should be noted that a large part of the text of this unofficial dissenting opinion was not directed against the decision or its arguments but against the order of the President of the LiCC "on the Appointment of a Judge of the LiCC of the Republic of Lithuania as the Temporary President of the LiCC". Šileikis criticized the procedure for the appointment of a temporary President. In response to Šileikis' criticism, it was stipulated that a dissenting opinion may only express disagreement with and argue against the majority decision in question and may only contain information directly related to the case under review.

It is likely that these changes to the Rules of Procedure, as well as certain established traditions of expressing dissenting opinions, have resulted in the decreasing number of dissenting opinions in recent years. Furthermore, it should be emphasized that analysis of individual dissenting opinions has received only episodic attention in the media or in legal scholarship. Exceptions are dissents in cases with strong political resonance. An example of this is the dissenting opinion of Judge Ruškytė on the LiCC's decision of 28 September 2011 concerning the definition of the family.[32] This decision has continued to spark debate in society about how the family should be understood. The public awareness of this decision has led to doubts about the motives behind

32 Dissenting opinion of Judge R. Ruškytė on the LiCC's ruling of 28 September 2011.

the dissenting opinion, as it was published five days after the ruling was issued, at the height of a public debate (Valuta 2019, 135).

7.6 Conclusions

The position of the Lithuanian Constitutional Court has gradually strengthened over time. In parallel with this, the Court's jurisprudence has had a huge influence on the strengthening of democracy in Lithuania and the stability of the constitutional order. Its decisions have sometimes caused controversy, discontent, and dispute, but after some time and after tempers cooled, they were accepted as the undisputed truth. The Court has acted both as a legal arbiter in political conflicts and as a protector of human rights. The latter function of the LiCC was further strengthened by the introduction of the mechanism for bringing constitutional complaints before the Court in 2019. These amendments opened another phase of the LiCC's activity and paved the way for the further strengthening of the LiCC's role in the future.

References

Brewer-Carías, Allan. 2011. *Constitutional Courts as Positive Legislators: A Comparative Law Study*. Cambridge: Cambridge University Press.

Chochrin, Tomas. 2014. "Cenzūra demokratinėje visuomenėje neturėtų būti pateisinama (dėl E. Šileikio atskirosios nuomonės) [Censorship should not be justified in a democratic society (on the dissenting opinion of Mr Šileikis)]." *Tomo Chochrin Tinklaraštis*, March 28. http://jurisprudencija.wordpress.com/2014/03/28/cenzura-nera-demokratineje-visuomeneje-neturetubuti-pateisinama/

Constitutional Court of the Republic of Lithuania. 2021. "Visuomenės pasitikėjimas Konstituciniu Teismu išlieka aukštas." [Public confidence in the Constitutional Court remains high] Accessed October 23, 2021. https://lrkt.lt/lt/naujienos/ivykiai/visuomenes-pasitikejimas-konstituciniu-teismu-islieka-aukstas/1837.

Danėlienė, Ingrida. 2019. "Konstitucinių ginčų teisena [Adjudication of Constitutional Disputes"]. In *Konstituciniai ginčai*, edited by Vytautas Sinkevičius, 379–563. Vilnius: Mykolas.

Jarašiūnas, Egidijus. 2003. *Valstybės valdžios institucijų santykiai ir Konstitucinis Teismas [Relations between state authorities and the Constitutional Court]*. Vilnius: Teisinės informacijos centras.

Kelemen, Katalin. 2011. "The Road from Common Law to East-Central Europe: The Case of the Dissenting Opinions." In *Legal and Political Theory in the Post-National Age*, edited by Peter Cserne and Miklos Könczöl, 118–134. Frankfurt: Peter Lang Publ.

Kūris, Egidijus. 2003. "Konstitucinė justicija Lietuvoje: pirmasis dešimtmetis [Constitutional justice in Lithuania: the first decade]." *Justitia* 3–4: 45–46.

———. 2011. "Konstitucinės justicijos proceso teisės klausimu [On the Issue of Law of Constitutional Justice Procedure." *Teisė* 78: 7–27.

———. 2012b. "Apie Konstitucinio Teismo teisėjų atskirąsias nuomones: keli bihevioristiniai aspektai [On dissenting opinions of the judges of the Constitutional Court: Some bihevioristical aspects]." *Jurisprudencija* 19 (3): 1031–1058.

Masnevaitė, Elena, Dovilė Pūraitė-Andrikienė, and Dainius Žalimas. 2015. "The Independence of Courts and Legal Dispute Resolution." In *Crisis, the Rule of Law and Human Rights*, edited by Egidijus Kūris, 450–506. Šiauliai: Titnagas.

Pūraitė-Andrikienė, Dovilė. 2017. "Konstitucinės justicijos procesas Lietuvoje: optimalaus modelio paieška [Constitutional Justice Procedure in Lithuania: The Search for an Optimal Model]." PhD diss., Vilnius university.

———. 2020. "Objects of Verification of the Constitutionality of Legal Acts in the LiCC of the Republic of Lithuania." *Teisė* 116: 72–91.

———. 2021. "The Developments and Prospects of the Lithuanian Constitutional Justice Model." In *Legal Developments during 30 Years of Lithuanian Independence: Overview of Legal Accomplishments and Challenges in Lithuania*, edited by Gintaras Švedas and Donatas Murauskas, 225–245. Cham: pringer International Publishing.

Račas, Artūras. 2014. "Atskiroji E. Šileikio nuomonė, kurios KT kažkodėl skelbti nenori [Separate opinion of E. Šileikis, which for some reason the CC does not want to publish]." *Artūras Račas*, March 24. http://racas.lt/atskiroji-siliekio-kazkodel/.

Sadurski, Wojcek. 2008. *Rights Before Courts. A Study of Constitutional Courts in of Central and Eastern Europe*. Leiden: Springer.

Staugaitytė, Viktorija. 2007. "Konstitucinio Teismo nutarimų tipai ir jų poveikio teisės sistemai bei teisės taikymo praktikai ypatumai [Types of Constitutional Court rulings and their impact on the legal system and the practice of law application]." *Konstitucinė jurisprudencija* 4 (8).

Valuta, Andrius. 2019. "Atskirosios nuomonės institutas Lietuvos konstitucinės justicijos procese: Raida ir tobulinimo perspektyvos [The Institute of Separate Opinion in the Lithuanian Constitutional Justice Procedure: its development and prospects for improvement]." *Teisė* 110: 132–146.

Žalimas, Dainius. 2019. "Konstitucinio Teismo baigiamųjų aktų specifinės teisinės pasekmės [Specific legal effects of final acts of the Constitutional Court]." In *Konstituciniai ginčai*, edited by Vytautas Sinkevičius, 527–539. Vilnius: Mykolas Romeris University.

8 The Polish Constitutional Tribunal

Encountering politics

Artur Wołek and Iga Jeziorska

8.1 Introduction

The story of the Polish Constitutional Tribunal (PCT), whose plot is full of twists and turns, might be considered a stress test for the method of judicial politics analysis proposed here. The PCT was established in 1982 as a measure to enhance the legitimacy of the collapsing communist regime, more as a support than a check on the façade Parliament (the *Sejm*). In the 1990s it became a major co-author of the democratic transformation, only to quickly lose its political importance once the new democratic constitution was introduced in 1997. After 2015, the PCT was taken over by the ruling populist majority and ceased to function as an effective check on the Parliament. If the relations between the constitutional court and the parliament are a good indicator of judicial politics, the turbulent fortunes of the PCT might be better understood once the PCT decisions are analysed with the tools offered by the methodology developed in this chapter. One would expect the crooked path taken by the PCT to be mirrored in its decisions which might make the successive curves of its judicial policies possibly easier to explain.

The main question of this chapter concerns what the PCT does when it encounters politics and how politics and adjudication interact. The scope and means by which the PCT restricts the Parliament would help to answer that question. We argue that in the Polish case, it is political or partisan change that is the most important variable for explaining the fluctuations in judicial behaviour as reflected in judicial decisions. Therefore, the focus of this chapter is on politics. Our analysis suggests that, since the political process of the PCT judges' nomination has been highly partisan, party politics is a major factor behind the PCT strategy *vis-à-vis* the Parliament. The Tribunal was activist when there was no clear majority in the *Sejm* but became more deferential when a parliamentary majority succeeded in electing judges more amenable to the requirements of political governance. The extreme endpoint of this continuum is a PCT that has been fully incapacitated since December 2016, when it was taken over by the ruling majority.

The character of the PCT has fluctuated over time, with the Tribunal acting as a Kelsenian negative legislator and arguably a neutral professional

DOI: 10.4324/9781003399483-8

adjudicator for most of the time period under scrutiny. This was in accordance with its proclaimed legitimacy doctrine. However, the PCT's political neutrality was questionable, especially during crisis situations and in the period of bipolar politics in Poland after 2005. When it came to politically divisive issues, the judges acted as the third chamber of the Parliament and apparently took into account political/partisan considerations. This behaviour of the PCT was used as a justification for packing the Tribunal with loyalists of the government after 2015, who effectively converted the PCT into an obedient tool of the ruling majority.

To explain this trajectory of the PCT, the chapter begins with a short description of the PCT's peculiar origins and institutional setup, and a reconstruction of the Tribunal's legitimating ideology of political neutrality or purported role as a professional negative legislator. The main part of the chapter is based on the empirical analysis of judicial decisions, attempting to answer the questions of what judges do when they encounter politics and why their activities during specific periods might be described as following the model of the constitutional court as the third chamber of Parliament. The activism of the early 1990s, the deep deference of the period from 1994 to 2005, and the polarization in the court after 2006 are all modes in which judges dealt with politics while gravitating towards one of the two poles: negative legislator or the third chamber. The period since 2015 can hardly be analysed with the tools developed in this volume because the gap between the formal rules regulating the PCT's activities and the actual rules followed by judges is too wide. After 2016 the PCT turned into the government's aide rather than a constraint on the parliamentary majority. As such, we argue, it should be researched using the methods developed for studying post-Soviet constitutional courts.

8.2 Origins and institutional setup

Unlike the constitutional courts in all the other Central and Eastern European countries, the PCT was not a product of the democratic transformation of the early 1990s. In fact, it was a product of the transformation of the communist regime that began in the early 1980s. The change in the political and intellectual climate which resulted in the Solidarity (*Solidarność*) revolution of 1980–1981 emboldened law professors and legal professionals. Even though they generally remained supporters of the communist regime, they started to raise the possibility of re-establishing communist power on legal rules rather than on political will, not to say outright violence. Quite paradoxically, the military suppression of the Solidarity movement in 1981–1982 created a legitimacy vacuum which the legal proceduralization of communist rule promised to fill. In this atmosphere of an acute legitimacy crisis, the Constitutional Tribunal was soon created by the constitutional amendment of 1982. It took the communist authorities another three years to clarify the details of the new institution and to select judges for the PCT, so the first ruling was delivered only in May 1986 (Czeszejko-Sochacki 2001; Garlicki 2003).

The delay was telling. If the Tribunal was to address the deep deficit of legitimacy, the institution had to be granted real powers; the judges could not simply be another set of communist apparatchiks. On the other hand, the entire communist legal system was based on the assumption of unrestricted sovereignty of the "working people" embodied in the Parliament. The solution developed to address this contradiction was to grant the newly created PCT the power to strike down parliamentary legislation, yet such rulings had to be accepted or dismissed by the *Sejm* with a two-thirds majority. A general conception of the PCT was that it should act as a counsel and not an opponent of Parliament, and its real field of activity should be secondary legislation, where the Tribunal had a final say. In the period 1986–1988, the PCT dealt with four acts of Parliament and 22 sub-statutory acts, with only one statute declared unconstitutional (Garlicki 1999, 283). During this period, the PCT gained some recognition within the legal profession – if not among the general public. The majority of the 12 judges elected by the *Sejm* in December 1985 were law professors and former Supreme Court judges, and only a few of them had previously been directly involved in politics. On the other hand, half of the judges were elected for a short, four-year term, a provision which did not exactly lend them judicial authority.

Thanks to this back-door arrangement, secured by the communists in case the Tribunal became too independent, the PCT played an instrumental role when the political transformation gained momentum after the roundtable talks (spring 1989), the partly free parliamentary elections (June 1989), and the appointment of the first non-communist prime minister (September 1989). When the term of six of the judges expired in December 1989, the new *Sejm* elected five judges who were clearly linked to the Solidarity movement and a former Supreme Court judge to the sixth seat. One of the new judges became the president of the Tribunal, a position crucial to the day-to-day functioning of the PCT.

The institution gained a completely new dynamic. Not only did the Tribunal become more assertive towards the Parliament, declaring the unconstitutionality of more than half of the statutes it dealt with in 1990–1993, but it also developed an extensive jurisprudence based on the new constitutional definition of the state. Article 1 of the 1952 Constitution amended in December 1989 pronounced Poland to be "a democratic state ruled by law realizing the principles of social justice" (henceforth: the *Rechtsstaat* clause). This clause was often referred to in rulings presenting an abstract authoritative binding interpretation of statutes, a competence taken over from the communist-era collective Presidency of the Republic and used extensively during the political transition – there were 29 such rulings in 1990–1992, and 101 until 1997 (Czeszejko-Sochacki 1996).

In one such ruling the Tribunal further strengthened its position *vis-à-vis* Parliament, declaring that the statutes deemed unconstitutional by the PCT cease to be legally binding, even if the *Sejm* does not accept or dismisses the ruling (W 6/93), i.e. when the *Sejm* is passive, the President of the PCT pronounces the abrogation of the act. This ruling, delivered in 1994, was a visible sign of the strong self-confidence of the PCT stemming from the substantial legitimacy capital it had accumulated in the period of transition. No less important from a legitimacy perspective was the fact that in February 1993 the first democratically elected *Sejm* selected its own judge (after an early resignation), and Solidarity judges effectively became the majority in the court. A change in the composition of the PCT following the elections of 1993, which were disastrous for the post-Solidarity parties, did not change the general outlook of the institution, even though they changed its adjudication strategy (see Section 8.4.1). The Tribunal was held in high esteem among legal professionals, respected by politicians, and viewed as legitimate by the general public. As such, it was an important actor in the legislative-political process leading to the preparation of the new constitution.

The new constitution of 1997 (in force from 17 October 1997), followed by the new Constitutional Tribunal Act in the same year, stabilized the position of the PCT for the next 20 years. The new Constitutional Tribunal Act of 2015 barely changed the established practice of the PCT, but rather refined its procedures. The post-1997 legal framework upheld the competences of the PCT: (i) deciding on the conformity of statutes with the constitution; (ii) deciding on the conformity of the secondary legislation issued by national executive organs with the constitution and statutory law; (iii) resolving competence (authority) disputes between state organs (*Organstreitverfahren*); and (iv) vetting the constitutionality of the goals and activities of political parties. It also retained the relatively long list of actors entitled to petition the PCT: Parliament, a group of 50 members of the *Sejm* or 30 senators, the government, the President of the Republic, courts of law, or the ombudsman. Local authorities, trade unions, and churches were also eligible if they perceived their legal interests to have been infringed by legislation. Only in the latter type of cases did the PCT have the power over its docket to dismiss any application as inadmissible. The PCT also retained the competence of the *a priori* review of statutes before their promulgation on the motion of the President of the Republic (Garlicki 2016, 406–429). The constitutional complaint was a new institution introduced in 1997. It was defined in a rather restrictive way as a grievance against a legal regulation which constituted a basis for a final court's decision that infringed the rights or freedoms of the applicant (but not against the court's decision itself).

The most significant change in the new formal legal framework concerned the final character of the PCT decisions. This applied to both statutory and sub-statutory legal acts, *a priori* and *a posteriori* review, competence disputes, and all other forms of procedures (see Section 8.4.1). At the same time, the PCT was deprived of the competence to issue binding interpretations of statutes. This competence was vehemently contested by the Supreme Court in the 1990s, as it encroached on the court's own competence to declare binding principles of legal interpretation in the application of law. Only minor changes took place concerning the Tribunal's composition and *modus operandi* at this time. The number of judges was increased from 12 to 15, and their term of their office was extended from eight to nine years, without the possibility of re-election.

Judges are elected by the *Sejm* in a strictly political procedure: candidates are proposed by groups of deputies (*de facto* by political parties) and elected with an absolute majority of those present. The only real threshold for candidacy is the requirement to have worked in the legal profession for at least 10 years. In practice, the elected judges are almost always candidates selected by the ruling majority. Broader coalitions or non-partisan candidacies are extremely rare (only two judges elected during the whole 28-year period studied were not simply from the ranks of the parliamentary majority). Among all 57 judges effectively elected by democratic parliaments, there were only 13 with weak political ties, of whom 8 were elected in the period from 2007 to 2015 (Wiaderek 2016). This does not mean that politicians elect politicians, although 15 judges jumped into judges' robes directly from politicians' suits. Out of 44 judges elected between 1993 and 2015, there were 17 active politicians and 38 law professors who constantly dominated the bench. There were also 12 judges originating from the courts of law, although they were also sponsored by political parties. Even the populist ruling majority which packed the PCT with its loyalists after 2015 took care to uphold the tradition of legal scholars and judges dominating the Tribunal. Of 16 judges elected by the post-2015 majority[1] 4 were outspoken politicians, 11 were law professors, 2 were judges, and several were legal professionals, although these categories often overlapped. Even so, the professional backgrounds of the judges selected after 2015 included a law professor running unsuccessfully in the parliamentary election and immediately receiving a proposal to join the PCT, government officials working simultaneously as academics, or a former secret service officer making a career in academia. This suggests that the judges' professional career is not a crucial factor when we analyse the PCT's political strength *vis-à-vis* Parliament and its neutrality or partisanship.

A peculiar feature of the PCT involves decision-making by benches (councils) created *ad hoc* for each case. A five-member bench is a basic mode of operation of the PCT, and minor cases are decided by a bench of three. The only exceptions are in matters previously adjudicated by the full Tribunal and as such reserved by the law for the full Tribunal, and "especially complicated cases" (as decided by the PCT President). The allocation of judges to cases involves a crucial power – this competence belongs once again to the President of the Tribunal, who is selected by the President of the Republic from two candidates proposed by the PCT judges' assembly. Before 2006, the Tribunal's President could allocate judges at their will, although a practice of there being more or less stable benches evolved. Since 2006, the internal rules and regulations of the PCT have required the Tribunal's President to allocate cases

1 Three new judges died in office in the period 2015–2020.

according to the alphabetical order of judges. This provision restricted the power of the President significantly, at least in theory. In practice, the President is the sole employer and superior of all clerks serving the Tribunal, so the scope for the informal influence of the President is still very broad. For example, the PCT's presidents during the period of the polarized court (up until 2010) were accused of manipulating cases allocation, and in the post-2016 period the presidents have used political criteria quite openly when choosing judges to adjudicate "sensitive" cases (on the importance of benches see Section 8.4.3).

8.3 Legitimation by political neutrality

In the early communist period of the PCT, an ostentatious detachment from politics was a deliberate strategy to gain legitimacy for the new institution and to fulfil the expectations of the PCT's creators, namely, to strengthen the legitimacy of the whole regime. This strategy proved to be useful during the transition period, as the PCT was eager to play the role of a neutral, professional facilitator of the legal changes leading to the *Rechtsstaat* construction in Poland. The PCT could claim to be neutral because judges had significant cultural capital and were perceived as independent from the political capital of the old communist guard: they were law professors and/or law professionals with few immediate political links (Dębska 2015a, 35–37; Dębska 2015b, 204–217). This high prestige and an image of political neutrality were apparently transferred from the law professors to the institution itself. Dębska (2015a, 36) claims that "the constitutional court, similarly to the supreme court, is located on Poles' mental maps close to universities and not the law or politics".

The Tribunal cultivated its image as a neutral "negative legislator". However, Warczok and Dębska (2014, 472), examining the discourse of and about the PCT, observed frequent dichotomies that were used for framing the role of the constitutional court in the Polish polity. They involved not only a juxtaposition of the law (legal science, professionalism) and (partisan) politics, but also a confrontation between the universal (common interest) and the particular (political, ideological interests); reflexiveness and a long-term perspective against short-sighted hand-to-mouth thoughtlessness; rationality opposed to emotionality; impartiality versus political engagement; and formality serving objectivity contrasted with informality in the service of subjectivity.

This kind of "it's the law, stupid" legitimating ideology was for a long time an effective deterrent when it came to empirical studies on the role of the PCT in Polish politics. For a long time "the power of the Constitutional Tribunal [became] a 'denied power', an apolitical legal professionalism denying politics" (Warczok and Dębska 2014, 472), not only for political actors and legal scholars, but also for social scientists. The judges might be entangled in power processes; they might be selected by politicians; they might even have political views; but being, first and foremost, professionals they "leave them in the cloakroom of the Tribunal", as the popular sound bite went. As this claim could not be empirically examined due to the secrecy of the most important parts of the Tribunal's proceedings, one is left with a black box model with "politics" on the input side and the "neutral law" claim on the output side, a model constructed by the legal community for its own use (Stone Sweet 1992, 115–116).

However, some light is shed on the inside of this box by the judges themselves. Marek Safjan, the PCT President from 1998 to 2006, writing about constitutional courts as positive legislators, quite openly admitted that adding new normative content in relation to the existing legal situation "remains somewhat concealed, never being openly proclaimed or clearly expressed in a legal solution, as doing so would transgress the boundaries of the ethos and ideology of constitutional justice" (Safjan 2013, 703). He recalled the sole case when the PCT directly told Parliament what the deputies should do, ordering the restoration of a provision that had been in force before the statute found unconstitutional by the PCT was passed by the *Sejm* (K 4/99). Safjan acknowledges, however, that during the transition "when adequate constitutional norms were still missing, [the PCT was] practically pushed toward substantial creativity, which consisted in decoding the standards of rights and freedoms – which were not directly expressed in the constitutional norms – from the axiology of a new democratic system" (Safjan 2013, 710), and this apparently involved some extra-legal sources. He argued that "social and political revolution justified such an attitude" but continued that after the new constitution of 1997 was ratified, "the scale and direction of judicial activism changed, [but] the nature of the phenomenon of creation of norms of constitutional significance did not"; this consisted of the "process of decoding rules (and, *de facto*, their creation) and finding a new normative content" (712).

Overall, only a few openly political statements had been made by the PCT judges by 2016. However, the judges were often ready to admit that they might have struck down some clearly unconstitutional statutes yet did not do so for some prudential/political reasons. Judge Biruta Lewaszkiewicz-Petrykowska recalled "Act 203" of December 2000, in which Parliament raised the salaries of the medical staff in the public healthcare system without allocating extra money to their employers (K 43/01). "We had to do a lot of balancing and stretching in order to keep the act. It was all about weighing different values, and the act itself was very badly written". It could have been easily deemed unconstitutional as encroaching on the "principles of correct legislation", a part of the *Rechtsstaat* principle often cited by the PCT (*Sąd czy ustawodawca* 2009, 22).

Despite these confessions, both Polish judges and the legal scholars deeply involved in the PCT's legitimacy doctrine-building would never admit that that they are playing politics: making policy choices and not just the subsumption of statutory acts to a rule of the constitution. They would be indignant if confronted with an argument that an institution which can invalidate a decision of the Parliament in abstract terms rather than in the process of litigation, which can suggest to the Parliament positive solutions that would remove the defect from the law, which decides between contested policy options where the constitutional norms in question are highly indeterminate, and which acts as a result of a political initiative by Members of Parliament should be called "the third chamber" rather than a part of the judicial system. The "third chamber" characterization, used by Alec Stone Sweet (1992, 209–219) in relation to the French Constitutional Council, also fits the Polish Tribunal in some periods of its functioning much more than the legal-professional "negative legislator" term. Moreover, the conceptualization of the PCT as the " 'chamber of reflection', the purpose of which is to reconsider the bill in a more dispassionate manner, removed one step further from specific political controversies" (Sadurski 2008, 57) or "juridically institutionalized part of the political processes" (Böckenförde 2017, 195) might be a source of a stronger legitimacy than reiterating the claims that judges do not bring their political preferences into the courtroom.

8.4 PCT political trajectory: empirical analysis

If the judges themselves admit (albeit not in their rulings) that they make policy choices based on certain extra-legal considerations, it opens up a legitimate field for the empirical research of their behaviour. We may accept the challenge of Jerzy Stępień, one time PCT President (2006–2008) and former deputy interior minister and senator that "if one would analyse the judicial behaviour . . . one would be surprised how often the cleavages in substantial issues that are the subject of rulings are absolutely athwart so-called political affiliations" (*Sąd czy ustawodawca* 2009, 53).Without going into a discussion on the nature of the constitutional court's activities (Segal 2010; Lax 2011; Sadurski 2008, 27–63), we ask how judges' policy choices restrict parliament: how often they contradict the will of deputies, how far they go, and what patterns of interaction between the institutions exist over time. Moreover, we can bracket the legitimation ideology of the PCT and disaggregate both the world of politics and the PCT itself, asking which parliamentary majorities were restricted by which majorities in the PCT and what tools were used in the adjudication.

In the following sections, we propose such an analysis for the period from 1993 to 2020. The survey begins when the first judge was selected by the first democratically elected Parliament in 1993 and ends in 2020, when the conflict over the PCT drew to an end as the governing majority successfully took over the Tribunal.[2] The analysis focuses on four encounters between the PCT

2 The beginning date of the analysis is arbitrary to a certain degree as there was a clear continuity of the PCT operation in the pre-democratic and democratic period. Even though the 1993 full democracy caesura is necessary in order to have comparative data from different countries, we often refer to the earlier PCT strategies and adjudication lines since they continued after 1993.

and politics, four crucial periods which disclose how politics and adjudication interact and which therefore reveal the role of the PCT in the Polish politics.

8.4.1 *From early activism to infused deference: the early 1990s*

A dominant periodization of the PCT activity that is present in the scholarship corresponds to the widely accepted official legitimation doctrine of the PCT as a professional politically neutral negative legislator. The presumed watershed is the adoption of the new democratic constitution in 1997, with the crucial argument for its importance being the final character of the Tribunal rulings introduced by the new basic law. Additionally, whereas the PCT had felt obliged under the 1989–1997 provisional constitutional regulations to fill gaps in the constitutional system, the new basic law was founded on an assumption of completeness. The PCT could therefore assume the role of a self-restraining guardian of the constitutional order and abandon the role of activist co-author.

The empirical analysis of the PCT rulings, however, gives credibility to such a narrative only in part. It does not confirm that the 1997 change was in fact "a final victory of the Constitution over politics and acknowledgment that nothing can justify keeping unconstitutional legal provision in the legal system" (Safjan 1999). On the contrary, it suggests another story of the PCT trajectory in which party politics is a much better explanatory tool than constitutional changes.

First and foremost, the analysis shows that the competence of Parliament to overrule the Tribunal's decisions of unconstitutionality was not a significant barrier for the PCT in having a final say in the period from 1986 to 1999.[3] During these 13 years, the *Sejm* overruled 11 of the PCT's decisions (some of them only in part), which constituted 11.3% of all decisions declaring the unconstitutionality of a statute (Garlicki 1999, 283–289). It would be difficult to argue that any of these "restored" acts were important from the constitutional point of view. Many of them were statutes concerning financial matters, and the *Sejm's* majority managed to convince the opposition (a two-thirds majority was required) that acceptance of the PCT's decision would be disastrous for the state budget. Other decisions overruled by Parliament dealt with social rights, and a strong interest group stood behind the prevailing parliamentary majority on these matters. The *Sejm* was successful in reversing a fairly random selection of policies – no pattern could be traced, and in fact, the result of the chamber vote was always uncertain. The Parliament's approach to PCT decisions does not indicate a lasting institutional conflict about the sphere of the PCT's influence or its political and constitutional position. On the contrary – there were solid arguments that it was the *Sejm*, or at least some of the deputies, who wanted "to see if a pending statute would run afoul of

3 A two-year transitional clause was included in the constitution.

any previous decisions of the Tribunal and if the *Sejm* would again run the risk of having its legal acts questioned" (Zoll 1997, 78), as the PCT president recalled.

An institutionalist might argue that the mere possibility of overruling the Tribunal's decision could influence its strategy and curb its activism. Certainly, the PCT, like any court in the world, strove not only for its policy preferences but also for compliance, and this influenced its strategy. Nevertheless, the early 1990s can be considered a period of the steady strengthening of the PCT's position in relation to the Parliament. When the real problem with non-compliance arose in the form of the Parliament passively ignoring the Tribunal's decisions, in 1993 the PCT granted itself the power to declare that a statute ceased to be valid if the *Sejm* had failed to deal with the respective PCT ruling (W 6/93). The PCT also established that *a priori* reviews could not be subject to a reversal vote by the Parliament (W 1/95). Eventually, the PCT attributed to itself the power to review not only international agreements but also the standing orders of Parliament (Prochazka 2002, 89–91). Overall, Poland in the early 1990s could probably be characterized as being close to the "judicial supremacy" situation in terms of Vanberg's model (2005), with legislative self-censorship, a powerful or rather steadily strengthening constitutional court, and strong public support for the PCT. The formal constitutional framework restraining the PCT proved to be of secondary importance.

What was especially significant with respect to the power of the PCT during this period was an extreme fragmentation of the Parliament. In the first democratic elections of 1991, 28 groupings received seats in Parliament; there were 18 parliamentary factions in the *Sejm* in 1993 when the chamber was dissolved, and early elections followed. The deputies had difficulty forming a simple majority to support the cabinet, so the two-thirds majority required to override a ruling of the Tribunal was normally beyond their reach. Therefore, the first encounter of the PCT with democratic politics was marked by the weakness of Parliament, which gave space for the activist Tribunal to assertively claim co-authorship in the Polish transformation. This observation is in line with the findings of Santoni and Zucchini (Santoni and Zucchini 2004, 447–454) that the effective number of parties in Italian Parliament correlates positively with judicial independence and corresponds with Franck's research (Franck 2009) on cohabitation and judicial independence in France.

In this context it is easier to understand why a more detailed empirical analysis of the PCT rulings raises doubts about the ground-breaking character of the adoption of the 1997 constitution. If we compare the period from 1993 to 1997 with the PCT's behaviour in the later period, and to the whole sample of rulings, clear differences can indeed be found. The average rate of rejections of petitions was 47.6% for the period 1993–1997, 54.8% for the period 1998–2020, and 54.4% for the whole 27 years under scrutiny. This is a robust difference but definitely not a watershed. Moreover, the most telling indicator of the court's assertiveness *vis-à-vis* Parliament – the frequency of substantive unconstitutionality rulings – was even less impressive for the early PCT. The

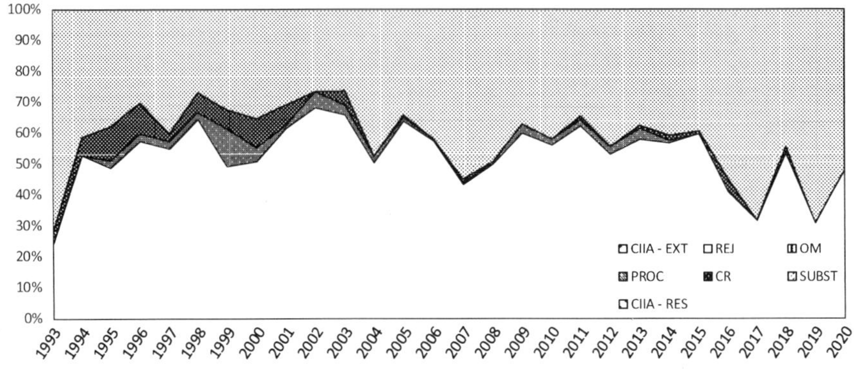

Figure 8.1 Frequency of the ruling types (1993–2020) (PCT)

Tribunal abrogated 42.1% of the clauses questioned in the 1993–1997 period and 41.6% of 1998–2020 rulings.

In fact, a closer examination reveals that a much greater change in judicial behaviour took place in 1994 than in 1997–1998. This change is responsible for many of the differences between the period from 1993–1997 and from 1998–2020. Whereas in 1993 the PCT declared 72% of the statutes it dealt with unconstitutional, in 1994 this proportion had fallen to only 41.2% and on average 35.8% by 1997. However, in 1993 the PCT rejected only 24% of the Parliament's motions, and in 1994–1997 it was 53.7% on average (see Figure 8.1). Despite the dominant narrative of the importance of the 1997 changes, a much clearer break can be identified in 1994. This break is also reflected in the change of the average strength of judicial rulings as measured by the methodology of the JUDICON-EU project (see Figure 8.2).[4] Furthermore, there is no clear discontinuity from 1997 to 1998 or 1999, despite the change of the constitutional framework, even though the tendency beginning in 1994 was reinforced after 1997.

What happened in 1994, then? In an early election in September 1993, the *Sejm* of two dozen political groupings was reduced (due to the newly introduced electoral threshold) to a six-party parliament with a stable governing coalition of two post-communist parties. In late autumn of 1993, the new coalition elected half of the PCT, and in May 1994 the seventh judge, all of them linked to the new left-wing governing parties. The professional authority of the new judges could not be questioned, but their links to partisan politics were significantly stronger than those of previous judges (two Members of Parliament, one unsuccessful candidate in the elections). In short, until late 1993 there was a prevailing majority of Solidarity-nominated judges: out of

4 For a more detailed analysis of the strength of majority decisions see Wolek and Jeziorska 2019.

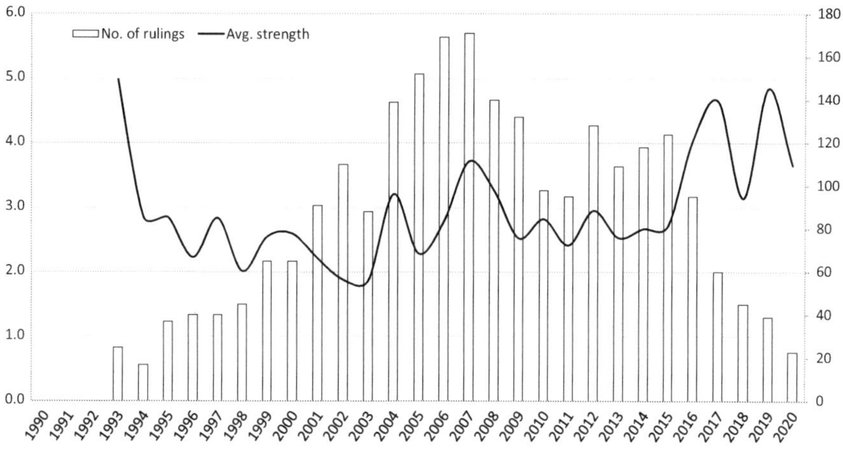

Figure 8.2 Number and average strength of rulings (1993–2020) (PCT)

25 rulings taken by the PCT in 1993, 16 were decided by a bench where Solidarity judges were majority (64%). By contrast, in 1994 58% and in 1995 76% of rulings were delivered by benches with the new left-wing coalition-nominated judges in the majority.

Apparently, the change in the PCT's adjudication policy is also reflected in its jurisprudence. The presumption of constitutionality is obviously a dogma in all constitutional courts which follow the "negative legislator" model. This had always been a working assumption of the PCT as well, but more elaborate consequences of this principle resulting in deference to Parliament appeared as late as 1994 (Oniszczuk 1998, 36–37; Sadurski 2008, 99–100). The principle stating that the PCT is limited to the scrutiny of constitutionality and is not interested in "the wisdom" of legal acts (K 19/96, K 18/95), the principle of parliamentary freedom to choose any constitutionally acceptable policy (K 2/94, K 6/94, K 12/94), and the very self-definition of the PCT as "the negative legislator" (K 13/95) were formulated in 1994–1996 by the Tribunal with a majority of judges elected by the first strong parliamentary majority after 1989. Arguably, such judges were more responsive to the troubles of everyday governing and ready to leave more space for politicians.

This argument does not contradict a more general interpretation of the PCT of the 1990s as a "constitutional emergency-unit . . . fixing the gap-ridden texture of Poland's pre-1997 constitutional law", constructing missing rules instead of evading hard cases. Thus, the PCT was generally more activist and positively creative, while at the same time understanding that the particular needs of the systemic transition needed to be taken into account in its decision-making (Prochazka 2002, 87, 206). Indeed, the PCT was ready "to exhibit considerable self-restraint in reviewing transition-related policies" (84), but only after the first parliamentary majority succeeded in electing friendly judges in 1993. Earlier, the judges were more often prone to "fix the gaps" according to their own vision of the new democracy.

8.4.2 Between deference and polarized Tribunal: 1997–2006

Those early phases of the PCT's trajectory may be aptly interpreted with the tools supplied by institutionalist approaches to judicial politics research. These are based on the assumption that judges are policy-seekers, although in pursuing their policy goals they are severely constrained by the institutional environment, e.g. the formal status of the court *vis-à-vis* Parliament (Dyevre 2010, 304–311). Indeed, the PCT's judges did play a collegial game *vis-à-vis* the Parliament when they were expanding the PCT's competences in the period of the highly fragmented *Sejm* and when they became more deferential after 1994. Even if the engine behind the PCT's position was partisan politics, a dominant group of judges (first Solidarity-sponsored, then post-communist-elected) was able to persuade the other judges to follow suit.

Even if there are no major differences between the post-1994 adjudication of benches with a majority of Solidarity-sponsored judges and those dominated by post-communist-nominated ones (see the quite steady performance of the strength of majority decisions in Figure 8.2), another indicator suggests that institutional models may have limited explanatory power as they focus less on politics. This indicator considers the dissenting opinions of the judges (Figure 8.3). The first dissenting opinion in the history of the PCT was delivered in 1995, and until 2000 almost 13% of all rulings were accompanied by at least one dissenting opinion. The dissenting opinion as a practice appeared when a group of judges nominated by the first strong (post-communist)

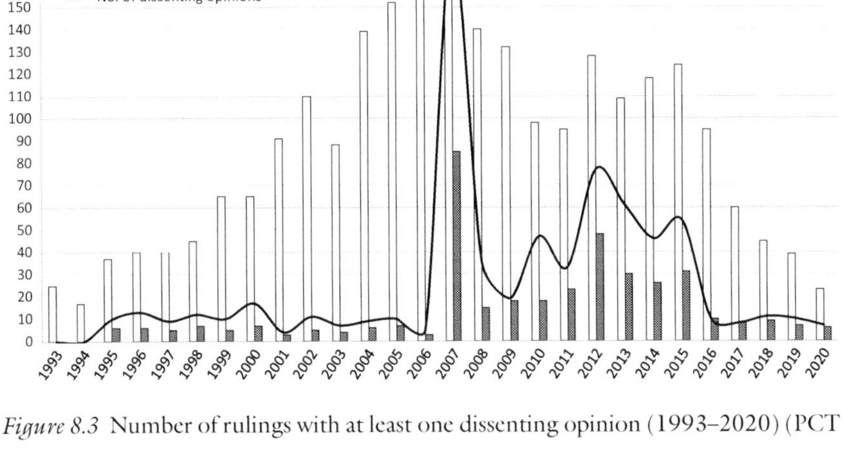

Figure 8.3 Number of rulings with at least one dissenting opinion (1993–2020) (PCT)

majority were sitting on the bench. Apparently, the need to demonstrate dissent became stronger than the logic of the collegial game among the Solidarity-nominated judges, who authored 9 out of 10 dissenting opinions in 1995. By the very fact of disclosing a disagreement and proposing an alternative, judges questioned the legitimating ideology of decision-making by professional consensus and unveiled existing conflicts, as well as the parties involved. Once the practice became accepted, the political origin of judges did not differentiate their readiness to openly express a dissent.

The ratio of dissenting opinions decreased in the period between 2001 and 2006 (3.8% of rulings with a dissenting opinion), which is – again – explainable in political terms. Specifically, not only were the Solidarity-nominated judges replaced in 1997 by the nominees of the fragile centre-right coalition of Solidarity Electoral Action (*Akcja Wyborcza Solidarność*, AWS) and the Freedom Union (*Unia Wolności*, UW) which did not have a strong ideological identity or high political profile, but the post-communist judges also began to disappear as their terms came to an end. This resulted in a lack of a clear majority in the PCT. This happened in the context of a weakened 1997–2001 *Sejm*, where the majority was at first unstable and later hardly existed. The situation in the *Sejm* changed after the 2001 election, although at that time the PCT was already a multi-player game and not a bipolar competition. The new left-wing coalition elected six new judges between 2001 and 2003, but they were still in a minority (due to the total number of judges being increased by the new constitution), even if one could not identify a coherent majority.

The indicator of dissenting opinions skyrocketed from 1.8% in 2006 to 49.7% in 2007 and equalled 22.4% on average in the period between 2008 and 2015. This indicates another era in the PCT political trajectory – a strongly politically polarized court. The drastic increase in the number of dissenting opinions at this time was a result of the 2005 election when the Law and Justice (*Prawo i Sprawiedliwość*, PiS) dominated coalition formed the government. They succeeded in selecting six PCT judges from 2006 to 2007 before losing power in the early elections of 2007.

The group of judges sponsored by PiS and its allies, however diversified it was internally, proved to be the most unified set of judges in the pre-2016 history of the PCT. Even though it is not possible to determine how they voted in the court, when it came to divisive issues, as indicated by dissenting opinions, they very often stood together. A network analysis of the dissenting coalitions reveals the uniqueness of the PiS-sponsored group of judges (see Figure 8.4). The hexagon Gintowt-Jankowicz-Hermeliński-Kotlinowski-Cieślak-Liszcz-Granat co-operated to a degree which can hardly be compared to the next period of more intensive co-operation – the post-communist judges of the 2001–2010 term (Zdziennicki-Mazurkiewicz-Łętowska-Grzybowski-Wyrzykowski-Jamróz). However, the network analysis also reveals that the PiS-sponsored judges were not an isolated group and co-operated quite frequently with judges elected by the next ruling coalition,

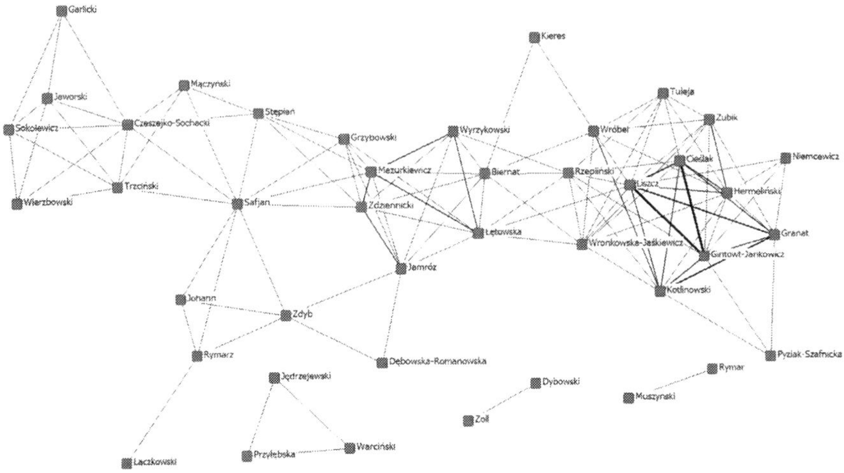

Figure 8.4 Dissenting coalitions 1993–2020 (PCT)

which suggests that the narrative of a deeply divided, polarized Tribunal might be not the whole story.[5]

8.4.3 *Polarized Tribunal: 2006–2015*

Institutionalist models of judicial behaviour do little to illuminate our understanding of such politically polarized courts. The attitudinal model, on the other hand, is not viable in most European countries due to the strict rules concerning judges' conference secrecy (Dyevre 2010, 300–302). An institutional peculiarity of the PCT, which will be discussed in the following paragraphs, however, supplies data which might serve as a proxy of individual judges' behaviour and help to explain the dynamics behind the closed door of the judges' conference. The PCT adjudicates, when it comes to legislative acts, in three modes: (i) whole Tribunal for *a priori* review and "notably complicated cases"; (ii) five-member benches for petitions concerning statutory law; and (iii) three-member benches for secondary legislation. The President of the Tribunal decides whether to conduct adjudication by the whole Tribunal and, in practice, highly publicized and divisive issues are most often decided by the whole Tribunal. This means that a majority of dissenting opinions concern decisions taken by the whole Tribunal.

To illustrate this, during the period of high polarization (2007–2015), which was marked by a high number of dissenting opinions, 333 out of 1,061

5 For details see Wołek and Jeziorska 2019.

rulings (31%) were decided by the whole Tribunal; 217 (65%) of them were accompanied by at least one dissenting opinion. If we deduct the special case of the lustration act of 2007 (K 2/07, with 77 rulings, and 160 dissenting opinions) from this number, it turns out that the deliberation of the whole Tribunal is a relatively rare procedure, reserved mostly for highly visible and divisive cases (16% of all rulings, but 69% of rulings with dissenting opinions; in the 2016–2020 period there were 19.8% of rulings by the whole Tribunal and 37% of rulings with dissenting opinions).

On the other hand, the daily activity of the PCT is undertaken by five-member benches: between 2007 and 2015, 69% of the rulings (728 instances) were decided by such benches. Even though only 8.6% of them were accompanied by at least one dissenting opinion, the sheer number suggests that these could not be confined to politically irrelevant matters only. Indeed, various politically salient issues were decided by five-member benches between 2007 and 2015. These included the establishment of the special service Central Anti-Corruption Bureau (K 54/07), the question of the (il)legality of communist and fascist propaganda (K 11/10), the (un)constitutionality of shooting down a hijacked passenger aircraft (K 44/07), the constitutionality of compensatory redistribution payments incurred by richer municipalities (the so-called Robin Hood tax [K 14/11]), the conditional annulment of court decisions delivered during the Stalinist era (P 8/11), and various aspects of the act on higher education (K 40/12, SK 61/12, K 16/13, K 35/11).

As mentioned earlier, adjudicating benches are created *ad hoc*, and since 2006, as a rule, the cases have been assigned to judges in alphabetical order; therefore, there is a high probability of a random allocation of cases to judges. This means that there should be a sizeable group of rulings where the judges who were nominated by PiS in 2005–2006 were in the majority. In fact, they formed a majority in 221 rulings in 2007–2015, which comprised 30% of all the rulings delivered by five-member benches. Our hypothetical reasoning, informed by the attitudinal approach to judicial politics is as follows: if we assume that the level of partisanship (policy preferences maximization) in judicial decision-making is strong, the PiS-nominated minority – whose strategic co-operation was proved by the dissenting coalitions analysis – would take the opportunity to realize its policy preferences whenever it becomes a majority in a five-member bench. This would mean that there should be a robust difference between the rulings by PiS-dominated benches and those by all other benches, and especially that the PiS-nominated judges should declare statutes adopted by the Civic Platform (*Platforma Obywatelska*, PO) dominated *Sejm* to be unconstitutional more often, and more often reject petitions concerning statutes from the period of the *PiS* government.[6]

Analysis of the data generates a few surprising observations, however. First of all, only 28.6% of the rulings by five-member benches concerned acts

6 For an earlier assessment see Kantorowicz and Nuno 2016.

adopted by the parliaments with either a PiS or a PO majority, due to the time lag. Almost all the constitutional complaints and petitions by courts of law concerned pre-2005 legislation, and astonishingly few "fresh" statutes were referred to the PCT by the numerous possible actors authorized by the constitution. The relatively small number of instances not only makes our observations dubious in terms of statistics rules but also indicates that the political sphere relatively rarely has access to the docket, mostly due to the time-lag. Once it appears on the docket, it is channelled through the full Tribunal procedure.

Nevertheless, the analysis of the nearly one-third of five-member rulings discloses interesting trends. There were proportionally more cases of PiS-sponsored legislation (99 rulings for the two-year period of PiS majority) than of PO-sponsored legislation (109 rulings for almost eight years of PO-dominated government). Moreover, PiS legislation was declared unconstitutional much more frequently: 40% as opposed to the PO's 30%. Benches with a majority of PiS-nominated judges adjudicated in 38.5% of PO-sponsored legislation cases and delivered 36% of the unconstitutionality rulings.

This result, which undermines the hypothesis of judges' partisanship, gives a good context for the next observation: PiS-nominated majorities adjudicated on only 11% of PiS-sponsored legislation in 2007–2015. The probability of them receiving such a meagre share of cases to decide is extremely low. A reasonable explanation is that the sequence of incoming cases was manipulated in order not to allow PiS-nominated judges to adjudicate over PiS legislation. This explanation may be corroborated by the fact that PiS-nominated majority benches were more numerous after 2011 when the PiS-PO conflict seemed to have been settled in favour of the PO governing majority. This date also overlaps with the election of the new PCT president, Andrzej Rzepliński, the judge recommended by the PO. The ratio of unconstitutionality rulings for PiS legislation delivered by PiS-nominated judges (54.5%) cannot lead to any conclusions due to the very low overall number of cases (6 out of 11 rulings).

This data may suggest that non-PiS judges (led by the non-PiS President) preferred not to take the risk that PiS-nominated judges would be swayed by their partisan political preferences and decided to adjudicate on PiS legislation themselves, even if this involved bending PCT procedures. Once they got the legislation into their hands, they did not seem to be excessively partisan, however. The ratio of unconstitutionality rulings (40%) is on par with the averages of such rulings for the consecutive years from 2007–2015 and for PCT rulings as a whole. This strategy precludes a positive verification of the partisanship hypothesis, but it strongly supports the argument that, when it comes to politics, it is political/partisan logic that is a primary point of reference for the judges. This observation is striking especially when juxtaposed with the fact that roughly 60% of the PCT's work involved adjudicating over legislation from the period before the PiS-PO clash. No differences can be found between the behaviour of PiS-nominated and non-PiS oriented judges here. It should be also noted that no such attitudinal analysis is viable for the period of PiS domination (2017–2020). Even though non-PiS judges formed a majority in 24% of the five-member benches, they did not have a single chance to adjudicate on PiS-sponsored legislation, and almost half of the cases they dealt with were constitutional complaints, typically of minor political importance and with a substantial time lag.

8.4.3 From incapacitation to the take-over: 2015–2020

These conclusions sketch a background on which the fourth and final encounter of the PCT with politics may be better understood. Despite the generally deferential jurisprudence of the post-1994 Tribunal, the institution had proved to be an active and effective counterweight to the PiS-led majority in 2005–2007, with indicators of restraints on the *Sejm* almost returning to 1993 levels (see Figures 8.1 and 8.4). This episode rejuvenated the myth of the strong Tribunal and obscured the visible trend of deference which began in 1994–1995 and to which the PCT returned soon after the 2005–2007 interlude. As a result, the PCT in the rhetoric of PiS politicians was targeted as one of the main pillars of the Polish version of *impossibillismo*, a doctrine or maybe a practice prohibiting any radical changes in the pernicious post-transitory *status quo* (Zajadło 2017). On the other hand, politicians of the PO-dominated coalition also learnt the lessons of 2005–2007. When it came to giving up the power in 2015 presidential and parliamentary elections, they decided to secure a friendly majority in the PCT for as long as possible and elected five new judges two weeks before the coalition was set to lose the parliamentary election. The problem was that the places they were to fill became vacant only after the elections, and in the case of two judges even after the end of the parliament term. In other words, at least two judges were elected "in advance". The PCT itself decided in December 2015 that these two judges had been elected in a flawed and unconstitutional procedure but confirmed the election of three judges whose term would commence during the formal term of the *Sejm* that elected them (K 34/15). However, when this ruling was delivered, the new majority's operation aimed at taking over the PCT was already underway.

While a detailed account of the process by which the PiS government took control over the PCT exceeds the limits of this chapter, it is worth recalling the major moves in the operation, which consisted of two phases. In the first phase (2015–2017) the Tribunal, with a majority of non-PiS judges, was incapacitated. First, the new President of the Republic refused to swear in any of the five judges elected by the PO-dominated *Sejm*. The new Parliament hastily elected five new judges, and the president swore them in on the late night of their election. Subsequently, the government refused to publish the PCT ruling (K 35/15) which declared the Constitutional Tribunal Act amendment which had resulted in the re-election of new judges to be unconstitutional. All these measures were either legally controversial or openly illegal. Nevertheless, they could not be effectively challenged since the PiS controlled all the power centres. The Parliament then passed a series of "remedial" amendments changing the PCT's procedures and aimed at blocking the Tribunal.[7] According to the new procedures, as a rule the PCT was to proceed in full court and take decisions by a two-thirds majority, hearing cases in the order of their registration on the docket, although petitioners were given at least six months to prepare for the first hearing. As a result of these changes, the PCT would be able to tackle any PiS legislation only after the Parliament had elected two more new judges, giving PiS a majority in the Tribunal. The amendments were declared unconstitutional by the Tribunal (K 47/15 and K 39/16) but the government, again, refused to publish its decisions. The PCT, however, proceeded as if their decisions were legally binding, and courts of law also accepted the rulings as part of the Polish legal system.[8]

It should be stressed that the efforts to hamstring the Tribunal should not be understood in terms of institutional rivalry between the PCT and Parliament. The PCT President Andrzej Rzepliński accepted all new judges sworn in by the President as members of the Tribunal – even though he did not allocate to benches those three judges who had been elected unlawfully according to the PCT ruling (soon dubbed popularly "double judges"). They were given offices, monthly salaries, and the right to participate in the general assembly of the PCT judges but could not adjudicate. This decision was contested by the government and the PiS-sponsored judges elected lawfully in late 2015 and 2016. They tried to act strategically and boycotted sittings where their absence could block a decision. An interesting testimony of this strategy may be found in the reasoning part of PCT decision K 44/16, which reports that three judges participated in deliberations but that once the conclusion was reached, they refused to take part in the final sitting, hence preventing the Tribunal from taking the decision as a full bench. The PCT President decided to transfer the case to a bench of five judges, and eventually the ruling was delivered.

These kinds of problems for the governing majority ended in 2017. First, the term of Andrzej Rzepliński came to an end, and Parliament accepted a special act giving the PCT President's powers to "the person substituting the President" instead of to the Vice President of the PCT (despite the constitutional status of the Vice President). The President of the Republic immediately named one of the new judges, Julia Przyłębska, to be "the person substituting the president". Within weeks she was elected as the President of the PCT (in a flawed procedure), whereupon she admitted new judges to the bench

7 There were six amending acts between November 2015 and December 2016.

8 The rulings were eventually published under the European Commission pressure, however the politically most sensitive of them were changed when PiS built the majority in the PCT in 2017.

and effectively suspended three old judges.[9] By these means the government-friendly majority took over the control of the PCT. In uncertain cases president Przyłębska openly manipulated the compositions of adjudicating benches. In 2017 alone, she changed the composition of benches 53 times (96% of the changes involved nominating a judge elected in the unlawful procedure in 2015), 52% of the judge rapporteurs were changed, and 80% of the new rapporteurs were "double judges" (*Funkcjonowanie Trybunału* 2018, 130–133). In extreme cases, Przyłębska was prepared to change the whole bench and compose the new one entirely of PiS-sponsored judges (U 2/16).

In 2017, the ruling majority succeeded in electing two more judges. Hence, even without breaking procedures, the PCT could be reshaped into an active supporter of the PiS government. This may be called phase two of the takeover. Even though the governing majority enjoyed full legislative and executive power it might be expedient for them to refer decisions on controversial issues to the PCT in order to shift the blame. The best example of this was the October 2020 decision (K 1/20) to outlaw abortion in all cases except for rape or incest and when a pregnancy poses a threat to the life or health of the woman. The ruling broke a moderate anti-abortion compromise achieved in 1991 (which also allowed an abortion in cases of the severe or irreversible impairment of the fetus), which was supported by the vast majority of Poles and by nearly the whole political elite. It was, however, contested by radical anti-abortion groupings linked to the ruling party. In order to satisfy their demands, it was expedient not to change the law via Parliament, which would spark a widespread and emotive debate, but instead to dress the decision as a matter of unconstitutionality of the 30-year-old practice. Thanks to leaks by a radical anti-abortion judge, the public learnt that the abortion case had been handled in full concertation with the PiS leadership and that electoral considerations were of major importance while adjudicating. Blame-shifting, however, works if the public believes in at least the relative independence of the court. In this case, the massive and violent demonstration which broke out in October 2020 not only protested against the Tribunal's decision but also sent a strong message to PiS.

The ruling majority also used the PCT as a legitimation tool when its legislation was criticized as amounting to a change of the constitution without altering the text of constitution and especially if the legislation was contested by the EU organs. For instance, the PCT legitimized the major element of the "court system reform" – the act which allowed the parliamentary majority to choose

9 Minister of Justice-Attorney General questioned in January 2017 the procedure in which three judges were elected in 2010 even though the same procedure was used earlier, and its legality was never questioned before. President Przyłębska decided not to allocate the three judges to adjudicating benches and postponed consideration of the Minister of Justice-Attorney General motion till the end of the three judges' term.

all the members of the National Judicial Council, the body responsible for the selection of judges (K 12/18). In this ruling, the PCT openly ignored the constitutional setup of the Council as a partly corporate representation of judges.

At times, the PCT worked as the third chamber of Parliament for the ruling majority in cases when the legislation accepted by the *Sejm* and Senate had unexpectedly proved to be embarrassing to the government. In 2018, the Parliament amended the National Remembrance Institute Act including clauses penalizing those who claim that "contrary to the facts . . . the Polish Nation or the Republic of Poland is responsible or co-responsible for Nazi crimes committed by the Third Reich" (Art. 55a) and adding to the mission of the Institute the aim of prosecuting and commemorating "the crimes of Ukrainian nationalists. . .. One of the crimes of Ukrainian nationalists and members of Ukrainian organizations collaborating with the Third German Reich is (was) their involvement in the extermination of the Jewish population and genocide on citizens of the Second Polish Republic in Volhynia and Eastern Lesser Poland" (Art. 2a). The first amendment caused a major uproar as an attempt to deny the complicity of Poles in the Holocaust. It was soon diluted by the *Sejm* after an open diplomatic confrontation with Israel and the United States. Ukrainian diplomatic pressure was less effective, in part due to the fact that the issue of Volhynia WWII atrocities was championed by an influential lobby in the governing camp. The government could not simply back out, but the issue was harmful enough for the country's relations with Ukraine, and PiS decided to solve the problem by involving the PCT. The Tribunal ruled in Solomon-like fashion that the expressions "Ukrainian nationalists" and "Lesser Poland" did not satisfy the constitutional requirement of normative clarity (determination), and in this respect the clauses were declared unconstitutional (K 1/18).

A separate category has also emerged of what former Vice President of the PCT called "artificially created" cases for constitutional review (Zoll and Wortham 2019, 930). These include issues which have not caused a legal controversy, but where the government needed to break with an established legal practice, or when an immediate political need appeared. One such instance occurred when the Supreme Court decided in full bench (in a privileged procedure that allows it to establish binding legal principles) that benches of the courts of law which included judges recommended by the new National Judicial Council would always be procedurally flawed. As a reaction to this decision, the government filed a case before the PCT referring to an alleged conflict of competences (*Organstreitverfahren*). The Tribunal immediately suspended the questioned resolution and quickly decided that the Supreme Court does not have competence in "the interpretation of the law leading to the change of the normative status of the constitution and organization of the administration of justice" (Kpt 1/20) – a competence the Supreme Court has never claimed. Sadurski (2019, 84) sums up these changes in the functioning of the PCT, stating that "for all practical purposes, the PCT as a mechanism of constitutional review has ceased to exist: a reliable aide of the government and parliamentary majority has been born".

Public opinion surveys are not a reliable measure of the standing of relatively unknown and opaque institutions like constitutional courts in the eyes of the wider public. However, the results of public opinion polls about the PCT are telling. Between 2015 and 2020 the percentage of respondents judging PCT activities positively decreased from 40% to 20%. The number of negative opinions rose from 12% to 59%, while the share of those undecided decreased from 50% to 21% (CBOS 2020). The fall in the PCT caseload, measured both as the number of applications received and the number of decisions taken, suggests that potential claimants also swiftly realized the change in the nature of the institution. In 2014, the PCT received 530 applications, in 2015 it received 623, while in 2016 the number suddenly dropped to 360, with further decreases in subsequent years to 235 and 240, in 2017 and 2018 respectively. There can be no doubt that the open questioning of the PCT's authority by various actors (for instance the ombudsman who withdrew his motions from being assessed by the "double judges") contributed to this delegitimating process. On the other hand, the number of statutes challenged before the Tribunal was more or less stable during the period 1997–2020 (between 30 and 40 on average). The categories of petitions which increased almost exponentially in 1997–2015 were "questions of law" addressed to the PCT by courts of law and constitutional complaints. The latter were introduced in 1997, and the number of filed complaints increased rapidly until 2008 (with a record 405 complaints), after which they were quite abruptly cut by the stricter policy on admitting individual complaints to the docket. All these categories of applications have decreased since 2015 to reach record-low levels in 2020. Only 173 constitutional complaints were filed in 2020 (compared to 375 in 2014 and 408 in 2015), and other categories of motions numbered two dozen at most.

In the context outlined here, the fall in the number of cases the PCT took a substantive decision on, and the number of PCT rulings is understandable. The number of rulings grew steadily throughout the 1990s (1993: 25 rulings, 1997: 39 rulings) and in the first decade of the new millennium (2007: a record 171 rulings), before falling slightly and stabilizing at 95–125 rulings per year afterwards (Figure 8.2). After 2015, the number of PCT rulings returned to the level of the early 1990s when the Tribunal was only beginning to build its political importance (2019: 39 rulings, 2020: 23 rulings). Other indicators of the constitutional court's importance *vis-à-vis* parliament that are used in this study (such as the strength of the rulings) may point to misleading conclusions, however. With respect to accepting motions and declaring unconstitutionality, an analysis of the period 2017–2020 suggests that the PCT was highly assertive and restrictive towards the Parliament. The number of refusals is very low (39.5%, as compared to 56.1% for 1993–2015) paralleled only by a short period in the early 1990s when the PCT dealt with an extremely fragmented *Sejm*. Similarly, the percentage of substantial unconstitutionality rulings is 59.9% as compared to 39.7% for 1993–2015 and 72% in 1993 (see Figure 8.2). In terms of the strength of the PCT rulings, the period

2017–2020 also deviates from the 25-year-long PCT practice. The average ruling in the whole period surveyed scored 2.97 on the 10-point scale used in this study, with 2.73 for 1993–2015. During the PiS supremacy period after 2015, the score was 4.07. The only comparable score is 4.98 in 1993. This is even more impressive if compared to other countries of the region during last three decades: Slovakia with the average at 3.8 points, Germany at 3.6 points, Lithuania at 3.5 points, the Czech Republic at 2.9 points, Hungary at 2.8 points. On this basis, the PiS-dominated PCT seems to be the strongest, most assertive constitutional court in the region, excluding the highly atypical Estonian case.

The high scores in terms of the court's strength *vis-à-vis* Parliament did not entail a change in the tools of adjudication by the "new" PCT. Weak and average-strength substantive unconstitutionality were the dominant types of ruling, and only in roughly 4% of cases did "unconstitutionality" mean something other than weak or average substantive unconstitutionality (see Figure 8.1). A combination of several factors can be identified behind this extremely high proportion of substantive unconstitutionality for the whole time period under scrutiny. First, there is the self-image of the PCT as a negative legislator, which most often means two default options: either constitutionality (zero score on the scale) or unconstitutionality on substantive grounds. Weak and average forms of the latter ruling were first of all consequences of the PCT institutional setup: no *ex tunc* rulings were admissible in the Polish legal system, and the Parliament's assent was needed for PCT decisions to have binding force until 1999. Second, prescriptions or positive policy directives in rulings were unthinkable. Third, the PCT almost never used the tool of the complete annulment of an act of Parliament (34 cases in the whole period under research). The Tribunal more often found only some parts of an act unconstitutional, but most frequently declared unconstitutionality of the specific usage or application of some parts of regulations. Finally, the constitution of 1997 introduced a new measure for judicial self-restraint (effective since 1999) by allowing rulings with *pro futuro* temporal effect. Of all rulings in the period under research, 29% were *pro futuro* substantive unconstitutionality rulings; this explains to a degree why the strength of the PCT's decisions was less than moderate until 2017. The "weakness" of a PCT ruling, then, is most often a combination of its partial character and the time it allows the legislator to find an alternative to the questioned policy. Interestingly enough, these two characteristics of PCT rulings did not change in the era of PiS supremacy. Therefore, the growth of the average strength of the PCT rulings in that period is mostly a result of the domination of substantive unconstitutionality decisions over rejections and constitutionality decisions.

The qualitative analysis presented here indicates that the post-2015 PCT protects and legitimizes the parliamentary majority, whereas the quantitative indicators appeared to show a strong, assertive constitutional court restricting the parliament. The easiest explanation for this would be that time lag is responsible for this highly counterintuitive result which contradicts previous findings, as the PiS-dominated PCT adjudicated mainly on earlier legislation from the time when PiS was in opposition. However, there is more to it than that. The apparent contradiction highlights the limits of the methodology used in this study, which assumes that judges take seriously the formal rules of the constitution, as well as the formal rules of the court's operation and legal order as a whole. Without engaging in a deeper discussion on the essence and definition of the regimes established in the past decade in Turkey, Hungary, or Poland, one has to agree that formal rules are not a priority for these regimes. They uphold the main constitutional structure in their states but lack a normative commitment to placing constraints on public power. "There is an established and to a certain extent, functioning mechanism of checks and balances, which may be effective in cases of no importance to the political decision-maker" (Drinóczi and Bień-Kacała 2019, 1164), but once politics and power are involved, informal rules take precedence. In such a situation the governing majority does not hesitate to change the constitution through ordinary legislation (e.g. declaring binding decisions of the previous parliament null and void, incapacitating the very institution of the PCT Vice President despite its constitutional character), and the constitutional court is there to authorize those decisions taken by the majority. This act of authorization may take a form of strong PCT decisions on the unconstitutionality of previous parliaments' acts or strong PCT decisions mending present governing majority "mishaps" when the government changes its strategy (e.g. the National Remembrance Institute Act). In short, the method used in this study does not work well in studying a political environment where the written law is significantly different from actual practice.

Such situations are not unheard of. A substantial part of the literature on democratization is devoted to situations

> when the fit [between rules and institutions formalized in constitutions, and behaviour] is loose or practically non-existent, [and] we are confronted with the double task of describing actual behaviour and discovering (usually informal) rules that behaviour and expectations do follow. Actors are as rational in these settings as in highly formalized ones, but the contours of their rationality cannot be traced without knowing the actual rules . . . that they follow. . . . One may define this situation negatively, emphasizing the lack of fit between formal rules and observed behaviour . . . [but] this is no substitute for studying the actual rules that are being followed.
>
> (O'Donnell 1997, 46)

We have become accustomed to the idea that such a situation is not typical for successfully consolidated democratic regimes, but apparently institutionalization is a two-way street.

Scholarship on constitutional courts in the post-Soviet area may therefore provide useful inspiration for those researching the PCT. In those (semi-)

authoritarian regimes, courts that do not have a veto power whatsoever played a meaningful role as agents of ruling politicians who exploited the courts for various strategic purposes. The courts may be a tool for shifting or spreading responsibility for unpopular decisions or may be used to mislead domestic opponents or deceive external counterparts (Mazmanyan 2015, 212). All those functions sound familiar to an observer of the Polish Tribunal after 2017, but none of them can be captured using the method developed for consolidated democracies in which the constitutional court can meaningfully restrict the parliamentary majority.

8.5 Conclusions

Constitutional review in Poland is in a position where there is no easy way for it to regain its credibility, and on this fact, we close this review of the quarter-century long experience of the PCT as we have known it. The reasons for the PCT's failure are numerous, and our research emphasizes its inability to maintain a healthy relationship with politics. Such a relationship would preclude politicians from perceiving the Tribunal as a dangerous encroachment on their field and make them respect the identity of the institution. The obvious contradiction between the legitimation doctrine of professional neutrality on the one hand, and the judges' partisan behaviour in the periods of PCT activism on the other, proved to be disastrous for the institution once politicians contesting the post-1989 order took power in 2015. From the apparent tension between the self-proclaimed negative legislator doctrine and its role as a third chamber in practice, the politicians understood only this: the PCT is just another instrument in the toolbox of the ruling majority, a tool which is especially dangerous because it acts behind the veil of a legal-professional ideology of neutrality.

The data analysed in this chapter suggests that the story of the PCT is much complicated; the neutral negative legislator vs. the third chamber is not a dichotomy but a frame for a space in which the PCT tried to find its place in the changing world of Polish politics. The shape the PCT took at each stage of this winding road depended on the parliament's ability to create a stable majority as well as on the respect for the Tribunal's specific role in political life. On the one hand, then, the PCT did function as a significant restraint on the *Sejm*, especially in the early period of the democratic transition. The PCT quickly established its authority over a fragmented parliament and effectively co-authored the legal framework of Polish democracy, filling the gaps created by a pace of change that was proving too rapid for the *Sejm*. The multi-layered doctrine of the *Rechtsstaat* developed by the PCT was especially instrumental in this enterprise.[10] This development in the early 1990s generated a high level of esteem for the PCT, not only among the legal profession but also among

10 For more detail on this see Wolek and Jeziorska 2019.

politicians. However, once the politicians were able to build a coalition strong enough to curb the power of the PCT, they did not miss the opportunity and packed the Tribunal with judges more responsive to the requirements of political governance. Nevertheless, the politicians still accepted a specific mode of reaching decisions by the Tribunal and even if the judges followed their party preferences the whole process was kept at arm's length from partisan politics. This second wave of judges, first post-communist and then centre-right-nominated, skilfully used the myth of the powerful Tribunal but steered its jurisprudence in the direction of deference. At the same time, the resources the PCT amassed in the early 1990s enabled it to become a very active counterforce for the PiS-led majority government in 2005–2007. This episode reactivated memories of a strong Tribunal, even though the PCT soon returned to the trend of deference.

Deference did not mean that the PCT jurisprudence was weakened *vis-à-vis* the Parliament, but once the Tribunal decided to stay in its niche of the negative legislator and refrain from encroaching on the field of politics, it was "encysted" by politicians. The PCT might have issued whatever ruling it wished, but the Parliament had developed methods to circumvent the barriers the Tribunal erected. After its 2006 ruling politicians no longer questioned the authority of the PCT, but its jurisprudence had a meagre influence on law making, unlike in the early 1990s. The diminishing number of openly partisan nominations to the Tribunal in the period 2008–2015 was probably the clearest proof that politicians had learnt how to live with the PCT. Having become fully predictable, the PCT became harmless for politicians.

Harmless, that is, for those politicians who were ready to maintain the *status quo*. The PiS government elected in 2015 had an acute understanding of the PCT's mode of operation as a third chamber: it may be either subordinated to the *Sejm* majority, or it must be incapacitated as a potential threat to the will of the rulers. First incapacitated and later taken over, the PCT became an entirely different institution, keeping its old form while transforming its institutional identity. Studying the judicial behaviour of the court might reveal the character of this new PCT, but it is not the interaction between the PCT and Parliament that would be the salient indicator. The new PCT is neither a negative legislator nor the third chamber but the helpmeet of the ruling majority. It operates mostly according to informal rules, and therefore it should be studied using the research methods developed for post-Soviet constitutional courts.

References

Böckenförde, Ernst-Wolfgang. 2017. *Constitutional and Political Theory. Selected Writings*. Oxford: Oxford University Press.

CBOS. 2020. *Ocena działalności Trybunału Konstytucyjnego [The Assessment of the Constitutional Tribunal Activity]*. CBOS Survey Press Release 150/2020.

Czeszejko-Sochacki, Zdzisław. 1996. "O niektórych problemach powszechnie obowiązującej wykładni ustalanej przez Trybunał Konstytucyjny ["On Selected Problems of Generally Binding Interpretation by Constitutional Tribunal"]." In

Konstytucja i gwarancje jej przestrzegania. Księga pamiątkowa ku czci prof. Janiny Zakrzewskiej [Constitution and Guarantees for Its Enforcement. A Festschrift for Janina Zakrzewska], edited by Janusz Trzciński and Adam Jankiewicz, 39–54. Warsaw: Wydawnictwa Trybunału Konstytucyjnego.

———. 2001. "Trybunał Konstytucyjny w PRL (zagadnienia wybrane) ["Constitutional Tribunal in PPR (Selected Issues)"]." *Państwo i Prawo* 56 (6): 3–15.

Dębska, Hanna. 2015a. "Trybunał Konstytucyjny w poszukiwaniu legitymizacji ["Constitutional Tribunal in Search of Its Legitimacy"]." *Studia Prawnicze* 4 (204): 23–41.

———. 2015b. *Władza – Symbol – Prawo. Społeczne tworzenie Trybunału Konstytucyjnego [Power – Symbol – Law. Social Construction of Constitutional Tribunal]*. Warsaw: Wydawnictwo Sejmowe.

Drinóczi, Tímea, and Agnieszka Bień-Kacała. 2019. "Illiberal Constitutionalism: The Case of Hungary and Poland." *German Law Journal* 20 (8): 1140–1166.

Dyevre, Arthur. 2010. "Unifying the Field of Comparative Judicial Politics: Towards a General Theory of Judicial Behaviour." *European Political Science Review* 2 (2): 297–327.

Franck, Raphaël. 2009. "Judicial Independence Under a Divided Polity: A Study of the Rulings of the French Constitutional Court, 1959–2006." *The Journal of Law, Economics, and Organization* 25 (1): 262–284.

Funkcjonowanie Trybunału Konstytucyjnego w latach 2014–2017. Raport Zespołu Ekspertów Prawnych Fundacji im. Stefana Batorego. [*The Functioning of the Constitutional Tribunal, 2014–2017. Report of the Stefan Batory Foundation Legal Expert Group*] 2018. Warsaw: Fundacja im. Stefana Batorego.

Garlicki, Lech. 1999. "Odrzucanie orzeczeń Trybunału Konstytucyjnego przez Sejm ["Rejection of the Constitutional Tribunal Rulings by the Sejm"]." In *Państwo prawa, administracja, sądownictwo: prace dedykowane prof. dr. hab. Januszowi Łętowskiemu w 60. rocznicę urodzin [Rechtsstaat, Administration, Judiciary: A Festschrift for Professor Janusz Łętowski on the Occasion of the 60th Birthday]*, edited by Adam Łopatka, Andrzej Wróbel, and Stefan Kiewlicz, 281–293. Warsaw: Scholar.

———. 2003. "The Experience of the Polish Constitutional Court." In *Constitutional Justice, East and West. Democratic Legitimacy and Constitutional Courts in Post-Communist Europe in a Comparative Perspective*, edited by Wojciech Sadurski, 265–282. The Hague: Kluwer.

———. 2016. *Polskie prawo konstytucyjne. Zarys wykładu [Polish Constitutional Law. An Outline]*. Warsaw: Wolters Kluwer.

Kantorowicz, Jaroslaw, and Garoupa Nuno. 2016. "An Empirical Analysis of Constitutional Review Voting in the Polish Constitutional Tribunal 2003–2014." *Constitutional Political Economy* 2016 (27): 66–92.

Lax, Jeffrey R. 2011. "The New Judicial Politics of Legal Doctrine." *Annual Review of Political Science* 14: 131–157.

Mazmanyan, Armen. 2015. "Judicialization of Politics: The Post-Soviet Way." *International Journal of Constitutional Law* 13 (1): 200–218.

O'Donnell, Guillermo. 1997. "Illusions about Consolidation." In *Consolidating Third-Wave Democracies. Themes and Perspectives*, edited by Larry Diamond, 40–57. Baltimore: Johns Hopkins University Press.

Oniszczuk, Jerzy. 1998. *Orzecznictwo Trybunału Konstytucyjnego w latach 1986–1996 [Jurisprudence of the Constitutional Tribunal 1986–1996]*. Warsaw: Wydawnictwo Sejmowe.

Prochazka, Radoslav. 2002. *Mission Accomplished: On Founding Constitutional Adjudication in Central Europe*. Budapest: CEU Press.

Sąd czy ustawodawca? Legitymizacja sądownictwa konstytucyjnego we współczesnej Polsce i Europie. Trzecia debata Tocqueville'owska. 2009. [A Court or a Lawgiver? The Legitimacy of Constitutional Courts in Contemporary Poland and Europe. 3rd Tocquevillean Debate]. Łodź: Centrum Myśli Polityczno-Prawnej im. Tocqueville'a.

Sadurski, Wojciech. 2008. *Rights Before Courts: A Study of Constitutional Courts in Postcommunist States of Central and Eastern Europe*. Dordrecht: Springer.

———. 2019. *Poland's Constitutional Breakdown*. Oxford: Oxford University Press.

Safjan, Marek. 1999. "Epitafium dla nieostatecznych orzeczeń ["An Epitaph for Non-final Rulings"]." *Rzeczpospolita*, October 4, C-2.

———. 2013. "Poland. The Constitutional Court as a Positive Legislator." In *Constitutional Courts as Positive Legislators. A Comparative Law Study*, edited by Allan R. Brewer-Carias, 701–720. Cambridge: Cambridge University Press.

Santoni, Michele, and Francesco Zucchini. 2004. "Does Policy Stability Increase the Constitutional Court's Independence? The Case of Italy During the First Republic (1956–1992)." *Public Choice* 120 (3–4): 439–401.

Segal, Jeffrey. 2010. "Judicial Behavior." In *The Oxford Handbook of Law and Politics*, edited by Keith Whittington, 19–32. Oxford: Oxford University Press.

Stone Sweet, Alec. 1992. *The Birth of Judicial Politics in France: The Constitutional Council in Comparative Perspective*. Oxford: Oxford University Press.

Vanberg, Georg. 2005. *Constitutional Politics in Germany*. Oxford: Oxford University Press.

Warczok, Tomasz, and Hanna Dębska. 2014. "Sacred Law and Profane Politics. The Symbolic Construction of the Constitutional Tribunal." *Polish Sociological Review* 4 (188): 465–478.

Wiaderek, Grzegorz, ed. 2016. *Procedury nominacji na wybrane stanowiska publiczne – przejrzystość, standardy, rekomendacje [Nomination Procedures for Selected Public Positions: Transparency, Standards, Recommendations]*. Warsaw: Instytut Prawa i Społeczeństwa INPRIS.

Wolek, Artur, and Iga Jeziorska. 2019. "The Polish Constitutional Tribunal: Deference beyond the veil of activism." In *Constitutional Politics and the Judiciary. Decision-making in Central and Eastern Europe*, edited by Kálmán Pócza, 126–155. London and New York: Routledge.

Zajadło, Jerzy. 2017. "Pojęcie "imposybilizm prawny" a polityczność prawa i prawoznawstwa ["The Concept of Legal Impossibilism and the Politicisation of Law and Jurisprudence"]." *Państwo i Prawo* 72 (3): 17–30.

Zoll, Andrzej. 1997. "Interview with Professor Andrzej Zoll, Chief Justice of the Polish Constitutional Tribunal (Interview by Irena Grudzinska-Gross)." *East European Constitutional Review* 6 (1): 77–79.

Zoll, Fryderyk, and Leah Wortham. 2019. "Judicial Independence and Accountability: Withstanding Political Stress in Poland." *Fordham International Law Journal* 42: 875.

9 The Romanian Constitutional Court

Layers of constitutional adjudication

Csongor Kuti

9.1 Introduction

This chapter presents an analysis of the variation in the strength of the rulings of the Romanian Constitutional Court (RCC) issued in the period from 1992 to 2020. It represents a follow-up to the JUDICON pilot project for assessing the degree of judicial constraint on legislatures by mapping the strength and diversity of judicial decisions (Kuti 2019). Completing the initial dataset with an analysis of the decisions issued in the 2015–2020 period, it does not depart from the previous study's general conclusions with regard to the RCC's self-constructed role and positioning in the constitutional structure of Romania. Instead, focusing on the distinct review procedures ("layers of adjudication") of the RCC, it attempts to explain the variation in success rate of petitions and in strength of rulings. The chapter argues that the various competences of the RCC in reviewing normative acts adopted by Parliament produce different outcomes in terms of success rates and ruling strength. This reflects the different role and positioning of the RCC in the various procedures that arguably represent distinct layers of constitutional adjudication. While, as we argued in the conclusions of the pilot project's analysis (Kuti 2019), in *a posteriori* review procedures one cannot demonstrate a constitutionalization of politics, the RCC mostly refrains from overriding Parliaments' normative choices and leaves it up to them to correct faulty legislation, in *a priori* review procedures the RCC demonstrate a higher degree of willingness to censor legislative attempts. The existence of distinct layers of constitutional adjudication might be explained by contextual factors, such as the general political (in)stability at the time or the political affiliation of constitutional judges. However, and perhaps more significantly, it might also be considered the product of a conscious design and of the general perception – endorsed and to some extent enforced by the RCC – with regard to its role in the blueprint of the government. The chapter begins with a brief presentation of the institutional arrangements of the RCC to familiarize the reader with the contexts of Romanian constitutionalism before continuing with an overview of methodology and of country-specific issues, a summary of the pilot project study, and finally it

DOI: 10.4324/9781003399483-9

attempts to analyse the trends in the strength of rulings and the factors that might determine these trends.

9.2 Organization and functioning of the RCC

Besides the Constitution, the organization and functioning of the RCC is regulated by an organic law.[1] Both have been amended over the years, altering to some degree the initial institutional arrangements of the RCC. At the outset, the RCC's review powers comprised the *a priori* review of bills, the review of Parliaments' rules and regulations, the *a posteriori* review of laws and governmental ordinances, and the *ex officio* review of constitutional revision bills. *A priori* review motions could be lodged by the President of Romania, the presidents of the two chambers of the Parliament, Members of Parliament (at least 50 deputies or 25 senators), the government, and the President of the Supreme Court. *A posteriori* review of laws or governmental ordinances was possible only by way of objection (as a procedural defence, similar to the French "*exception d'inconstitutionnalité*") raised before ordinary courts of justice during regular litigation proceedings by the parties, the prosecutor, or by the court.[2] While decisions on *a priori* review motions had to be taken by the full court, with no possibility of appeal, decisions on *a posteriori* review motions were taken by a panel of three judges, with the possibility of appeal before a panel of five judges.[3] The decisions of the RCC were mandatory and had effect starting from the moment of their publication in the Official Gazette.

The law on the organization and functioning of the RCC was significantly amended for the first time in 1997.[4] The most important modifications on this occasion concerned *a posteriori* review proceedings: the system of panels was abolished, and from then on, all decisions were taken by the full court. The possibility of appeal was also withdrawn, and since then, proceedings before ordinary courts of justice are halted until the RCC decides about the objections of unconstitutionality raised during regular litigation. The 2003 constitutional revision[5] broadened the sphere of persons authorized to bring a

1 Law no. 47/1992 on the organization and functioning of the Constitutional Court, Official Gazette no.101/1992.

2 The referring court could but did not necessarily have to suspended litigation until the objection was decided upon by the Constitutional Court.

3 If procedures had not been halted before the referring court, admission decisions constituted grounds for retrial upon the request of the party which raised the exception in civil litigation and *ex officio* in penal litigation, if the conviction had been passed on the basis of a provision declared unconstitutional.

4 Law no. 138/1997 on amending and supplementing of Law no. 47/1992 on the organization and functioning of the Constitutional Court, Official Gazette no. 187/1997.

5 Constitution Review Act 2003 and Law no. 232 of 2004, amending and supplementing Law no. 47 of 1992 on the organization and functioning of the Constitutional Court.

complaint directly before the RCC, so as to include the President of the Superior Council of Magistracy,[6] the Prime Minister, the President of Romania, and the presidents of the two chambers of Parliament, the Ombudsman, and a group of at least 50 deputies or 25 senators. Furthermore, it also extended the RCC's jurisdiction to juridical conflicts of constitutional nature between different public institutions (parliament, executive, and presidency). Finally, but perhaps most important, the RCC's decisions became generally binding in both *a priori* and *a posteriori* review procedures, eliminating Parliament's power to veto its *a priori* review decisions. (It must be noted that this power of the legislature, which could have been exercised by a qualified majority vote, was never used in practice.)

In *a posteriori* review proceedings, the constitutional revision introduced a 45-day term from the date of the publication of the RCC's decision, within which period the parliament (or the government, in case of ordinances) may "correct" the provisions that were found to be unconstitutional to bring them in line with constitutional requirements. For this period of 45 days, the provisions at stake are suspended, and if the aforementioned actors fail to act, the provisions will be annulled. However, Parliament retained a trump card to compensate for the loss of its power to override the RCC's decisions. The article of the Constitution dedicated to the RCC's jurisdiction was appended with the phrase "other duties stipulated by the organic law of the Court" – hence allowing a certain degree of legislative control over the RCC's jurisdiction, with Parliament being able to alter (or at least to add to) the RCC's sphere of competence, with a qualified majority vote. The legislature played this card for the first time in 2010, when the organic law of the RCC was revised.[7] The RCC's special *a priori* (mandatory) review powers over constitutional revision bills, which enable the RCC to adjudicate on the revision bills after their adoption, were introduced in their current form by an amendment to Law no. 47/1992 on the organization and functioning of the RCC, in 2004. Before then, the RCC mandatorily reviewed such bills *ex officio*, only prior to their first reading.[8] Thus, the RCC can exert an uncommonly high degree of control over constitutional revisions, being obliged to scrutinize such bills twice, once prior to their first reading – the bill can be presented on first reading

6 The Superior Council of Magistracy is a representative body of the judicial authority, the guarantor of the independence of judiciary, which oversees the careers of magistrates and prepares and keeps professional records of the magistrates.

7 Law no. 177/2010 for the revision of Law no. 47 of 1992, Official Gazette no. 672/2010, of the Code of Civil Procedure and of the Code of Criminal Procedure.

8 Law no. 232/2004 on amending and supplementing of Law no. 47/1992 on the organizing and functioning of the Constitutional Court, Official Gazette no. 502/2004; Decision no. 356/2003, published in the Official Gazette no.686/2003.

only together with the RCC's decision – and once (if it is the case) after their adoption.[9]

The provisions on the appointment of judges and their term of office have remained unchanged from the outset. Accordingly, the RCC is composed of nine judges, of whom six are appointed by Parliament (three judges by each chamber) and three by the President of Romania. Judges are appointed for a single, non-renewable mandate of nine years, and the first Court was appointed in such a way as to ensure that every three years one-third of the mandates would expire. The constitutional judges themselves are responsible for electing the President of the RCC, who holds office for three years. Although the RCC is not part of the judicial system, constitutional judges must hold a law degree, have at least 18 years of professional experience (either as practitioners or as academics), and enjoy "a high degree of professional competence". Several judges of the first Court were also members of the constitution drafting committee, and it has been a constant practice ever since to appoint Members of the Parliament as judges (Kuti 2019).

9.3 Some methodological considerations

9.3.1 Peculiarities

Romanian constitutional adjudication is characterized by certain specific features that need to be addressed in order to nuance the conclusions of the research: the issue of executive law-making via governmental ordinances, the specifics of individual complaints, the effects of RCC decisions, the rather unique caseload of the court, and the dual – *a priori* and *a posteriori* – review competence.

First, Parliament may mandate the government to enact *ordinances* within a specified domain and period of time. The government is also able to enact *emergency ordinances*, in extraordinary and urgent situations, without any parliamentary mandate, but without affecting the domains reserved for constitutional laws, the fundamental institutions of the state, constitutional rights, liberties and duties, electoral rights, and the regime of expropriations. As this research is concerned with the constraints that constitutional adjudication exerts upon legislature, it will focus solely on the review of acts of parliament. Government-made normative acts appear in the dataset only in those cases in which either: (a) the RCC reviewed a law approving, rejecting, amending, or supplementing a governmental ordinance (with some exceptions); or

9 Thus far Parliament has managed only once to pass a revision bill, on the occasion of the 2003 constitutional revision. The RCC however, has made use of its review power several times, striking out provisions from revision bills before their first reading on two occasions: Decision no. 148/2003, published in the Official Gazette no. 317/2003, and Decision no. 799/2011, published in the Official Gazette no. 440/2011. However, it has yet to review a revision bill after being adopted by the Parliament.

(b) provisions of ordinances are addressed inseparably, together with various articles of law, in a single ruling. Similarly, judgments on the constitutionality of treaties or other international agreements, as well as decisions concerning disputes of a constitutional nature between public authorities and those pertaining to house rules of the parliament have also been disregarded. This represents an important difference from the pilot project, which also included disputes of a constitutional nature between the Parliament and other public authorities. However, in the period analysed in this paper, as political conflicts between various authorities became more embittered (culminating in the conviction of the former Prime Minister for corruption-related crimes and the dismissal from office of the Chief Prosecutor of the National Anti-Corruption Directorate), claims of constitutional conflict tended to be used mostly for strategic purposes, rather than simply for settling disputes over normative competences. These included for example the refusal of the National Anti-Corruption Directorates' (DNA) Chief Prosecutor to appear before a parliamentary commission,[10] the method used by the High Court of Cassation and Justice for establishing its panels in penal matters,[11] the protocols concluded between the Prosecutor's Office alongside the High Court of Cassation and Justice and the Romanian Intelligence Service (SRI),[12] or the prosecution of the President of the Senate for failing to present to the plenum the National Integrity Agency's (ANI) request to terminate the mandate of a member of the Senate.[13] Therefore, with little to no connection to limiting Parliament's legislative powers, the constitutional conflict claims of this period seem to represent attempts to involve the RCC (and provisions of the constitution) in the settling political accounts, and thus appear less relevant for the purposes of the present study.

Second, individual complaints can reach the RCC solely by way of objections raised before regular courts during judicial litigation, in connection with the constitutionality of the legal norms applicable in a given case. This leads to the RCC facing recurring complaints, regarding the same issues – this is obvious especially when norms addressing salient issues such as property restitution, mortgage loans, public pensions, etc. – are at stake, either when an unfortunate regulation (e.g. the post-communist property restitution process) results in a flood of desperate claims, or when interested institutions attempt, arguably, to exert pressure on the state (e.g. credit institutions, in the case of legislation amending mortgage loans rules). Things are complicated by the fact that the RCC has no preliminary screening mechanism, thus all complaints are currently decided upon by the full court. All these, in practice, lead to a large number of rejections, creating a distorted image of the relative power of the constitutional court. Therefore, recurring complaints have not been taken into consideration, except if they invoked the breach of distinct constitutional provisions, or the RCC changed its jurisprudence and implemented a different approach.

10 Decision no. 611/2017, published in the Official Gazette, no. 877/2017.
11 Decision no. 685/2018, published in the Official Gazette, no. 1021/2018.
12 Decision no. 26/2019, published in the Official Gazette, no. 193/2019.
13 Decision no. 775/2020, published in the Official Gazette no. 1094/2020.

Third, and in connection with the lack of preliminary screening, one must note the peculiar issue of refusals. The JUDICON project classifies constitutional court rulings into admissions, rejections, and refusals – the last meaning, by and large, that the courts decide, usually through a preliminary ruling, that they do not need to discuss the case on its merits. Unfortunately, the specific legal language used by the RCC distinguishes between only two categories of rulings: admissions and rejections. The RCC may decide to reject a claim either on its merits, due to the lack of a breach of the constitution – since, in its own wording, it was "unfounded" (*respinge ca nefondată*) – or without discussing the merits, on some procedural grounds – in its own wording as "inadmissible" (*respinge ca inadmisibilă)* – such as lack of standing, lack of jurisdiction, *res judicata* (but only if the contested provision has already been ruled unconstitutional, as previous rejections are not taken into consideration), or if the claim is considered to be unsubstantiated (failure to indicate the reasons for the invoked unconstitutionality).

In practice, however, the RCC's jurisprudence is not completely unequivocal with regard to the two types of rejections, therefore some compromise had to be made while selecting cases for the purpose of the present research. It was eventually decided to consider the second type of rejection rulings (rejection as inadmissible) to be "refusals" and thus to be omitted from the database, unless they occurred in an *a priori* review procedure or produced dissenting opinions (this is why, for example, the database contains only an extremely reduced number of "no competence" – lack of jurisdiction – rulings). Furthermore, some of the "proper" rejection rulings (rejection as unfounded), appear to be in practice more akin to refusals than rejections, lacking a detailed discussion of the merits of the case and relying on very scant reasoning. Such summary, single-ruling decisions were also considered to be "refusals" from the perspective of the present research, and omitted from the database, unless they occurred the *in a priori* review procedure or produced dissenting opinions. Acknowledging the perils of arbitrariness, rejection rulings were considered to lack detailed discussion or to give incomplete reasons each time their reasoning part was shorter than one page and 10 numbered paragraphs (RCC decisions may extend to over 100 numbered paragraphs). Fourth, according to the fundamental law,[14] the decisions of the RCC are generally binding from their publication and take effect only in the future. Consequently, unconstitutional provisions become inapplicable from the day the decision is published, and thus the rulings of the RCC may only have an *ex nunc* effect.

Finally, the RCC has the power to adjudicate also *a priori* on the constitutionality of laws. Comparable competences, concerning the review of laws before their entry into force, are enjoyed also by other European constitutional courts; however, the *a priori* review powers of the RCC have some peculiar characteristics. On the one hand, the circle of persons authorized to lodge a complaint for *a priori* review is uncommonly large, including the

14 Art. 147 sect. (4) Constitution of Romania

President of the Republic, the presidents of the two Chambers of Parliament, a group of MPs (at least 50 deputies or 25 senators, i.e. members of the opposition), the Ombudsman and the President of the High Court of Cassation and Justice (Romania's highest court of law). In the case of the government-made normative acts (ordinances), it is not possible to review their constitutionality through an *a priori* procedure.

The situation regarding *a priori* review of laws approving, rejecting, amending, or supplementing governmental ordinances is somewhat peculiar. In some of these rulings, the RCC does not actually analyse the bill adopted by the Parliament, but instead it examines the formal and/or substantive constitutionality of the governmental ordinance that forms the object of the bill. Thus, the constitutionality of the bill depends on the constitutionality of the governmental ordinance. As such rulings analyse acts of the executive, rather than acts of the legislator, and therefore arguably represent only a remote constraint upon parliament, they have been excluded from the dataset. (This explains the difference between the number of *a priori* review decisions issued by the RCC and the number of such decisions included in the research.)

Due to the reasons outlined here, this research covers only a fraction of the RCC's case law from the given timeframe (1992–2020). The dataset includes 3,184 decisions out of total 21,056, consisting of 3,300 individual rulings, but it can be considered representative of the RCC's jurisdiction concerning the analysed aspects. The number of decisions from each year included in the research fluctuates and is not necessarily proportionate with the overall number of decisions issued by the RCC. (In fact, the largest number of decisions per year were issued, to date, in the period from 2007 to 2012.) Nevertheless, it is notable that the last five years of the timeframe produced the largest number of decisions (and consequently rulings) included in the research. This increase is attributable on one hand to the dynamics of the claims – for instance there was a considerable increase in the number of *a priori* review claims – and the dynamics of the rulings – a decrease in the percentage of refusal rulings. On the other hand, it can also be explained by the use of strategic litigation tactics: for instance, Law no. 77/2016 on the offering of certain property to extinguish debts arising from loans (altering the regulations so as to support mortgage loan debtors) flooded the courts with complaints from banks and other credit institutions. Objections on the grounds of unconstitutionality were constantly raised in these cases, with well over 1000 claims being filed with the RCC in the 2016–2020 period; 68 of the rulings concerning these complaints were included in the present research.

9.3.2 Workload of the Court

The RCC has quite a remarkable workload. According to its own official statistics, during the timespan (1992–2020) and the subject matter covered by this research, the Court received a total of 48,482 unconstitutionality complaints, of which 581 were *a priori* review (including mandatory review of constitutional revision bills), 47,801 represented objections raised during litigation before ordinary courts, and another 100 claims were filed by the ombudsman's office – adding up to 47,901 *a posteriori* review claims (Constitutional Court of Romania Statistics 2022a). Of the decisions issued in the same period, and according to the subject matter covered, 405 *a priori* review and 2,743 *a posteriori* review decisions (made up of one or more rulings) were included in the database that represents the basis of the research.

The number of *a priori* review claims did not fluctuate dramatically over the years for a long period, generally settling at around 10–20 claims per year, but there were clearly a low number of claims in the period from 1998 to 2004 (two to eight claims per year), with the clear peak being 24 claims in 2010. However, there was a significant increase in the number of such claims in last five years of the project, with 289 claims filed in this timespan, the lowest annual number being 24 in 2016, the highest 105, in 2020. This increase in the number of claims might also be attributed to an increase in political conflicts (Section 9.3.1), when explaining the increase in constitutional conflict claims. As will be argued (Section 9.5.3), they may be considered to represent an alternate means of political dispute and are more likely to be deployed in situations when members of opposition feel incapable of influencing normative decisions during parliamentary proceedings.

The number of *a posteriori* review claims grew steadily from 24 in 1992 to 2,458 in 2006, with a smaller peak in 1997 (570 claims). After 2006, the trend became more erratic, fluctuating from 888 in 2013 to almost 10 times that number: 8,823 in 2009. In the last five years of the timeframe, there was a somewhat lower degree of fluctuation, but overall, a relatively higher number of claims were registered, ranging from 2,260 (in 2018) to 3,556 (in 2016). It should be noted that the methodology elaborated by the JUDICON project uses rulings as its unit of analysis instead of decisions, since in a single decision a Court may address more than one legal provision and can offer various solutions. As regards the RCC, the analysis did not find a dramatic difference between the number of rulings and the number of decisions, with the former usually exceeding the latter by a narrow margin (Figure 9.1).

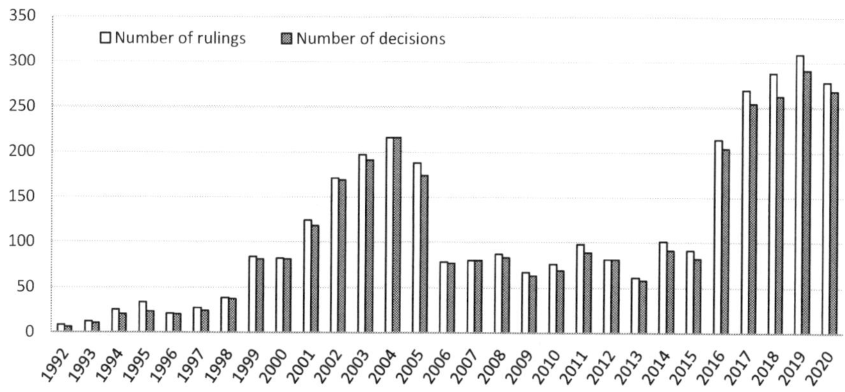

Figure 9.1 Number of decisions and rulings (1992–2020) (RCC)

9.4 Muddling through the democratic transition

The pilot project covered the period between 1992 and 2015. To be able to identify the factors that might be linked with the evolution of the average strength of the RCC's rulings, the research focused especially on two periods – 2001 to 2004 and 2009 to 2012 – in which rulings present a constant difference in average strength (constantly low or constantly high, compared to the average of the RCC). Both periods were chosen so as to fall exactly between two periods of general elections. The study concluded (Kuti 2019) that the RCC's case law exhibits a deferential attitude towards the legislator, demonstrated by the high rate of rejection rulings and the relatively low rate of dissenting opinions. Moreover, in periods of higher general political stability, *a priori* review claims tend to produce a low success rate, while substantive unconstitutionality rulings are mostly average or weak.

In relation to majority opinions, three factors were identified that were considered to influence the trends in the strength of rulings: general political stability, the political affiliation of the judges, and the character of the constitutional review.

In assessing general political stability, the stability of the governing coalition (i.e. whether it managed to stay together for the whole term of its parliamentary mandate or whether it was subject to changes), the stability of the government (i.e. whether the Prime Minister managed to fulfil his whole term of office), the stability of the President (i.e. whether the president managed to fulfil his term of office; whether he had to face impeachment or not), and finally, the number of seats held by the largest of the governing parties were taken into consideration. The Prime Minister and the President are both relevant players in this equation, as Romania is a semi-presidential republic, where the president is elected directly and possesses significant executive powers. The study argued that the strength of the rulings can be linked to general political stability, i.e. in periods of stability rulings tend to be weaker while in periods of unrest they tend to be stronger (Kuti 2019).

Regarding the second factor, the study found that a politically more balanced (polarized) court, in periods of lower general political stability, will issue more rulings of unconstitutionality. At the same time, the proportion of procedural unconstitutionality rulings was considerably higher in such periods. Similarly, when the majority of the judges were nominated by the same (governing) party, which enjoyed a relatively high general level of political stability, a low average strength and a low degree of variation of rulings could be observed. However, the claims of political partisanship made by some scholars were not supported by the study. It should also be noted that a study on conflicts of a constitutional nature between state organs, which arguably represent the most politically sensitive issues, found that judges tend to form dissenting coalitions according to their formal political affiliation and publish dissents in line with their nominating party's interests (Kuti 2020).

The third factor was the type of constitutional review. *A priori* reviews represent a low proportion of the case law of the RCC, but their success rate – in comparison with *a posteriori* review rulings – is remarkably high. The study found that in those periods of time when the success rate of *a priori* review claims was low, the average strength of rulings was also low, and this relationship was more prominent than that of *a posteriori* review claims. Moreover, the data also demonstrated that the relative rate of *a priori* review claims was the highest in periods of reduced general political stability, and this holds true also for the success rates. These intriguing conclusions of the pilot-project pertaining to *a priori* and *a posteriori* review rulings called for a more detailed investigation, while the temporal broadening of the scope of original research offered the opportunity to explore this issue more extensively, and it is this which lies at the core of the current chapter.

9.5 Trends in the strength of majority rulings

Due to the principles of case selection, only a small number of rulings were included in the dataset from the first seven years of the timeframe. In fact, the number of *a priori* review rulings exceeds the number of *a posteriori* review rulings in the period between 1992 and 1996 (most *a posteriori* review claims did not target laws or were lodged against laws adopted under the previous regime – prior to the 1991 democratic Constitution), thus the average strength of these early rulings appears somewhat distorted in comparison to the rest of the dataset. As the total number of rulings per year increased and the proportion of *a posteriori* review rulings began to significantly exceed that of *a priori* review rulings, the average strength of the rulings became relatively stable in the second half of the timeframe, with only two notable peaks that will be briefly addressed in the following text. As the number of *a posteriori* review decisions exceeded the number of *a priori* review decisions by a very large margin – 19,993 decisions to 476 in the full docket of the RCC and 2,743 decisions to 405 in the dataset (which translates to 2,837 rulings to 493) – the average strength of the RCC's decisions is clearly determined by these rulings. It appears however, fairly evident from the dataset that in the second half of the timeframe there was a clear and constant difference between the average strength of *a priori* and *a posteriori* review rulings, suggesting that the two represent distinct layers of constitutional adjudication.

Regarding the two peaks, an explanation for the increase in the average strength of *a posteriori* review rulings in 2015 can be found in the reform of the Code of Penal Procedure, adopted and implemented between 2010 and 2013, which led to a cohort of constitutional review claims, with almost half of the strong unconstitutionality rulings in 2015 (13 out of 31) targeting the Code of Penal Procedure, while some other rulings involved provisions of the Penal Code, or of other connected legislation, pertaining to protection of

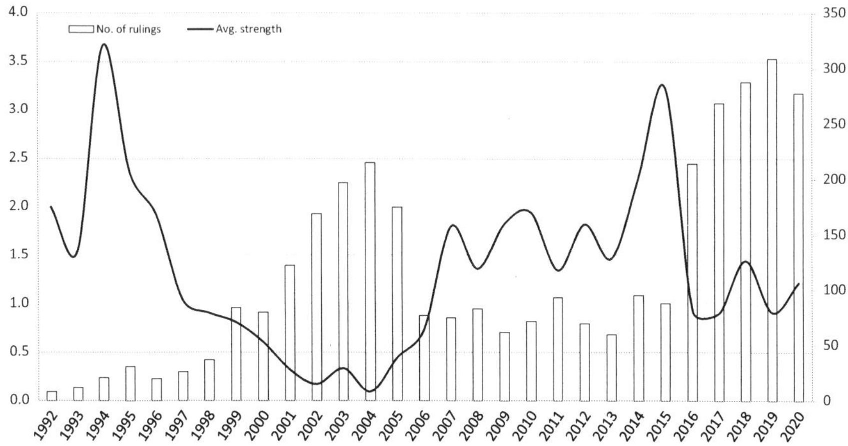

Figure 9.2 Number and average strength of rulings (1992–2020) (RCC)

witnesses, the execution of sentences, tax evasion (Figure 9.2). To understand the unusually high average strength of the *a priori* review rulings of 2012, one has to take into consideration the turbulent political context,[15] which characterized that year, and during which political actors attempted to alter significant pieces of legislation to secure short-term gains.[16] The pilot project, as already mentioned in Section 9.4, identified three factors that might explain the trends in the average strength of majority rulings: political stability, the political affiliation of judges, and the distinction between *a priori* and *a posteriori* review procedures. This chapter argues that these factors are mostly applicable also for the extended timeframe.

9.5.1 *Political stability*

The pilot project identified a single period of high political stability, lasting from 2001 to 2004. This finding is valid also for the extended timeframe, as

15 In a single year, a former Prime Minister and president of the Social Democratic Party were sentenced to prison for corruption, the Prime Minister in office resigned after weeks of protests, his successor was dismissed by Parliament via a vote of no confidence, the election-winning and reigning Prime Minister was accused of plagiarism (upheld years later by the courts of law), one minister of education resigned after accusations of plagiarism, and one nominated minister of education had to withdraw after being accused of lying about her studies.

16 Efforts were undertaken to amend legislation pertaining to the organization of local and parliamentary elections (both being held in 2012), the law on the organization and conduct of referenda (the President of the Republic underwent – and survived – a suspension procedure, an essential part of which was a referendum for his dismissal from office), and the law on the organization and functioning of the RCC. In the latter case, there were attempts to eliminate the RCC's jurisdiction over individual decisions of the Parliament and over resolutions taken either by the Senate or the Chamber of Deputies, or by both chambers sitting in a joint session – these in the context of the rising anti-corruption campaign that began to also target MPs.

in the 2016–2020 period only the President of the Republic managed to complete his term of office. However, governing coalitions proved just as fluid as earlier: there were six Prime Ministers in a five year-period between 2016 and 2020 (general elections being held in 2016 and 2020).

According to the pilot project's findings, in politically more stable periods, the RCC's rulings tend to be weaker, while in periods of turmoil they tend to become stronger. In the extended timeframe, these conclusions seem to remain valid but only with respect *to a priori* review rulings, as in the 2016–2020 period a relatively higher average strength of rulings can be observed, paired with a lower degree in the variation of the average strength, similarly to the figures characterizing the 2008–2012 period examined in the pilot project. This holds true, even if the 2016–2020 period contained a significantly larger number of rulings than the reference period from the pilot project.[17]

However, if *a posteriori* review rulings are considered, the results are no longer as similar: even if the period of unrest remained constant until the end of the timeframe, in the last five years of the period the average strength of *a posteriori* review rulings (and, consequently, of the rulings in general) decreased significantly, approaching the average strength of the *a posteriori* review rulings (and of the rulings in general) of the period characterized by general political stability. It would be tempting to argue that the difference in the strength of *a posteriori* review rulings is due to the fact that a significantly larger number of rulings were included in the dataset from the last five years of the timeframe (Figure 9.3). However, the proportion of *a priori* review rulings in the last five years is almost identical to the proportion for the entire dataset (204 out of 1,325 in the 2016–2020 period and 493 out of 3,330 in the entire dataset) and only 3% lower than in the 2009–2012 period (54 out of 2,297), a time considered highly unstable in the pilot project.

All this makes it appear that the political stability factor might explain the trends in the strength of *a priori* review rulings, but it proves an insufficient argument with regard to the trends in the strength of the *a posteriori* review rulings, underpinning the perception that the two types of procedures might be considered to be distinct layers of constitutional adjudication. This finding may lead one to draw a cautious conclusion on the different nature of the two review procedures, according to which the RCC seems to allow, in the *a priori* review procedure, more room for political/ideological perspectives (hence the average strength of such rulings decreases in periods of relative political stability), while in the *a posteriori* review procedure it seems to allow more room for a judicial approach (hence the average strength of such rulings is seemingly unrelated to the political context).

It should also be noted that in the second half of the timeframe the constitutional conflict procedure which allows the RCC to become an arbitrator of institutional conflicts (resembling the "*Organstreitverfahren*" proceedings before

17 See explanations provided under Section 9.3.1. for the larger number of rulings (dynamics of the claims and of the rulings, strategic litigation).

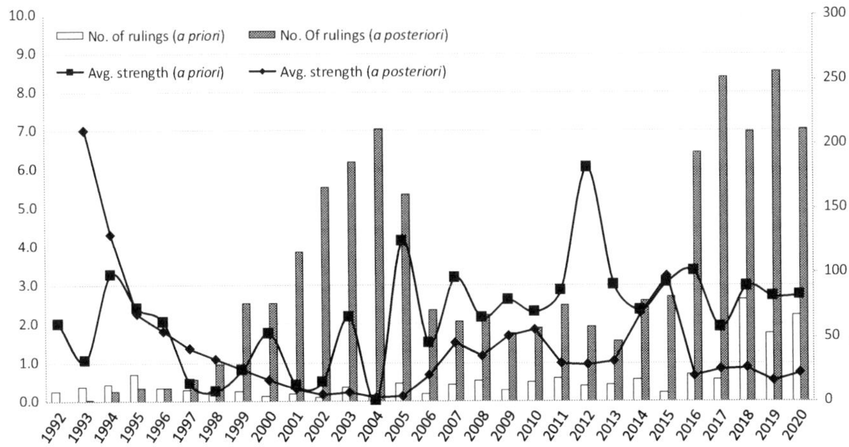

Figure 9.3 Number and average strength of rulings (*a priori* vs. *a posteriori* review) (1992–2020) (RCC)

the German Federal Constitutional Court but exceeding the notion of conflicts of competence) gradually increased in importance as a major tool for settling political disputes between various actors. (As mentioned in Section 9.3, decisions of the RCC in this specific procedure have been ignored by the present research.)

9.5.2 *Political affiliation of judges*

Being nominated by a party does not necessarily mean that the nominee is affiliated to the nominating party, and this is especially true in the case of judges appointed by the President of Romania (except when a Member of Parliament is nominated or appointed). The appointment of politician-judges has been a traditional practice since the founding of the RCC, when the majority of judges were former MPs, but this tradition has faded over the years. For instance, in the 2001–2004 period, out of 11 judges involved in the rulings included in the dataset, 5 were politician-judges, while later, in the period from 2009 to 2012 period, there were also 5 politician-judges, but out of 16 involved in the analysed rulings, and finally, in the last four years of the timeframe, only 3 out of 15 judges were former politicians.[18]

18 In the 2001–2004 period, four politician-judges came from the Social Democratic Party (PSD) and one from the Democratic Alliance of Hungarians in Romania (RMDSZ), while another three were former counsellors of the President of Romania (also coming from the PSD). In the period from 2009 to 2012, three politician-judges came from the PSD – one from the RMDSZ, one from the Democratic Party (PD), while another judge was a former minister of justice (in a government led by the PSD). In the 2017–2020 period, two politician-judges came from the PSD, one from the RMDSZ, while another one judge was a former counsellor of the President of Romania (coming from the National Liberal Party – PNL), and one was a former minister of justice (in a government led by the PSD), while another two judges embraced a political career after the termination of their mandate (one as minister of justice in a government led by the PSD, another as MP for PSD).

Since the voting behaviour of the judges is not public, indicators about the judges' voting behaviour can be inferred only from dissenting opinions. As the composition of the court and the dissenting or concurring opinions are usually available, decisions which produced a maximal number of dissents (three or four, depending on whether the bench was made up of eight or nine judges) and which were accordingly adopted by the lowest possible majority, provide the best information about the individual judges' votes. The dataset contains only 20 such decisions (taken by a five-to-four or a five-to-three majority with all the minority judges publishing a dissenting opinion),[19] but in none of these cases do politician-judges constitute a decisive majority. Moreover, there is a single decision in which all four dissenting judges can be linked to the same party (coalition), but in this case, their nominating parties formed the governing coalition.

However, if these 20 decisions are clustered according to the type of the review procedure in which they were issued, it turns out that minimal majority rulings are arguably connected to the (political) balance (polarization) of the RCC. The more balanced (polarized) the bench is, the more likely it is to produce increasingly disputed *a priori* review rulings. Conversely, an imbalanced, less-fragmented bench is less likely to generate controversial disputes over *a priori* review claims and more likely to result in minimal majority rulings in *a posteriori* reviews. This finding is in line with the cautious conclusion proposed in the previous sub-section, and it seems to support the idea that *a priori* review rulings are characterized by a stronger political/ideological approach (hence, judges are more unified on political/ideological grounds), while *a posteriori* review rulings are characterized by a stronger judicial approach (hence, judges are more unified on legal theory/interpretation grounds). Thus, six out of a total of eight *a priori review* minimal majority decisions were issued in the period between 2008 and 2013, which according to the pilot project was characterized by a relative equilibrium of left-wing and right-wing judges (at least according to their formal political affiliation and nominating parties), while all the *a posteriori* review minimal majority decisions were issued in the 1999–2007 (four rulings) and 2013–2018 (eight rulings) periods, characterized by a relative imbalance of the left-wing and right-wing judges (at least as per their formal political affiliation and nominating parties).[20]

Conclusively, even if in its most-debated rulings the Court was not, as a rule, split along the lines of formal political affiliation or the nominating parties of the judges, and the majority was not, as rule, formed by judges nominated by the governing party (coalition), still, a connection may arguably be established between how disputed individual rulings are under different

19 Decisions demonstrably taken by the lowest possible majority, without excluding the possibility of the existence of other decisions taken with a similar majority.

20 The majority of the politician-judges come from the Social Democratic Party (PSD), and most of the formally not-affiliated judges were nominated by the same party (or the coalition led by it).

review procedures and the composition of the Court, suggesting that the two types of procedures belong to distinct layers of constitutional adjudication.

9.5.3 A priori and a posteriori review

The total number of *a priori* review rulings in the dataset is significantly lower than the number of *a posteriori* review rulings (493 to 2,837), although the difference in their outcome is inversely proportionate: 49.5% of all *a priori* review rulings represent admissions, while a mere 12.9% of all *a posteriori* review rulings had a similar result (Figure 9.3). According to the RCC's own statistics (in which the units of analysis are decisions, not rulings), in the same timeframe there were 476 *a priori*, and 19,993 *a posteriori* review decisions, with an admission rate of 52.9% for *a priori*, and 2.77% for *a posteriori* review rulings (Constitutional Court of Romania Statistics 2022b). While the numbers in the dataset of the research are lower due to case selection, the differences between the two types of review procedure remain outstanding.

Some constitutional scholars have proposed the elimination of the *a priori* review powers of the Court, arguing that *a priori* motions are in essence the expression of political conflicts and are used by the opposition as an alternative means of political dispute, after being defeated in parliamentary voting procedures (Perju 2010). This view finds some degree of support in the present analysis, as the data show that the relative rate of *a priori* review rulings was the highest when the general level of political stability was relatively lower (66.5% of the total of 493 rulings being issued in the last 12 years), while their success rate was also significantly higher in comparison with periods of relatively higher general political stability (55.4% versus 37.5% in the first 17 years). The perception that *a priori* review motions are induced by political conflicts is also supported by the fact that claims coming from the office of the President of the Republic were extremely low in the periods of relative general political stability (two motions were filed in the 2001–2004 period), while they appeared more regularly in the politically less stable periods (13 motions filed in the 2009–2012 period) and their frequency rocketed in the last few years of the timeframe (96 motions filed in the 2017–2020 period) (Constitutional Court of Romania 2022a).

These enumerated differences in the number of motions filed in distinct political contexts, and the difference in their admission rates between *a priori* and a *posteriori* review rulings is also reflected in the average strength of the rulings issued (Figure 9.3). Even if the RCC's rulings seem to be rather modest in strength, there is still a considerable difference between the two types of rulings: in the entire dataset, *a priori* review rulings have an average strength of 2.59, while *a posteriori* review rulings have a strength of only 0.79, a difference that is almost equal to that established in the ratio of the restraining rulings (49.1% to 12.9%). From all these it appears, again, that *a priori* and *a posteriori* review procedures might be regarded as representing separate layers of constitutional adjudication.

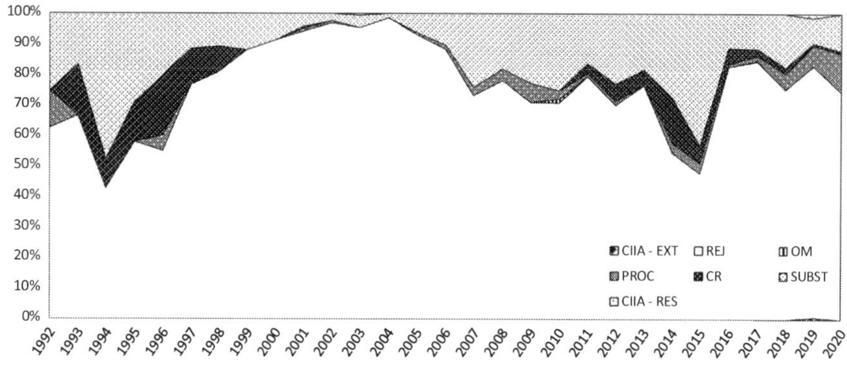

Figure 9.4 Frequency of the ruling types (1992–2020) (RCC)

9.6 Trends in the strength of unconstitutionality rulings

The RCC's rulings are less differentiated, as the bulk of them qualify as either rejections/refusals or substantive unconstitutionality, implying that the RCC's role was – as an instrumentalist interpretation put it – to enforce the Constitution, without any "creativity" or activism (Tănăsescu 2013, 20).

There are, however, at least two tendencies worth noting: there was a significant increase in constitutional requirement rulings in the last decade of the timeframe, after a period of 12 years in which such rulings were almost completely absent; and there was a massive eruption of procedural unconstitutionality rulings in the last three years of the dataset (70 out of a total of 101 rulings) (Figure 9.4). An explanation for this increase in the number of constitutional requirement rulings might be sought in the RCC's self-perceived role in the constitutional architecture. The RCC is careful not to be perceived as a "positive legislator", so it avoids grounding its rulings on reasons outside the constitutional text and is rather reluctant to play the role of arbitrator[21] or to assume an activist stance. Instead, the RCC seeks to offer, when possible, an interpretation for the contested norm that is in line with the provisions of the constitution, instead of declaring it unconstitutional. The pilot project also concluded that these types of rulings are more frequent during periods of relatively lower general political stability (a conclusion confirmed also by the extended timeframe). As regards procedural unconstitutionality rulings, the pilot project found that in periods of relatively lower general political stability, seemingly less attention is paid to procedural rules by the lawmakers – as if the

21 However, in later years political actors attempted to force the RCC to arbitrate conflicts of competence ("juridical conflicts of constitutional nature") between various organs of the state or branches of government, with 25 out of totally 55 such claims being lodged in the last five years of the timeframe.

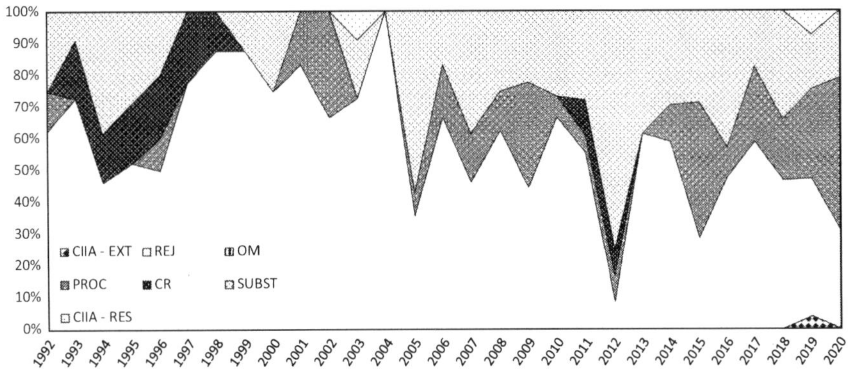

Figure 9.5 Frequency of the ruling types (*a priori* review) (1992–2020) (RCC)

unrest somehow also affects the quality of normative output – combined with an arguable decrease in the general quality of the political elite.[22]

A more nuanced picture of the trends in these rulings emerges if the unconstitutionality rulings are clustered according to the type of the procedure in which they were issued. The variations in the unconstitutionality rulings are quite intriguing. First, when it comes to substantive unconstitutionality rulings, with 295 out of a total of 427 (i.e. 69%) having been issued in *a posteriori* review procedures. Second, similar proportions can be found for constitutional requirement rulings, with 58 out of a total of 74 (i.e. 78.3%) also issued via *a posteriori* review proceedings. Third, in contrast, procedural unconstitutionality rulings are significantly more specific to *a priori* review procedure, with 89 out of a total of 101 (i.e. 88.1%) rulings pronounced during a preliminary examination of constitutionality (Figure 9.5).

These numbers may be regarded as a confirmation of the pilot project's findings and are also in line with the instrumentalist view of the RCC's activity. The Court prefers to strike out as unconstitutional norms that are already in force (and which were presumably adopted by a previous legislature), but only if it cannot find a constitution-compatible interpretation of the norm, so as to avoid suspicions of "activism". Conversely, it is content to find procedural grounds for unconstitutionality and to bypass a substantive analysis in the case of bills, thus allaying suspicions of "creativity" and "partisanship" (and perhaps sidestepping a conflict with the reigning legislature).[23]

22 Some studies argue that the degrees (B.Sc., master or PhD.) held by the members of the Parliament are increasingly obtained from the lowest ranking Romanian universities. While in 2004, 77% of the MPs with a law degree graduated from the highest-ranking Romanian universities or abroad, by 2012 this number decreased to 29% (Muntean and Preda 2016).

23 A study on the conflict of competence rulings found that the admission record of the claims seems to differ depending on the authority that lodged them; here the executive is considered the strongest player, as if the RCC were somehow attempting to compensate for the instability of cabinets (Kuti 2020).

In conclusion, the analysis of the strength of unconstitutionality rulings also supports the claim that *a priori* and *a posteriori* review procedures might be considered to represent different layers of constitutional adjudication.

9.7 Analysis of dissenting opinions

During the timeframe covered by the dataset, 41 judges were involved in the rulings passed by the RCC. Six of these judges did not formulate a single dissenting opinion. All six of them served in the first decade, five of them being members of the initial composition of the RCC. Besides them, there were six other judges, whose dissenting opinions were of lower than the average strength of the majority opinions.[24] As regards the remaining 29 judges, the average strength of their dissenting opinions exceeded the average strength of the majority opinions, usually by quite an appreciable margin. At the other extreme were three judges, who stand out with regard to the percentage of dissents formulated (5.2, 6.3, and 7.1). All three sat on the benches in the most recent decade of the Court, none of them were politicians, but all are legal professionals; one of them a distinguished professor and currently appointed by Romania as a judge at the ECHR, while one is a former president of the High Court of Cassation and Justice (the highest ranking court in the Romanian justice system) and the other is a lawyer and professor.[25] Concerning the strongest dissenting opinions, the judges who achieved the highest rankings for these also published a low number of dissenting opinions (fewer than 10), a statistically rather foreseeable outcome (Figure 9.6).

Generally, the number of dissenting opinions published was relatively modest, especially if compared to the overall number of decisions issued over the years. In the first five years of the functioning of the Court, only two dissents were registered in the dataset used for the present research, although the numbers increased moderately over the years, peaking at 60 in 2018 (Figure 9.7). Out of a total 3,330 rulings, only 219 were accompanied by at least one dissent, while the total number of dissents amounted to 436 rulings over the entire timeframe. Unfortunately, the RCC does not provide any statistics regarding dissenting opinions, therefore the data from the timeframe cannot be measured against the full docket of the Court. In the initial years, at least according to the number and frequency of dissenting opinions, the RCC appears to have been more unanimous, or it at least attempted to convey such an image (which can be explained on the one hand by the fact that it had to assert its own legitimacy, and, on the other, by the fact that it was less diversified and polarized than in later years). The pilot project found no unequivocally demonstrable

24 Individual judges' voting pattern cannot be determined, except for in those situations in which they formulated dissenting or concurring opinions.

25 Holding a law degree is a mandatory criterion, but no adjudicatory experience is necessary, nor a significant career as legal professional. Some judges had only a brief professional career, followed by several parliamentary mandates, while others have an academic rather than practitioner background.

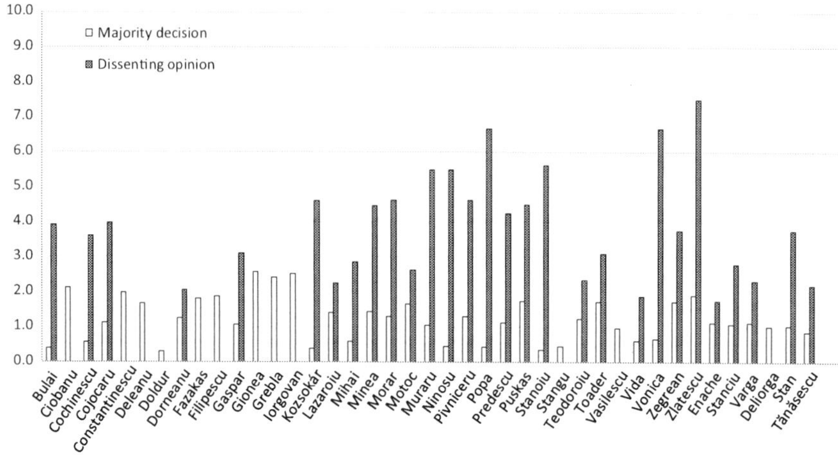

Figure 9.6 Average strength of rulings by judges (RCC)

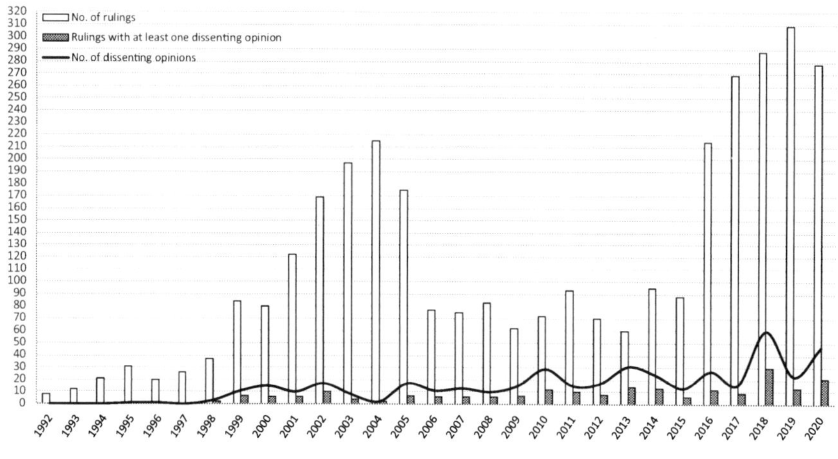

Figure 9.7 Number of rulings with at least one dissenting opinion (1992–2020) (RCC)

connection between the number of dissenting opinions and the directions and strength of majority rulings, but it suggested that in periods when the Court seemed to be politically more balanced, and there was generally a lower degree of general political stability, rulings were more frequently disputed, producing a larger number of dissents.

The 219 rulings mentioned here, which feature at least one dissenting opinion, are made up of 82 rulings pronounced in an *a priori*, and 137 pronounced in an *a posteriori* review procedure. The difference is remarkably low, especially if compared to the total number of rulings issued in both review procedures (493 and 2,837 respectively), which means that 16.6% of *a priori* review rulings were accompanied by at least one dissent, while a mere 4.8% of *a posteriori* review rulings had one. These proportions remain largely similar, if all dissenting opinions are taken into consideration: 183 were expressed in connection with an *a priori* review, and 253 with *a posteriori* review rulings.

So far, all the findings reported have been in line with and supported by previous findings: *a priori* review rulings are more disputed than *a posteriori* review rulings, and they have a higher admission rate, which generates a proportionally higher number of dissenting opinions. Further, one might expect on the basis of the statistical rule observed with respect to the strength of individual judges' dissenting opinions (more dissents leading to a lower average strength) to find a higher average strength for dissents expressed in connection with *a priori* review rulings and a lower average strength for dissents expressed in connection with *a posteriori* review rulings. However, the dataset contradicts these statistical expectations, as the more numerous *a posteriori* review dissents feature a higher average strength (3.7) than the somewhat scarcer *a priori* review dissents (2.9). This somewhat unexpected finding can be explained by the RCC's rather prudent, instrumentalist stance described in the previous section, confirming the impression that the Court attempts to avoid being labelled as "activist" or "creative".

9.7.1 Network analysis of dissenting opinions

The rulings selected for inclusion in the dataset involve 41 judges. The RCC had seven presidents, of whom three were former MPs who presided over the Court for all 13 years. Of the 41 judges, 15 (36.5%) were politicians, i.e. they had been elected as an MP at least once prior to their appointment to the RCC. The other 26 had no formal party affiliation, even though some of them had previously been ministers or counsellors of the President of the Republic. All the judges were nominated by political players (parties represented in the Parliament or by the President of the Republic) who, even if formally independent from the political parties, in fact retained strong ties with the party that supported their campaigns. Thus, as regards the remaining 26 judges with no formal party affiliation, the identity of their nominators might appear relevant as an indicator of ideological preference. Except for 6 judges (appointed in the early years of the RCC) whose nominators were not identified, 11 were nominated by the left-wing and 9 by the right-wing political camps. In total, 41% of the judges involved in the analysed rulings can reasonably be linked to the left-wing parties.

Analysing the network of dissenting opinions, no significant trends of partisanship can be identified, as judges formally affiliated with or nominated by the same political parties do not seem to consistently form majority or dissenting coalitions (at least in rulings accompanied by multiple dissenting opinions). Certain trends can be discerned, but they are too discrete and insular to be considered decisive. As the composition of the RCC became more balanced (polarized) the occurrence of smaller coalitions of two or three judges grew more noticeable (Figure 9.7).[26] Although they are not the subject of the present research, rulings on "juridical conflicts of constitutional nature" show a more serious polarization of dissenting coalitions. Arguably constituting the most politically sensitive issues, these rulings led to dissenting coalitions that tended to form in line with the formal political affiliation of judges, with the single ideologically and pragmatically centrist judge (nominated by the Democratic Alliance of Hungarians in Romania and who is always a former MP) representing the bridge between the two wings of the political spectrum (Kuti 2020).

The picture does not look any different even if dissenting opinions are clustered according to the type of procedure in which they were issued. No major difference can be observed between dissenting coalitions in *a priori* or *a posteriori* reviews. A slight difference might be spotted in the proportion of politician-judges involved in dissents: in *a priori* review rulings, 11 out of the 27 dissenting judges are former politicians (40.7%), while this proportion is 13 of 34 (38.2%) in the case of *a posteriori* review rulings. Thus, it is perceivable that in more disputed rulings (which generate at least one dissenting opinion) politician-judges are more likely to voice their disagreement, this involvement being the highest in relation to *a priori* review rulings. A network analysis of dissenting opinions can be taken one step further by focusing on minimal majority rulings, i.e. those rulings demonstrably taken by the minimal possible votes (usually five out of nine or five out of eight, depending on how many judges were sitting on a particular bench), "demonstrably" meaning that all the minority judges expressed a dissenting opinion. As the question of minimal majority rulings has already been discussed in Section 9.5.2, it is enough to restate that major dissenting coalitions were formed against *a priori* review procedure rulings in periods when the RCC's bench was arguably more politically balanced or polarized, while they were more likely to occur against *a posteriori* review procedure rulings in periods when the RCC's bench was arguably less politically balanced or polarized. In conclusion, it may be stated that an analysis of dissenting opinions also reveals a distinction between *a priori* and *a posteriori* review procedures, as distinct layers of constitutional adjudication.

9.8 Layers of constitutional adjudication

Unlike the Supreme Court of the United States, which carved out for itself the federal courts' power to interpret the Constitution and impose their interpretation upon the legislator, even if such powers were never expressly conferred

26 For instance, judges Predescu, Cojocaru, and Gaspar (two of them former MPs, the third nominated by the left wing), Zegrean, Minea, Morar (one former MP, the other two nominated by the right wing), or lately Stanciu and Tănăsescu (both nominated by the President in office) were/are prone to forming dissenting coalitions.

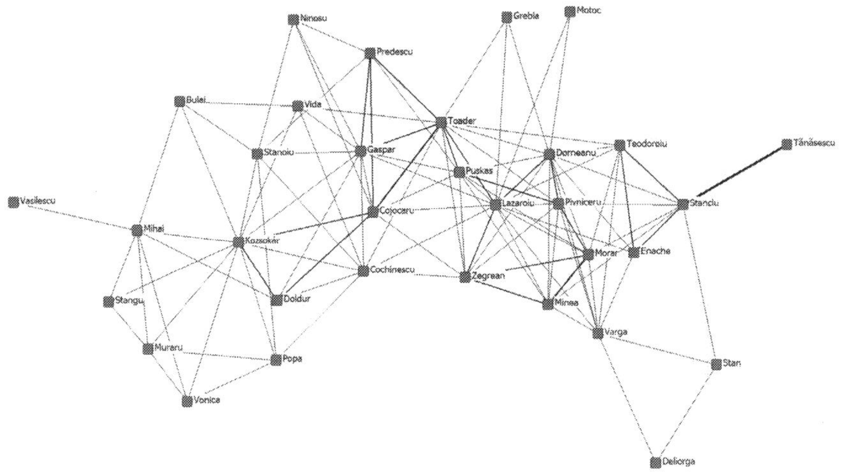

Figure 9.8 Dissenting coalitions 1992–2020 (RCC)

on them by the Constitution, post-communist constitutional courts' powers stemmed from the Constitution and were determined by the legislator (Kuti 2013). According to a former president of the RCC, there was barely a consensus in the constituent assembly about the necessity of a constitutional court (Mungiu-Pippidi 1997). Many perceived it as an undemocratic form of political authority, while the judicial system feared that the new court was an attempt to limit their powers especially since in 1990, before the adoption of the new Constitution, the Supreme Court had attempted to perform judicial review on several occasions (Tănăsescu 2013).

The initial design established two distinct jurisdictions: an *a priori* review, to control the constitutionality of bills before their promulgation, and an *a posteriori* review, to scrutinize the constitutionality of legal provisions (attaching, accordingly, also a different weight to the decisions issued). This instituted a system of weak constitutional review, in which the Court could declare a bill or a law (or a provision of it) unconstitutional but could not instantly invalidate it (Kyritsis 2020). The validity of a norm that had been found unconstitutional still depended on Parliament's action or omission: it was up to Parliament, on the one hand, to override the RCC's decision by a qualified majority, and, on the other hand, to correct faulty legislation; the unconstitutional norm would only be set aside if Parliament had failed to make use of these possibilities.

Even if subsequent revisions of the relevant constitutional and legal provisions corrected some weaknesses of the initial system, the general impression remains that the review powers of the RCC were designed to enable two different types of control over the legislative power: a political form of control, in the form of *a priori* review of bills (also of constitutional revisions, plus the competence to resolve legal conflicts of constitutional nature between state organs), and judicial control, in the form of the *a posteriori* review of laws. This impression is supported by the overriding power of Parliament in connection with *a priori* review rulings, which did not exist in the case of *a posteriori* review procedures (here the Parliament can only correct the provisions declared unconstitutional), and also by the practice of appointing politician-judges.

Apart from its design, the specific features that emerge from the analysis of the RCC's case law, as presented in this chapter, also support the idea that the two jurisdictions (review procedures) represent different layers of constitutional adjudication. The difference in the number of motions filed in distinct political contexts, the difference in admission rates (49.5% to 12.9%) between *a priori* and a *posteriori* review rulings, in their average strength (2.59 to 0.79) and in the ratio of restraining rulings among them (49.1% to 12.9%), demonstrates the higher relevance and higher degree of controversy characterizing *a priori* review motions.

Narrowing the analysis to admission (unconstitutionality) rulings and clustering them according to the proceeding type, the proportion of substantive unconstitutionality rulings (80.3% in *a posteriori* review and 54% in *a priori* review) of constitutional requirement rulings (15.8% in *a posteriori* review and 36.4% in *a priori* review) and of procedural unconstitutionality rulings (3.2% in *a posteriori* review and 36.4% in *a priori* review) demonstrate that the RCC acknowledges the higher relevance and higher degree of controversy attached to *a priori* review motions. It therefore considers these motions more carefully, finding substantive breaches of the Constitution more rarely than in the case of *a posteriori* control and preferring to resort more often to procedural reasons when striking down bills than in the case of laws. Further support for the theory of distinct layers of constitutional adjudication can be found in an examination of the dissenting opinions. First, there is a significant difference in the number of rulings accompanied by at least one dissenting opinion (16.6% for *a priori* review rulings and 4.8% for *a posteriori* review rulings). Second, further disparity can be found in the average strength between dissents published in *a priori* and *a posteriori* review proceedings (2.9 to 3.7), confirming the RCC's cautiousness in relation to the more sensitive, controversial nature of *a priori* review motions. Also, a slight and less relevant difference may be noticed in the proportion of politician-judges involved in dissents, according to the type of review in which they were formulated (40.7% in the case of *a priori*, and 38.2% in the case of *a posteriori* review dissents), as politician-judges are more prone to voice their disagreement in more disputed rulings. Third, major dissenting coalitions occur more often to oppose *a priori* review procedure rulings in periods when the RCC's bench is more politically balanced or polarized, and against *a posteriori* review procedure rulings in periods when the bench is politically less balanced or polarized, which suggests that the *a priori* review procedure exercises a more political type of control, while *a posteriori* review procedure is closer to a legal control of legislation.

As constitutional scholars have observed, *a priori* review might bring stability to the legal system, strengthening the law and protecting it from future challenges. However, when *a posteriori* review is also made possible within the same system, this stability-promoting character diminishes, and *a priori* review becomes more or less a political tool for obstructing the legislative procedure (Sadurski 2011). It should be mentioned in this regard that the case law of the RCC in its later years hints that the constitutional conflict procedure may be the ultimate tool for settling political disputes, in a manner that appears more efficient and timelier than the review of bills. The discussion of this topic, unfortunately, exceeds the limits of the present writing, however.[27] Interestingly, even if the Court has recently been subject to severe criticism, being depicted as intensely politicized and unable to transcend political disputes (Perju 2010; Gilia 2012), the problematic coexistence of *a priori* and *a posteriori* review has not been raised. However, a commission charged with analysing the political and constitutional regime, set up by the Presidency (Presidency 2008) made an exciting proposal, recommended as a possible approach to the rationalization of constitutional justice. The commission envisaged a system of dual competence, in which the RCC should retain the power to adjudicate *a priori*, while regular courts could exercise *a posteriori* review powers over the constitutionality of laws. The commission thus, arguably, not only recognized that *a priori* and *a posteriori* reviews form distinct layers of constitutional adjudication but also made a proposal to separate them to improve review procedures.

9.9 Conclusions

Using the methodology developed by the JUDICON pilot project for assessing the judicial constraints on legislatures by mapping the strength and diversity of judicial decisions, the present chapter assessed the performance of the Romanian Constitutional Court from the time of its establishment to almost the present day (1992–2020). As the RCC's case law, due to a number of specific features, amounts to an incredible number of decisions, a selection method had to be applied to reduce the quantity of cases to a manageable number of rulings, which formed the dataset of the present research. The goal of the research was to evaluate the constraint exercised by RCC on the legislature by evaluating its decisions considering factors such as the admission rate of claims, the strength of constitutional review rulings, the strength of admission rulings, the dissenting opinions, and the individual performance of the constitutional judges. As a similar analysis had already been performed in the JUDICON pilot project, albeit over a shorter timeframe, this research – which besides the extended timeframe also features a few minor adjustments to the case selection and evaluation criteria – focused on the trends in the strength

27 The reasons are explained in Section 9.3.1.

of constitutional review as they relate to the two main review procedures: the control of the constitutionality of bills before promulgation (*a priori* review) and the control of the constitutionality of laws (*a posteriori* review).

By clustering the rulings of the RCC compiled in the dataset in terms of the review procedure in which they were issued, this chapter argues that the two procedures represent in practice distinct layers of constitutional adjudication. The argument finds support in the analysis of the admission rate and strength of rulings, the strength of admission (unconstitutionality) rulings, dissenting opinions, and dissenting networks. This conclusion is also supported by the peculiarities of the initial constitutional design, which attributed different strengths and different consequences to the decisions adopted by the RCC in the different procedures. Finally, further arguments to support the theory have emerged from relatively recent research which, recognizing the distinct character of the two procedures, proposed a complete separation of jurisdiction. The RCC has never constituted a strong check on the legislature. In the second half of the timeframe of the research, during which period tensions between the parliament, the executive, and the presidency escalated, the RCC had several opportunities to become an arbitrator, a role it was not particularly enthusiastic to take on.

The Court was traditionally considered to be highly deferential, constantly striving to avoid being accused of "activism" or "creativity". This conclusion is also supported by the low occurrence of remedies in the rulings and the court's constant preoccupation with seeking those interpretations for the contested norm that can be considered in line with constitutional provisions, so as to avoid declaring it unconstitutional. However, the present research, which constantly builds on the differences between the layers of constitutional adjudication, leans towards the idea that this cautious-deferential stance is more characteristic of the RCC's rulings in *a priori* review procedures. In the later years, the Court has shifted from its initial stance, and it is gradually becoming a stronger player, especially in settling political conflicts through adjudicating "juridical conflicts of constitutional nature". Becoming less cautious, it is moving from general recommendations towards concrete remedies, not merely recommending, but sometimes already dictating desirable conduct.

References

Constitutional Court of Romania. 2022a. *Statistics on the Activity of the Constitutional Court from Its Establishment Until 31.12.2021*. Accessed January 15, 2022. www.ccr.ro/wp-content/uploads/2022/01/ActivitateRo_dec.pdf

———. 2022b. *Statistics on the Acts of the Constitutional Court from Its Establishment Until 31.07.2017*. Accessed January 15, 2022. www.ccr.ro/wp-content/uploads/2022/01/SinRoNew_dec.pdf.

Gilia, Claudia. 2012. "Curtea Constitutionala sub imperativul reformei [The Constitutional Court Under the Imperative of Reform]." *Sfera Politicii* 20 (6): 21–34.

Kuti, Csongor. 2013. "In Courts We Trust?" *Acta Iuridica Hungarica* 54 (4): 384–392.

———. 2019. "Muddling Through Democratic Transition. The Romanian Constitutional Court." In *Constitutional Politics and the Judiciary: Decision-making in Central and Eastern Europe*, edited by Kálmán Pócza, 155–183. London: Routledge

———. 2020. "Between a Rock and a Hard Place: Constitutional Conflict Cases before the Romanian Constitutional Court." *Acta Iuridica Hungarica* 60 (3): 281–295.

Kyritsis, Dimitros. 2020 "Justifying Constitutional Review in the Legitimacy Register." *Revus – Journal for Constitutional Theory and Philosophy of Law* 2020 (42).

Mungiu-Pippidi, Alina. 1997. "Interview with President of the Romanian Constitutional Court, Ion Muraru." *East European Constitutional Review* 6 (1): 78–83.

Muntean, Ioana, and Marian Preda. 2016. "Why Does Romania Have a Negative Selection in Parliamentary Elections? An Analysis of the Recruitment and Selection System During the Last Three Legislative Terms." *Transylvanian Review of Administrative Sciences* No.48E/2016: 84–103.

Perju, Vlad. 2010. "A sosit timpul pentru reformarea Curtii Constitutionale? [Has the Time Come for Reforming of the Constitutional Court?]." *Contributors.ro*, November 29. Accessed January 15, 2022. www.contributors.ro/idei-si-solutii/a-sosit-timpul-pentru-reformarea-curtii-constitutionale-partea-i.

Presidency. 2008. *Raportul Comisiei Prezidențiale de Analiză a Regimului Politic și Constituțional din România. [Report of the Presidential Commission for the analysis of the political and constitutional regime – To consolidate the rule of law]*. Accessed January 15, 2022. http://old.presidency.ro/static/rapoarte/Raport_CPARPCR.pdf.

Sadurski, Wojciech. 2011. "Constitutional Review in Europe and in the United States: Influences, Paradoxes and Convergences." *Legal Studies Research Paper No.* 11/15. Sydney: Sydney Law School.

Tănăsescu, Simina. 2013. "Constitutional Review of Judicial Activism?" *International Journal of Law and Jurisprudence Law Review* 3 (2): 19–36.

10 The Slovak Constitutional Court

The promise of Dworkinian adjudication?

Max Steuer and Erik Láštic

10.1 Introduction

This chapter updates and refocuses the study of the Slovak Constitutional Court (SCC) as a key decision-maker in the Slovak political system with the potential not only to constrain the legislator, but also to address wider societal problems via the key tool at its disposal: interpretation.[1] The previous study ended by posing the question of whether the tensions we identified in the SCC towards the early second half of its third term were caused by the clashing of two sets of partisan mindsets or by an opposition between partisan and principled views of the Slovak Constitution (Láštic and Steuer 2019, 205).[2] By addressing this question, we suggested moving beyond the Kelsenian idea of the SCC as a (negative or positive) "third" legislator in the constitutional system.[3] The reference to principled views echoes the contribution of Ronald Dworkin from over half a century ago, in which he challenged the positivist view of law, advocated by his mentor, HLA Hart (Dworkin 1967; Hart 2012). Dworkin's interpretivist position places high demands on (constitutional) judges and acknowledges the significance of legal interpretation for politics, while not shying away from recognizing judges as political actors (Zreik 2019). Against this backdrop, we argue that the legislator's response to the SCC's verdict on the 2014 constitutional amendment with unconstitutional provisions embraces a Hartian position for the Court, whereby textually clear rules are needed for a competence to be recognized, and with the legislator wielding a constitutional majority occupying a supreme systemic, even dominating position over the Court.

An overview of the Court's case law in this period suggests that, while it did not subscribe to a perceived subordinate position, it leaned towards a Hartian interpretation of the Constitution, thus reducing its own potential to respond

1 This chapter (excluding the JUDICON-EU data collection, coding, and charts) was supported by the Slovak Research and Development Agency under the contract no. APVV-21-0484.

2 This chapter considers developments until February 2023, but its empirical data only cover ground until the end of 2021.

3 In addition to the people and the Parliament (Art. 2 sec. 1 of the Constitution).

DOI: 10.4324/9781003399483-10

to the actions of the legislature as well as to potential future illiberal majorities. Nevertheless, the data from the first years of the "fourth SCC" (see Section 10.2.1) indicate the promise of the Fiačan Court overcoming this shadow while being painfully aware of the responsibilities associated with the Court's unique interpretive position.

Firstly, we map selected key developments of the SCC's organization and operation including the judges of the "fourth" Court. An important challenge for the functioning of the Court is the 2020 constitutional amendment, which is why we critically scrutinize the parliamentary debates leading up to its enactment. Secondly, we discuss the impact of the formal legislative (including constitutional) changes on the methods of assessment and interpretation employed in the project. Thirdly, we evaluate the quantitative data obtained via the JUDICON-EU methodology, that, when read together with the pre-2015 developments, allow us to complete the chapter of the "third" SCC and discuss the similarities and differences that arose in the last three years of its mandate. Fourthly, we discuss selected landmark cases, generating several dissenting opinions and offering an insight into the interpretive practice of the Court's decision-making, before concluding with an outlook based on the 2021 data and selected subsequent developments (until early 2023). It should be kept in mind that while our earlier study (Láštic and Steuer 2019) analysed the three previous terms of the SCC, this chapter focuses mainly on the developments in the fourth term and compares the Court's performance at the early stage of this term with its practice in previous terms.

10.2 Institutional settings and changes in 2018–2021

This section provides a brief overview of the SCC to help understand its positioning in the constitutional system in the early 2020s and the challenges it faces. In February 2023, as this chapter was being revised, the Court celebrated its 30th anniversary, ahead of its Czech counterpart which was established slightly later in 1993 (Constitutional Court of the Slovak Republic 2023a).[4] Thus, three decades of the Court's operation provides an opportunity to offer a few remarks on the foundational framework governing the Court's operation, followed by a discussion of the key changes it has undergone since (focusing on the period of the collection of empirical data, i.e. until 2021).

10.2.1 Organization of the SCC and its four terms: a brief overview

The SCC was established in 1993, following the model of constitutional review that was also adopted in the neighbouring countries (Sadurski 2014). Since 2001, it has had 13 judges who usually serve a 12-year, non-renewable term.

4 The Slovak public television channel broadcasted a short documentary on the Court, entitled, tellingly, "The Most Powerful Institution" (Košťová 2023).

The Court is endowed with a wide range of competences including *a posteriori* constitutional review, *a priori* review of international agreements, review of the constitutionality of referendum questions, constitutional interpretation *in abstracto*, and the review of some electoral disputes (Steuer 2019a; Láštic and Steuer 2019, 184–186). The latter competence was curtailed with the establishment of the Supreme Administrative Court (SAC) in 2021, which is charged with decisions on electoral disputes in local elections alongside other competences transferred to it from the Supreme Court of Slovakia. This includes the decision-making on the dissolution of a political party or a political movement, with the SCC retaining the competence to review decisions which result in such a dissolution (Art. 129 sec. 4). Complaints on individual human rights violations remain the most common items on the SCC's agenda.

Most cases continue to be decided by the four three-member senates of the SCC, which publishes its schedule of operations every year including slight changes in the composition of the senates (Constitutional Court of the Slovak Republic 2023c). The senate chairperson positions may thus change while the same judges continue to serve their terms. The President of the SCC is typically assigned to one of the senates but participates in their proceedings only when they are the judge rapporteur. This serves the purpose of allowing enough time for the President to fulfil their responsibilities, including the representation of the Constitutional Court as a whole (although, since 2019, other judges may also interact with the media). The most visible cases of the Court are, with the exception of a few mediatized constitutional complaints, decided by the plenum. This is also the case for the decisions analyzed in the JUDICON-EU project; the exceptions are constitutional interpretations *in abstracto* before the constitutional amendment of 2001, which were decided in senates, illustrating the lack of awareness on the part of the constitution-makers of the significance of (and potential controversies embedded in) these types of proceedings.

The Court's 30+-year history is typically divided into four terms, corresponding to the four SCC Presidents who have held the office to date. The era of the Fiačan Court began in April 2019 with the appointment of Ivan Fiačan alongside other judges and was preceded by the first (Čič) Court (1993–2000), the second (Mazák) Court (2000–2007), and the third (Macejková) Court (2007–2019). The periodization is not exact; for example, President Mazák resigned in 2006, and the Court was without a President for almost five months; there was no President for two months in 2019 (mid-February to mid-April) either. Still, it provides a relatively straightforward periodization that aids comparison. From a historical perspective, it might be difficult to categorize some individual judges based on this periodization if they served under two SCC Presidents. An example is Judge Mojmír Mamojka, who was appointed in 2017 but resigned in May 2020, due to suspicions of contact with corrupt actors, notably Marián Kočner, who is accused of ordering the murder of journalist Ján Kuciak (Kuzmány and Cuprík 2020). The website of the SCC listed him as member of the plenum during the SCC's third term,

Table 10.1 The SCC's and the Slovak executive's terms in office

Court term	*Executive term*
Čič (1993–2000)	Mečiar II (1992–1994)
	Moravčík (1994)
	Mečiar III (1994–1998)
	Dzurinda I (1998–2002)
Mazák (2000–2007)	Dzurinda I (1998–2002)
	Dzurinda II (2002–2006)
	Fico I (2006–2010)
Macejková (2007–2019)	Fico I (2006–2010)
	Radičová (2010–2012)
	Fico II (2012–2016)
	Fico III (2016–2020)
Fiačan (2019–2031 [estimated])	Fico III (2016–2020)
	Matovič (2020–2021)
	Heger (2021–2023)
	Fico IV (2023–)

even though he also adjudicated during part of the Fiačan term (Constitutional Court of the Slovak Republic n.d.a). The fourth Court has had only two female judges, following the trend of the majority of judges being male from the previous three terms. Table 10.1 provides an overview of the executives who were in office during the Court's four terms, showing that, typically, one term on the Court spanned several, often ideologically opposed, executives.

10.2.2 *Changes in 2018–2021*

Three milestones are key for understanding the Court's development between 2016 and 2021: the new Constitutional Court Act of 2018 and the subsequent gridlock in SCC appointments after the end of the term of the majority of judges of the third Court in early 2019. This gridlock was ultimately resolved and followed by a constitutional amendment in 2020 that (for a time) completed the reform of the SCC. We discuss each of these milestones in turn.

10.2.2.1 *The Act on the Constitutional Court of 2018*

Beginning in 1993, the SCC operated according to the Act on the Organization of the SCC (No. 38/1993 Coll.). Seven constitutional amendments later affected the functioning of the SCC (Fiačan 2020, 9). In March 2019, a new Act on the Constitutional Court (Act No. 314/2018 Coll.) came into effect. Without providing a comprehensive assessment of this Act, it is worth noting that its impact was affected by the rejection of the associated constitutional amendment which primarily concerned the selection of constitutional judges (Steuer 2018). This rejection meant, for example, that the regulation that would have allowed the senates of the SCC to send cases they deem particularly significant to the plenum was not included (Baricová 2020, 111).[5] The new Act on the Constitutional Court has, however, introduced live hearings of the candidates for constitutional judges. While leaving some aspects to be desired (Steuer 2019c), the live hearings of the candidates have improved the transparency and "throughput legitimacy" of the selection process (Ľalík, Baraník, and Drugda 2018, 270). Still, live hearings in 2019 did not result in a sufficient number of appointments, and no less than five rounds of elections were needed to generate enough candidates who could be sent to the President of the Republic for review (Steuer 2019b). The failed bid of (at the time) former PM Robert Fico, who resigned from office in 2018 after the murder of the journalist Ján Kuciak, seems to have contributed to the lack of willingness on the part of coalition actors to come to an agreement.

10.2.2.2 *Gridlock in electing new judges in 2018–2019*

> "The sky did not fall upon Slovaks! For god's sake, the Constitutional Court, that does not mean that it is closed, that nothing is happening there."[6]

This statement by a former Chairman of the National Council[7] refers to the period in 2018–2019, when the SCC did not operate in its full composition due to a gridlock in the selection process. A constitutional amendment that was intended to improve the selection process of constitutional judges was tabled for October 2018 (alongside the Act on the Constitutional Court), but failed due to unexpected modifications to the draft bill being made in Parliament and their subsequent rejection by democratic actors, as well as a last-minute shift in the position of the extreme political party that had promised to support the government.

Prior to this episode, the SCC had rejected the President's petition for the abstract constitutional interpretation of the presidential competence to substantively review candidates for constitutional judges (Láštic and Steuer 2019, 204). Moreover, on St. Nicholas' day, 6 December 2017, the first senate of the Court annulled the decisions of the then President, Andrej Kiska, who had declined to appoint three constitutional judges from among the candidates submitted to him by the National Council, and required him to reconsider (I. ÚS 575/2016). Although, as a senate decision, this does not appear in the JUDICON quantitative assessment, it had a considerable *de facto* effect of strengthening the Parliament, as it confirmed the limited leeway

5 The 2020 constitutional amendment introduced such a possibility, however, with effectiveness only from 1 January 2025 (Orosz 2021, 89–90).

6 See Janščová (2019).

7 Andrej Danko. He has become known in popular discourse for his way of speaking, adopting a very "liberal" approach to Slovak grammar and style.

Table 10.2 Selected basic information about the judges of the "fourth SCC"

Judge	*Entered office*	*Doctoral degree*	*Previous occupation*	*Gender*
Ivan Fiačan (chairperson)	17.4.2019	Yes	Attorney	Male
Ľuboš Szigeti (vice-chairperson)	17.4.2019	No	Judge (district court, experience at the Supreme Court)	Male
Jana Baricová	10.7.2014	No	Judge (Supreme Court, interim SCC President in 2019)	Female
Jana Laššáková	14.12.2017	No	MP for Smer-SD	Female
Miroslav Duriš	14.12.2017	Yes (in social work)	Notary	Male
Peter Molnár	17.4.2019	Yes	Academic	Male
Libor Duľa	10.10.2019	No	Judge (Supreme Court)	Male
Peter Straka	10.10.2019	No	Judge (regional court)	Male
Ladislav Duditš	10.10.2019	No	Judge (regional court)	Male
Rastislav Kaššák	10.10.2019	Yes	Attorney and academic	Male
Martin Vernarský	10.10.2019	Yes	Academic	Male
Miloš Maďar	10.10.2019	Yes	Academic	Male
Robert Šorl	30.9.2020	Yes	Judge (district court) and academic	Male

for the President of the Republic to vet the candidates. Six days later, on 12 December 2017, Kiska appointed three judges (Duriš, Laššáková, Mamojka), although he accompanied this announcement with a harsh critique of the verdict of the first senate (Štiavnický and Steuer 2020, 197).

After the expiration in February 2019 of the term of the majority of the judges appointed in 2007, it took until late 2020 for the Court to be back at its full composition. Table 10.2 provides an introductory overview of the bench as of 31 December 2022. (Judge Laššáková resigned in September 2023.)

The conflicts and the multiple rounds of the appointment procedures resulted in the new bench not containing a single prominent Slovak constitutional lawyer or academic.[8] The closest fit to this profile is Judge Vernarský,

8 President Zuzana Čaputová did not appoint a Yale-educated associate professor of constitutional law, Radoslav Procházka, who is regarded as one of the most original (if controversial) constitutional thinkers in the country. The probable reason for this was Procházka's engagement with partisan politics, in which his track record is questionable, as he has admitted (e.g. Mikušovič 2018). The academic expertise of several of the candidates appointed is significantly lower than that of Procházka. However, other constitutional experts with equally prominent academic track records but without a morally questionable past decisions in partisan politics were not even nominated by the parliament, and so Procházka's success in this regard could be seen also as a remnant of his earlier connections, which could have cast a shadow on the new Court. Moreover, given his specialist expertise and skills, Procházka had the potential to dominate the Court with his theory of constitutional interpretation (e.g. Procházka 2011).

who possesses the academic rank of associate professor in administrative law.[9] The two more junior academics (assistant professors) on the bench have not previously specialized in constitutional law either – one focused on administrative law (Judge Kaššák) and the other on criminal law (Judge Maďar). A fifth judge (Robert Šorl) has academic experience (in the discipline of legal history). In total, seven judges hold a doctoral degree. Even though the collective strength of the bench appears to lie more in their experience with legal and judicial practice and private law matters, the judges' biographies generally emphasize their academic experience and publications.[10] This emphasis might be intended to compensate for what may be seen as a weakness of the bench: a lack of advanced expertise in constitutional theory.[11]

10.2.2.3 The constitutional amendment of 2020

The adoption of a constitutional amendment in 2020 was a key milestone for the Court's position in the Slovak constitutional system, and hence it is worth analyzing it more extensively. At the end of 2020, amidst a raging pandemic and during a state of emergency, the Slovak Parliament adopted a constitutional amendment (National Council of the Slovak Republic 2020n),[12] which had as its most striking feature the declared removal of the competence of the SCC to review the constitutionality of constitutional amendments. That competence had been found in the Constitution just a year earlier, when, during the final days of the presidency of Ivetta Macejková, the SCC declared a constitutional amendment unconstitutional on the basis of the Court's designation as the independent judicial guardian of constitutionality (Art. 124, PL. ÚS 21/2014). The story of the amendment of this provision in the Act. No. 422/2020 Coll. is non-linear: it was proposed by the Ministry of Justice,[13] though the Minister of Justice did not see the need to flag the provision in her introduction of the amendment during the first parliamentary reading on 21 October, where she argued that the amendment exemplifies the 'values that unite us' (National Council of the Slovak Republic 2020j).

9 Judge Molnár also holds the title of associate professor, although he specializes in private (civil) law.

10 For example, the biographies for the most part do not include references to major cases the judges were involved in in their previous careers as judges of general courts or attorneys.

11 Of course, this does not mean that no expertise on constitutional theory would have been present at the Court altogether: several clerks, including some who themselves applied for the CC judge position, are notably qualified from this perspective.

12 The final wording of the amendment is in Act No. 422/2020 Coll.

13 Analyzing the explanatory report, Ľalík (2021) notes that the SCC used Art. 124 (that stipulates its general role as the guardian of constitutionality), in addition to Art. 125 sec. 1a) to exercise its competence of constitutional amendment review. This dual reference was missed by the explanatory report and opens up the possibility of the competence of constitutional amendment review remaining in place even with the new provision prohibiting it in Art. 125 sec. 4.

Furthermore, the provision was excluded from the scope of the public consultations that preceded the constitutional amendment. The initial wording of the amendment aimed to add the phrase *constitutional act*[14] to the wording of the provision.[15] As noted by the Constitutional Committee of the National Council, however, this wording would also have excluded the competence of the Court to review the compatibility of constitutional acts with international law that is binding for Slovakia and that (according to the Committee) encompasses EU law, as well as other constitutional acts. Hence, the Committee proposed a different wording (a separate sentence saying that the "SCC shall not decide also on the conformity of a constitutional act with the Constitution") (Constitutional Affairs Committee of the National Council of the Slovak Republic 2020). These and other modifications were introduced at short notice, making the revisions more questionable than the initial proposals (Orosz 2021, 82–86).

Two other, more technical competence changes were also introduced in the constitutional amendment. The first one relates to the establishment of the SAC, with the rationale including the reduction of the workload of the SCC (see Section 10.2.1). However, at the same time, the SCC gained the new competence of adjudicating disputes between the newly created SAC and the Slovak Supreme Court (Art. 126 sec. 1). The Court was also restricted in its competence to review and provide consent for the imprisonment of judges and the Attorney General, a reaction to the upsurge of such cases the SCC needed to deal with at short notice, due to the uncovering of judicial corruption networks in Slovakia in 2019–2020 (Čuroš 2023, 638–639). Last but not least, a sentence on the procedural rejection of plenary cases in case the necessary majority (of seven votes) is not reached was removed from Art. 131 sec. 1, thus obliging the Court to reach a consensus. While this eliminates a legitimacy deficit that the Court had triggered in the past due to procedural rejections of important cases (see Láštic and Steuer 2019, 192), it raises the question of what happens if the judges, due to the internal polarization of their philosophical disagreement, are unable to reach consensus. In an extreme situation, it may require the case in question to remain undecided until new judges are sworn in, which would create another legitimacy deficit due to the excessive delay in reaching a decision.

Secondly, the amendment modified the appointment process for constitutional judges, limiting the risks stemming from the collaborative model that requires the President of the Republic to confirm the nominees voted for by

14 A "constitutional act" is a broader category in Slovak constitutional law that encompasses constitutional amendments and legislation adopted by a constitutional majority (such as the Constitutional Act No. 227/2002 Coll. on State Security).

15 "The Constitutional Court shall not decide on conformity of a draft law or a proposal of other generally binding legal regulation with the Constitution, with an international treaty that was promulgated in the manner laid down by a law or by a constitutional law" (Constitution of the Slovak Republic Art 125 (4)).

the Parliament (Steuer 2017). As a series of vacancies for the bench both in 2006 and in 2019 demonstrate, the collaborative model in the Slovak practice risks either a gridlock resulting in prolonged periods with empty seats at the Court, or a single party or a coalition having the capacity to pack the Court with its nominees if the President of the Republic is favourably inclined. Hence, the amendment introduced a selection system, in which the candidates initially need the support of a three-fifth majority of the MPs. If some positions still cannot be filled via such a consensual process, a smaller majority (but still of all deputies, rather than just the present deputies as it used to be the case) may decide in the subsequent rounds of voting (Art. 84 sec. 5). The risk of a gridlock is further reduced by the amendment allowing the President of the Republic to appoint judges without waiting for the Parliament if the MPs fail to provide the full number of nominees within given time intervals (Art. 134 sec. 2). However, there is a risk that a future parliamentary majority may intentionally postpone the appointment process of new judges, in order for the President to be subjected to informal pressure to select from the more limited pool of candidates (Orosz 2021, 94). Thus, the mechanism that appears to enhance the President's position *vis-à-vis* the legislature might *de facto* weaken it, depending on how it is applied by the legislature.

The constitutional provision regulating the composition of the SCC was further amended to enable outgoing judges to remain in office until their replacement is sworn in (Art. 134 sec. 3). Even though the prevention of gridlock is at the core of this segment of the amendment, it also tries to ameliorate the accompanying risk of a party gaining supremacy at the Court by introducing variable tenure lengths for constitutional judges appointed after 1 January 2021 (Art. 154g sec. 9). A relatively complicated regulation applies to the term limits of the judges (Art. 154g sec. 10) that is likely to result in new appointments being more spread out instead of becoming clustered in a particular year. Another factor to consider is the newly introduced age limit for occupying the bench – the term of the judges now ends when they turn 72 years old (Art. 138 sec. 3). However, none of the 10 judges appointed in 2019–2020 were born before 1959, so this provision will have no bearing on the majority of the positions on the bench becoming vacant in 2031–2032, assuming that the current judges complete their terms. As the remaining judges' terms will expire earlier, provided there are no resignations or further amendments, 12 appointments remain clustered within the three-year interval (2029–2032), with the first three judges appointed to the bench only set to serve until 30 October 2037. It is only after the appointments of 2031–2032 that this clustering would dissipate.

The effort to limit the SCC's competence to review constitutional amendments prompted the second-ever speech in the National Council by the President of the SCC, Ivan Fiačan, who assumed office in 2019 to head a Court that was still understrength, with several vacancies (National Council of the Slovak Republic 2020h). On 3 December, six days before the second reading and subsequent approval of the amendment, Fiačan introduced his speech as an attempt to promote an "authentic understanding of the initiator of these legal acts as well as to the legislator, or the constitution-maker", while respecting the need for self-restraint and wishing to avoid the impression of picking a fight with the constitution-maker by intervening in a "politically motivated deliberation". Welcoming the initiative for the amendment, Fiačan raised doubts both about the procedure (excluding public discussion) and the rationale of the amendment, arguing that it would prevent intervention even in extreme cases. The tone throughout Fiačan's speech remained respectful to the authority of the legislator and its commitment to constitutionalism, and explicitly claims that it "does not aim to . . . protest against the unconstitutionality of the constitutional change in this part", but merely to recognize that the Constitution and its "fundamental key principles" are above both the Parliament and the Constitutional Court, as in most European jurisdictions. Hence, it is not a defence of a "usurped (*privlastnená*) competence" but of "the modern European standard".

The Minister of Justice, in her response, rejected this interpretation. Arguing that the comparative references are invalid and that the SCC had exceeded its competences, she invoked "publications, which were . . . devoted [to the SCC's verdict]" as a supporting reason for the executive intervention (National Council of the Slovak Republic 2020i). However, these publications are ambivalent on the legitimacy of the SCC's competence, with some academics also arguing in support of it (see overview in Štiavnický and Steuer 2020, 198–199). One legal expert, MP Dostál, endorsed the Minister's view by arguing for "ground zero" to be the "original definition of the Constitution", which did not set this competence for the SCC in his view (National Council of the Slovak Republic 2020k).

The parliamentary opposition were largely unenthusiastic about the amendment.[16] Ján Podmanický, a former member of the governing party Smer-SD who declared his ambition to unite conservative forces in the Parliament (TASR 2020), proposed an addition to the sentence formulated by the Committee, saying "this [the prohibition of review of constitutional amendments] does not apply when it comes to essential components of a democratic state governed by the rule of law" (National Council of the Slovak Republic 2020a). In the justification, he noted the need to address, similarly to the Czech Constitution, those situations in which the constitution-makers act arbitrarily and undermine the spirit of the Constitution.[17] However, his second argument

16 During the first reading of the bill in October, the opposition members were passive. The only comment came from coalition MP Juraj Šeliga, who expressed his appreciation for the Minister "finding a solution that is completely in compliance with the Constitution and at the same time will have a practical impact on these judges" (National Council of the Slovak Republic 2020l).

17 He offered the examples of the death sentence and the extension of the mandate of MPs from 4 to 15 years. At least the former amendment would clearly violate Slovakia's international obligations, hence it is plainly reviewable under the current wording.

was much more pragmatic. Referring to the decision of the Indian Supreme Court in *Minerva Mills*,[18] he argued that his proposal would eliminate the risk of the SCC declaring the amendment unconstitutional, an impression he had gathered from Fiačan's speech. Another amendment, initiated by the Smer-SD deputies, went even further and required the abolishment of the provision altogether, claiming that it would undermine the possibility for the SCC to defend the substantive core of the Constitution (National Council of the Slovak Republic 2020b).

In the deliberations on 3 December, a defence of a robust notion of constitutionalism was ostensibly mounted by the opposition parties, headed by the extreme right *Kotleba – People's Party Our Slovakia*. Their member on the Committee of Constitutional Affairs noticed that the Minister of Justice had failed to mention the amendment in her introductory speech,[19] and he castigated this omission of the "most serious amendment to the Constitution in its history". The MP did not question whether, via the amendment, the SCC's competence would indeed "disappear"; in this sense, he (possibly inadvertently) subscribed to the Minister's view of the law. However, his standing was discredited by the later segments of the speech, which portrayed the amendment as a final step towards "dictatorship" and as a "betrayal of the Slovak nation" (National Council of the Slovak Republic 2020f). MP Podmanický shared the preference of all speakers for "determining clearly what the competence of the Constitutional Court is . . ." (National Council of the Slovak Republic 2020g) but requested the postponement of the discussion. He also hinted darkly that a "constitutional crisis" would arise if the SCC invalidated the amendment. MP Ľuboš Blaha, arguably the closest connecting link between the party of (at the time) former PM Robert Fico (Smer-SD) and the extreme right, delivered a passionate speech on the Minister undermining the separation of powers and clearing the way for institutional changes by future non-democratic actors, if they attain power, without court scrutiny (National Council of the Slovak Republic 2020m).[20]

18 In this 1980 case, revolving around a challenge to the nationalization of a textile mill by the Indian government during the emergency period declared by Indira Gandhi, the Supreme Court invalidated the constitutional amendments initiated by Gandhi. It represented a major victory of constitutionalism over unrestrained executive power in the context of a state of emergency. See e.g. Chandrachud (2020).

19 This was also missing from her concluding speech (National Council of the Slovak Republic 2020e).

20 The speech is a dangerous combination of sound arguments, including a positive reception of the SCC President's intervention as one made by an expert who is not affected by partisan politics, and of claims accusing the Minister of Justice of building a dictatorship for COVID-19-related restrictions during the state of emergency, along with a celebration of certain features of the state socialist regime. The references to the constitutional amendment are thus combined with a critique of rights restrictions during the pandemic. On the latter, see Steuer (2022).

These initiatives were unsuccessful, however. To some of them, the Minister responded by referring to her experts' assessments of the prevailing views in Slovak constitutionalist scholarship, claiming that most academics consider the declaration of the competence to review constitutional amendments by the SCC as an "excess" (National Council of the Slovak Republic 2020c).[21] It appears that a single publication, a monograph that had appeared the year before and was critical of the SCC's verdict (Káčer and Neumann 2019), influenced the government's interpretations of what the position of the academic community actually is. Other claims made by the minister referred to the lower legitimacy of the SCC compared to the directly elected Parliament – a classic reiteration of the counter-majoritarian difficulty (Bickel 1986). MP Dostál reiterated the Hartian argument regarding the competence being absent from the Constitution before the SCC's 2019 decision and the coalition's initiative merely representing a return to the previous state of affairs, which is "implicitly clearly in the Constitution" (National Council of the Slovak Republic 2020d). The hopes of achieving a consensus remained unfulfilled: a narrow constitutional majority of 91 MPs from the coalition parties (a three-fifths majority of 90 out of the 150 MPs being the required minimum) carried the amendment; all opposition MPs voted against, without a single MP abstaining (National Council of the Slovak Republic 2020o). The amendment can be seen as a parliamentary retaliation to the SCC's decision, attempting to curtail its powers (see Sajó and Uitz 2017, 357–366 for more on this strategy and its variants).

10.3 Methodological and contextual specifics

Turning to the quantitative assessments, the following methodological caveats should be kept in mind. Firstly, only those rulings pertaining to specific legal provisions were included in the coded database. The Court occasionally decides to dismiss elements of a petition without specifying the relevant provisions in the headnote (for example, PL. ÚS 11/2010 includes a formulation on the Court refusing "the rest of the petition"). While we treated these as refusals, one could also interpret them as rejections, in which case the strength of the SCC decisions would decrease, and the gap identified between the quantitative and qualitative evaluation in the Slovak case (Pócza, Dobos, and Gyulai 2019) might be smaller.

Secondly, as regards statistical data, the Court, while placing considerable emphasis on presenting the statistics of its decision-making, has not done this in a consistent format since its establishment. Press releases are issued on an *ad hoc* basis, although they are grouped into a useful separate section for archival purposes (Constitutional Court of the Slovak Republic n.d.b). Court President Macejková arranged the publication of an annual report on

21 "I think that those of us, who are a little engaged with constitutional law, probably have a consensus on that, the way in which [the SCC] did it, was an excess".

Table 10.3 Selected statistics of SCC petitions and decisions

Year[1]	*No. of petitions*	*No. of decisions*	*No. of decisions on unconstitutionality according to Art. 125 (number of decisions in this type of proceeding)*
1993–2016	162,464	75,074	59 (142)
2017[2]	2,434	2,281	8 (17)
2018[3]	2,568	2,810	7 (10)[4]
2019[5]	2,373	1,581	8 (16)
2020[5]	2,963	2,857	4 (7)[6]
2021[7]	2,643	2,835	NA
2022[8]	2,876	2,995	NA
Total	**178,321**	**90,433**	**~86 (192) SUCCESS RATE 44,8%**

1 The overall statistics for Macejková's term are 148,941 petitions received, 148,256 petitions processed, and 685 pending (Ústavný súd Slovenskej republiky 2019a). It is important to note that the SCC may combine several petitions into one decision, and so the discrepancy that appears in the table between the number of petitions received and the number of decisions does not amount to the number of petitions that await processing at the SCC. At the end of 2022, around 1,000 petitions awaited processing at the Court (see reference to the 2022 data that follows).

2 Macejková 2018, 15

3 Ústavný súd Slovenskej republiky 2020

4 Only proceedings based on Art. 125 sec. 1 (a) based on the JUDICON-EU database, due to unavailability of statistical information from the SCC materials.

5 Ústavný súd Slovenskej republiky 2021a

6 Only proceedings based on Art. 125 sec. 1 (a) based on the JUDICON-EU database, due to unavailability of statistical information from the SCC materials.

7 Ústavný súd Slovenskej republiky 2022

8 Ústavný súd Slovenskej republiky 2023c

the protection of constitutionalism by the Court, but this ceased publication in 2017 (Constitutional Court of the Slovak Republic 2019a). President Ivan Fiačan created a new format of a yearbook presenting the main developments and cases decided by the Court (Constitutional Court of the Slovak Republic 2023b). Table 10.3 shows that in 2019, the total number of decisions was considerably smaller than in the surrounding years. In contrast, in 2021 and 2022, more petitions were decided than received.

The explanation for the 2019 reduction lies in the vacancies on the bench in that year: after the expiration of the term of President Macejková and eight other judges, only four judges were left on the bench between 17 February and 17 April, when three judges, including the new President and Vice President, were eventually appointed. The SCC refers to the vacancies as a problem from the perspective of the sustainable practice of constitutional adjudication (Constitutional Court of the Slovak Republic 2019b). At the same time, the fact that the backlog was relatively limited indicates that the Court operated effectively in the background, particularly thanks to the clerks working on the draft decisions (see Macejková 2020, 130–134).

Thirdly, one should be mindful of the continued extension of the competences of the SCC and the limitations this imposes on understanding the judicial-legislative relationship through the JUDICON-EU methodology. In 2017, the SCC gained a new competence according to Art. 129a of the Constitution (Act No. 71/2017 Coll.), that of reviewing the constitutionality of the parliamentary resolution on the abolishment of amnesty or individual pardon according to a new competence that had been gained, in turn, by the Parliament. This competence was introduced in reaction to the controversies surrounding the constitutional procedure for the abolishment of the so-called Mečiar amnesties (Mazák and Orosz 2018). Only one decision was issued according to this procedure (PL. ÚS 7/2017), which differs from the SCC's other competences in that the Court needs to start the proceeding automatically, without a petition. By affirming the constitutionality of the Parliament's decision, the SCC exhibited a willingness to cooperate with the legislature over an issue of pressing societal concern, but the quantitative analysis does not reflect this decision. The COVID-19 context also needs to be accounted for, particularly in using the, until the pandemic only theoretical, competence to review the constitutionality of the state of emergency and related decisions taken by the public institutions (Art. 129 sec. 6). The reason is that the Parliament was granted the competence to endorse the prolongation of executive decisions on states of emergency[22] beyond the maximum time period that the executive can declare a state of emergency. Hence, by affirming the constitutionality of a prolonged state of emergency that was endorsed by the Parliament (PL. ÚS 2/2021),[23] the Court has legitimated the decision of the legislative majority.[24]

Last but not least, separating the legislative-judicial and the executive-judicial relationships becomes increasingly difficult at a time of a fusion of public powers, where a "neo-medieval" structure of overlapping competence areas (Albert 2010; Zielonka 2014) rather than a neat separation of powers may be observed. While the debate on the democratic legitimacy of judicial review has traditionally been conducted precisely in terms of its relation to the legislature (e.g. Waldron 2006), today, not only has the executive become more central

22 Via an amendment of the Constitutional Act No. 227/2002 Coll. on State Security.

23 This decision was issued in spring 2021 so, chronologically speaking, it falls outside the scope of the period under scrutiny. However, we refer to it due to its significance for the future developments of the legislative-SCC relationship. Furthermore, the Court delivered another decision in the same proceeding in Fall 2020 (PL. ÚS 22/2020), just at that time the decision reviewed only the executive declaration of the state of emergency, and so it did not pertain to the Court's relationship with the legislature.

24 A broad reading of the abstract constitutional interpretation (Art. 128 of the Constitution) that is included in the dataset could speak for including these cases in the dataset as well. However, to ensure methodological consistency, the list of procedures included has not been extended compared to the earlier JUDICON dataset.

(e.g. Lachmayer 2019, 39), but many more actors are involved, including the public at large. The collaborative model of appointing constitutional judges in Slovakia is just one indicator of this interconnectedness. The Court's public image is also shaped by more factors than its position to the legislator. In Slovakia, this was illustrated by the avalanche of proceedings relating to Art. 136 sec. 3 of the Constitution, which used to give the Court the competence to decide on the incarceration of judges upon the request of the Attorney General – if the judges are suspected of criminal activity and justified grounds exist for placing them in custody. The SCC was required to decide immediately in a plenary sitting, which left it with very limited time for thorough consideration of the case and for the preparation of a justification for the decision (Macejková 2020, 1448–1463). Exercising this competence, the Court found itself under pressure to justify why some of its decisions, issued during a series of prosecutions of judges suspected of corrupt activities as a result of the information that surfaced after the murder of the investigative journalist Ján Kuciak and his fiancée, granted consent for incarceration while others withheld it (Tódová 2021).[25]

10.4 Trends: first glimpses of a new era?

How do the trends during 2016–2020 compare to the preceding periods? The key finding is that "business as usual" seems to have continued at the Court. The number of cases it handled in the procedure according to Art. 125 did not exceed the average of the 1990–2015 period, nor did the strength of its decisions (Figure 10.1).[26] A mild increase is observable towards the end of the third term on the bench in February 2019, marked by the "unconstitutional constitutional amendment" verdict (PL. ÚS 21/2014). The significance of this judgment is such that it prevents one from drawing major conclusions based merely on the number of rulings with and without dissenting opinions (Figure 10.2). For example, in 2018, there were more rulings with a dissent than without one, but this does not allow us to conclude that 2018 was more significant in relation to dissents than 2019. The dissents of 2018 occur in less salient cases and pertain mainly to disagreements on the interpretation of the scope of fundamental rights in the Constitution and the SCC's interpretive powers related thereto. This may be a sign that less effort was expended on consensus-building at the Court via internal deliberative processes (cf. Lübbe-Wolff 2020) in this period.

Figure 10.3 shows the first results available on the strength of the majority rulings and dissenting opinions of the judges of the Fiačan Court. While the data are very limited, they indicate, firstly, that there have been no major

25 This competence has, however, been taken from the Court in December 2020.

26 Between 2016–2020, the SCC delivered a decision on the merits in a total of 42 cases according to Art. 125 sec. 1 of the Constitution.

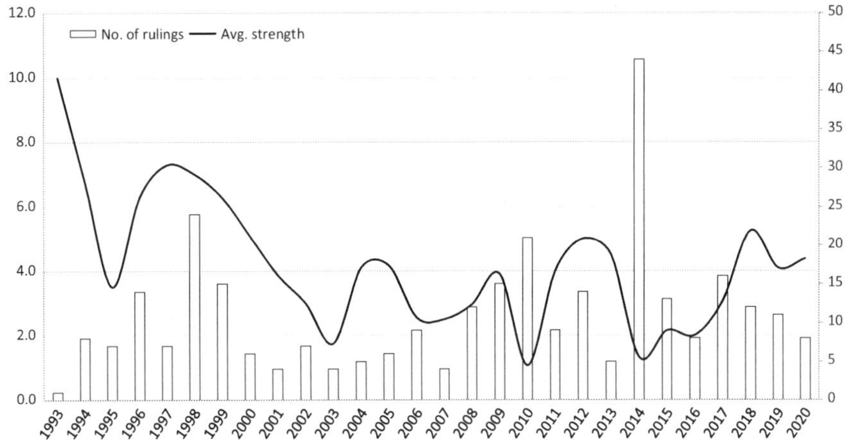

Figure 10.1 Number and average strength of rulings (1993–2020) (SCC)

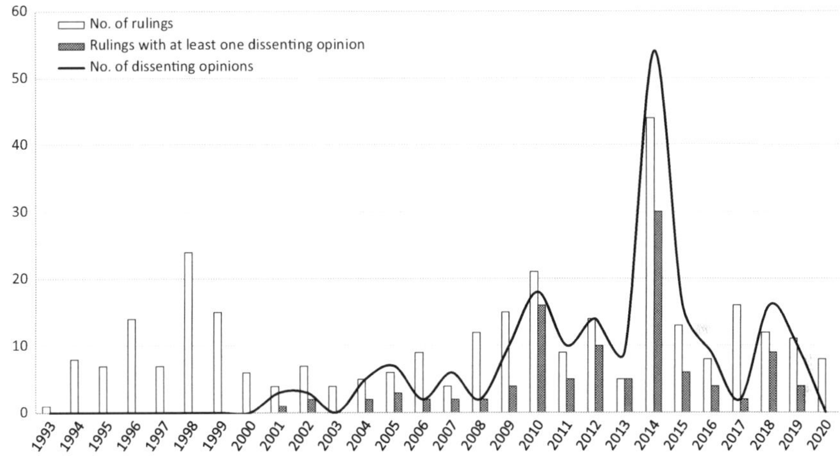

Figure 10.2 Number of rulings with at least one dissenting opinion (1993–2020) (SCC)

disagreements between the judges in the plenary cases under scrutiny. This finding is underscored by the absence of a single dissenting opinion in the period after the completion of the majority of the bench on 10 October 2019. Secondly and relatedly, the differences in the strengths of the rulings between the new judges are negligible but, on average, the values are higher than during the Macejková period and rather approximate the first period of the Court from 1993–2000 (while not reaching the strength levels of that period). This indicates a Court that is ready to assert itself in proceedings on the unconstitutionality of legislation, although the mere seven decisions included after

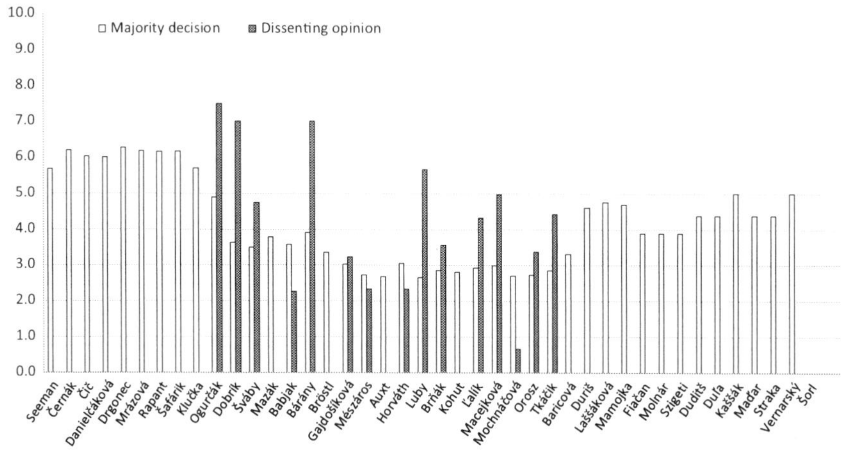

Figure 10.3 Average strength of rulings by judges (SCC)

June 2019 do not suffice to offer any definite conclusions.[27] Thirdly, the figures do, however, provide a conclusive picture about the judges of the Macejková Court (all judges to the right of Judge Gajdošíková and the left of Judge Mamojka, with judges Baricová, Duriš, and Laššáková from the previous period also continuing on the bench during part of the Fiačan period). It is clear that the period saw the lowest average strength of the three complete periods of the SCC (see Figure 10.1).[28] There are no major outliers either: all the judges except those who joined the bench in 2017 (Laššáková, Duriš, Mamojka) display an average strength of between 2.65 (Judge Luby) and 3.30 (Judge Baricová).

No conclusive trends are discernible in the depictions of dissenting opinions in terms of their proportion and strength or of their relative strength or frequency. Dissenting opinions tend to be stronger than majority decisions, but not by a wide margin, and judges whose dissents are weaker than the majority decisions have only a few dissents included in the database. An exception

27 As can be seen in the dataset, no plenary cases (Art. 125 sec. 1a) were decided between June 2019 and February 2020 (with only one case decided in June 2019 after the end of the Macejková term in February 2019, a rejection based on procedural reasons). The reason for this is again the low number of judges; because the quorum for a binding plenary decision does not decrease with the increasing number of vacancies, deciding on plenary cases with a lower number of judges increases the risk of not reaching a binding decision.

28 Because the judges penned dissenting opinions with reference to a differing number of cases, such comparisons between judges are less feasible for dissenting opinions. Importantly, dissents could not be attached to judgments until 2000, which leaves the first Court out of consideration.

is Judge Mészáros, who issued 31 dissents (and is generally considered as an author of important and illuminating dissents),[29] but their average strength is below the minority. Mészáros frequently emphasizes the importance of self-restraint. If this is understood as greater reluctance to invalidate the constitutionality of legislation (in the context of the Art. 125 sec. 1a procedure), then the quantitative evidence confirms that he practiced as well as preached his normative preference. The lack of major gaps between the strengths of the majority and dissenting opinions indicates the generally "fair weather" in which the SCC found itself during its existence from 2000, compared to its regional counterparts that faced major challenges to the continuity of the democratic regime (Hungary, Poland). At the same time, the more dramatic chapters of its story are concealed by these statistics, as they pertain to procedures that are not captured by the dataset and hence do not *prima facie* speak to the relationship between the SCC and the legislator, but rather concern the SCC and a broader set of institutions including the public at large.

A somewhat monotonous picture emerges when it comes to the diversity of ruling types (Figure 10.4): the SCC uses almost exclusively rejections and declarations of substantive unconstitutionality. Only rarely does it declare a provision unconstitutional for procedural reasons, despite concerns over the quality of the legislative procedure in Slovakia, including the tendency to overuse fast-track legislative procedures (Láštic 2020) at the expense of proper deliberation on new legislation. Between 2016 and 2020, some substantive unconstitutionalities were categorized as referring to the violation of legal certainty or clarity. Thus, in a free speech case (PL. ÚS 5/2017), the Court's decision to invalidate the amendment to the Slovak Criminal Code that allowed the prosecution of spreading extreme speech on the grounds of "political conviction" or an "other characteristic" decried the vagueness that these formulations entail in the context of the fragile Slovak investigation and prosecution system, where there is limited expertise in dealing with sophisticated instances of extreme speech. In a 2018 case on the regulation of salaries of public officials (PL. ÚS 8/2017), the majority invalidated the freezing of certain salaries that had been introduced on the grounds of the economic crisis, arguing that since the crisis has passed, there are no legitimate grounds for sustaining the restriction. Interestingly, the case generated three individual dissents with similar arguments by judges who do not typically dissent on the

29 Mészáros (Prušová 2019) was writing a book collecting his various (concurring and dissenting) opinions. He commented that the separate opinions "gave [him] a degree of freedom. I always tried to be restrained and write only how I would have decided. But sometimes it was really impossible. I was bothered by the majority sometimes going completely on the edge [*absolútne nadoraz* in the original]".

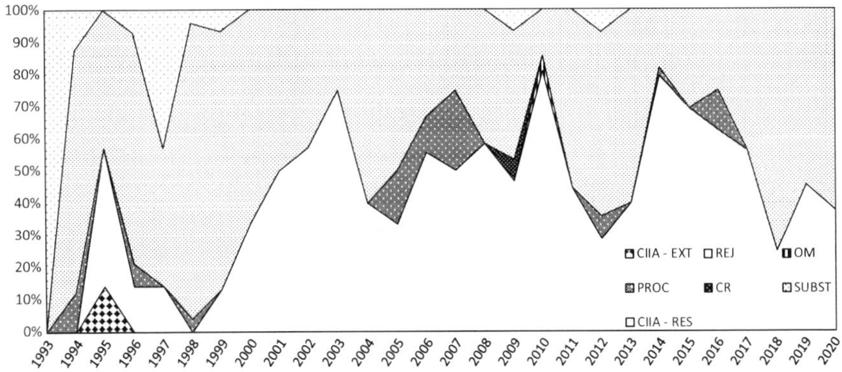

Figure 10.4 Frequency of the ruling types (1993–2020) (SCC)

same issues (Judges Ľalík and Brňák on the one hand and Judge Mészáros on the other hand).[30]

Turning to the patterns of affinity and the lack thereof in dissenting coalitions, no significant changes appear in comparison to the results based on the 1990–2015 data only (see Láštic and Steuer 2019). There are still two relatively stable dissenting coalitions of three judges each (Macejková, Ľalík, and Dobrík; and Gajdošíková, Mészáros, and Orosz). The one judge from among those depicted in Figure 10.5 who continued to sit on the bench after 2020 (Baricová) is connected to the coalition with Macejková and Ľalík because she joined them in issuing a dissent on a case (PL. ÚS 42/2015) concerning a violation (on the grounds of prohibition of expropriation of property) arising from the act on thermal energy, in that it offered only a single compensation for the establishment of easement for an unspecified time. The three judges all believed that the threshold for disproportionality was not exceeded by the legislator in this case, thus differing from the other three dissenters who either asked for a stricter scrutiny of the review (Mochnáčová) or identified a disproportionately beneficial legal position for commercial providers of thermal energy compared to those who wish to generate energy in their own heating system and called for the invalidation of a related provision (Mészáros,

30 This judge went further in his reasoning than the other two dissenters by stating that the majority "takes away from the democratic environment a topic that undoubtedly belongs there. . . . More than with its economic impacts [the majority decision] is problematic due to its *pro futuro* effects, because it can unaccountably constrain the parliament [and induce it to] avoid freezing the salaries of 'independent' state functionaries [in the long term]". This verdict on the controversy associated with salaries to public officials is but the last one in a chain, where the SCC's (generally) critical positions towards freezing salaries (including of judges) have been met with unease in the public reflections thereof.

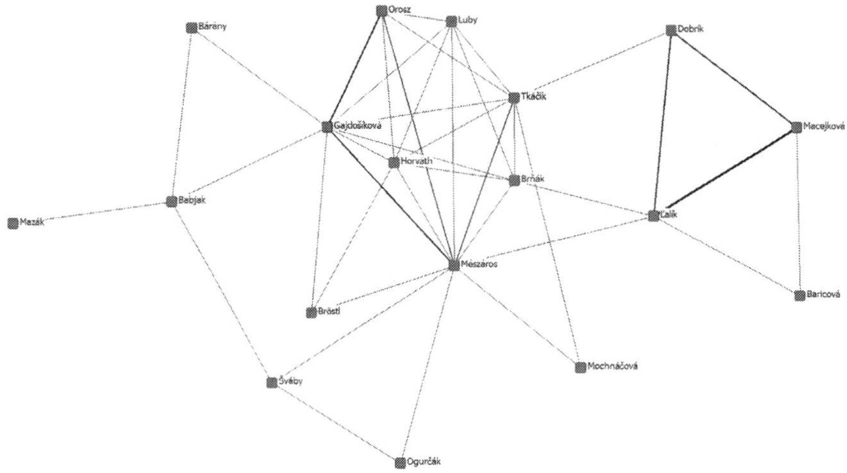

Figure 10.5 Dissenting coalitions 1993–2020 (SCC)

Tkáčik). However, no firm conclusions can be drawn on Judge Baricová carrying on the "legacies" of one of the two dissenting coalitions from this single case, which illustrates the disputes about the optimal scope of the right to property and the role of the market in regulating public affairs.

10.5 Landmark cases: not (yet) a bold step towards Dworkinian interpretivism

Previously, we labelled as particularly contentious cases those which generated at least four dissenting opinions (Láštic and Steuer 2019, 198). Among these was the invalidation of a provision of the Anti-discrimination Act (No. 365/2004 Coll.) that allowed the introduction of special compensatory measures for discrimination based on racial or ethnic origin, decided during the Court's second term. We interpreted both the majority decision and the concurring opinion as adopting a positivist reading of the Constitution, which sees the open-endedness of the provision as contradicting the rule of law due to its openness for further interpretation, unlike the dissents, which supported a more principled reading, emphasizing the injustices that necessitate the compensatory measures (Láštic and Steuer 2019, 200–201).

During the Court's third term from 2007 to 2015, the cases with four or more dissents revolved primarily around competence disputes (Láštic and Steuer 2019, 201–204). The Court's decision on abortion (PL. ÚS 12/01), encompassing a prominent human rights element, can be interpreted as being built primarily on a comparative analysis of the practice in other countries to argue for the legitimacy of the legislator's scope to permit abortion in the first 12 weeks of the pregnancy.[31] The majority decisions which appear as considerably constraining the legislature from a quantitative point of view (the Special Court case[32] and the Attorney General case[33]) appear to be closer to embracing Dworkinian interpretivism, although the extent to which they introduced broad principles (including a particular reading of judicial independence in the Special Court case) without in-depth elaboration (especially in the Attorney General case which had only 24 pages) raises questions about the judges trying to approximate the Dworkinian "Judge Hercules" in the process.

Thus, in these contentious cases, the Court can be seen as entering the final period of its third term without a clear position in the Hart-Dworkin debate, while perhaps leaning slightly towards Hart in attributing broader leeway to the legislature. Between 2016 and 2020, only two cases were accompanied by four or more dissents. One is the aforementioned case on the regulation of providers of thermal energy. The dissents (no fewer than six) may be clustered into two subgroups with three judges each, one standing more on the side of the providers and the other on the side of the customers. In this sense, however, the majority decision can be seen as a compromise between these competing positions that dissatisfied six judges enough for them to write or join a dissent. However, this does not represent an extreme position towards which all dissenters would align themselves. As the case pertained to the right to property, one may read the dispute between the judges as an effort to find an answer that best fits the Slovak constitutional system "seen as an unfolding political narrative" (Dworkin 1986, 225). Indeed, in fundamental rights cases, the Dworkinian narrative is at its most visible, including via the prominent and now standard use of proportionality analysis.[34] For example, in March 2017 the SCC adjudicated the mandatory secondary school education requirement for mayoral candidates.[35] Technically, the case revolved around several provisions of Act No. 180/2014 Coll. on the conditions of the implementation of the right to vote, adopted during the single-party cabinet of Robert Fico (2012–2016). In a dedicated section titled "Why we decided just this way" that can be seen as part of the SCC's communication strategy to explain complicated and notable decisions in a more straightforward manner, the SCC highlighted the violation of several constitutional provisions, including the principle of democracy and the right to vote (Constitutional Court of the Slovak Republic 2017). The unconstitutional provisions, however, did not have unconstitutional effects, as the SCC used its competence to suspend the effectiveness of the provisions shortly after it had received the relevant petition

31 The decision contains a reference to Dworkin's work (para. II.B.4, pp. 46–47), but in the context of this comparative analysis, rather than as a point clarifying the role of the judiciary *vis-à-vis* the legislature.

32 PL. ÚS 17/08.

33 PL. ÚS 4/2012.

34 E.g. PL. ÚS 5/2017, PL. ÚS 20/2014 from among the 2016–2020 cases.

35 PL. ÚS 18/2014; see also Drgonec 2019, 749–750.

(in 2014) (TASR 2014). Judge Ľalík penned a sole dissent to this decision, arguing that the "educational census" is akin to other forms of restriction on the right to vote, including age or place of residence. He did not persuade the other judges with this exclusionary view of democracy (cf. Brennan 2016, Chapter 1).

The second case with more than four dissents adjudicated in the 2016–2020 period is the notorious judicial clearance case (PL. ÚS 21/2014). The Parliament acting as the constitutional legislator adopted a constitutional amendment (161/2014 Coll.) in the name of judicial reform, subjecting judges to security clearances by the National Security Authority. The controversial amendment was practically operable only via implementing legislation. The SCC decided to invalidate not only the statutory but also the constitutional provisions in question, causing a major uproar both among dissenting judges and parts of the academia (e.g. Káčer 2019). A book-length "doctrinal dissent" to the decision claims that the SCC "violated the principle of the minimization of interference in the actions of other constitutional organs, and thereby also proportionality, the central principle of the rule of law" (Káčer and Neumann 2019, 16). While space does not permit a detailed engagement with its arguments, this represents a well-established tradition in Slovak constitutional scholarship that, following its Anglo-American counterparts (Waldron 2006), gives primacy to the legislature and envisions a deferential role for the SCC, indicating a degree of distrust in its significance as a constitutional guardian.

According to a dissenting judge who proposed an alternative verdict that would have invalidated only the implementing legislation, the Court unnecessarily triggered a "constitutional revolution" (Prušová 2019). Another scholar considered it to be a prime example of the "careless" application of the SCC's implied competences (Drgonec 2019, 1425). More favourable readings of the verdict praised it for, among other things, "returning" the constituent power into the hands of the people (Ľalík 2020). This is reflected particularly in the provision where the Court referred to the constitutional referendum (para. 177) as having made a non-reviewable change to the Constitution (and, hence, if such a mechanism existed, even if the people decided to abolish democracy, the Court could not act). However, this segment of the judgment can be read differently as yet another articulation of the deferential attitude of the Court, this time leaning towards a more Schmittian (Kelsen and Schmitt 2015) than Hartian reading, where democracy is attributed to the popular subject and is contrasted to constitutionalism.[36] In addition, while the majority decision contains a reference to Dworkin when highlighting the significance of

36 Káčer and Neumann (2019, 126) argue that this reading is unconvincing because the likelihood of such a referendum to pass given its high threshold is minimal, and so the SCC exhibits only "façade deference". Paradoxically, one of their opponents agrees that a revolution is highly unlikely to happen in Slovakia but uses this claim to question the "doomsday imagery" built up around the judgment (Ľalík 2021, 120–121). The SCC's approach is troubling, not because of façade deference but because of the loophole that it creates in constitutional guardianship in Slovakia.

the "constitutional principles" which form the "normative ground of not only the constitution, but the legal system as a whole" (para. 54), it soon resorts to Hart to highlight that the Court may develop a new competence in penumbral cases, the acceptance of which can only be determined *after* the decision (para. 60.2, see also Hart (2012, 153)).[37] The consequence of this position would be that if the competence is not accepted (as demonstrated by constitutional amendment No. 422/2020 Coll. claiming the removal of the Court's power to review constitutional amendments), it does not exist. In sum, *even* in this case, which undoubtedly represents a major constraint on the legislature according to the JUDICON-EU methodology, a more nuanced analysis reveals the tendency of the SCC to constrain its own powers, without these constraints necessarily having any convincing interpretive basis.

At the end of 2020, the Court remained very much alive and active, with several landmark cases on the horizon. Just a few days after the approval of the constitutional amendment (see Section 10.2.2.3), opposition MPs submitted the amendment to the SCC, petitioning its invalidation due to a violation of the substantive core of the Constitution (Constitutional Court of the Slovak Republic 2020).[38] Their arguments revolved around a "radical" view which held that the sovereignty of the people – *as articulated* via general elections – needs to give way to the legitimacy of the SCC because this legitimacy contains, in addition to that of the Parliament, "a component of the highest moral and professional standard" (p. 9). Those opposition politicians who considered the reduction of the thresholds needed for the parliamentary selection of SCC candidates, in this petition, cherish the interaction between the Parliament and the President during the appointment process and the support of the Constitutional Committee of the National Council in screening the candidates. Once again, constitutionalist rhetoric was appropriated by inauthentic speakers who had repudiated that very same rhetoric in their past actions.

If the Court agreed, rhetoric claiming "judicial overreach" or the undermining of democracy could have been expected. Deference to the legislature would have made Slovak constitutionalism more fragile, due to potential future illiberal majorities receiving a "rubber stamp" from the Court to do virtually anything. Commentators tended to neglect[39] a third way available to the Court, that is, a stipulation of a constitutional requirement constraining

37 "The truth may be that, when courts settle previously unenvisaged questions concerning the most fundamental constitutional rules, they get their authority to decide them accepted after the questions have arisen and the decision has been given. Here all that succeeds is success".

38 In 2021, another opposition petition was submitted to the Court that encompasses several provisions of the constitutional amendment, including the removal the SCC's consent requirement for imprisonment of a judge or attorney general for the decision of the general court to enter into effect, or the possibility of recall of the chairperson and members of the Judicial Council (Constitutional Court of the Slovak Republic 2021a).

39 For a partial exception, see Orosz (2021, 88–89), who argues that, even if explicitly prohibited, the SCC may go against "positive law" and articulate a position that specific decisions of other constitutional organs "substantially interfere with the identity of the Constitution and undermine the fundamental values it is built upon".

the incompatibility of review introduced in Art. 125 sec. 4 by the commitment of the SCC to protect constitutionality in Art. 124, and hence to invalidate those amendments that undermine democracy and its core related values. Despite the downside of the incompatibility of the remaining part of the constitutional text, such a requirement could not be changed by a future constitutional amendment that would subsequently be endorsed by a potential illiberal majority at the Court itself. Even extreme (and very theoretical) acts such as the abolishment of the SCC or the enactment of a new authoritarian constitution could legally be resisted in this form. In short, the Court has the tools to persuade considerable segments of the expert community as well as the public that its right to review constitutional amendments has to be retained at least for grave instances of the undermining of democracy by a partisan majority (with the "graveness" itself being subject to interpretation).[40]

This brief discussion of landmark cases conceptualized via the number of dissenting opinions they generated demonstrates that the SCC leans towards the interpretive picture of adjudication primarily in its human rights jurisprudence. We need to wait for the development of the adjudication of the "fourth Court" to see whether this commitment to self-restraint will become effectively dissociated from deference to the legislator and adherence to constitutional principles, even at times when partisan, academic, or even public opinion pressures make doing so uncomfortable for the Court.

10.6 Conclusions

The JUDICON-EU methodology retains its value in capturing the positioning of the SCC *vis-à-vis* the legislature as well as in tracing the evolution of individual judges' assessment thereof. As in our former analysis, however, one needs to look beyond the numbers to recognize the transformative value of landmark cases and uncover the broader web of relations that encompasses key political leaders,[41] political parties, and academics whose work becomes an argumentative tool in parliamentary and judicial deliberations. The range of relevant actors is even considerably broader than that and encompasses the media, civil society, and the public more broadly (participating, for example, in public consultations on draft legislation which, in the case of the 2020 constitutional amendment, took place over less than three weeks in July 2020 (Ministry of Justice of the Slovak Republic 2020)). Further research is needed to discuss how the media and public perception shape the legislative and judicial choices made at the Court. The Court's economic and social rights jurisprudence is also a relatively neglected field (see Steuer 2023), including

40 The Court ultimately retained a very narrow leeway for amendment review (PL. ÚS 8/2022, PL. ÚS 12/2022), but this would hardly qualify as a constitutional requirement, not least as it was articulated in the justification of a decision in preliminary proceeding, in which (the respective parts of) both petitions were refused (see Šipulová and Steuer 2023, 101).

41 In our story, these encompassed the Minister of Justice (2020–2022) (Mária Kolíková) and the chairman of Smer-SD and, as of 2023, again PM (Robert Fico).

in the context of its interaction with various forms of expertise (King 2012, 211–249). The inspirations that were determinative for the Court's pronouncements on the constitutionality of legislation would also benefit from further scrutiny.

This chapter suggests that the SCC struggles to square a principled, Dworkinian reading with a positivist, Hartian account. This is manifested in more deferential attitudes, including, prominently, in relation to the 2020–2021 declarations of states of emergency. The Court reviewed these twice using a dedicated competence in Art. 129 sec. 6 of the Constitution.[42] The second case, following an amendment of the Constitutional Act on State Security[43] included a parliamentary review of the emergency declaration; hence, by endorsing it, the SCC also showed deference *vis-à-vis* the legislature. It would be bold to fully embrace an interpretive account of law for a Central European constitutional court based in a civil law system with an overwhelming legacy of positivism, and to recognize politics as interconnected with law (Robertson 2010; Uitz 2007; Belov 2019), a connection that does not necessarily undermine judicial independence (cf. Friedman 1998; Petrov 2022). However, without such an embrace, the tension between what the Court says and what it does is likely to become more entrenched and weaken the argumentative quality of future decisions. Addressing this tension is a formidable task for the "fourth" Court.

References

Albert, Richard. 2010. "Presidential Values in Parliamentary Democracies." *International Journal of Constitutional Law* 8 (2): 207–236.

Baricová, Jana. 2020. "Nová zákonná regulácia konania pred Ústavným súdom Slovenskej republiky a jej (potenciálny) prínos pre rozhodovaciu činnosť Ústavného súdu Slovenskej republiky [New Legal Regulation of the Proceedings before the Constitutional Court of the Slovak Republic and Its (Potential) Contribution to the Decision Making of the Constitutional Court of the Slovak Republic]." In *Ústavná a zákonná úprava konania pred súdnym orgánom ochrany ústavnosti v štátoch V4 – VIII. Ústavné dni*, edited by Ladislav Orosz, Sabina Grabowska, and Tomáš Majerčák, 98–112. Košice: Univerzita P. J. Šafárika.

Belov, Martin. 2019. "Introduction." In *Courts, Politics and Constitutional Law: Judicialization of Politics and Politicization of the Judiciary*, edited by Martin Belov, 1–18. London: Routledge.

Bickel, Alexander M. 1986. *The Least Dangerous Branch: The Supreme Court at the Bar of Politics*. 2nd ed. New Haven: Yale University Press.

Brennan, Jason. 2016. *Against Democracy*. Princeton: Princeton University Press.

42 PL. ÚS 22/2020, PL. ÚS 2/2021.

43 Constitutional Act No. 227/2002 Coll. on State Security.

Chandrachud, Chintan. 2020. "How a Case on Minerva Mills Challenged and Undid Indira Gandhi's Damage to the Constitution." *ThePrint* (blog), January 12. https://theprint.in/pageturner/excerpt/how-minerva-mills-case-challenged-indira-gandhi-damage-to-constitution/348426/.

Constitutional Affairs Committee of the National Council of the Slovak Republic. 2020. "Uznesenie č. 140 z 24. novembra 2020" [Resolution No. 140 of 24 November 2020]. www.nrsr.sk/web/Dynamic/DocumentPreview.aspx?DocID=488036.

Constitutional Court of the Slovak Republic. 2017. "K rozhodnutiu Ústavného súdu Slovenskej republiky o podmienení kandidatúry na funkciu starostu obce/primátora mesta získaním vzdelania (vzdelanostný cenzus)" [On the Decision of the Constitutional Court of the Slovak Republic on the Conditioning of the Candidacy for Mayor of Village/Town by Education (Educational Census)]. www.ustavnysud.sk/-/k-rozhodnutiu-ustavneho-sudu-slovenskej-republiky-o-podmieneni-kandidatury-na-funkciu-starostu-obce-primatora-mesta-ziskanim-vzdelania-vzdelanostny-ce.

———. 2019a. "Ochrana ústavnosti a Ústavy Slovenskej republiky v rozhodovacej činnosti Ústavného súdu Slovenskej republiky" [The Protection of Constitutionalism and the Constitution of the Slovak Republic in the Decision Making of the Constitutional Court of the Slovak Republic]. www.ustavnysud.sk/ochrana-ustavnosti.

———. 2019b. "Tlačová informácia č. 15/2019" [Press Release No. 15/2019]. www.ustavnysud.sk/c/document_library/get_file?uuid=feae8a1e-e5c6-4084-b6f0-09a0e32ed49b&groupId=10182.

———. 2020. "Podanie č. 2879/2020" [Petition No. 2879/2020]. www.ustavnysud.sk/ussr-intranet-portlet/docDownload/f5393b8d-5a4f-4dbf-a870-4706eb5c7f87/Podanie%20-%20Podanie.pdf.

———. 2023a. "30. výročie Ústavného súdu Slovenskej republiky" [30th Anniversary of the Constitutional Court of the Slovak Republic]. www.ustavnysud.sk/30-vyrocie.

———. 2023b. "Ročenka Ústavného súdu Slovenskej republiky" [Yearbook of the Constitutional Court of the Slovak Republic]. www.ustavnysud.sk/rocenka.

———. 2023c. "Rozvrhy práce Ústavného súdu Slovenskej republiky" [Timetables of Operations of the Constitutional Court of the Slovak Republic]. www.ustavnysud.sk/predchadzajuce-rozvrhy-prace-ustavneho-sudu-slovenskej-republiky.

———. n.d.a "Galéria sudcov predchádzajúcich funkčných období" [Gallery of Former Judges]. www.ustavnysud.sk/galeria-sudcov-predchadzajucich-funkcnych-obdobi.

———. n.d.b "Tlačové správy – štatistické prehľady" [Press Releases – Statistical Overviews]. www.ustavnysud.sk/tlacove-spravy-statistiky#!pressReleaseView.

Čuroš, Peter. 2023. "Attack or Reform: Systemic Interventions in the Judiciary in Hungary, Poland, and Slovakia." *Oñati Socio-Legal Series* 13 (2): 626–658.

Drgonec, Ján. 2019. *Ústava Slovenskej republiky: Teória a prax [The Constitution of the Slovak Republic: Theory and Practice]*. 2nd ed. Prague: C. H. Beck.

Dworkin, Ronald. 1967. "The Model of Rules I." *The University of Chicago Law Review* 35 (1): 14–46.

———. 1986. *Law's Empire*. Cambridge: Harvard University Press.

Fiačan, Ivan. 2020. "Právna úprava konania pred Ústavným súdom Slovenskej republiky ako kľúčový predpoklad efektívneho výkonu jeho kompetencií [Legal Regulation of the Proceedings before the Constitutional Court of the Slovak Republic as a Necessary Condition for Effective Exercise of Its Competences]." In *Ústavná a zákonná úprava konania pred súdnym orgánom ochrany ústavnosti v štátoch V4 – VIII. Ústavné dni*, edited by Ladislav Orosz, Sabina Grabowska, and Tomáš Majerčák, 6–18. Košice: Univerzita P. J. Šafárika.

Friedman, Terry B. 1998. "The Politicization of the Judiciary." *Judicature* 82: 6.

Hart, Herbert L. A. 2012. *The Concept of Law*. 3rd ed. Oxford: Oxford University Press.

Janščová, Kristína. 2019. "Duchaplné myšlienky z poslednej tlačovky Andreja Danka [Witty Thoughts from the Last Press Conference of Andrej Danko]." *fici.sme.sk*, February 21, 2019. https://fici.sme.sk/c/22058444/vyroky-andreja-danka-16-myslienok-z-tlacovky-ktore-by-nemali-ostat-zabudnute.html.

Káčer, Marek. 2019. "Od ochrany pred hrôzami koncentračných táborov k ochrane "profesionálnej existencie" vydierateľných sudcov [From Protection against the Horrors of Concentration Camps to the Protection of the "Professional Existence" of Bent Judges]." *Acta Facultatis Iuridicae Universitatis Comenianae* 38 (1): 261–273.

———, and Jakub Neumann. 2019. *Materiálne jadro v slovenskom ústavnom práve. Doktrinálny disent proti zrušeniu sudcovských previerok [The Substantive Core in Slovak Constitutional Law: Doctrinal Dissent against the Abolishment of Judicial Clearances]*. Praha: Leges.

Kelsen, Hans, and Carl Schmitt. 2015. *The Guardian of the Constitution: Hans Kelsen and Carl Schmitt on the Limits of Constitutional Law*. Translated by Lars Vinx. Cambridge: Cambridge University Press.

King, Jeff. 2012. *Judging Social Rights*. Cambridge: Cambridge University Press.

Košťová, Silvia, dir. 2023." Najmocnejšia inštitúcia [The Most Powerful Institution]." *RTVS*. www.rtvs.sk/televizia/archiv/19969/391812.

Kuzmány, Andrej, and Roman Cuprík. 2020. "Mamojka končí ako ústavný sudca, pre kontakty s Kočnerom sa rozhodol vzdať funkcie [Mamojka Resigns as a Constitutional Judge, Gave Up Position Due to Contacts with Kočner]." *Sme*, May 13, 2020. https://domov.sme.sk/c/22403483/mamojka-sa-pre-kontakty-s-kocnerom-vzdava-funkcie-ustavneho-sudcu.html.

Lachmayer, Konrad. 2019. "Disempowering Courts: The Interrelationship between Courts and Politics in Contemporary Legal Orders or the Manifold Ways of Attacking Judicial Independence." In *Courts, Politics and Constitutional Law: Judicialization of Politics and Politicization of the Judiciary*, edited by Martin Belov, 31–54. London: Routledge.

Ľalík, Tomáš. 2020. "The Slovak Constitutional Court on Unconstitutional Constitutional Amendment (PL. ÚS 21/2014)." *European Constitutional Law Review* 16 (2): 328–343.

———. 2021. "K odňatiu právomoci Ústavného súdu SR posudzovať ústavné zákony – kritické reflexie [Nullifying the Power of the Slovak Constitutional Court to Review Unconstitutional Amendments – A Critique]." *Právny obzor* 104 (2): 116–140.

———, Kamil Baraník, and Šimon Drugda. 2018. "Slovakia: The State of Liberal Democracy." In *The I·CONnect-Clough Center 2017 Global Review of Constitutional Law*, edited by Richard Albert, David Landau, Pietro Faraguna, and Šimon Drugda, 249–254. Boston: I•CONnect and the Clough Center.

Láštic, Erik. 2020. "Slovakia in the Time of Pandemic." *V4 Human Rights Review* 2 (2): 38–40.

———, and Max Steuer. 2019. "The Slovak Constitutional Court: The Third Legislator?" In *Constitutional Politics and the Judiciary: Decision-Making in Central and Eastern Europe*, edited by Kálmán Pócza, 184–213. London: Routledge.

Lübbe-Wolff, Gertrude. 2020. "Why Is the German Federal Constitutional Court a Deliberative Court, and Why Is That a Good Thing? A Comparative Assessment." In

Collective Judging in Comparative Perspective: Counting Votes and Weighing Options, edited by Birke Häcker and Wolfgang Ernst, 157–179. Cambridge: Intersentia.

Macejková, Ivetta. 2018. *Ochrana ústavnosti a Ústavy Slovenskej republiky za rok 2017. Prehľad rozhodovacej a ďalšej činnosti Ústavného súdu Slovenskej republiky za rok 2017 [The Protection of Constitutionality and the Constitution of the Slovak Republic in the Year 2017. An Overview of the Decision Making and Other Activity of the Constitutional Court of the Slovak Republic in the Year 2017]*. Košice: Ústavný súd Slovenskej republiky.

———, ed. 2020. *Zákon o Ústavnom súde Slovenskej republiky: Komentár [The Act on the Constitutional Court of the Slovak Republic: A Commentary]*. Bratislava: C. H. Beck.

Mazák, Ján, and Ladislav Orosz. 2018. "Quashing the Decisions on Amnesty in the Constitutional System of the Slovak Republic: Opening or Closing Pandora's Box?" *The Lawyer Quarterly* 8 (1): 1–21.

Mikušovič, Dušan. 2018. "Procházka v prvom rozhovore po roku a pol: Koniec v politike som si zaslúžil, bol by som dobrý ústavný sudca [Procházka in the First Interview after a Year and a Half: I Deserved the End in Politics, I Would Be a Good Constitutional Judge]." *Denník N*, February 20. https://dennikn.sk/1034919/prochazka-v-prvom-rozhovore-po-roku-a-pol-koniec-v-politike-som-si-zasluzil-bol-by-som-dobry-ustavny-sudca/.

Ministry of Justice of the Slovak Republic. 2020. *LP/2020/267 Ústavný zákon, ktorým sa mení a dopĺňa Ústava Slovenskej republiky č. 460/1992 Zb. v znení neskorších predpisov* [Constitutional Act Amending the Constitution of the Slovak Republic No. 460/1992 Coll. as Amended]. www.slov-lex.sk/legislativne-procesy/-/SK/LP/2020/267.

National Council of the Slovak Republic. 2020a. *Pozmeňujúci návrh k vládnemu návrhu ústavného zákona, ktorým sa mení a dopĺňa Ústava Slovenskej republiky č. 460/1992 Zb. v znení neskorších predpisov* [Altering proposal for the government Bill Amending the Constitution of the Slovak Republic No. 460/1992 Coll. as Amended]. www.nrsr.sk/web/Dynamic/DocumentPreview.aspx?DocID=488509.

———. 2020b. *Pozmeňujúci návrh k vládnemu návrhu ústavného zákona, ktorým sa mení a dopĺňa Ústava Slovenskej republiky č. 460/1992 Zb. v znení neskorších predpisov* [Altering proposal for the government Bill Amending the Constitution of the Slovak Republic No. 460/1992 Coll. as Amended]. www.nrsr.sk/web/Dynamic/DocumentPreview.aspx?DocID=488508.

———. 2020c. "Transcript, No. 28 [Mária Kolíková]." https://tv.nrsr.sk/transcript?id=233632.

———. 2020d. 'Transcript, No. 34 [Ondrej Dostál]." https://tv.nrsr.sk/transcript?id=233634.

———. 2020e. "Transcript, No. 55 [Mária Kolíková]." https://tv.nrsr.sk/transcript?id=233662.

———. 2020f. "Transcript, No. 71, 73 [Rastislav Schlosár]." https://tv.nrsr.sk/transcript?id=233503.

———. 2020g. "Transcript, No. 85 [Ján Podmanický]." https://tv.nrsr.sk/transcript?id=233518.

———. 2020h. "Transcript, No. 103 [Ivan Fiačan]." https://tv.nrsr.sk/transcript?id=233538.

———. 2020i. "Transcript, No. 107 [Mária Kolíková]." https://tv.nrsr.sk/transcript?id=233559.

———. 2020j. "Transcript, No. 108 [Mária Kolíková]." https://tv.nrsr.sk/transcript?id=230558.

———. 2020k. "Transcript, No. 109 [Ondrej Dostál]." https://tv.nrsr.sk/transcript?id=233544.

———. 2020l. "Transcript, No. 112 [Juraj Šeliga]." https://tv.nrsr.sk/transcript?id=230563.

———. 2020m. "Transcript, No. 142 [Ľuboš Blaha]." https://tv.nrsr.sk/transcript?id=233579.

———. 2020n. "Vládny návrh ústavného zákona, ktorým sa mení a dopĺňa Ústava Slovenskej republiky č. 460/1992 Zb. v znení neskorších predpisov" [Government Bill Amending the Constitution of the Slovak Republic No. 460/1992 Coll. as Amended]. www.nrsr.sk/web/Default.aspx?sid=zakony/zakon&MasterID=7962.

———. 2020o. "Hlasovanie č. 219" [Voting Call no. 219]. www.nrsr.sk/web/Default.aspx?sid=schodze/hlasovanie/hlasklub&ID=45141.

Orosz, Ladislav. 2021. "Justičná novela Ústavy Slovenskej republiky (solídne zámery – rozpačité závery) [Judicial amendment to the Constitution of the Slovak Republic (solid intentions – embarrassing conclusions)]." In *Úvahy o zmenách v ústavnej úprave súdnej moci a ich dopady na rozhodovaciu činnosť Ústavného súdu Slovenskej republiky – IX. ústavné dni*, edited by Ladislav Orosz, Sabina Grabowska, and Tomáš Majerčák, 79–97. Košice: Univerzita P. J. Šafárika.

Petrov, Jan. 2022. "(De-)Judicialization of Politics in the Era of Populism: Lessons from Central and Eastern Europe." *The International Journal of Human Rights* 26 (7): 1181–1206.

Pócza, Kálmán, Gábor Dobos, and Attila Gyulai. 2019. "Courts Compared: The Practice of Constitutional Adjudication in Central and Eastern Europe." In *Constitutional Politics and the Judiciary: Decision-Making in Central and Eastern Europe*, edited by Kálmán Pócza, 213–246. London: Routledge.

Procházka, Radoslav. 2011. *Ľud a sudcovia v konštitučnej demokracii [The People and Judges in a Constitutional Democracy]*. Plzeň: Aleš Čeněk.

Prušová, Veronika. 2019. "Bývalý ústavný sudca Mészáros: Ak chcete byť slobodný, musíte byť samotárom [Former constitutional judge Mészáros: If you want to be free, you have to be a loner]." *Denník N*, Februar 23, 2019. https://dennikn.sk/1391363/byvaly-ustavny-sudca-meszaros-ak-chcete-byt-slobodny-musite-byt-samotarom/#?ref=menu.

Robertson, David. 2010. *The Judge as Political Theorist: Contemporary Constitutional Review*. Princeton: Princeton University Press.

Sadurski, Wojciech. 2014. *Rights Before Courts: A Study of Constitutional Courts in Postcommunist States of Central and Eastern Europe*. 2nd ed. Dordrecht: Springer.

Sajó, András, and Renáta Uitz. 2017. *The Constitution of Freedom: An Introduction to Legal Constitutionalism*. Oxford: Oxford University Press.

Šipulová, Katarína, and Max Steuer. 2023. "From Minimalism to the Substantive Core and Back: The Slovak Constitutional Court and (the Lack of) Constitutional Identity." In *The Jurisprudence of Particularism: National Identity Claims in Central Europe*, edited by Kriszta Kovács, 81–104. Oxford: Hart.

Steuer, Max. 2017. "Kto a ako vyberá strážcov? Legitimita výberu sudcov Ústavného súdu Slovenskej republiky v komparatívnej perspektíve [Who Selects the Guardians and How? Legitimacy of the Selection of Constitutional Court Judges of the Slovak Republic in a Comparative Perspective]." *Právník* 156 (4): 338–356.

———. 2018. "On the Brink of Joining Poland and Hungary: The Night of Surprises in the Slovak Parliament." *Verfassungsblog* (blog), October 25. https://verfassungsblog.de/on-the-brink-of-joining-poland-and-hungary-the-night-of-surprises-in-the-slovak-parliament/.

———. 2019a. "Constitutional Court of the Slovak Republic." In *Max Planck Encyclopedia of Comparative Constitutional Law*, edited by Rainer Grote, Frauke Lachenmann, and Rüdiger Wolfrum. Oxford: Oxford University Press.

———. 2019b. "The Guardians and the Watchdogs: The Framing of Politics, Partisanship and Qualification by Selected Newspapers during the 2018–2019 Slovak Constitutional Court Appointment Process." *Právny Obzor* 102 (Special Issue): 34–54.

———. 2019c. "The First Live-Broadcast Hearings of Candidates for Constitutional Judges in Slovakia: Five Lessons." *Verfassungsblog* (blog), February 5. https://verfassungsblog.de/the-first-live-broadcast-hearings-of-candidates-for-constitutional-judges-in-slovakia-five-lessons/.

———. 2022. "The Extreme Right as a Defender of Human Rights? Parliamentary Debates on COVID-19 Emergency Legislation in Slovakia." *Laws* 11 (2): 17.

———. 2023. "Democracy, Procedural and Social Rights, and Constitutional Courts in Hungary and Slovakia." *Constitutional Review* 9 (1): 28–76.

Štiavnický, Ján, and Max Steuer. 2020. "The Many Faces of Law-Making by Constitutional Courts with Extensive Review Powers: The Slovak Case." In *Judicial Law-Making in European Constitutional Courts*, edited by Monika Florczak-Wątor, 183–200. London: Routledge.

TASR. 2014. "Ústavný súd stopol zákon, že starosta musí mať strednú školu [The Constitutional Court Halted the Law Stipulating that Mayors Must Have Graduated High School]." *domov.sme.sk*, September 10. https://domov.sme.sk/c/7376713/ustavny-sud-stopol-zakon-ze-starosta-musi-mat-strednu-skolu.html.

———. 2020. "Poslanec Podmanický, ktorý opustil Smer, chce v parlamente spájať konzervatívcov [MP Podmanický, Who Left Smer, Wants to Unite Conservatives in Parliament]." *HNonline.sk*, May 22. https://slovensko.hnonline.sk/2151371-poslanec-podmanicky-ktory-opustil-smer-chce-v-parlamente-spajat-konzervativcov.

Tódová, Monika. 2021. "Predseda Ústavného súdu Fiačan: Po troške sa začala obnovovať dôvera občanov v justíciu [Constitutional Court President Fiačan: Bit by Bit, the Citizens' Trust in the Judiciary Has Started to Be Restored]." *Denník N*, May 20, sec. Audio. https://dennikn.sk/2396748/predseda-ustavneho-sudu-fiacan-po-troske-sa-zacala-obnovovat-dovera-obcanov-v-justiciu/.

Uitz, Renáta. 2007. "Constitutional Courts in Central and Eastern Europe: What Makes a Question Too Political." *Juridica International* 13: 47–59.

Waldron, Jeremy. 2006. "The Core of the Case against Judicial Review." *The Yale Law Journal* 115 (6): 1346–1406.

Zielonka, Jan. 2014. "The Rise of a Neo-Medieval Order in Europe." In *Civilizations and World Order: Geopolitics and Cultural Difference*, edited by Fred Dallmayr, M. Akif Kayapinar, and Ismail Yaylaci, 193–204. Lanham, Maryland: Lexington Books.

Zreik, Raef. 2019. "Ronald Dworkin and Duncan Kennedy: Two Views of Interpretation." *Canadian Journal of Law & Jurisprudence* 32 (1): 195–234.

11 The Slovenian Constitutional Court

Courage in times of political instability

Polona Batagelj

11.1 Introduction

In 1991, the Constitutional Court of the Republic of Slovenia (hereinafter: SloCC or Court) assumed its current role as the constitutional court of an autonomous state (Mavčič 1999, 13; Božič et al. 2016, 9). During the 30 years of its existence, the Court has made a significant contribution to the transformation of an authoritarian regime into a new socio-political order based on the rule of law, the defence of human rights, and human dignity (Slovenija 2016, 8). As the present chapter shows, it can be argued that the SloCC was able to exert the greatest influence on the legislature during periods of political instability due to political fragmentation. Moreover, the SloCC used a variety of instruments in its decisions. This diversity was most pronounced in the early years, when the SloCC was tasked with supervising the building of the entire Slovenian legal system and ensuring compliance with basic legal principles. Only rarely did the Court decide to invalidate an entire piece of legislation. Instead, it often added a prescription and a remedy. In this way, it acted as an active legislator while placing great emphasis on the separation of powers. This chapter first gives a brief overview of the history and organization of the Court, then it outlines the trends in majority decisions in terms of their diversity and strength. Finally, dissenting opinions and the dissenting coalitions of judges are analysed, followed by a conclusion with general remarks.

11.2 History of constitutional review in Slovenia

The former Socialist Federal Republic of Yugoslavia (hereafter SFRY) and the Socialist Republic of Slovenia (hereafter SRS), as its federal unit, established their constitutional courts as early as 1963, which was a peculiarity among Eastern European countries (Accetto 2010, 132). The former Slovenian Constitutional Court of the Socialist Republic of Slovenia (hereafter also SRSLCC) thus belonged to a federal entity. The SRSLCC was established by the 1963 Constitution of the SRS which, by contrast, also declared the principle of the unity of state powers (Mavčič 1999, 13). This Constitution introduced some basic principles that are binding on the activity of the SRSLCC and

DOI: 10.4324/9781003399483-11

represented a step towards the enforcement of the principle of the supremacy of the constitution over the parliament (Mavčič 1995, 82). The establishment of the SRSLCC thus entailed a new kind of judicial review, which initially led to serious discussions about its compatibility with the principle of the unity of state power. It was emphasized at the time that constitutional review did not involve any element of separation of powers in the constitutional system. Rather, it is an integral, essential part of the parliamentary system, in which the principle of the supremacy of parliament still prevails (Mavčič 1995, 82–83).

The characteristic features of the SRSLCC, which at that time was responsible for protecting the constitutionality of the laws and legal acts of the Socialist Republic of Slovenia, as Mavčič (1995) notes, were somewhat different than today. These peculiarities included, for example, the fact that the SRSLCC could initiate proceedings *ex officio*, a power which is rarely granted to constitutional courts nowadays. The "letter to the Parliament" was also an important instrument of the Court in enforcing the constitutionality of legal acts of the SRS. This tool was most frequently used in connection with inaction on the part of the legislature or of a particular body in regulating an area within its competence. The SRSLCC informed the Parliament about such lapses in the form of a letter. Even more astonishing was the fact that anyone had the right to appeal to the SRSLCC without having a personal interest in a specific case (*actio popularis*). Furthermore, the SRSLCC was empowered to protect constitutional rights and fundamental freedoms. Nevertheless, it was also established that the judgments of the ordinary courts cannot be appealed to the SRSLCC and that the SRSLCC is therefore not hierarchically superior to the ordinary courts. In principle, the SRSLCC was responsible for protecting the rights of individuals if no other legal protection was provided.

It should be stressed, however, that even under the 1974 Constitution of the SRS, the SRSLCC did not have the competences of real constitutional review because it could not declare a law unconstitutional. Consequently, the Parliament of the SRS remained the only power centre. This meant that if the SRSLCC decided that a law passed by the Parliament of the SRS was inconsistent with the Constitution, this decision was communicated to the Parliament, which had six months to ensure that the law was harmonized with the Constitution of the SRS. If this did not happen, the law became ineffective, which meant that the SRSLCC only performed the task of indirect cassation. Upon the proposal of the Parliament, the SRSLCC could extend the deadline for the harmonization of the law by a maximum of six months (Mavčič 1995, 85).

It should also be emphasized that the SRSLCC was not in a hierarchical position *vis-à-vis* the Federal Constitutional Court of the SFRY. Therefore, the Federal Constitutional Court of the SFRY did not have the power to rule on the constitutionality of the constitutions of the member states or to intervene directly in the content of any legal regulation adopted by the parliaments of the member states of the federation. It could only issue an opinion for consideration by the Parliament of the SFRY, which, moreover, was not empowered to make a binding decision on the legal regulations of the federated states (Accetto 2010, 132, 133; Sadurski 2002, 214).

11.3 Organization of the Slovenian Constitutional Court

More than 30 years ago, on 25 June 1991, the Republic of Slovenia became an independent state with the adoption of the Basic Constitutional Charter on the Sovereignty and Independence of the Republic of Slovenia. With this Charter, Slovenia reaffirmed its commitment to respecting human rights and fundamental freedoms. Six months later, on 23 December 1991, a new Constitution was adopted.[1] The adoption of these documents led to the secession of the Republic of Slovenia from the SFRY (Slovenija 2016, 7). As a result of this process, the new Constitutional Court of the Republic of Slovenia became the constitutional court of a sovereign state and the highest organ of the judiciary for the protection of constitutionality, legality, human rights, and fundamental freedoms (Mavčič 1999, 13; Božič et al. 2016, 9).[2] This meant that the SloCC could rule on the unconstitutionality of a law and had the final say in the constitutional review processes.

Today the SloCC operates as an independent and autonomous state organ, regulating its internal organization and procedures by its own rules. The Court's position was further strengthened by the adoption of the Constitutional Court Act (CCA) in 1994, which expanded the scope of the review of the constitutionality of legal regulations and other legal acts to include (*a posteriori*) abstract and concrete review (Mavčič 2000, 51). The SloCC's competences include deciding on the compatibility of laws and regulations with ratified international treaties and the general principles of international law; on constitutional complaints of violations of human rights and fundamental freedoms; on jurisdictional disputes between the National Assembly, the President of the Republic, and the government; on charges against the President of the Republic, the government, and ministers for violations of the Constitution and laws; on complaints against the confirmation of the parliamentary mandate and on the unconstitutionality of the activities of political parties. The Slovenian system thus followed the German model in structuring the competences of the Constitutional Court (Mavčič 1995, 71). Since 2013, the SloCC has also had the power to decide on disputes over the admissibility of referenda.

In principle, the SloCC has jurisdiction only to review regulations that are in force, but under certain circumstances it may review legal acts that are no longer in effect. International treaties, in contrast, are reviewed by the SloCC

1 Constitution of the Republic of Slovenia (Official Gazette of the Republic of Slovenia, No. 33/91-I, 42/97, 66/2000, 24/03, 69/04, 68/06, 47/13, and 75/16).

2 See Article 1 of the CCA (Official Gazette of the Republic of Slovenia, No. 64/07 – official consolidated text, 109/12, 23/20, and 92/21).

before they will be ratified (Božič et al. 2016, 38–39) – following the French model of preventive constitutional review (Mavčič 1995, 71; Škrk 2006, 73–96).[3] In these latter procedures, the SloCC does not issue a decision, but an opinion binding on the National Assembly. As the SloCC explained in detail in its Opinion No. Rm-1/02: "The *a priori* constitutional review of treaties is intended to prevent the State, by ratifying a treaty, from entering into an obligation under international law that is incompatible with the Constitution, or from being forced, after ratification, to bring the treaty into conformity with the Constitution, which could lead to serious complications".[4]

Unlike the SRSLCC, the SloCC cannot initiate a constitutional review process *ex officio*. Pursuant to Article 23a of the CCA, proceedings to review the constitutionality of a legislative provision or law may be initiated by the National Assembly, one-third of the deputies, the National Council, the Government, the Ombudsman, the Information Commissioner, the National Bank of Slovenia and the Court of Audit, the Prosecutor General, a representative body of the local community (when it interferes with the constitutional status or constitutional rights of the local government), or a representative association of the local community (if the rights of the local community are threatened). In addition, a procedure to review the constitutionality of a legal provision or law may also begin with a petition filed by anyone who demonstrates a legal interest. Such an interest exists when a legal provision or act directly interferes with his or her rights or legal position (Article 24 of the CCA). Proof of a legal interest by the applicant serves to limit the instrument of *actio popularis*. Given the increasing congestion at the SloCC and the fact that individuals have access to the Court through a constitutional complaint process, one could argue that a restrictive approach to the interpretation of legal interest is justified (Nerad 2005).

Another peculiarity is the so-called declaratory decision, which is provided for in Article 48 of the CCA. This type of decision is issued by the SloCC when it finds that the law is unconstitutional because: (1) it does not regulate a certain issue that it was supposed to regulate (legislative omission); or (2) it regulates it in a way that does not allow for repeal or abolition (Čebulj 2000, 191–196; Mavčič 1995, 72–74, 2000, 270–272; Testen 2000b, 1130–1137). These cases are presented in more detail in the text that follows.

Petitions on the basis of which the SloCC initiates proceedings are first examined by the Court in a preliminary procedure (Article 27 of the CCA).[5] If a case has been declared admissible, the SloCC shall decide whether to deal

3 According to the second paragraph of its Article 160 (Powers of the Constitutional Court), the Slovenian Constitution regulates the preventive (a priori) constitutional review of treaties only.

4 See opinion no. Rm-1/02.

5 As for the petition, the SloCC has the following preselection procedure according to Article 26 of the CCA: it shall first be examined by a judge of the Constitutional Court as determined by the work schedule, who shall collect the data and explanations necessary for deciding whether the Constitutional Court should initiate proceedings.

with it in closed session or, exceptionally, in a public hearing (Article 29 of the CCA). The President of the SloCC may initiate a public hearing either on his own initiative or at the request of the parties. However, the President of the SloCC must convene a public hearing if at least three judges request it (Article 35 of the CCA). The SloCC always takes its decisions in closed sessions (*in camera*) (Article 40 of the CCA). The default rule for decision-making is a majority vote, and judges may not abstain from voting (Article 41 of the CCA).

A judge who disagrees with a decision or the reasoning of a decision may submit a separate opinion (dissenting or concurring), which he or she must submit within the time limit specified in the Rules of Procedure of the Constitutional Court, i.e. seven days from the date on which the judges receive the text of the decision confirmed and signed by the Secretary General. A separate opinion may be submitted only by those who, after voting on the decision, have declared that they will submit such an opinion (Articles 71–72 of the Rules of Procedure of the Constitutional Court).

Pursuant to Articles 163 and 165 of the Constitution, the SloCC is composed of nine judges, including the President of the SloCC, who are elected for a term of nine years, without the possibility of re-election. Parliament elects the judges by a majority of all deputies on the proposal of the President of the Republic (Articles 10–15 of the CCA). Every citizen of the Republic of Slovenia who is a legal expert and is at least 40 years old is eligible for these positions (Article 9 of the CCA).[6] There are no restrictions on who may propose candidates to the President of the Republic, no limit on the number of candidates for any office, and no substantive restrictions on the President of the Republic regarding eligible candidates (Avbelj and Šušteršič 2019, 142; Avbelj et al. 2021a, 290–296). The President of the Republic may informally consult with experts of his or her choice, which in practice means that he or she usually consults parliamentary groups before proposing candidates, which reinforces the political nature of the selection and election of candidates (Avbelj et al. 2021a, 293).

The confirmation and election of constitutional judges is therefore politically coloured (Grad 2008, 10; Jevšek 2021, 175), which in practice is often reflected in right-wing and the left-wing political camps electing judges primarily according to their political orientation. Consequently, the selection and election of judges usually depends on the current political context (Jevšek 2021, 175–176). For this reason, many scholars have proposed adopting a

6 The CCA does not specify what the term "legal expert" means, i.e. in specific terms of education, work experience, or the legal field of work. This is reflected in the very different profiles of Slovenian constitutional judges. In principle, the profile of a constitutional judge with a previous career as a supreme judge prevails in the Slovenian Constitutional Court. It is followed by law professors and former employees of the Constitutional Court (advisers, secretaries-general) (Jevšek 2021, 186).

different approach to the election process (Avbelj et al. 2021a, 290–296; Jerovšek 1998; Kaučič 2006; 2007; 2014; Tratar 2017; Zalar 2008), which would, however, require amending the Constitution. Most of these proposals envisage a larger number of nominees, which would mean that, for example, in addition to the President of the Republic and the Parliament, the Judicial Council would also have the right to nominate and elect candidates. Of course, even such a system would not guarantee that those nominated would not follow political interests, but it is still expected that this would lead to a more politically balanced composition of the SloCC (Avbelj et al. 2021a, 291). Thus, one of the ways to protect the SloCC from being subordinated to the political parties and majorities would be to tighten the criteria for judicial office and to establish an independent panel of experts (following the practice of the ECJ) to assess the professional suitability of candidates instead of the President of the Republic. This body would hear each candidate, assess his or her competence, and send a detailed but non-binding opinion to the President of the Republic. The President and the Parliament should assume political responsibility if they contravene it (Avbelj et al. 2021a, 292–293).

It would also make sense to introduce a staggered procedure for the appointment of constitutional judges, as is used in France, Spain, and Italy, meaning that every three years, three constitutional judges whose term of office has expired should be replaced. This is to prevent all nine judges from being appointed by the same or a politically and ideologically very similar parliamentary majority (as was the case in the second term of the SloCC). Moreover, when only one judge is appointed, it is more difficult to expect that the opinions of the parliamentary minority will be taken into account (Avbelj et al. 2021a, 295).

11.4 Trends in majority rulings

The SloCC played an important role at the beginning of the democratic transition and consolidation process (Slovenija 2016, 8). It elaborated basic doctrines and established the formal legal standards of constitutional democracy and the rule of law (Slovenija 2016, 8; Letnar Černič 2021, 57). Of course, the Court later adhered to these basic values and developed or significantly supplemented the principles adopted by the first Court (Slovenija 2016, 21).

The JUDICON project coded 799 decisions and 1,055 rulings of the SloCC. The SloCC thus makes more than one ruling per decision, or more precisely 1.3 rulings per decision (Figure 11.1). The number of decisions and rulings peaked in 1998, which is also related to the adoption of the first set of Rules of Procedure of the Constitutional Court, by which it independently regulated its organization and work, as well as the rules of procedure before the SloCC.

The activity of the SloCC can be divided into four periods, interrupted by interim periods: the first period lasted from 1993 to 1998; the second from

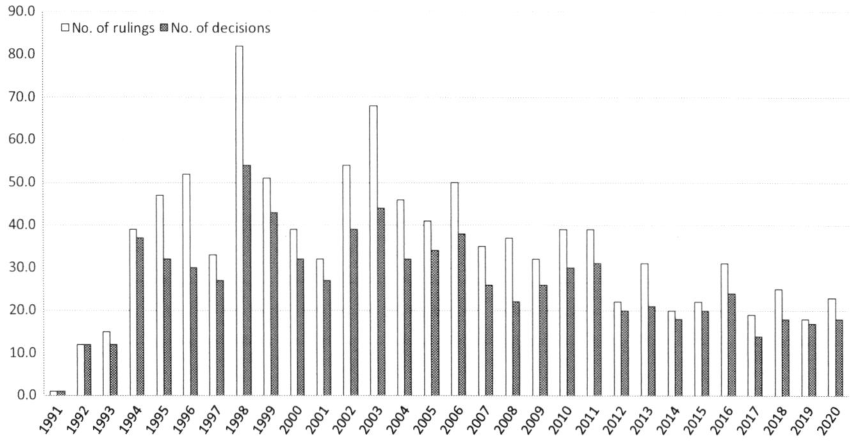

Figure 11.1 Number of decisions and rulings (1991–2020) (SloCC)

2002–2007; the third from 2011–2017; and the fourth period lasted from 2021 to the present day. The judges of the first period were nominated by Milan Kučan, who was President of the Republic from 23 December 1991 to 22 December 2002. The first six judges were elected by the first centre-right coalition, but all of them were also supported by opposition parties (Avbelj, Polona, and Janez 2020, III; Jevšek 2021, 187–191).[7] The other three judges (Lojze Ude, Boštjan M. Zupančič, and Franc Testen) were elected by a centre-left coalition led by Janez Drnovšek, who was prime minister from 14 May 1992, to 19 December 2002 (except for the second half of 2000). Moreover, Judge Testen was also supported by the opposition parties, which means that no less than seven judges in the first period enjoyed cross-party support.

Which political parties support or oppose the nomination of a candidate can be seen most clearly in the vote and (if it takes place) the discussion of the MPs in the parliamentary session. Thus, despite the secret ballot, it is possible to determine whether or not a constitutional judge received broader political support (Jevšek 2021, 176, 191). When the debate takes place, it focuses mainly on the candidate's past work while considering any concerns about his or her political and ideological affiliation (Jevšek 2021, 176, 191). Thus, the voting results show that the coalition and opposition parties were more united in the appointment to the court of the first judges than at any later time (Jevšek 2021, 187–191). Probably because of this, and due to the fact that until 2004 the governing coalitions always included a party with a divergent ideological background (Zajc 2013, 757), there were no significant fluctuations in the strength of rulings of the SloCC until 2003 (Figure 11.2).

7 Janez Šinkovec, Lovro Šturm, Peter Jambrek, Tone Jerovšek, Matjaž Krivic, Janez Snoj.

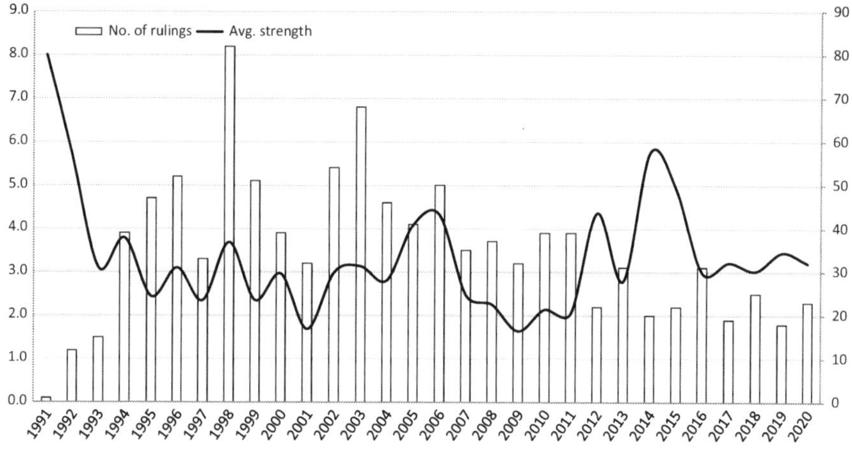

Figure 11.2 Number and average strength of rulings (1991–2020) (SloCC)

The strength of the SloCC's rulings started to increase between 2004 and 2006.[8] At this point, the composition of the court was quite homogeneous. All nine judges had been elected by a centre-left coalition. Since Slovenia had a right-wing government during this period, it is not surprising that the strength of its decisions increased. In contrast, as shown in Figure 11.2, the strength of rulings decreased again in 2007 and 2008, after new judges were appointed, and the SloCC gained a more diverse composition. Six judges (who served on the third court) were appointed by the same centre-right government. Then, from 2011 until the end of 2014, the trend of increasing ruling strength can be observed again. This may be due to the political instability in Slovenia at that time. At the end of 2011 the first early elections in Slovenia's history were called. This happened mainly due to external circumstances, as the government began its term at a time of escalating economic crisis. This recession hit Slovenia much harder than other EU member states, as the state continued to hold shares in companies and banks (Zajc 2013, 758). Even the next centre-right government under Janez Janša was in power for just over a year. The work of this government was again affected by the deteriorating economic situation, under the pressure of which the government took austerity measures (Zajc 2013, 761). Many laws were prepared and passed in a hurry, which resulted in many provisions violating the constitution (Zajc 2013, 761). In addition to the economic crisis, many clashes and the formation of new governing coalitions can be explained by the fact that they were not formed on the basis of the previously well-coordinated interests and identifiable common goals (Zajc 2013, 765).

8 Judges: Dragica Wedam Lukić, Mirjam Škrk, Janez Čebulj, Lojze Janko, Milojka Modrijan, Zvonko Fišer, Ciril Ribičič, Marija Krisper Kramberger, Jože Tratnik.

Consequently, it could be argued that the SloCC had its strongest constraining effect on the legislature in times of political instability caused by political fragmentation. Under such circumstances, courts usually assume institutional power to replace representative actors (Musella and Rullo 2021, 100), because the more dysfunctional or gridlocked the political system, the more likely the judiciary is to expand (Guarnieri and Pederzoli, 2002, 160–181). Consequently, space opens up for stronger court rulings because the constitutional court need not fear a backlash. The strongest rulings during this period are mainly in the areas of taxation, public finance, and social affairs, which could primarily be due to the economic crisis happening during this period and the government's reaction to it. While these are the areas in which the legislature otherwise has a great deal of discretion, government measures must still comply with human rights (especially the principle of equality), non-retroactivity, and clarity (Podlipnik 2019, 367–372). The particular combination of the economic and social crisis and political fragmentation, however, allowed the SloCC to intervene in areas originally reserved for the executive and legislative branches. All in all, we can conclude that changes in the government and in parliamentary majorities influenced the evolution of the strength of rulings. The rulings were strongest in times of political instability.

11.4.1 Trends in ruling types

The dominant form of SloCC's rulings during the whole time period under scrutiny was rejection. In addition to substantive unconstitutionality (37.5%), legislative omission was also declared quite frequently (9.6%). Procedural unconstitutionality (0.6%), constitutional requirement (2.1%), and restrictive constitutional interpretation *in abstracto* (0.1%) were, in contrast, very rare rulings.

Of all "non-rejections", 75% were findings of substantive unconstitutionality. It should be noted that the SloCC has repeatedly found unconstitutionality based on various aspects of the rule of law principle: accessibility, clarity, predictability, necessary preparation time, or retroactivity. Substantive unconstitutionality is followed by legislative omission (19.2 %). Slightly over 5% of the "non-rejections" were distributed among procedural constitutionality, constitutional requirement, and restrictive constitutional interpretation *in abstracto*.

Figure 11.3 shows the distribution of ruling types over time. The use of different decision-making approaches was somewhat more pronounced in the early years of the court. Until 2006, the court quite frequently declared constitutional requirements, a ruling type that later disappeared. By contrast, legislative omission was a popular tool throughout the period under scrutiny. The relative diversity of rulings in the first period (especially until 1998), i.e. the frequent use of constitutional requirements and declarations of legislative omission, can be attributed to the aforementioned fact that the first court was active in the early period of the new state, when the aim was to ensure respect for constitutional values and the rule of law.

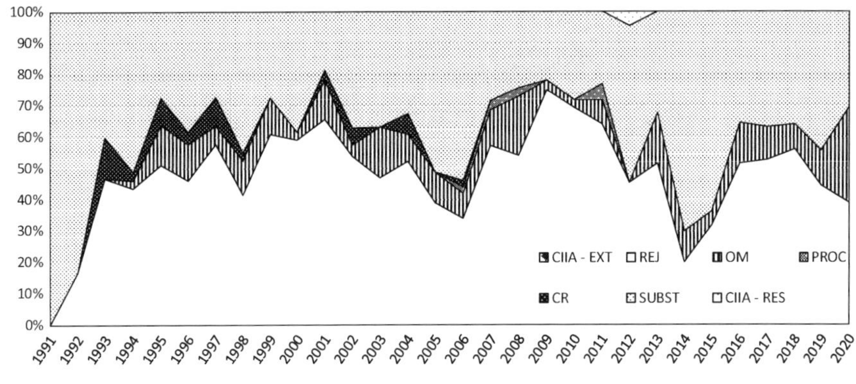

Figure 11.3 Frequency of the ruling types (1991–2020) (SloCC)

Nevertheless, in doing so, it opted for milder forms of rulings, thus giving the legislature more room to manoeuvre in order to avoid confrontation with the Parliament. This was also necessary to respect and consolidate the principle of separation of powers, which replaced the principle of unity of powers enshrined in the previous socialist constitution. A particularly significant decline in rejections is observable between 2011 and 2014. This can be explained by the economic crisis, political instability, constantly changing governments and parliamentary majorities, the hasty passage of laws and, consequently, the growing inclination of the SloCC to intervene in legislation. There seem to be two periods when rejection is exceptionally high. These are the period from 1999–2001 and again from 2008–2010, i.e. the transition years between the first and second court and the second and third court, i.e. the period of appointment of new judges. The performance of the SloCC during these interim years suggests that court became less active with the arrival of new judges.

11.4.2 Prescription and completeness

Turning to prescriptions, it should be noted that SloCC included a prescription in 15% of all the rejections. These are the cases in which the SloCC found that a law is unconstitutional and explicitly abandoned the law's annulment but set a deadline for the legislature to remedy the unconstitutionality. These are the so-called declaratory decisions provided for in Article 48 of the CCA (Čebulj 2000, 191–196; Mavčič 1995, 72–74, 2000, 270–272; Testen 2000b, 1130–1137). They may be based on various reasons, which may also be interwoven. Nerad (2011, 1491–1502) describes these reasons in detail: (a) grammatical grounds (a contested provision cannot be annulled on the basis of the rules of grammar, otherwise the rest of the text would be linguistically incorrect or meaningless); (b) nomotechnical grounds (an unconstitutional provision cannot be removed from the legal order in such a way that the rest of the provision retains its legal meaning); (c) the reason of it leading to more adverse consequences (the court does not repeal the challenged provision because it would lead to an even more serious unconstitutionality); and (d) the intention of the legislator (the court does not annul the law because the rest of the legal text would be contrary to the legislator's objective). These are, in fact, mere decisions that, apart from the legislature's duty to change the rule within a certain period of time, have no effect on the continued application of an unconstitutional law (Nerad 2011, 1491–1502).

Focusing on "non-zero" rulings, we can see that the SloCC used some kind of prescription in more than 50% of cases. This means that it added a remedy in every second "non-zero" decision, thus playing an active role as a positive legislator. The positive legislator function of the SloCC should thus be strongly emphasized. Undoubtedly, the SloCC also exercises negative legislative powers in reviewing the constitutionality of laws, as decisions by which the SloCC annuls or establishes the unconstitutionality of a law are binding and have *erga omnes* effect (Nerad 2019, 451–452).[9] Moreover, through the so-called determination of the manner of implementation of the SloCC decision the SloCC directly, albeit temporarily, assumes the function of the legislature (Pavčnik and Mavčič 2000, 163–164), since such decisions have the same legal force as a law (Krivic 1999; Nerad 2011, 1502–1505).

Thus, as long as the legislator does not eliminate the established unconstitutionality, the ordinary courts and other institutions must act as if the SloCC's decision were a law. Even in cases that are still pending, the SloCC's decision should be used as the legal basis for the final decision. In cases where the decision of an ordinary court does not follow the SloCC's guidance, this can later be challenged by a constitutional complaint. Thus, the power to determine the manner of enforcement of its decisions strengthens the position of the SloCC in relation to both the legislature and the judiciary (Nerad 2011, 1502–1505). It should be noted, however, that the legislature is not bound by the (provisional) prescriptions of the SloCC, i.e. it can also adopt rules that are different from the prescriptions of the SloCC. Nevertheless, the legislator, by and large, changes the legal regulation in accordance with the Constitutional Court's prescriptions, since it usually has no other options, as there is only one way to eliminate the unconstitutionality (Nerad 2011, 1502–1505).[10]

9 See Article 40 of the CCA and, for example, decision no. U-I-60/03, U-I-61/00, U-I-198/03.

10 See, for example, decision no. U-I-248/08, paragraph 20: "In order to suspend the unconstitutional state of affairs until the necessary act is adopted, on the basis of the third paragraph of Article 40 of the CCA the Constitutional Court determined the manner of the implementation of its decision and thus it determined that as of the day following the publication of the decision in the Official Gazette of the Republic of Slovenia, the President of the National Council was to perform his office professionally (paragraph 3 of the operative provisions). Thereby, the Constitutional Court has taken into consideration that the legislature could not have regulated the matter differently".

The SloCC very rarely annuls a complete law (in only 1.8% of all rulings, i.e. in 19 cases). The last time a complete law was annulled was in 2020 in its decision U-I-194/19, when the SloCC again underlined two important elements of the principle of separation of powers, stating that "the legislature has essentially enacted a concrete single act. In doing so, it impermissibly assumed the typical function of the executive branch and interfered with the powers of it". Since the SloCC hardly ever repeals a complete law, but often applies some sort of prescription and adds a remedy, we can conclude that it plays an active role as a positive legislator while attaching great importance to the principle of separation of powers.

11.4.3 Temporal effect

Pursuant to Article 161 of the Constitution and Article 43 of the CCA, the annulment of a law may take effect immediately (*ex nunc*) or within a time period determined by the SloCC (*pro futuro*). This period may not exceed one year. The SloCC pronounced *pro futuro* annulments in 10.2% of cases. As a rule, the Court makes use of this option when immediate annulment would have more serious consequences than postponement. As stated by the SloCC in its decision U-I-330/97: "Pursuant to Article 43 of the CCA, the Court may annul a law, the incompatibility of which with the Constitution it has determined, by means of a suspensive period, if there are constitutional grounds for which it must be permissible for the unconstitutional law to continue to be applied for a certain period of time". It is not surprising that in all other cases the Court annulled laws with *ex nunc* effect, since the *ex tunc* annulment of laws is not permissible. According to Article 161 of the Constitution, such annulment is possible only for other regulations or general legal acts, but not for laws.[11]

11.4.4 Constitutional requirements

Finally, this section will focus on constitutional requirements, i.e. interpretive decisions of the SloCC for which there is no specific legal basis in the Constitution.[12] Such decisions are necessary and useful when the challenged norm is understood and applied in practice in different ways. An interpretive decision preserves a challenged norm while excluding the unconstitutional application or definition of a norm with *erga omnes* effect (Testen 2000a, I-V; 2000b, 1131–1132). Due to its legal consequences, the SloCC in these cases does not annul legal provisions or parts thereof, but only excludes unconstitutional interpretations. However, this technique is rarely used by the SloCC (in only 22 cases). In temporal terms, interpretive decisions have the same effect

11 See Article 161 of the Constitution of the Republic of Slovenia.

12 See decision no. U-I-108/91.

as normal annulments (Nerad 2011, 1475–1478). Interpretive decisions can be divided into *positive* and *negative* decisions. A typical tenor of a positive interpretive decision is that the challenged provision "is not inconsistent with the Constitution" if interpreted in the manner described by the court in the operative part of the decision or in the reasoning (Nerad 2011, 1475–1478).[13]

It is important to note that the *negative* interpretive decisions appeared only later. In these negative interpretive decisions, only the interpretation that is unconstitutional and should not be used is determined. The choice between all other legally possible interpretations is thus left to the ordinary courts (Nerad 2003, 84–85): "The provision violates the Constitution" if it is interpreted in the manner described in the operative part of the decision (Nerad 2011, 1475–1478).

In his concurring opinion to decision U-I-308/02 from 2004, Judge Ribičič was the first judge to present a negative interpretative decision. He regarded as a disadvantage of positive interpretative decisions the fact that they allow only one constitutional interpretation of a regulation, thus excluding all other legal interpretations. Indeed, a *positive* interpretative decision excludes all legal interpretations (those that conform to the Constitution and those that do not) from the legal order, except for those that the SloCC makes in its decision. This makes positive interpretative decisions more compelling. The advantage of negative interpretative decisions is that they exclude only what is necessary and leave open other possible interpretations and the question of their compatibility with the Constitution. This type of decision thus interferes less with legislation and ordinary courts.

11.5 Trends in dissenting opinions

According to Article 71 of the Rules of Procedure of the SloCC, a judge may issue a separate opinion.[14] A separate opinion may also be issued by a group of judges, or a judge may join in support of the separate opinion of another judge. It can be argued that the publication of dissenting opinions is relatively rare at the SloCC. Of 1,055 rulings coded in this project, only 161 rulings contained at least one dissenting opinion. This means that judges decided to publish dissenting opinions in only 15% of the cases considered.

13 See, for example, decision no. U-I-301/95: "The provision of last indent of Paragraph 3 of Article 1 of the Amendments and Supplements to the Act on Privatization of Legal Persons Owned by the Fund of the Republic of Slovenia for Development and on Obligations of the Agency of the Republic of Slovenia for Restructuring and Privatization Act is not in conflict with the Constitution if interpreted in the sense that the imposed 60-day period started to run on the date of the coming into force of the Act".

14 The Rules of Procedure (Official Gazette of the Republic of Slovenia, No. 86/07, 54/10, 56/11, 70/17 and 35/20).

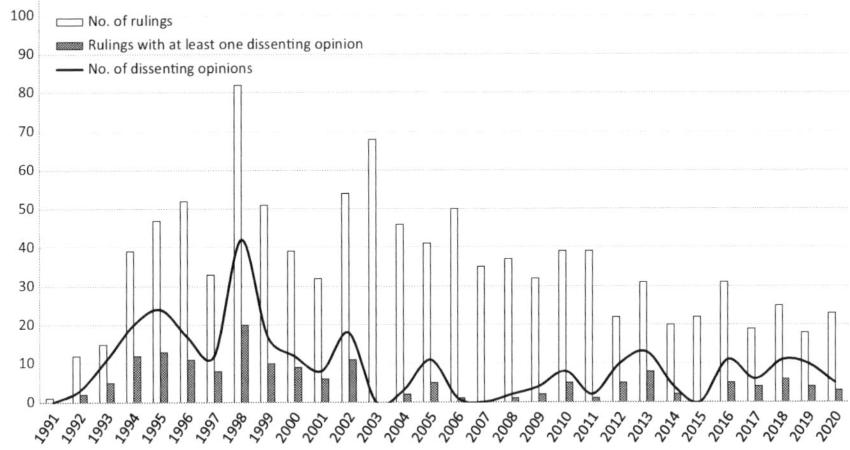

Figure 11.4 Number of rulings with at least one dissenting opinion (1991–2020) (SloCC)

The publication of dissenting opinions has been allowed since the beginning of the SloCC's activity. Interestingly, many dissenting opinions were published during the first 10 years of the Court's activity. The high number of dissenting opinions in the first court (Figure 11.4) can be explained by the fact that most of the judges had pursued academic careers (as law professors) before being elected to the SloCC. It is also generally accepted that most Slovenian judges (not only those of the first Court) who have had an academic career have issued more dissenting opinions than others who worked in other fields before being elected to the SloCC. Of the 285 total dissenting opinions, "academic" judges issued 162 (57%). At the top of the scale are Matjaž Krivic (49) and Lojze Ude (36), followed by Dragica Wedam Luké (13), Etelka Korpič Horvat (13), Boštjan M. Zupančič (12), Ciril Ribičič (12), Janez Čebulj (10), Peter Jambrek (7), Lovro Šturm (6), and finally Ernest Petrič and Mirjam Škrk with a total of 4 dissenting opinions.

11.5.1 *Judges clustered*

A few judges consistently issued dissenting opinions only in cases where they would have rejected the motion, implying that otherwise they would not have constrained the legislation in any way (Škrk, Klampfer, Zobec, Deisinger, Petrič, Knez, and Šugman Stubbs). At the other end of the scale, we find five judges – Tratnik, Šorli, Geč-Korošec, Šturm, and Snoj – who would have constrained the legislature more than the majority of the court. However, considering the fact that these judges issued only a minimal number of dissenting opinions, we cannot draw any clear conclusions from this data.

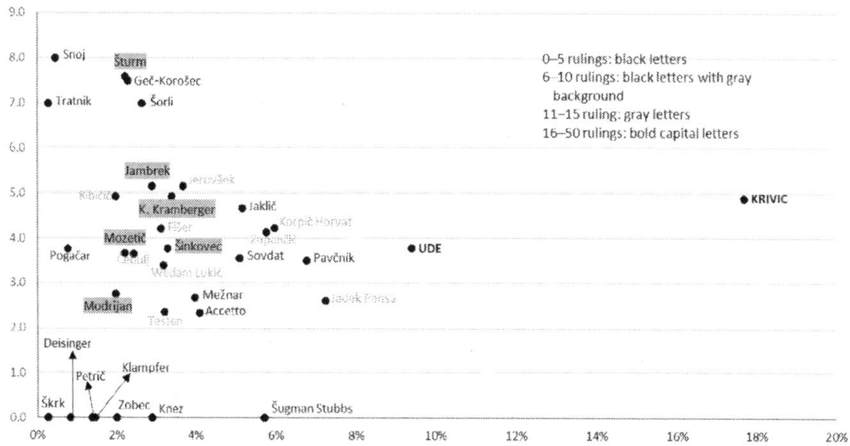

Figure 11.5 Proportion and strength of dissenting opinions (SloCC)

The highest number of dissenting opinions were issued by Judge Krivic (49) (Figure 11.5). He added a dissenting opinion in 17.7% of his rulings. Furthermore, his dissenting opinions were most of the time more constraining than the majority rulings. This could be explained by the fact that he was appointed by a centre-right governing coalition but served during the tenure of a centre-left government and parliamentary majority. The same applies to other judges of the first court – Šturm, Jambrek, Jerovšek, and Snoj – who, however, issued significantly fewer dissenting opinions during the same period. Judge Ude issued the second most dissenting opinions. His dissenting opinions also constrained the legislature more than those of the majority. The same is true for Judge Zupančič, while Judge Testen's dissenting opinions would have constrained the legislature less than the majority. This could be explained by the fact that these judges were appointed by the left-wing coalition parties, which were also in office during these judges' term, and for this reason they would have exerted less constraint against the left-wing parliamentary majority.

The trend of issuing fewer and fewer dissenting opinions continued during the Court's third term. As noted, there were four judges (Klampfer, Zobec, Deisinger, and Petrič) who did not want the legislator to be constrained by their dissenting opinions. They added dissenting opinions to the majority rulings only if they would have rejected the motion. Even the judge with the most dissenting opinions within this group, Jadek Pensa (14), would have constrained the legislature less than the majority. The dissenting opinions of the judges of the last court, on average would have constrained the legislature less than the majority. However, this is not true for Judges Šorli and Jaklič. Their appointment was the result of a political compromise, as these two clearly "right-wing" judges were appointed under the centre-left parliamentary majority (Avbelj, Šušteršič, and Batagelj 2021). At the same time, their dissenting opinions would have constrained the legislature more than the majority rulings. Of course, it must be pointed out that these are only five individual opinions in total. All in all, we should emphasize that due to the small percentage of dissenting opinions we cannot draw any clear conclusions regarding the judges' dissenting attitude.

The role of SloCC presidents should also be considered when examining trends in dissenting opinions. Since the judges elect the President of the SloCC from among themselves for a term of three years, this means that in most cases the President of the SloCC acts in a very neutral manner (Avbelj et al. 2021b, 162), but at the same time he encourages the judges to make unanimous decisions. Fundamentally, his leadership qualities, personality, and attitudes toward unanimity, as well as his behaviour are thought to influence the likelihood of dissenting opinions (Corley, Steigerwalt, and Ward 2013; Eisenberg and Miller 2009; Haynie 1992; Lanier 2011; Walker, Epstein, and Dixon 1988). This is also indicated by the fact that most presidents have issued 10 or fewer dissenting opinions (Figure 11.5).[15] As noted in other research projects, unanimous decision-making is an important driver of SloCC judges' behaviour. Judges are therefore willing to invest effort in negotiation and discourse to reach a consensus and to support decisions that differ from their ideology (Avbelj et al. 2020). Another reason for this inclination towards reaching a consensus is that judges are reluctant to publicly express their disagreement with the majority, as this could (in some cases) be understood as political support for the government (Avbelj et al. 2018, 23).

11.5.2 Dissenting coalitions

Figure 11.6 shows the divergent coalitions of 38 SloCC judges. On the right side of the figure are the judges of the first (and second) court. As noted earlier, they formulated dissenting opinions more frequently than judges in later time periods. The judges of the first court formed cross-party coalitions regardless of which governing coalition (left or right) appointed them. It is also true, however, that almost all judges in the first period enjoyed bipartisan support from the political elite. In the second court, when judges were appointed by centre-left coalition parties, there were fewer coalitions – the only strong coalition was between Fišer and Ribičič. However, the judges of the second court formed coalitions with the judges of the first court, regardless of whether they were appointed by left-wing parties (Ude and Testen) or right-wing coalition parties (Krivic).

15 Presidents: Jambrek, Jerovšek, Šturm, Testen, Wedam Lukić, Čebulj, Tratnik, Petrič, Mozetič, Sovdat, Knez.

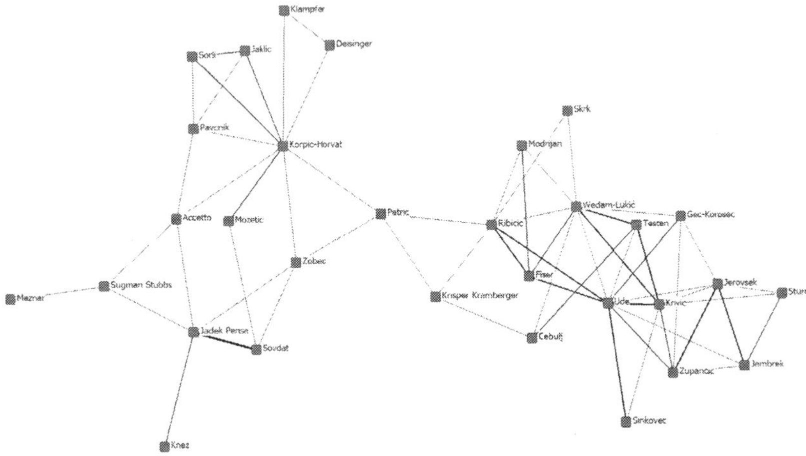

Figure 11.6 Dissenting coalitions 1991–2020 (SloCC)

11.6 Conclusions

The Constitutional Court of the Republic of Slovenia became the constitutional court of an independent state and the highest organ of the judiciary in 1991 (Božič et al. 2016, 9; Mavčič 1999, 13). During the 30 years of its existence, constitutional adjudication was shaped by 38 judges, and the Court contributed significantly to the transition from an undemocratic regime to a new socio-political system harmonized with European and international legal standards based on the rule of law and the protection of human rights and human dignity (Slovenija 2016, 8). Some trends can be observed in the strength of rulings as they related to the political situation. Most obviously, changes in governing coalitions have influenced the development of the strength of rulings. One could argue that the SloCC had the strongest restrictive effect on the legislature during periods of political instability caused by political fragmentation. On the other hand, because of the small proportion of dissenting opinions, we cannot draw firm conclusions about the attitudes of dissenting judges. The SloCC used a variety of instruments when it made its decisions. This practice was more pronounced in the early years, when the goal was to establish the entire legal system and to ensure respect for constitutional values and the rule of law. The Court very rarely decided to annul a complete law but often applied some kind of prescription and added a remedy. It thus played an active role as a positive legislator, while attaching great importance to the principle of the separation of powers.

References

Accetto, Matej. 2010. "Sodstvo in medetični odnosi v nekdanji Jugoslaviji [Judiciary and interethnic relations in the former Yugoslavia]." In *Historični seminar 8*, edited by Katarina Keber and Luka Vidmar, 127–150. Ljubljana: Založba ZRC, ZRC SAZU.

Avbelj, Matej, and Šušteršič Janez. 2019. "Conceptual Framework and Empirical Methodology for Measuring Multidimensional Judicial Ideology." *DANUBE: Law, Economics and Social Issues Review* 10 (2): 129–159.

———, Batagelj Polona, and Šuštaršič Janez. 2020. "Ali je slovensko Ustavno sodišče res politično ugrabljeno, sodniki pa sprti kot še nikoli? [Has the Slovenian Constitutional Court been politically hijacked, and the judges are divided like never before?]." *Pravna praksa* 3 (44): II–VII.

———, Batagelj Polona, Cigoj Maja, Letnar Černič Jernej, Jevšek Pezdir Ana, Šušteršič Janez, Šušteršič Snežana, and Vatovec Katarina. 2020. "Obvladovanje ideologije in politike na ustavnem sodišču [Controlling Ideology and Politics in the Constitutional Court]." *Pravna praksa* 39 (33): II–VIII.

———, Batagelj Polona, Cigoj Maja, and Vatovec Katarina. 2021b. "Vladna in parlamentarna dimenzija ideologije Ustavnega sodišča [The governmental and parliamentary dimension of the Constitutional Court's ideology]." In *Ideologija na sodiščih*, edited by Matej Avbelj and Janez Šušteršič, 143–173. Nova Gorica: Nova univerza.

———, Šušteršič Janez, Letnar Černič Jernej, Šušteršič Snežana, Batagelj Polona, Cigoj Maja, Vatovec Katarina, Jevšek Pezdir Ana, Doljak Anja, Remškar Kristian, and Stanišič Maja. 2021a. *Ideologija na sodiščih [Ideology at Courts]*. Nova Gorica: Nova univerza.

———, Šušteršič Janez, Vatovec Katarina, Jevšek Pezdir Ana, Letnar Černič Jernej, and Šušteršič Snežana. 2018. "Pojmovni okvir in empirična metodologija za merjenje večdimenzionalne ideologije na sodiščih [Conceptual Framework and Empirical Methodology for Measuring Multidimensional Judicial Ideology]." *Pravna praksa* 37 (44): II–VIII.

Božič Štajnpihler, Vesna, Leohar Simon, Novak Lidija, Prešeren Tina, Kambič Miran, Novakovič Daniel, Schmidt Ajda, and Stojko Tone. 2016. *Constitutional Court of the Republic of Slovenia: 25 Years*. Ljubljana: Ustavno sodišče Republike Slovenije.

Čebulj, Janez. 2000. "Učinki ugotovitvenih odločb Ustavnega sodišča na uporabo podzakonskih aktov [The effects of declarative decisions of the Constitutional Court on the application of by-laws]." In *VI. dnevi javnega prava, Portorož, 5.–7. junij 2000*, 191–196. Ljubljana: Inštitut za javno upravo.

Corley, Pamela C., Amy Steigerwalt, and Artemus Ward. 2013. *The Puzzle of Unanimity – Consensus on the United States Supreme Court*. Stanford, CA: Stanford University Press.

Eisenberg, Theodore, and Geoffrey P. Miller. 2009. "Reversal, Dissent, and Variability in State Supreme Courts: The Centrality of Jurisdictional Source." *Boston University Law Review* 89 (5): 1451–1504.

Grad, Franc. 2008. "Kako razbremeniti ustavno sodišče [How to relieve the Constitutional Court?]." *Revus* 8: 7–10.

Guarnieri, Carlo, and Pederzoli Patrizia. 2002. *The Power of Judges: A Comparative Study of Courts and Democracy*. New York: Oxford University Press.

Haynie, Stacia L. 1992. "Leadership and Consensus on the U.S. Supreme Court." *The Journal of Politics* 54 (04): 1158–1169.

Jerovšek, Tone. 1998. "Ustavno sodstvo in funkcija sodstva v luči (prepotrebnih?) ustavnih sprememb [Constitutional judiciary and judicial functions in the light of (necessary?) constitutional changes]." *Podjetje in delo* 6 (24): 1202–1209.

Jevšek, Ana. 2021. "Sociologija slovenskega Ustavnega sodišča [Sociology of the Slovenian Constitutional Court]." In *Ideologija na sodiščih*, edited by Matej Avbelj and Janez Šušteršič, 175–204. Nova Gorica: Nova univerza.

Kaučič, Igor. 2006. "Volitve in mandat sodnikov ustavnega sodišča [Elections and mandate of judges of the Constitutional Court]." In *XII. dnevi javnega prava. I. Dnevi javnega sektorja: Portorož, 7.–9. junij 2006*, 411–436. Ljubljana: Inštitut za javno upravo.

———. 2007. "Spremembe položaja in volitev sodnikov Ustavnega sodišča [Changes in the position and elections of judges of the Constitutional Court]." *Podjetje in delo* 33 (6–7): 1013–1024.

———. 2014. "Election of Judges of Constitutional Courts in Slovenia and Comparatively." *Strani pravni život* 58 (3): 323–343.

Krivic, Matevž. 1999. "Odločbe ustavnih sodišč kot pravni vir [Decisions of constitutional courts as a legal source]." In *V. dnevi javnega prava: Portorož, 7.–9. junij 1999*, 523–542. Ljubljana: Inštitut za javno upravo.

Lanier, Drew Noble. 2011. "Acclimation Effects and the Chief Justice: The Influence of Tenure and Role on the Decisional Behavior of the Court's Leader, 1888–2007." *American Politics Research* 39 (4): 682–723.

Letnar Černič, Jernej. 2021. "Avtoritarna dimenzija sodniške ideologije v praksi slovenskega Ustavnega sodišča [The authoritarian dimension of judicial ideology in the practice of the Slovenian Constitutional Court]." In *Ideologija na sodiščih*, edited by Matej Avbelj and Janez Šušteršič, 57–78. Nova Gorica: Nova univerza.

Mavčič, Arne. 1995. *Slovenian Constitutional Review, Its Position in the World and Its Role in the Transition to a new Democratic System*. Ljubljana: Nova revija.

———. 1999. *Ustavno sodišče Republike Slovenije = The Constitutional Court of the Republic of Slovenia = La cour constitutionnelle de la République de Slovénie = Verfassungsgericht der Republik Slowenien*. Ljubljana: Ustavno sodišče Republike Slovenije.

———. 2000. *Zakon o Ustavnem sodišču s pojasnili [Constitutional Court Act with explanations]*. Ljubljana: Nova revija.

Musella, Fortunato, and Luigi Rullo. 2021. "The Expansion of the Constitutional Court in Italy: Ruling the Void in Times of Political Instability." *Review of Constitutional Studies* 25 (1): 79–101.

Nerad, Sebastian. 2003. *Pravne posledice in narava odločb Ustavnega sodišča v postopku ustavnosodne presoje predpisov. [Legal consequences and nature of decisions of the Constitutional Court in the process of constitutional review of regulations]*. Ljubljana: Pravna fakulteta Univerze v Ljubljani.

———. 2005. "Legal Standing for the Constitutional Review of Statutes and Other Regulations." *Revus* 4: 42–73.

———. 2011. "161. člen [Article 161]." In *Komentar Ustave Republike Slovenije: dopolnitev komentarja – A*, edited by Lovro Šturm, 1462–1510. Ljubljana: Fakulteta za državne in evropske študije.

———. 2019. "161. člen [Article 161]." In *Komentar Ustave Republike Slovenije II. del*, edited by Matej Avbelj, 444–452. Nova Gorica: Nova univerza, Evropska pravna fakulteta.

Pavčnik, Marijan, and Arne Mavčič, eds. 2000. *Ustavno sodstvo [Constitutional judiciary]*. Ljubljana: Cankarjeva založba.

Podlipnik, Jernej. 2019. "147. člen [Article 147]." In *Komentar Ustave Republike Slovenije II. del*, edited by Matej Avbelj, 367–372. Nova Gorica: Nova univerza, Evropska pravna fakulteta.

Sadurski, Wojciech. 2002. *Constitutional Justice, East and West: Democratic Legitimacy and Constitutional Courts in Post-Communist Europe in a Comparative Perspective*. Hague: Kluwer Law International.

Škrk, Mirjam. 2006. "Constitutional Review of International Treaties." *Revus* 6: 73–96.
Slovenija, U. sodišče. 2016. *Izbor odločitev: 1991–2015 [Selection of decisions 1991–2015]*. Ljubljana: Ustavno sodišče Republike Slovenije.
Testen, Franc. 2000a. "Interpretacija v odločbah ustavnega sodišča [Interpretation in decisions of the Constitutional Court]." *Pravna praksa* 34: I–V.
———. 2000b. "Razveljavitev z rokom in gola ugotovitev protiustavnosti – podlage za izrek in razlike v učinkih [Annulment with a deadline and bare finding of unconstitutionality – grounds for the ruling and differences in effects]." *Podjetje in delo* 6–7: 1130–1137.
Tratar, Boštjan. 2017. "Independence of Judges from the Perspective of their Election or Nomination." *Pravnik* 72 (7–8): 495–534.
Walker, Thomas G., Lee Epstein, and William J. Dixon. 1988. "On the Mysterious Demise of Consensual Norms in the United States Supreme Court." *The Journal of Politics* 50 (2): 361–389.
Zajc, Drago. 2013. "Razpad vlad in oblikovanje novih koalicij v Sloveniji v obdobju 2008–2013 [Government collapses and the formation of new coalitions in Slovenia 2008–2013]." *Teorija in praksa* 50 (5–6): 753–769.
Zalar, Boštjan. 2008. "Izbiranje ustavnih sodnikov [Selection of constitutional court judges]." *Dignitas* 37–38: 160–192.

12 Central and Eastern European constitutional courts in comparative perspective 1990–2020

Kálmán Pócza, Márton Csapodi, Gábor Dobos and Attila Gyulai

12.1 Introduction

What does the big picture of constitutional adjudication in CEE between 1990 and 2020 look like? This is certainly the question that has come to the reader's mind as he or she has begun reading this volume with the first chapter and continued with the country studies. While answering such a profound and fundamental question should certainly be the task of a comparative study, we do not think we can really live up to such expectations simply because there are so many aspects that could and should be analysed that a concluding chapter can only select a few basic questions and make a first attempt to answer them. Consequently, we have deliberately narrowed the scope of this chapter to a few pressing questions, and, at the same time, we want to emphasize that in-depth qualitative and sophisticated quantitative analysis is desperately needed to provide a more comprehensive picture of judicial behaviour and judicial-legislative relations in Europe.

While the JUDICON-EU research project formulated two aims, mapping the diversity and strength of judicial decisions, the results of the coding process present only one side of the story. The original data created by the project can answer the question as to what extent judicial decisions constrained the room for manoeuvre of the legislation. Nevertheless, it is only one way to approach judicial-legislative relations by focusing on the constraint exerted *by* the courts *on* the legislatures. The other side of the story tells us which factors might have influenced courts and judges in taking strong or weak decisions. While there are several theoretical models which try to explain judicial behaviour and, indirectly, the strength of judicial decisions, here we will focus only on some selected models and summarize the main findings of the country studies in this respect. Keeping in mind these limitations, we will focus on three basic factors which can explain judicial behaviour and ruling strength after presenting descriptive statistics on the diversity and strength of the courts' rulings in Europe.

While *institutional design* can create a powerful court, securing the potential of highly restrictive rulings *vis-à-vis* the legislator, sometimes these formal powers do not reflect the court's actual power. For various reasons, courts

DOI: 10.4324/9781003399483-12

simply do not want to, or are unable to, exercise the powers granted them. By contrast, other courts have not been vested with very forceful tools to control legislatures, yet they have either been able to empower themselves to exert control on elected politicians or have creatively used the formal tools available, sometimes causing serious turmoil in the political sphere. In addition to institutional design, the *political context* is usually considered a crucial factor in explaining judicial behaviour and judicial-legislative relations. In this regard, our research project also yielded mixed results. A third explanatory factor, *event-related variables* (such as democratic transformation or financial crisis), also did not prove to be crucial in all circumstances. After the democratic transformation or the financial crisis, courts chose different strategies. Some severely constrained the legislature immediately after the democratic transformation process or became guardians of social rights (in the context of austerity measures), while others held back and did not participate in either consolidating democracy or pushing back against austerity measures of the governments.

In what follows, we first provide a comparative overview of the JUDICON-EU dataset at a very basic level (Section 12.2). The descriptive statistics presented here can serve as a starting point for formulating various hypotheses for future research. In addition, it provides an overview of how (if at all) institutional design, political context, or various social/political events influenced the strength of judicial decisions and the propensity of judges to publish dissenting opinions (when they were entitled to do so).

With regard to *institutional design*, Section 12.3 examines whether the power to overturn court decisions, the institution of *actio popularis*, or the relatively narrow circle of potential petitioners, voting quorums, and super-majority requirements have an impact on the strength of the courts' decisions, but also whether different types of procedures (*a priori* and *a posteriori*) have an impact on the type of obstacles imposed on the legislature by the court. The competence to review constitutional amendments and various instances of competence creeping by acts of self-empowerment would suggest that courts engaged in expanding their scope of action are activist in the sense that they constrain the lawmakers more heavily. While the previous chapters have already reflected on these questions at country level, Section 12.3 puts the findings in a comparative perspective.

Regarding the *political context*, Section 12.4 summarizes the main findings of the country studies, focusing on whether political fragmentation, political instability, judges' political affiliation, or changes in government had an impact on the courts' decisions. While the widely held hypothesis is that political fragmentation paves the way for judicial interference and means that courts are more willing to constrain legislatures than in the case of a more homogeneous or bipartisan political landscape, analysis of the performance of European constitutional courts from this perspective has shown that the political context alone does not explain the strength of judicial decisions. Some courts are more inclined to interfere and strike down laws when the political landscape is more fragmented, but we also have examples that show that other factors besides political fragmentation can have a more profound influence on judges' minds when deciding mega-political issues or even relatively simple cases. It is also not so obvious that judges' political affiliation or a change in government is a crucial element in the judicial decision-making process. While the election of judges appears to be a thoroughly politicized process in several countries, judges have repeatedly disappointed their nominating parties.

Section 12.5 examines whether courts took a leading role in *democratic consolidation processes* by severely limiting the room for manoeuvre of parliamentary majorities and how they behaved *in times of austerity measures* in the wake of the 2008–2009 financial crisis. As for the thesis of democratic consolidation, legal scholars have formulated two contradictory hypotheses: drawing on the experience of the backlash against the Russian Constitutional Court in the early 1990s (Epstein, Knight, and Shvetsova 2001), several scholars argued that courts should be cautious about constraining political actors too much after democratic transformation processes. Instead, they should first build up their authority to be respected by the electorate, which could protect them from political backlash from the political elite. The implication (or normative expectation) of this hypothesis is that courts should not constrain the legislature too heavily after the democratic transformation process. By contrast, another hypothesis states that constitutional courts play (or should play) a crucial role in democratic transformation and consolidation, which would imply that courts should be strong in terms of both their formal power and their actual performance. Courts are set up to constrain political actors, and since the political landscape in new democracies generally lacks a tradition of self-restraint, courts should set limits on politicians' aspirations. This thesis implies that courts take strong decisions and constrain legislators very heavily directly after the democratic transformation process. The country studies in this volume and the following analysis have shown that the story is more complicated, and we cannot find indisputable arguments and irrefutable results that confirm or refute the first or the second hypothesis. The same is true for a second, event-related variable, the economic crisis and its well-known effects of austerity measures. Some courts became ardent guardians of social rights, while others displayed passive virtues by giving legislators more leeway to deal with the financial and economic crisis.

Section 12.6 puts the judges' dissenting opinions in comparative perspective. It examines the strategies chosen by the judges after the democratic transformation processes, whether they wanted to strengthen the authority of the court by holding back on publishing dissenting opinions and creating the image of a unified court or whether they tended to behave in a more individualistic manner and did not really care about the interests of the institutions. In addition, this section also takes a look at dissenting coalitions and summarizes the main findings of the country studies on the effects of party affiliation on dissenting coalitions. But before we turn to these explanatory variables, let us turn to the basic statistics on court performance!

12.2 Courts by numbers

The country experts of the JUDICON-EU project identified more than 15,000 constitutional court decisions that fall within the scope of the study (Table 12.1).[1] These decisions were broken down into nearly 25,000 rulings handed down by court majorities. In some countries, such as Ireland and Germany, courts issued fewer than 10 decisions per year. Although there are some institutional features that could explain the differences between countries (e.g. the fewest decisions per year were issued in countries with a decentralized judicial system in Cyprus and Ireland), the results are rather mixed. It seems that the total number of decisions is higher in Western Europe than in Central and Eastern Europe, but it is worth noting that in most Eastern European countries constitutional courts were established only two to three years after the beginning of the period under scrutiny (i.e. 1990). With this in mind, the courts in the two groups of countries have about the same activity when looking at the sheer number of decisions (WE countries: 27.2 decisions per year; CEE countries: 29.1 decisions per year).

Table 12.1 Number of decisions, rulings, and dissenting opinions (all countries)

	Country	*No. of decisions*	*No. of rulings*	*Rulings with at least one dissenting opinion*	*No. of rulings in dissenting opinions*
Western Europe	**AUS**	841	956	0	0
	BEL	733	2,518	0	0
	CYP	82	129	37	124
	FRA	1,230	2,851	0	0
	GER	254	334	21	35
	IRL	216	250	2	3
	ITA	3,233	4,857	0	0
	POR	234	343	166	504
	SPN	771	1,128	314	754
Central and Eastern Europe	**CRO**	808	896	70	106
	CZH	361	437	167	478
	EST	190	207	77	297
	HUN	747	1,476	449	1,154
	LAT	244	337	46	81
	LIT	305	872	43	51
	POL	1,337	2,460	398	714
	ROM	3,148	3,330	219	436
	SLK	204	309	109	196
	SLN	799	1,055	161	285
SUM		15,737	24,745	2,279	5,218

1 The descriptive statistics in this section cover all countries and are identical to Section 11.2 of the twin volume Kálmán Pócza (ed): *Constitutional review in Western Europe. Judicial-legislative relations between 1990–2020* (London/New York: Routledge, 2024).

In terms of the average strength of rulings, courts have constrained legislatures in relatively different ways (Figure 12.1). As with the number of decisions and rulings, the West-East divide appears to have limited explanatory power, with countries from both groups at either end of the scale. Of course, it would be foolish to claim that courts with roughly the same score have the same profile. Country studies of this volume also make clear that these numbers may mask different, country-specific contextual factors. For example, both Romania and Ireland are at the lower end of the scale, but for different reasons. In Romania, the institutional framework shapes the way the Romanian Constitutional Court operates. As there is no preliminary screening mechanism to filter petitions, the proportion of rejections is quite high, which gives a distorted picture of the relative power of the court (Chapter 9). The low strength value of Ireland, on the other hand, can be explained more by political and cultural factors. While the provisions of the Irish Constitution have an indirect (and reverse) effect on the propensity of the apex courts to strike down legislation, the Irish judiciary has also adopted a self-imposed principle of restraint and deference. Finally, Irish party politics (with two parties that do not differ heavily in their policies and with a low degree of polarization) also leads to a lack of political partisanship in judicial decision-making (Chapter 7 of the twin volume).[2]

At the other end of the scale, both the Cypriot and Estonian courts exert strong restraint on legislators but, once again, for different reasons. In Cyprus, many laws that the President of the Republic submits to the Supreme Court for preliminary review are completely annulled, meaning that the entire law is declared unconstitutional, not just part of it. However, a closer look at these cases reveals that these unconstitutionality decisions review laws that include only a single paragraph, and they merely amend a previous law (Chapter 4 of the twin volume).[3] Therefore, following the methodology of JUDICON-EU project, they were coded as complete annulments, even if the laws contained only a single paragraph.

On the other hand, to understand Estonia's position on this scale, we need to consider the procedural design of the judiciary. In Estonia, there are several review mechanisms that filter cases before they reach the Constitutional Review Chamber of the Estonian Supreme Court, making judicial review of legislative acts only an "ultima ratio" instance. Moreover, norm control proceedings can only be initiated by a limited group of state institutions, which indirectly affects the number and quality of petitions. Few petitioners submitting high-quality petitions often result in a finding of unconstitutionality by the Estonian Supreme Court (Chapter 4). These examples show that the

2 Kálmán Pócza (ed): Constitutional review in Western Europe. Judicial-legislative relations between 1990–2020 (London/New York: Routledge, 2024).

3 Kálmán Pócza (ed): Constitutional review in Western Europe. Judicial-legislative relations between 1990–2020 (London/New York: Routledge, 2024).

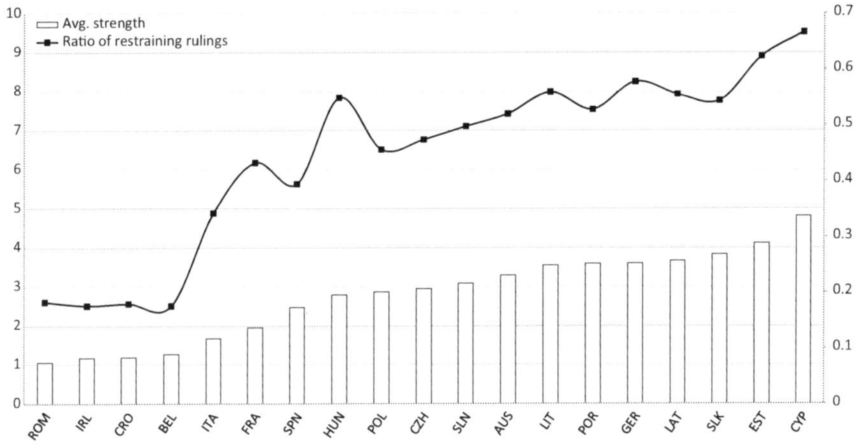

Figure 12.1 Average strength and proportion of restraining rulings (CEE)

quantitative analysis of the JUDICON-EU project can rather serve as a framework for a qualitative analysis that can be used to explore the contextual differences behind the similarities.

Figure 12.1 shows that the proportion of restrictive rulings more or less follows the trend of average strength scores. Nevertheless, there are at least two outliers: both France and Hungary are above the trend line because their constitutional courts tend to use softer restrictive rulings (constitutional requirements, omissions, and procedural unconstitutionalities), so while these courts are activist in the sense that they issue non-zero (restrictive) rulings quite frequently, the softer instruments they use keep the overall strength of their rulings lower. Both courts constrain the legislature relatively frequently but in a more generous way that gives the legislature more room to manoeuvre.

Looking at the performance of the courts longitudinally, the annual average of ruling strength shows a clear difference between the Eastern and Western blocs (Figure 12.2). The early years of the Central and Eastern European courts can be characterized with stronger rulings, although it must be emphasized that the constitutional courts were active in only two countries (Hungary and Slovenia) in 1990–1991, and the high restraint resulted from only a few rulings. In any case, the courts of the Central and Eastern European countries tended to issue more restrictive rulings (with the exception of countries with consistently weak rulings, such as Romania) in the first decade.

Regarding the diversity of rulings, Figure 12.3 shows the aggregate proportion of the two predominant types of provisions by country – that is, substantive unconstitutionality and rejection in each country. The figure shows that the original hypothesis of the JUDICON-EU project, that constitutional adjudication in Europe is more diverse than a dichotomous striking down/upholding of the reviewed laws, can only be partially confirmed. Most

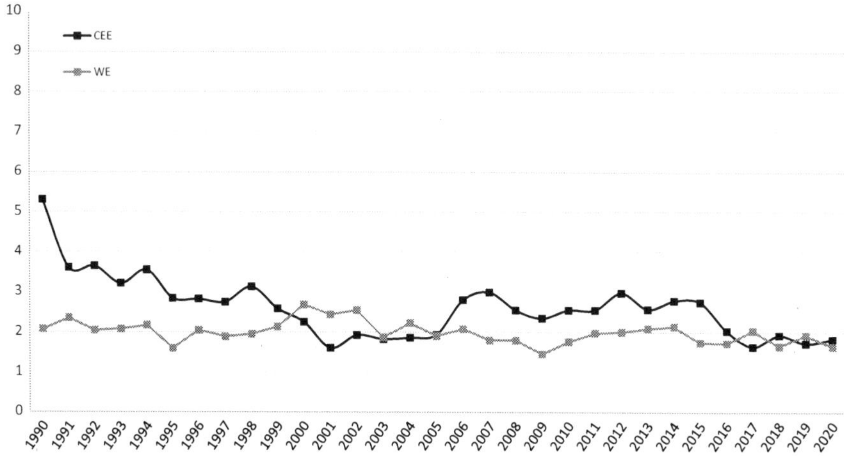

Figure 12.2 Average strength of rulings (CEE vs. WE)

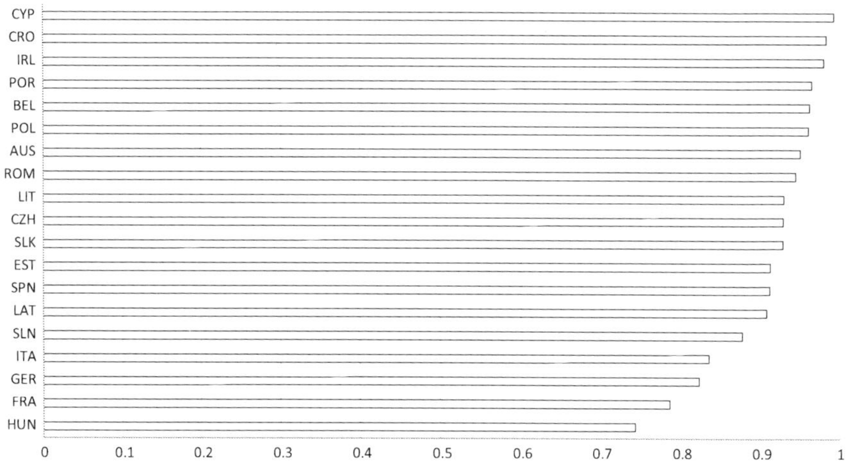

Figure 12.3 Cumulative ratio of the two most frequent provision types (REJ + SUBST)

countries have adhered well to the dichotomous approach, i.e. almost every ruling of the courts falls into either the category of rejection or substantive unconstitutionality. Across Europe, there are only a few examples where constitutional courts use a more colourful set of tools, such as in Italy, Germany, France, and Hungary. Several countries even prohibit declaring a particular type of provision, but most courts, which could theoretically choose from a wide range of provisions, tend to use only substantive unconstitutionality or rejections.

A breakdown of provision types (Figure 12.4) shows that in countries that rarely use provisions other than rejections and substantive unconstitutionalities,

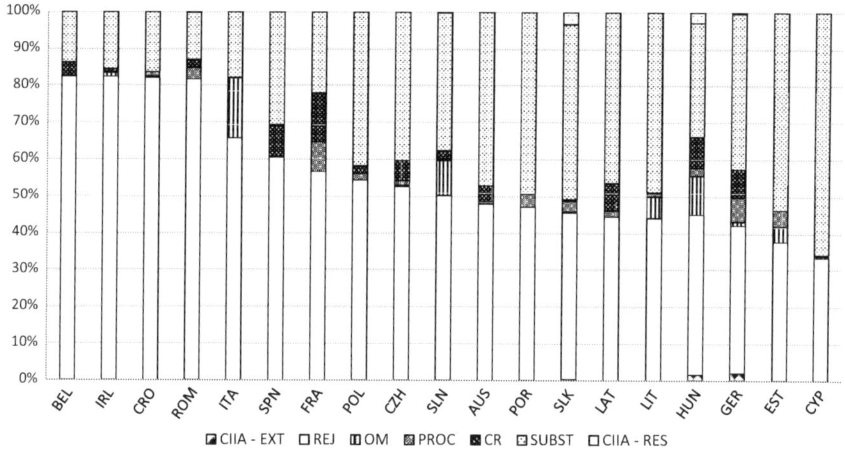

Figure 12.4 Frequency of ruling types (all countries)

differences are found depending on whether the former or the latter are predominant. In a few countries with greater diversity, constitutional courts tend to use a third type of provision in addition to the two dominant types – usually either an omission (in Italy and Slovenia) or a constitutional requirement (in Spain, Czechia, Austria, and Latvia). The use of more than three types of provisions is characteristic of only a handful of countries (France, Germany, Hungary).

Finally, as far as dissenting opinions are concerned, there is a clear difference between Western and Eastern European countries. First of all, there are Western countries where constitutional judges are explicitly forbidden to publish a dissenting opinion (Austria, Belgium, France, Italy), while there are no (or no longer) such restrictions in any Central and Eastern European countries. But even if we exclude the countries where it is not possible to express a dissenting opinion, the number of rulings with dissenting opinions seems to be much higher in Central and Eastern European countries (Figure 12.5).

However, when numbers in Figure 12.5 are broken down by country, it becomes apparent that neither group of countries can be considered coherent (Table 12.2). Among the Western European countries, a gap can be observed between the "Mediterranean" and the "Northern" countries. The proportion of rulings with dissenting opinions is quite low in Ireland and Germany, while in the Mediterranean countries (Spain, Cyprus, and Portugal) at least a quarter of rulings have dissenting opinions. The fact that Spain and Portugal perform similarly to the countries of CEE in terms of the number and proportion of dissenting opinions could be partly explained by their past, as both countries experienced a democratic transition in the 1970s. The cases of Cyprus and Ireland show that the political context of the countries is sometimes more important than the institutional framework of the courts (e.g. both the Irish

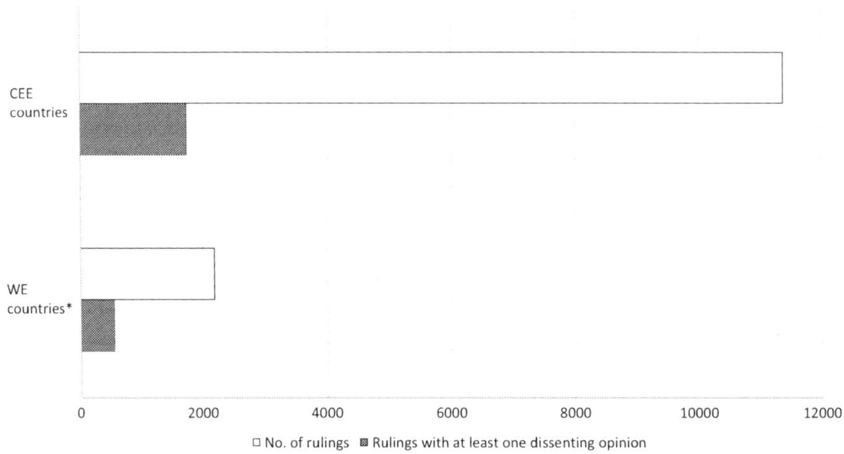

Figure 12.5 Rulings with at least one dissenting opinion (CEE vs. WE)

Table 12.2 Proportion of rulings with at least one dissenting opinion (all countries)

	Country	*Proportion of rulings with at least one dissenting opinion (%)*
WE countries*	IRL	0.8%
	GER	6.3%
	SPN	27.8%
	CYP	28.7%
	POR	48.4%
CEE countries	LIT	4.9%
	ROM	6.6%
	CRO	7.8%
	LAT	13.6%
	SLN	15.3%
	POL	16.2%
	HUN	30.4%
	SLK	35.3%
	EST	37.2%
	CZH	38.2%

* Countries where judicial dissent is forbidden are excluded.

and Cypriot judiciaries operate under a decentralized judicial system but show very different approaches to dissent).

Among Central and Eastern European countries, the establishment of the new political systems in the 1990s clearly affected the behaviour of the courts in terms of dissents. In most countries, judges were reluctant to attach dissenting opinions to majority rulings in the early period after the democratic transition. The reason for this is probably to be found in an institutional strategy based on uniform decision-making to build and protect the reputation of the newly created institution. Moreover, attaching dissenting opinions to majority rulings was explicitly forbidden in Slovakia and Lithuania until 2000 and 2008 (respectively). As with average strength, it appears that the frequency of dissents can be explained by a variety of reasons. Based on the country studies in this volume, differences across countries can be attributed to factors such as institutional settings, court strategy, political context, or even personal characteristics (for a more detailed analysis of the CEE region in this respect, see Section 12.6).

12.3 Institutional design

The subject of descriptive statistics in itself is of interest in a comparative research project, as the comparative data helps to formulate new research questions while answering some others. Nonetheless, the data from the JUDICON-EU project also inspired the project participants, and we asked them to try to provide a first approximate answer to several questions about judicial behaviour. As noted in the introduction, most authors refer to three explanatory models of judicial behaviour and provide detailed reflections on whether *institutional design*, *political context*, or *event-related factors* might have influenced judges in their highly restrictive or, conversely, highly lenient decisions.

To start with, a crucial aspect to consider in our analysis is the influence of the institutional settings on the strength of judicial decisions. Several theories point to the potential explanatory power of some institutional variables on judicial behaviour and the strength of rulings (Bumin 2017; Gardbaum 2018). At first glance, overriding mechanism, a small set of actors with the right to initiate review process, would imply that judicial decisions are more likely to be deferential. Contrary to expectations, country studies in this volume have refuted these assumptions. On the other hand, jurisdiction to review constitutional amendments, the initiation of review processes *ex officio*, or a broad range of actors who can file a petition would mean that courts will make very restrictive decisions. Again, these expectations have been refuted by the country studies in this volume. Nevertheless, there are other types of institutional constraints that appear to strongly influence court performance: a high voting quorum at the court or the type of the review process (*a priori* or *a posteriori*) obviously had an impact on the strength of the Czech and Romanian judges' decisions. Let us start with the latter examples and continue with counterexamples showing that institutional arrangements have a rather limited impact on the strength of court decisions.

12.3.1 Voting quorum and the type of review process

In the case of the Czech Republic, the presence of a high voting quorum and supermajority requirements in court proceedings leads to a dense combination of procedural constraints. These constraints result in the frequent inability of the Czech Constitutional Court (CzCC) to render rulings on sensitive political and social issues. A supermajority of nine votes is required for a finding of substantive unconstitutionality; therefore, it is much more difficult to obtain a vote on substantive unconstitutionality than it is to reject a case or declare a constitutional requirement. As a result, activist judges in the Czech Republic have turned to a less direct approach, relying on declaring constitutional requirements, a trend that has been vaguely evident since 1995 and in full effect since 2012. This shift can be seen as a reaction to the constraints imposed by the high voting quorum and supermajority requirements. It should be also stressed that judges of the CzCC are reluctant to challenge the Parliament with claims of unconstitutionality by legislative omission. Notably, legal scholarship in the Czech Republic tends to consider such claims as a highly assertive judicial attempt of positive legislation (Chapter 3).

Another example of institutional design playing a role is the Romanian practice of constitutional adjudication and the difference between an *a priori* and an *a posteriori* review process. Romania uniquely distinguishes between *a priori* and *a posteriori* procedures in terms of the average strength of their outcomes. The Romanian Constitutional Court (RCC) is more inclined to restrain legislative attempts in *a priori* procedures. Although *a priori* proceedings represent only a small portion of the RCC's total case law, they have a remarkably high success rate compared to the results of *a posteriori* review proceedings. Examining the entire data set on the RCC, we notice that *a priori* review rulings have an average strength of 2.59, while *a posteriori* review rulings have a much lower average strength of 0.79. This discrepancy suggests that *a priori* review rulings tend to be more controversial, resulting in a higher number of dissenting opinions compared to *a posteriori* review rulings. The relative rate of petitions for *a priori* review (and also their success rate) is highest during periods of low political stability. In politically stable times, RCC's rulings tend to be weaker, while in times of instability they are stronger. However, these conclusions seem to apply only to decisions under *a priori* review. It appears that political stability may explain the trends in the restraining nature of *a priori* review rulings, but it is not sufficient to explain the trends in *a posteriori* review rulings. One explanation for this trend may be that the RCC appears to leave more room for political and ideological considerations in the *a priori* process, leading to a decline in the average strength of such rulings during periods of relative stability, while the *a posteriori* review process leaves more room for a judicial approach (Chapter 9).

12.3.2 Overriding mechanisms

Continuing with examples that show that institutional factors can have rather *limited* explanatory power, we turn to the case of overriding mechanisms.

In the case of Poland, the analysis reveals that the competence of the Parliament to overrule decisions of unconstitutionality made by the Polish Constitutional Tribunal (PCT) did not significantly impede the court's powers between 1986 and 1999. Although the lower chamber of the Parliament (*Sejm*) did in fact overrule 11 decisions of the PCT (at times only partially), accounting for 11.3% of all decisions declaring statutes unconstitutional of the given time period, the impact and constitutional significance of these overrides are debatable. The Parliament's approach to the overriding mechanism did not suggest a long-standing institutional conflict concerning the court's influence or its position in the political and constitutional system. This implies that, in practice, the formal limitation on the PCT's powers inscribed in the constitutional framework was found to be of lower significance (Chapter 8).

In the case of Romania, the 2003 constitutional amendment first made the rulings of the Romanian Constitutional Court generally binding with respect to both *a priori* and *a posteriori* constitutional review, effectively eliminating the legislator's ability to override. However, this legislative competence, which can only be exercised by a qualified majority, was never used in practice until 2003. Parliament did, however, retain a strategic "trump card" to compensate for the limited power of overriding the RCC's decisions. By amending the constitutional article on the court's jurisdiction, the legislature added the provision "other duties stipulated by the organic law of the Court", which still gives the legislature a degree of control over the court's jurisdiction and empowers it to amend and expand the court's powers. In practice, this legislative control was evident in the exercise of this power in 2010, when the organic law of the RCC was revised. But again, as in the case of Poland, overriding power does not affect the strength of judicial decisions (Chapter 9).

12.3.3 Access to courts

The institution of *actio popularis* existed exclusively in Hungary, which is why the Hungarian Constitutional Court was often considered institutionally strong, although in practice it did not make consistently restrictive rulings (Chapter 5). In other countries, the circle of petitioners has been narrower. The question arises as to whether the limited number of petitioners or the broader accessibility can provide an explanation for the more restrictive or permissive attitude of the courts.

While the restriction of the circle of petitioners can, according to a certain view, weaken constitutional court decisions, in the case of Estonia it leads to one of the most stringent practices of constitutional review (Chapter 4). In contrast, in Hungary, where access to the HCC was much broader (*actio popularis*), the court did not consistently make very restrictive decisions. In Estonia, the initiation of norm control proceedings is limited to a select group of state actors. It can be inferred from this that the total number of proceedings initiated is relatively low, as applicants to the review process carefully consider the likelihood of success before filing an application. This circumstance potentially contributes to the strength of court decisions, as petitions go through a rigorous filtering process. Moreover, the combination of limited types of proceedings and a narrow group of potential petitioners further reduces the likelihood of an unsuccessful constitutional review in Estonia (Chapter 4).

However, the ruling strength of the Latvian Constitutional Court (LaCC) shows a different pattern: when the circle of petitioners was expanded by an amendment in 2001, this resulted in significantly more restrictive rulings, showing that limiting the circle of potential petitioners can actually increase the strength of judicial decisions (Chapter 6), while *actio popularis* does not necessarily mean that the court meets expectations and constrains the legislature more heavily (Chapter 5). Again, the comparative research shows mixed results and suggests that further (qualitative) research is needed to determine under what conditions courts are more likely to make restrictive rulings against legislators.

The thesis that institutional design alone does not imply a strong court is further supported by the example of the Croatian Constitutional Court (CrCC). The CrCC can not only be invoked through a limited *actio popularis* process, but the court has even the right to initiate constitutional review process *ex officio*. Limited *actio popularis* means that while any natural or legal person may initiate the review process, the Croatian Constitutional Court can decide whether to accept the petition and proceed. Moreover, the CrCC also has the power to initiate procedure and to review the constitutionality of a law *ex officio*. Nevertheless, the CrCC has apparently shown self-restraint and exercised this right only three times, which shows a restrictive interpretation of its own competence, since it preferred that the petition came from another actor. It is noteworthy that in the cases where the CrCC initiated the review process *ex officio*, this always resulted in a partial annulment of the law for substantive unconstitutionality. When the possibility of *ex officio* initiation was introduced in 2002, concerns were raised that the CrCC might assume a legislative role and interfere in political matters that fall within the competence of Parliament. In contrast to these fears, however, statistics from the JUDICON-EU dataset show a rather restrained attitude on the part of Croatian judges (Chapter 2).

In summary, the country studies using the JUDICON-EU dataset have shown that if a wide range of actors has the right to initiate the review process (including the court itself), it does not guarantee that the court will take an uncompromising position toward the legislature. Obviously, other factors should also be considered when explaining the behaviour of courts with strong formal powers.

12.3.4 Reviewing constitutional amendments

Another example that proves that strong formal empowerment does not imply strong courts and court decisions is the right to review constitutional amendments. To be sure, this is a highly controversial power (Roznai 2013; Roznai 2019; Barak 2011, Albert 2015; Albert, Nakashidze, and Olcay 2019; Abeyratne and Bui 2023), and courts are rarely entrusted with the task of being a negative constituent power. Nevertheless, even in the CEE region, it is not uncommon to have courts with such jurisdiction. In Romania, the Romanian Constitutional Court exercises unusually strong competence to review such amendments. It is mandated to review constitutional amendments twice: once before the first reading and once after adoption. To date, the Romanian Parliament has succeeded in passing a constitutional amendment only once, during the constitutional revision in 2003. The RCC has actively exercised its power of review by deleting provisions from amending laws before their first reading, but the opportunity to review an amending law after its adoption has not yet arisen. Consequently, the figures do not seem to reflect the exceptionally strong institutional empowerment (Chapter 9).

In Lithuania, the Lithuanian Constitutional Court (LiCC) has granted itself broad powers, sometimes even contradicting written legal sources. It has expanded its jurisdiction to review not only ordinary laws but also, among other things, laws amending the constitution, constitutional laws, or laws adopted by referendum. Although the LiCC claims to be able to exert strong influence, it relies predominantly on softer methods, such as the equally self-created ability to declare a legislative omission, which has a significant impact on the strength of its decisions (Chapter 7). It should be stressed that it is not uncommon for courts to secure some powers without an explicit mandate in written legal sources. Thus, it is worthwhile to survey acts of self-empowerment in the CEE region and consider whether such moves affect judicial-legislative relations and, in particular, the strength of judicial decisions.

12.3.5 Self-empowerment

The absence of certain powers does not necessarily mean that courts sit back and behave in a disciplined manner. Sometimes courts are very creative and use their interpretive powers to empower themselves to do things that are not explicitly addressed in the constitution or in laws on the operation of the courts. Again, the question is whether such acts of formal self-empowerment affect the strength of judicial decisions one way or another.

By "self-empowerment" we refer to the use of a given ruling type despite not explicitly having the competence, but at the same time not being prohibited to do so. Of course, a much more blatant example of self-empowerment is when the court finds a way to use a ruling type despite an explicit statutory prohibition. An interesting combination of self-empowerment and self-restraint may arise when, after self-empowerment, the constitutional court makes only occasional use of the self-created legal instrument or uses it in a self-restraining manner. Here again, the question arises whether acts of self-empowerment and the resulting legal instrument have a significant impact on the strength of decisions.

12.3.5.1 Creating new ruling types

The case of Hungary may be a prime example of how self-empowerment affects the behaviour of the constitutional court in constraining the legislature. The HCC used the tools of legislative omissions and constitutional requirements on numerous occasions in its first decade, which led it to be, on average, less restrictive towards the legislature. These widely used tools were later legally added to the competence list of the HCC with the comprehensive constitutional reforms after 2010, and they can still be considered regularly used ruling types today. The self-empowerment of the HCC to enact legislative omissions and constitutional requirements has also had a long-term impact on its jurisprudence and ruling strength (Chapter 5).

In the Czech Republic, on the other hand, the self-empowerment of the Czech Constitutional Court (CzCC) has not had a lasting effect on the relationship with the legislature. As far as legislative omissions are concerned, there is a strong aversion in Czech constitutional scholarship to prescriptions for the legislature, as this is seen as a violation of the principle of separation of powers. There were only two instances in which the CzCC deviated slightly from this tradition in cases related to democratic and economic transition, but still in a very restrained manner, declaring only the absence of legislative action unconstitutional and not prescribing any specific policy change. Although the CzCC had significantly increased its influence on the Czech political landscape by assuming the power to review so-called constitutional laws in the *Melčák* case, this self-assumed power was rarely used in practice and therefore had no significant impact on the jurisprudence of the CzCC (Chapter 3).

Similarly, the few examples where the Constitutional Court of Croatia (CrCC) contravened its own explicit position of not being authorized to declare legislative omissions did not have any considerable impact in the long run due to their infrequency. In these cases, the CrCC decided to circumvent the self-imposed restriction and did assess the question of constitutionality of whether the legislature failed to prescribe something. Notably, on a few occasions the CrCC also issued some directives on necessary legislative amendments, although not as a separate ruling type, but as a part of unconstitutionality rulings (Chapter 2).

12.3.5.2 Determining ex tunc or pro futuro temporal effects

Temporal effects of judicial decisions are another venue where courts might expand their own (and the legislators') leeway, or, alternatively, can narrow down the room for the legislature to manoeuvre. In Latvia, in addition to the general rule of invalidating unconstitutional norms as of the publication of the decision (*ex nunc*), the Latvian Constitutional Court (LaCC) has the power to invalidate an unconstitutional norm either retroactively (*ex tunc*) from the date of its adoption or prospectively (*pro futuro*) from a future date. Case law indicates that a challenged legal norm is invalidated *ex tunc* if it was enacted *ultra vires* or has significant procedural violations. However, the LaCC has developed a special discretion in this regard: if it deems the legislation unconstitutional, it may generally annul the norm *ex nunc*, but it may make exceptions for certain persons who filed the constitutional complaint and decide to invalidate the norm *ex tunc* with respect to them. It is important to note that the consequences of such decisions apply only to the parties involved in the specific case and do not have far-reaching *erga omnes* effects, so this discretion does not have a significant impact on constraining the legislature (Chapter 6).

As mentioned, the self-empowerment of the Lithuanian Constitutional Court (LiCC) has at times been quite far-reaching: although the constitution provides that the temporal effect of the LiCC's decisions is *ex nunc*, the LiCC itself has created exceptions to this general rule. These exceptions, defined in various decisions, allow the temporal effect of rulings to occur retroactively (*ex tunc*) and even *pro futuro*, although this possibility is not mentioned in the constitution. Nevertheless, it should be emphasized that the LiCC has never declared a legal act unconstitutional with temporal retroactivity (*ex tunc*), but several times it has declared *pro futuro* decisions. The latter means that the LiCC has tended to mitigate its decisions through an instrument created by itself (Chapter 7).

In Estonia, the Constitutional Review Chamber (CRC) of the Estonian Supreme Court has the power to issue rulings with retroactive effect (*ex tunc*). In the past, constitutional review decisions had *ex nunc* effect, but a court ruling from 2008 necessitated the possibility of retroactive constitutional review ruling (*ex tunc*). This decision marked a decisive change, and since then *ex tunc* effect has become the general rule in practice. Although this change is not reflected in the ruling strength due to the small number of cases, it is of great importance because it represents a significant restriction on the legislature (Chapter 4).

12.4 Political context of judicial decisions

Several factors of the political environment can potentially affect the courts' ruling strength. The fragmentation thesis suggests that greater fragmentation of the political field (in terms of parliamentary parties) might result in larger room for manoeuvre for the constitutional court, as there is less fear of political backlash (Magalhes 2003; Rios-Figueroa 2007; Brouard 2009; Hönnige 2007; Dyevre 2010). Political instability could have similar effects, as there is a strong correlation between fragmentation and instability, but fragmentation alone does not necessarily mean instability, so other factors must also be considered. The change in government could also affect the behaviour of constitutional judges, as judges could respond to these political changes by imposing tighter restrictions on the new government or legislative majority (Spaeth and Segal 1992; Segal and Spaeth 2002; Gillman and Clayton 1999). The effects of these variables of the political environment can be seen in the behaviour of constitutional courts in Poland, Romania, or Slovenia, while in other countries, such as the Czech Republic, Estonia, or Croatia, the political context does not seem to have much influence on the strength of decisions.

12.4.1 Political fragmentation with significant impact

The strong fragmentation of the Polish Parliament in the first years after the democratic transition enabled the Polish Constitutional Tribunal (PCT) to assert its authority and actively shape the legal framework of Polish democracy. Because Parliament was barely able to achieve a simple majority (28 factions after the 1991 elections), the two-thirds majority required to override PCT rulings was typically out of reach. This created a space in which the PCT could play a crucial role in the Polish transition process. The analysis suggests that the transformative effect of the adoption of the 1997 constitution on the strength of the PCT rulings might be questioned because a more significant change in the behaviour of the PCT occurred in 1994, when the newly introduced electoral threshold reduced the number of factions in Parliament to only six. Furthermore, the new ruling coalition of two post-communist parties had the opportunity to elect the majority of judges in PCT at times with stronger political ties than the previous judges. The decline in the strength of PCT decisions in 1994 is visible, while there were no significant changes in the years following the amendment of the constitutional framework in 1997, which abolished the right of the legislature to override decisions of PCT with a two-thirds majority. In summary, the degree of party fragmentation in Parliament appears to have a decisive influence on how PCT limits the legislature (Chapter 8).

In the case of the Romanian Constitutional Court (RCC), the influence of political stability on the strength of *a priori* review rulings can be clearly observed. However, this factor alone is not sufficient to explain the trends in the strength of *a posteriori* review rulings. As a result, and as noted earlier, it appears that the RCC allows more room for political and ideological perspectives in the *a priori* review procedure. Consequently, the average strength of such rulings tends to decrease during periods of relative political stability. Conversely, the *a posteriori* review procedure seems to reflect a more judicial approach and the average strength of rulings appearing unrelated to the political context (Chapter 9).

In Slovenia, it can be argued that the Slovenian Constitutional Court (SloCC) restrained the legislature more in times of political fragmentation and instability. Fragmentation combined with economic and social crises allowed for the SloCC to gain influence in areas reserved for the legislature, and the strength of its ruling tended to peak during instability (Chapter 11).

12.4.2 Political fragmentation without any impact

In contrast, in other countries the connection between political stability/instability and the strength of court rulings may not be as pronounced. The Czech Republic presents an interesting case, as do the Baltic countries, where coalition governments are more widespread and legislatures tend to be fragmented (often with 8–10 political groupings), but constitutional courts do not seem to present a major obstacle to legislatures (Chapter 3). Estonia could be mentioned as an exception, but in the case of the Estonian CRC (Constitutional Review Chamber of the Estonian Supreme Court), the strength of rulings is more likely due to institutional variables, as described earlier. Estonia also presents an interesting case when it comes to the government change thesis, as no significant relationship between the strength of constitutional court rulings and political instability was found despite 14 governments over 27 years (Chapter 4). In Croatia, despite expectations of conflict between the new centre-left parliamentary majority and the centre-right majority of judges at the Croatian Constitutional Court, this did not occur after a change of government in the early 2000s. Qualitative analysis suggests that the reason may be that, because of the minority cabinet, legislation often required a left-right consensus in Parliament, making it less likely to be overturned by the Croatian Constitutional Court (Chapter 2).

Hungarian politics is generally characterized by a high degree of political stability. However, the Hungarian Constitutional Court has challenged both the socialist-liberal two-thirds majority and, between 2010 and 2013, the right-wing two-thirds majority, demonstrating its ability to assert itself in an extremely stable political environment and even in the face of a constitutional parliamentary two-thirds majority (Chapter 5).

12.5 Event-related variables

For the event-related variables, we examine two time periods. In the first period, we examine how constitutional courts constrained legislators' discretion during the transition to democracy and the early years of democratic consolidation. In the second period, we examine the constitutional courts' response to the 2008–2009 financial crisis and related legislative actions, particularly with respect to limiting legislators' austerity measures based on social rights considerations.

12.5.1 Democratic transition

Regarding the role of constitutional courts in the transition to democracy and in the first years of democratic consolidation, two hypotheses can be put forward (Sólyom 2003; Ginsburg 2013; Herron and Randazzo 2003; Jovanović 2015; Daly 2017; Bumin 2017; Smith 2023). The first hypothesis states that constitutional courts tend to avoid strict decisions, which corresponds to a cautious attitude in building authority. The second hypothesis states the opposite: constitutional courts could (and should) play a central role in the democratization process by making strong decisions and positioning themselves as a showcase institution of democratic transition.

If we look at the individual countries in the CEE region, we see that Hungary, Slovenia, Slovakia, and Croatia have a relatively small number of decisions, but those decisions are characterized by their strength (Figure 12.6). It

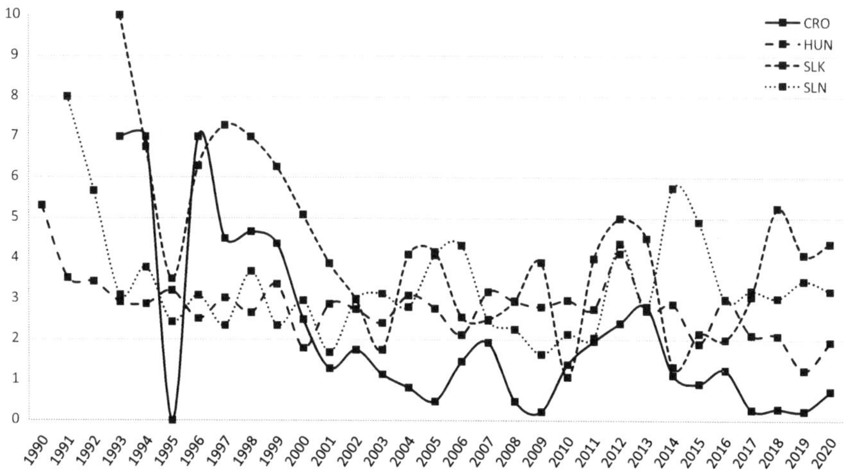

Figure 12.6 Average strength of rulings (1990–2020) (CrCC; HCC; SCC; SloCC)

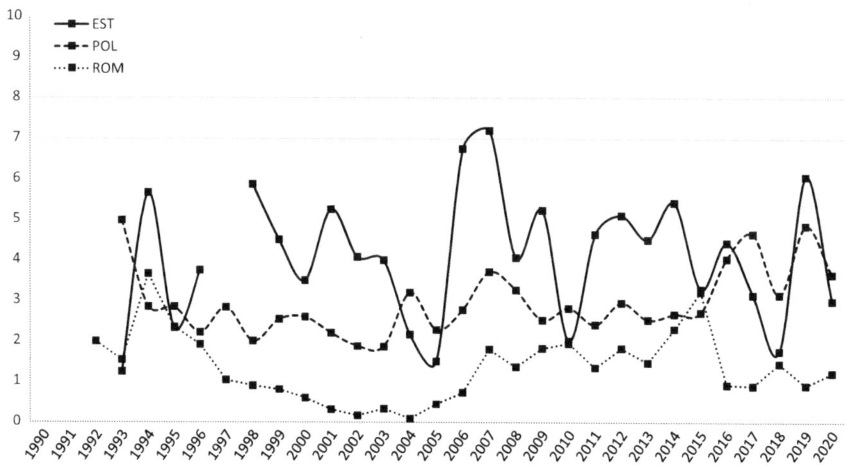

Figure 12.7 Average strength of rulings (1990–2020) (ESC; PCT; RCC)

is worth noting that Slovakia stands out because it was strong until the late 1990s and also had a relatively high number of rulings from the mid-1990s. On the other hand, Poland had a strong start with a considerable number of rulings in the first year, but the strength of decisions declined afterward (Figure 12.7).

Estonia had few and sporadic decisions in the early years of its democratic transition, but when the overall average of ruling strength is considered, it is still the strongest constitutional court in the CEE region (and the second strongest in Europe, after Cyprus) (Chapter 4). Latvia, on the other hand, had

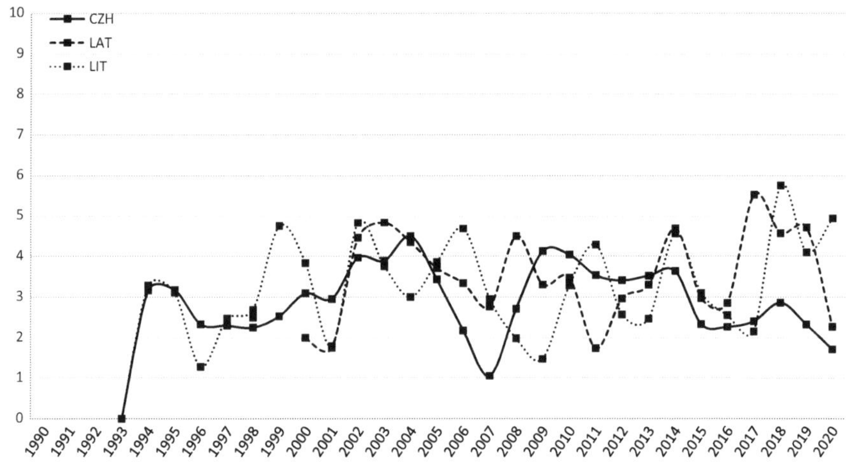

Figure 12.8 Average strength of rulings (1990–2020) (CzCC; LaCC; LiCC)

a weaker and delayed start (1997), with decisions gaining in importance from the 2000s onward, becoming more robust in terms of their restrictive nature and increasing in number (Figure 12.8) (Chapter 6). The Lithuanian and Romanian courts both had a weak start in terms of their rulings, and this trend continued over time, with the former issuing a moderate number of decisions and latter a substantial number of rulings (Chapter 7 and Chapter 9).

An interesting observation concerns the non-zero rulings, which refer to decisions finding some form of unconstitutionality. In this regard, the HCC took a softer approach in finding unconstitutionality by declaring legislative omissions and constitutional requirements (Chapter 5). The Slovak Constitutional Court (SCC), on the other hand, took a more assertive approach and intervened more strongly when it found some form of unconstitutionality (Chapter 10). This trend in non-zero rulings of the Hungarian Constitutional Court was also evident after 2014, when the number of constitutional requirements and legislative omissions increased (Chapter 5).

Overall, the results do not provide a clear indication of the hypotheses formulated in the literature. While some courts did not shy away from frequently striking down laws after democratic transformation, others developed more nuanced methods and attempted to "nudge" legislators to comply with constitutional rules rarely declaring unconstitutionality. This mixed result suggests that more comparative qualitative research should be conducted in this area.

12.5.2 *Financial crisis in 2008–2009*

In general, courts have historically been reluctant to intervene in legislative actions to correct fiscal imbalances. However, during and after the 2008–2009 financial crisis, several authors and advocacy groups urged judges to take a more uncompromising stance against austerity measures (King 2012; Pernice 2016; Ragnarsson 2019; Hinarejos 2015; Fabbrini 2016; Beukers, de Witte and Kilpatrick 2017). The country studies in this volume also addressed this issue; therefore, it is worth summarizing whether the courts in CEE took a bolder stance and struck down laws that violated social rights, or whether they took a more lenient stance in times of financial crisis, arguing that legislators have wide discretion in addressing crisis situations. The results of this survey show that some courts were more lenient, while others were quite active in policing legislators during and after the financial crisis.

The constitutional courts in Lithuania and Slovenia certainly belonged to this latter group (Chapter 7 and Chapter 11). The most restrictive decisions of the Slovenian Constitutional Court (SloCC) during this period were mainly in the areas of taxation, public finance, and social affairs. This can be attributed primarily to the economic crisis and the government's response to it. As analysed in Chapter 11, the combination of the economic and social crisis with a relatively high degree of political fragmentation provided the SloCC with the opportunity to assert its power and issue stricter rulings on the Slovenian parliamentary majority's austerity measures (Chapter 11). A similar attitude was evident in the Lithuanian Constitutional Court. Lithuanian judges dealt with a large number of cases concerning the constitutionality of austerity measures introduced by the legislative and executive branches as a result of the financial crisis. The increasing number of cases led to an increased number of decisions on unconstitutionality. Because some of the austerity measures related to the financial crisis were found to be unconstitutional, the LiCC faced some political backlash in the first half of the 2010s, with calls to abolish the court or to curtail its powers or budget (Chapter 7).

Constitutional judiciaries in Hungary and Poland showed similar tendencies in dealing with fiscal issues and austerity measures, as both courts showed some assertiveness in this regard in the early period after democratic transition but did not show significant strength during the 2008–2009 financial crisis (Chapter 5 and Chapter 8). The Hungarian Constitutional Court found itself at the centre of public debates in the mid-1990s, when it responded to the austerity measures of the left-liberal government with a series of restrictive decisions in 1995, issuing in that year the second-highest proportion of restraining rulings during three decades of its existence. These decisions were all the more surprising because the HCC faced a two-thirds parliamentary majority, so the left-liberal coalition could have simply overruled the decisions of the HCC. Nevertheless, a few years after the democratic transition, the post-communist prime minister feared that popular support would wane if the government overrode the HCC's decisions, not to mention the liberal coalition partner which resisted such moves (Chapter 5). In Poland, the activity of the Polish Constitutional Tribunal (PCT) on financial issues also resulted in some political fallout in the first decade. As noted earlier, the lower house of the Parliament (*Sejm*) had the power to override the PCT's decisions by a two-thirds majority. The government majority succeeded in gaining the support of the opposition (and thus the two-thirds majority) to overrule 11 decisions of the PCT by highlighting their allegedly disastrous consequences for the national budget, as most of these decisions concerned financial matters and social rights (Chapter 8). Conversely, and interestingly, the 2008–2009 financial crisis did not seem to cause any significant change in the ruling strength of the HCC or in the generally restrained behaviour of the PCT. Judges in both courts declared the austerity measures of both governments constitutional (Chapter 5 and Chapter 8).

Similar to the latter periods of the Hungarian and Polish courts, the Estonian Constitutional Review Chamber (CRC), the Latvian Constitutional Court (LaCC), and the Czech Constitutional Court (CzCC) have also taken a rather weaker stance on financial legislation in times of crisis.

The otherwise highly restrictive Estonian CRC was deferential in financial matters, recognizing that the legislature has exclusive competence in organizing public financial obligations. Therefore, the CRC limited its own jurisdiction in constitutional review proceedings in these matters, arguing that it can only assess the justifiability of financial measures in general terms (Chapter 4). Similarly, the Latvian Constitutional Court (LaCC) also accepted the legislature's broad discretionary power when it comes to fiscal regulations or the state budget. According to the consistent case law of the LaCC, the legislature has considerable discretion in the substantive implementation of social rights, provided that the actual economic circumstances of the state are adequately taken into account in these measures (Chapter 6). The Czech Constitutional Court's (CzCC) ruling strength in social issues seems to be declining (despite the growing number of cases in this area) due to the introduction of the reasonability test in cases involving social rights. When the CzCC shifted its focus to social issues, it introduced the reasonability test, which weighs the legislature's interference with social rights against reasonable competing interests. This test gives the legislature greater discretion than the proportionality test (Chapter 3). These approaches suggest a weaker encroachment by social rights adjudication and a more lenient attitude by constitutional courts.

12.6 Explaining dissenting opinions

When considering the internal dynamics of constitutional courts, the primary factors to examine are those related to dissenting opinions. However, statistics on dissenting opinions can be instructive not only in identifying the court's internal politics and fractures, but also in bolstering its authority before the public. Because of the initial backlash against the Russian Constitutional Court, it has become widely accepted that a constitutional court that does not make overly harsh decisions in its early years and whose judges show unity (i.e. avoid public dissent) can strengthen its authority in the long run (Kelemen 2013, 2018). However, there are constitutional courts that took advantage of the availability of dissenting opinions from the very beginning, while others followed the strategy of building authority slowly and started dissenting opinions only later.

12.6.1 Polarization from the outset

The Czech Constitutional Court (CzCC) has chosen a strategy that is rather unpopular among legal scholars who believe that courts should be very careful in showing signs of polarization in their early days. The percentage of rulings with at least one dissenting opinion ranged from 30% to 40% in the first seven years of the CzCC's operation, which are quite astonishing figures compared to other courts (Figure 12.9). Surely, the CzCC has been spared partisan fights, and the polarization measured by the proportion of dissenting opinions does not reflect partisan logic. Rather, frequent dissenting opinions seem to reflect judges' independence, meaning that judges may be more individualistic and less inclined to care about the court's reputation. Nevertheless, this strategy, which is mainly due to the political context in which the CzCC was embedded, paid off, as the authority of the CzCC was not affected by the apparent diversity of opinions on the bench (Chapter 3).

The publication of dissenting opinions is not only permitted but has also been practiced frequently since the establishment of the Slovenian Constitutional Court (SloCC). Especially in the first 10 years of its existence, numerous dissenting opinions were published. The high number of early dissenting opinions may be due to the academic background of some judges, as the majority of published dissenting opinions came from judges who had pursued an academic career before their election. However, the trend shows a gradual decline in the number of dissenting opinions in the third decade (Chapter 11).

The case of the Lithuanian Constitutional Court (LiCC) is somewhat different, as judges were not allowed to publish dissenting opinions until 2008. However, immediately after 2008, a large number of dissenting opinions were published. One explanation for this could be the lack of constitutional traditions

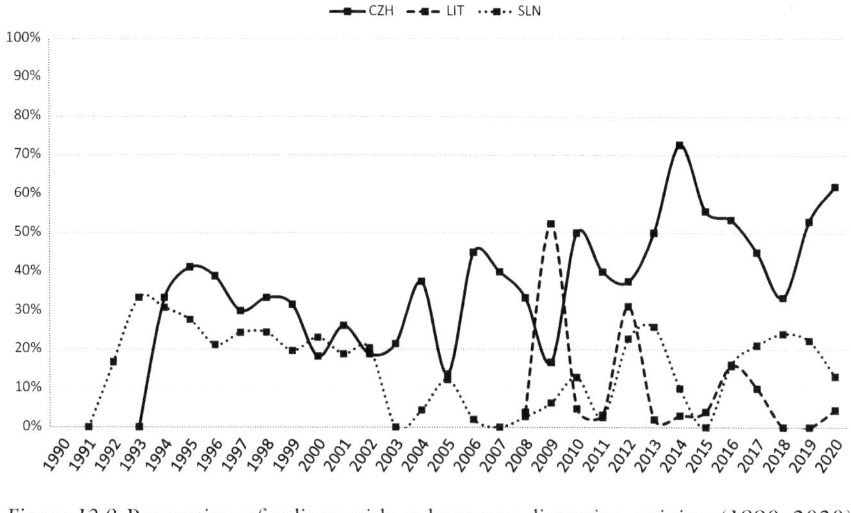

Figure 12.9 Proportion of rulings with at least one dissenting opinion (1990–2020) (CzCC; LiCC; SloCC)

in this regard, which probably led to judges often writing dissenting opinions in a rush and not always considering their necessity. Second, as mentioned earlier, the LiCC's unconstitutionality rulings during the economic crisis led to outright political backlash and public pressure, which may have increased tensions and intensified disagreements among judges. A third explanation could lie in the individual behaviour of the judges, as the same judge (Judge Šileikis) accounted for more than 50% of the dissenting opinions during those years (Chapter 7).

12.6.2 From unity to increasing polarization

Most constitutional courts in CEE seemed to be more cautious in the beginning and showed unity in the early years, which can be explained either by strategic considerations in building authority or by the political-ideological homogeneity of the court. In Poland, for example, the first dissenting opinions appeared only in 1995, mostly for political reasons, showing that the Solidarity-nominated judges disagreed with the post-communist majority. The wide fluctuations in the rate of rulings with dissenting opinions can also generally be attributed to the absence or presence of a clear political or ideological rift among PCT judges (Figure 12.10). For example, while in the first half of the 2000s the proportion of rulings with dissenting opinions remained low, at the beginning of the second half there was a sudden increase in this proportion (from 1.8% in 2006 to 49.7% in 2007) after the conservative coalition led by the Law and Justice Party was able to elect six new judges (Chapter 8). Similarly, in the case of the Croatian Constitutional Court, the low number of dissenting opinions in the first three election periods can be explained by the lack of political polarization among judges, as the rise of dissenting opinions only began in the first half of the 2000s, when the centre-left majority in Parliament

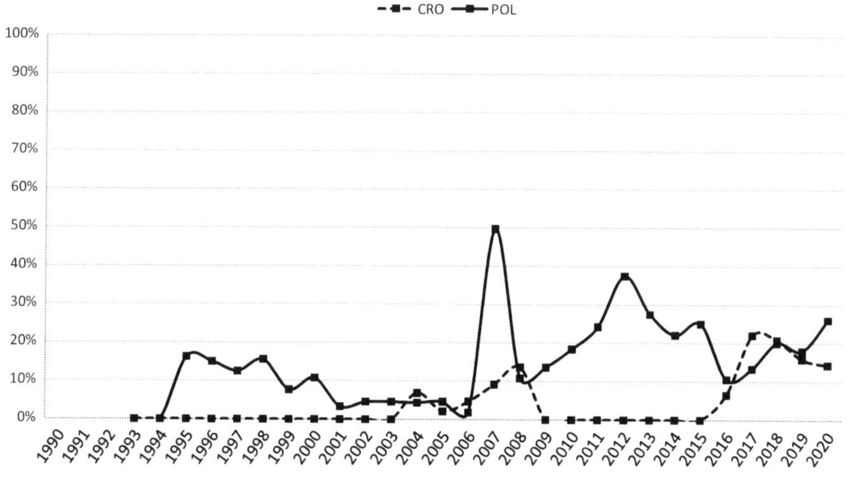

Figure 12.10 Proportion of rulings with at least one dissenting opinion (1990–2020) (CrCC; PCC)

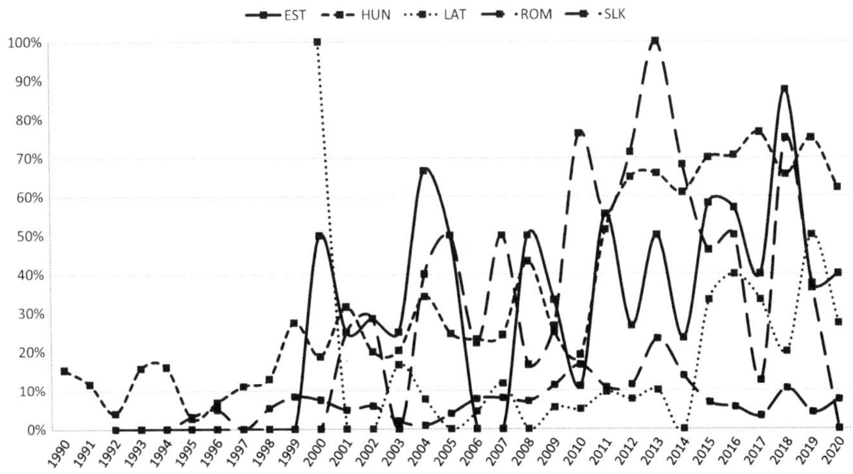

Figure 12.11 Proportion of rulings with at least one dissenting opinion (1990–2020) (ESC; HCC; LaCC; RCC; SCC)

was able to elect new judges to the bench, which previously consisted only of judges elected by the centre-right. In addition, the strategy of speaking with one voice and not making overly strict decisions and building authority may have played a decisive role (Chapter 2).

Other CEE courts such as the Latvian Constitutional Court (LaCC) and the Estonian Constitutional Review Chamber (CRC) in the Baltics and their Slovakian, Romanian, or Hungarian counterparts in Central Europe also seemed to adopt this strategic posture of authority building and avoided showing internal divisions in the early years (Figure 12.11). The two Baltic courts are a clear example of this approach. The LaCC judges completely avoided publishing dissenting opinions for four years, and the number of rulings with dissenting opinions remained low until 2015 (Chapter 6). Judges at Estonia's CRC did not write dissenting opinions for seven years after the court began operating in 1993, but over the past decade, the proportion of rulings with dissenting opinions rose steadily to over 50% (Chapter 4). The evolution of dissenting opinions at the Hungarian Constitutional Court is also instructive in this regard, as judges generally did not write dissenting opinions until 1998 (during the Sólyom era), and the court then saw a gradual, massive increase in both the number of dissenting opinions and the proportion of rulings with at least one dissenting opinion (Chapter 5).

12.6.3 Dissenting coalitions and party affiliation

An interesting pattern that emerges across CEE is that the party affiliation of judges does not seem to be strongly reflected in the dissenting coalitions, with a few exceptions in Central Europe such as Poland, Hungary, and Croatia.

Party affiliation is generally not considered a determining factor in the formation of dissenting coalitions in the constitutional courts of the Baltic region. As for the Latvian Constitutional Court (LaCC), for example, the data suggest that judicial coalitions are primarily due to the academic and professional backgrounds and careers of individual judges, as well as their different approaches to legal theory, interpretation, and methodology (Chapter 6). As mentioned earlier, judges of the Lithuanian Constitutional Court (LiCC) were not allowed to issue dissenting opinions until 2008. The analysis suggests that dissenting opinions in Lithuania are more likely to be related to the judges' personal character and other political circumstances, but not to political affiliation (Chapter 7). Similarly, in Estonia, dissenting coalitions do not appear to reflect political affiliation but rather individual background, academic career, and legal career (Chapter 4).

In Slovakia, no influence of party affiliation on judicial coalitions was found, mainly because there was no clear dissenting coalition, and there were also examples of judges with the same party affiliation (elected together) coming into conflict with each other in most cases (Chapter 10). In the Czech Constitutional Court, institutional variables make it more difficult than usual to trace ideological preferences and party affiliations: judges have a high degree of independence, as they are appointed by the President of the Republic and confirmed by the Senate, and these two political actors tend to be less involved in party politics. Moreover, most constitutional judges have a professional background in the judiciary, which means that they are not associated with politics. Of course, there are, nevertheless, some indirect indicators of individual ideological preferences, but these are not sufficient to infer party affiliation or to provide a comprehensive account. Therefore, the origins of judicial coalitions must be sought elsewhere, such as in judges' professional backgrounds or in their individual ability to form coalitions rooted in their jurisprudential authority, political legitimacy, or ideology (Chapter 3).

Analysis of the Slovenian Constitutional Court (SloCC) shows a tendency toward cross-party coalitions, and relations between judges do not seem to be strongly dependent on party affiliation. There are several examples of cross-party coalitions in the first and second courts, with most judges having cross-party support in the first period. Despite the absence of coalitions based on party affiliation, the behaviour of individual judges could skew these results, as there are examples of judges being more restrictive toward the opposing political side (or, conversely, casting more dissenting votes on decisions that restrict their own side) (Chapter 11). Similarly, the judges of the Romanian Constitutional Court (RCC) do not appear to form coalitions based on their previous political affiliation. As noted earlier, the analysis suggests that there are significant differences in the degree of politicization between the RCC's *a priori* and *a posteriori* review processes, but even in the more politicized or ideologically influenced *a priori* processes, majority or dissenting coalitions generally do not reflect political affiliations (Chapter 9).

In Poland and Hungary, there is evidence of judicial coalitions being based on political affiliation, but their voting records show a more complex network in cooperation that cannot be explained exclusively along political party lines. As for the Polish Constitutional Tribunal, we have already mentioned that the lack of dissenting opinions in the early years was probably due to ideological homogeneity, and conversely, the first dissenting opinions mostly belonged to Solidarity-nominated judges who publicly distanced themselves from the post-communist majority. Similarly, the striking increase in the number of dissenting opinions between 2006 and 2007 coincides with the election of a group of judges nominated by PiS. However, while the PiS-nominated minority generally stuck together on contentious issues prior to 2016, it did not represent a completely segregated group and collaborated with judges of other political affiliations, which adds nuance to the PCT's portrayal as a deeply politically divided court. Nonetheless, starting in 2016, after the PiS government took over the majority on the PCT, the number of rulings with dissenting opinions declined significantly (Chapter 8). The similarities and differences between the PCT and the Hungarian Constitutional Court (HCC) are worth highlighting in this regard. After building unity and authority during the Sólyom era (1990–1998), the rise in dissent paints a picture of a politicized court, with coalitions forming along political fault lines between the centre-left majority and centre-right minority judges in the 2000s – a similar pattern to the PCT. A marked difference emerges, however, regarding the impact of the conservative takeover in the 2010s on dissent rates. In the HCC, after the election of the first new judges by the conservative supermajority, coalitions primarily reflected differences between the minority of these "new judges" and the majority of "old" judges rather than primarily political/ideological affiliation. The same division remained crucial after 2013, when the new judges formed the majority as a result of the filling of vacancies, and the old judges mostly tended to form dissenting coalitions. Over time, all HCC judges have been replaced elected exclusively by the conservative supermajority in the legislature (with four exceptions due to a compromise in 2016). An interesting contrast emerges here: while in Poland the takeover of PCT by conservatives led to a rapid and visible decline in dissenting rates, the political homogeneity of the HCC is not reflected in these figures – on the contrary, the rate of rulings with at least one dissenting opinion even peaked at 75% in 2019 (Chapter 5).

The case of the Croatian Constitutional Court (CrCC) is an example of dissenting and majority coalitions that predominantly follow the lines of political affiliation. As mentioned, the lack of dissenting opinions until 2004 can be explained mainly in political terms, as the reluctance to publish dissenting opinions only began to wane with the election of three judges by the new centre-left government, whereas previously all judges had been elected by the centre-right. Similarly, the number of dissenting opinions increased after the election of eight new judges in 2016, five of whom were nominated by the opposition, and the subsequent period saw a higher number of dissenting opinions, mostly belonging to a coalition of judges nominated by the left-wing opposition party (Chapter 2).

12.7 Conclusions

Drawing on an original dataset, created by the JUDICON-EU project, authors of this volume tried to answer two basic questions: first, how differentiated are judicial decisions in Central and Eastern Europe? Second, to what extent have European constitutional courts constrained the room for manoeuvre of the legislator? First, while analysing the data, we asked the authors to follow the same structure and present the main characteristics of the court by outlining its historical origins, the court's position within the constitutional system, its main competencies, and institutional peculiarities or special processes unknown elsewhere in the region. Second, the chapters provided a general overview of the activities of the relevant court and at the same time clarified whether there are any country-specific phenomena relating to the selection of cases, the coding process, dissenting opinions, court decision-making processes, or other phenomena that differ from consistent coding rules. Third, the chapters evaluated the trends in majority decisions: the preferred or missing ruling types or the trends thereof and gave explanations to these trends. The authors also determined whether changes in the ruling types and ruling strengths are related to changes in political circumstances or changes in the composition of the courts. Some chapters used descriptive statistical analysis, while others used more advanced quantitative methods for evaluating and seeking explanations. The analysis of dissenting opinions provided information on whether trends are apparent in the publication of dissenting opinions. However, the authors also evaluated the performance of individual judges in terms of the frequency and strength of their dissenting opinions and the relative difference between the strength of majority decisions and their dissenting opinions. Surveys of dissenting coalitions found that the tendency of judges to join other colleagues in criticizing the majority's decisions depends on several factors and cannot be attributed simply to the judges' political affiliation – although the most important trigger for coalition formation may sometimes be the judges' political background. The qualitative assessment of selected cases concluded the country studies, which focused mainly on the most salient cases.

As a first summary of the research project, in this comparative chapter we have selected three questions on the determinants of judicial behaviour and presented the main findings based on the country studies. While judicial-legislative relations might be analysed from the perspective of the constraint exerted by the courts on the legislatures, in this final chapter we looked for judges' motives in taking heavily constraining or, contrary, more lenient decisions. We checked whether *institutional settings*, like the legislators' formal competence to overturn court decisions, the institution of *actio popularis* or the relatively narrow circle of potential petitioners, voting quorums and supermajority requirements in judicial decision-making, different types of procedures, the courts' competence to review constitutional amendments, or judicial self-empowerment had any effect on the ruling strength of the courts, but we also surveyed whether the *political context* (fragmentation, political instability, or change in government) influenced judicial decision-making. Furthermore, we were also interested in how judges behaved after the democratic transformation in CEE and how they reacted to austerity measures in the aftermath of the financial crisis of 2008–2009. Finally, we also gave an overview on the judges' predisposition concerning dissent and building dissenting coalitions.

As noted earlier, these are only the first steps, and we still have a long way to go in analysing the project's original dataset through more refined quantitative methods and/or in nuancing the key findings of the quantitative research through qualitative studies. While this volume along with its counterpart *Constitutional Review in Western Europe* close one chapter of the research project, they also open new avenues that could provide more nuanced answers about judicial behaviour in Europe. We hope that researchers have been inspired and will take advantage of the project's potential.

References

Abeyratne, Rehan, and Ngoc Son Bui. 2023. *The Law and Politics of Unconstitutional Constitutional Amendments in Asia.* London/New York: Routledge.

Albert, Richard. 2015. "The Theory and Doctrine of Unconstitutional Constitutional Amendment in Canada." *Queen's Law Journal* 41 (1): 143–206.

———, Malkhaz Nakashidze, and Tarik Olcay. 2019. "The Formalist Resistance to Unconstitutional Constitutional Amendments." *Hastings Law Journal* 70 (3): 639–670.

Barak, Aharon. 2011. "Unconstitutional Constitutional Amendments." *Israel Law Review* 44 (3): 321–341.

Beukers, Thomas, Bruno de Witte, and Claire Kilpatrick. 2017. "Constitutional Change through Euro-Crisis Law: Taking Stock, New Perspectives and Looking Ahead." In *Constitutional Change through Euro-Crisis Law*, edited by Thomas Beukers, Bruno de Witte, and Claire Kilpatrick, 1–24. Cambridge: Cambridge University Press.

Brouard, Sylvian. 2009. "The Politics of Constitutional Veto in France: Constitutional Council, Legislative Majority and Electoral Competition." *West European Politics* 32 (2): 383–403.

Bumin, Kirill M. 2017. "Judicial Institutionalization and Judicial Activism of the Post-Communist Constitutional Courts." *Journal of Politics and Law* 10 (2): 54–72.

Daly, Tom Gerald. 2017. *The Alchemists: Questioning Our Faith in Courts as Democracy-Builders.* Cambridge: Cambridge University Press.

Dyevre, Arthur. 2010. "Unifying the Field of Comparative Judicial Politics: Towards a General Theory of Judicial Behaviour." *European Political Science Review* 2 (2): 297–327.

Epstein, Lee, Jack Knight, and Olga Shvetsova. 2001. "The Role of Constitutional Courts in the Establishment and Maintenance of Democratic Systems of Government." *Law & Society Review* 35 (1): 117–164.

Fabbrini, Federico. 2016. *Economic Governance in Europe – Comparative Paradoxes and Constitutional Challenges.* Oxford: Oxford University Press.

Gardbaum, Stephen. 2018. "What Makes for More or Less Powerful Constitutional Courts?" *Duke Journal of Comparative & International Law* 29 (1): 1–40.

Gillman, Howard, and Clayton, Cornell W. 1999. "Beyond Judicial Attitudes: Institutional Approaches to Supreme Court Decision-Making." In *Supreme Court Decision-Making. New Institutionalist Approaches*, edited by C. Clayton, W. Cornell, and Howard Gillman, 1–12. Chicago: Chicago University Press.

Ginsburg, Tom. 2013. "The Politics of Courts in Democratization. Four Junctures in Asia." In *Consequential Courts. Judicial Roles in Global Perspective*, edited by Diana Kapiszewski, Gordon Silverstein, and Robert A. Kagan, 45–66. Cambridge: Cambridge University Press.

Herron, Erik S., and Kirk A. Randazzo. 2003. "The Relationship between Independence and Judicial Review in Post-Communist Courts." *The Journal of Politics* 65 (2): 422–438.

Hinarejos, Alicia. 2015. *The Euro Area Crisis in Constitutional Perspective*. Oxford: Oxford University Press.

Hönnige, Cristoph. 2007. *Verfassungsgericht, Regierung, und Opposition – Die vergleichende Analyse eines Spannungsdreiecks*. Wiesbaden: VS Verlag.

Jovanović, Miodrag A., ed. 2015. *Constitutional Review and Democracy*. The Hague: Eleven International Publishing.

Kelemen, Katalin. 2013. "Dissenting Opinions in Constitutional Courts." *German Law Journal* 14 (8): 1345–1371.

———. 2018. *Judicial Dissent in European Constitutional Courts: A Comparative and Legal Perspective*. Abingdon: Routledge.

King, Jeff. 2012. *Judging Social Rights*. Cambridge: Cambridge University Press.

Magalhes, Pedr. 2003. "The Limits of Judicialization: Legislative Politics and Constitutional Review in the Iberian Democracies." Diss., Ohio State University.

Pernice, Ingolf. 2016. "Domestic Courts, Constitutional Constraints and European Democracy: What Solution for the Crisis?" In *The Constitutionalization of European Budgetary Constraints*, edited by Maurice Adams, Federico Fabbrini, and Pierre Larouche, 297–319. Oxford: Hart Publishing.

Ragnarsson, Kári Hólmar. 2019. "The Counter-majoritarian Difficulty in a Neoliberal World: Socio-economic Rights and Deference in Post-2008 Austerity Cases." *Global Constitutionalism* 8 (3): 605–638.

Rios-Figueroa, Julio. 2007. "Fragmentation of Power and the Emergence of an Effective Judiciary in Mexico, 1994–2002." *Latin American Politics & Society* 49 (1): 31–57.

Roznai, Yaniv. 2013. "Unconstitutional Constitutional Amendments – The Migration and Success of a Constitutional Idea." *The American Journal of Comparative Law* 63 (3): 657–719.

———. 2019. *Unconstitutional Constitutional Amendments. The Limits of Amendment Powers*. Oxford: Oxford University Press

Segal, Jeffrey A., and Harold J. Spaeth. 2002. *The Supreme Court and the Attitudinal Model Revisited*. Cambridge: Cambridge University Press.

Smith, Brian C. 2023. *Judges and Democratization. Judicial Independence in New Democracies*. London and New York: Routledge

Sólyom, László. 2003. "The Role of Constitutional Courts in the Transition to Democracy: With Special Reference to Hungary." *International Sociology* 18 (1): 133–161.

Spaeth, Harold J., and J. Segal. 1992. *The Supreme Court and the Attitudinal Model*. Cambridge: Cambridge University Press.

Index

Note: Page numbers in *italics* indicate a figure and page numbers in **bold** indicate a table on the corresponding page.

Made in the USA
Las Vegas, NV
19 September 2026

4e74faa7-05fb-4733-8652-1e57f4dffa24R01